Five Filmmakers

Five Filmmakers

Tarkovsky
Forman
Polanski
Szabó
Makavejev

Edited by **Daniel J. Goulding**

Indiana
University
Press
BLOOMINGTON AND INDIANAPOLIS

Frame enlargements from *Ivan's Childhood, Andrei Roublev, Mirror, Nostalghia,* and *The Sacrifice* reproduced by permission of Artificial Eye Film Company, London, England. Frame enlargements from *Solaris* and *Stalker* reproduced by permission of Contemporary Films, London.

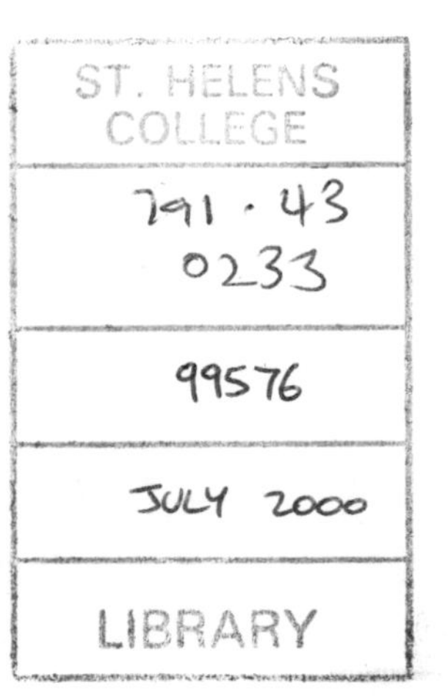

The paper used in this publication meets the minimum requirements of American National Standard for Information Sciences—Permanence of Paper for Printed Library Materials, ANSI Z39.48-1984.

MANUFACTURED IN THE UNITED STATES OF AMERICA

Library of Congress Cataloging-in-Publication Data

Five filmmakers : Tarkovsky, Forman, Polanski, Szabó, Makavejev / edited by Daniel J. Goulding.
p. cm.
Filmography: p.
Includes bibliographical references (p.) and index.
ISBN 0-253-32609-5 (cloth). -- ISBN 0-253-20825-4 (paper)
1. Motion picture producers and directors—Europe, Eastern.
I. Goulding, Daniel J., date . II. Title: 5 filmmakers.
PN1998.2.F555 1993
791.43'0233'092247--dc20 92-46312

1 2 3 4 5 97 96 95 94

Contents

ACKNOWLEDGMENTS

Gratitude must first be expressed to the five filmmakers included in this volume. Their works provided the intellectual stimulation, creative challenge, and sensory delight that made the ardors of critical inquiry, collective collaboration, and meeting publication deadlines for this project much more often a pleasure than a burden. I am especially grateful to my fellow collaborators for their unfailing cooperation in meeting and often exceeding the expectations and demands placed upon them.

In preparing my own chapter, I am especially grateful to Dušan Makavejev for the time he made available for our several meetings and conversations over the past two years. A strong debt of gratitude is also owed to Predrag Golubović, director of the Institut za film in Belgrade, and to Miroljub Vučković, program editor, for providing research assistance and for arranging special archival viewings of Makavejev's early amateur and documentary films during my visit to Belgrade in June 1991. Ann Amesbury of Cannon Pictures, Inc., was very helpful in locating and making available to me a high-quality 35mm print of Makavejev's film *Manifesto,* and Arlene and Bill Steel, co-managers of the Apollo Theater in Oberlin, generously provided me with several private screenings of the film. I received valuable guidance in locating and selecting stills for the chapter on Makavejev from Bridget Kinally, head of stills, posters, and designs for the British Film Institute, Doug Piwinski of MGM-Pathe, and Milos Stehlik (co-director) and Donald Gray of Facets Video.

Margaret S. MacDonald, senior writer-editor, provided expert editorial assistance in the preparation of all the manuscripts for the book. Karen D. Arcaba and Gretchen Higgins of the Oberlin College Irvin E. Houck Computing Center and Priscilla Scott, retired administrative assistant, efficiently and cheerfully provided technical assistance in ushering the book's manuscripts through their various iterations and revisions.

Daniel J. Goulding

INTRODUCTION BY DANIEL J. GOULDING

The five filmmakers selected for discussion in this volume all began their film directing careers in the political "East" and subsequently either moved their careers to the West or worked primarily in co-productions involving one or more Western film companies. They include Andrei Tarkovsky (from the former Soviet Union), Miloš Forman (Czechoslovakia), Roman Polanski (Poland), István Szabó (Hungary), and Dušan Makavejev (Yugoslavia). Each of these filmmakers, in his own unique way, has challenged the ideological and cultural boundaries that once separated East from West, and has helped to open the way for a newer generation of talented filmmakers from former East-bloc countries who wish to participate (and are participating) in growing numbers of cross-cultural film productions.

The present study is particularly timely now that the ideological and political barriers erected by both "Eastern" and "Western" countries have either crumbled or are in the process of crumbling. The cultural barriers were perforated long ago, and the filmmakers selected for discussion in this book were among the creative participants in that process. All of the filmmakers included in this study were born in the 1930s and were shaped, in part, by similar events and forces. They experienced the cruelties of the Second World War (which, in Polanski's case, were especially horrifying and traumatic). They began their careers when the iron grip of Stalinist cultural policy was progressively loosened and the sterile formulations of socialist realism were being challenged and laid to rest. They actively aligned themselves with these reform forces and helped to push even further outward the bounds of allowable artistic expression in their home countries, and to promote politically nonconformist cinematic critiques of existing societal conditions. Each of them imbibed the socialist legacy that assigns to film a much higher order of sociopolitical and artistic significance than it is often accorded in the West. They were all major artistic contributors to the remarkable "wave" of internationally acclaimed and awarded films that rolled out of East Europe during the late fifties and sixties, and all, therefore, had established significant international reputations before shifting their careers westward. In this book, each filmmaker is the subject of a chapter in which the authors explore continuities and discontinuities of artistic influences, thematic treatment, sociocultural content, and aesthetic form and imagery as the filmmakers moved from one film culture to another.

Andrei Tarkovsky (1932–1986) is perhaps the most original and certainly the most controversial filmmaker to emerge from the former Soviet Union since the Second World War. His films are eloquently crafted and imagistically rich, multilayered and densely textured. From the outset of his film career, Tarkovsky attracted significant international attention. Even his diploma film *Steamroller and Violin* (*Katok i skripka*) won first prize in 1960 at the New York Student Film Festival. His first feature film, *Ivan's Childhood* (*Ivanovo detstvo*, 1962)—released in English as *My Name Is Ivan*—won the Golden Lion at Venice in 1962; his second feature, *Andrei Roublev* (1966), though highly controversial at home, captured the International Critics' award at Cannes in 1969; his third, the metaphysical science-fiction film *Solaris* (1971), won the Special Jury Prize at Cannes in 1972. His next film, the autobiographical *Mirror* (*Zerkalo*, 1974), was heavily criticized in the Soviet Union for its labyrinthine structure and parabolic style, and was not offered for export until 1980. In 1979, Tarkovsky made *Stalker*, a complex allegory of decay and spiritual ennui that was interpreted by many Western critics as an indictment of Soviet repression of intellectual and artistic freedom. From 1983 until his untimely death by cancer in December 1986, Tarkovsky lived in Italy and Paris and worked abroad—making two of his most complex and important films, *Nostalghia* (1983), co-produced by Gaumont and RAI, Italy, and Sovin film, Moscow; and *The Sacrifice* (*Offret*, 1986), a French-Swedish co-production. Since his death in 1986, Tarkovsky has been the subject of increasing scholarly and critical attention.

In their chapter, Vida Johnson and Graham Petrie draw not only upon the significant and growing body of critical literature on Tarkovsky but also upon their own extensive original research and wide-ranging personal interviews. As Johnson's and Petrie's analysis reveals, Tarkovsky assumed the same uncompromising and intransigent stance toward his Western film producers as he had toward the Soviet film bureaucracy. He expressed only withering contempt for what he considered to be the crass materialism and bankrupt values of Hollywood, and showed no interest in ever working there. He even chafed and bristled under the mild capitalistic constraints that were gently imposed by Italy's RAI Television and the Swedish Film Institute. Johnson and Petrie present the interesting argument that Tarkovsky, with all of his well-publicized problems in the Soviet Union, might have been temperamentally better suited to that system (one that, while it might exact a political price, nonetheless respects artistic values and serious intellectual purpose, and shelters the artist from budgetary and other economic problems) than he was suited to a system that requires adapting to the nagging intrusions and requirements of "grubby" commercial considerations. None of these problems, however, prevented Tarkovsky from continuing to make artistically significant and impressive films. Johnson and Petrie have presented a sensitive and sophisticated analysis of the ways in which style, theme, and imagery in Tarkovsky's major films of the Soviet period are subtly and effectively transformed and expressed in his "Western" films *Nostalghia* and *The Sacrifice*.

Miloš Forman (1932–) was one of the most gifted and ultimately the most famous of a brilliant and versatile group of film artists who rose to international prominence in the 1960s during the flourishing period of the

Czech *new wave.* In his Czech period, Forman made three important and highly acclaimed feature films; *Black Peter* (*Černý Petr,* 1963), *Loves of a Blonde* (*Lásky jedné plavovlásky,* 1965), and *Firemen's Ball* (*Hoří, ma panenko!,* 1967). Shortly after the fall of Dubček in 1968, Forman came to the United States to continue his film career. His first film, *Taking Off* (1971), was made in the same *cinéma vérité* style and exhibited the same subtle, irreverent, witty, and penetrating satire as his Czech films—only this time directed against American mores. The film was a critical success and earned modest returns for its investors. It did not, however, lead to any further projects. Forman learned his lesson from this experience and subsequently made a series of highly successful commercial films—without losing his own cultural and artistic vision. His most important critical and commercial successes have included his acclaimed adaptation of Ken Kesey's novel *One Flew Over the Cuckoo's Nest* (1975) and his much heralded and critically discussed film version of Peter Shaffer's play *Amadeus* (1984). His most recent film, *Valmont* (1989), another screen adaptation of Laclos's novel *Les Liaisons Dangereuses,* received mixed reviews. It also suffered commercially, of course, because its release followed upon the heels of the immensely popular, award-winning film version of *Les Liaisons Dangereuses* directed by Stephen Frears.

In his chapter, Peter Hames situates Forman's early films within the sophisticated context of Czech *new wave* filmmaking and in relation to Czechoslovakia's rich and unique tradition of comedy and satire. In assessing Forman's American film career, Hames provides a thoughtful and reasoned response to those critics who argue that after Forman made *Taking Off,* he increasingly avoided taking the risks, both stylistically and thematically, that had made his Czech films so artistically fresh and politically daring.

Roman Polanski (1933–) has centered the greater part of his career in the West. He made his auspicious debut, however, with his precociously original and internationally recognized diploma film *Two Men and a Wardrobe* (*Dwaj ludzie z szafa,* 1958), made at the famous Polish film school at Łódź. His first feature film (the only one made in Poland), *Knife in the Water* (*Nóż w wodzie,* 1962), was singled out for harsh polemic attack domestically, even as it gained instant international recognition as a brilliant first work. Polanski left Poland shortly thereafter to make films in the West. Unlike Forman, however, he initially centered his film career in Great Britain rather than in Hollywood. Among his most substantive and critically significant films made in Great Britain are *Repulsion* (1965), *Cul-de-sac* (1966), *Macbeth* (1971), and the French-British co-production *Tess* (1979), based on the Thomas Hardy novel *Tess of the d'Urbervilles.*

Polanski's greatest commercial and critical successes in Hollywood are his films *Rosemary's Baby* (1968), based on the novel by Ira Levin, and *Chinatown* (1974), a stylish tribute to American *film noir* of the 1940s. The darkly absurdist, Kafkaesque, and surrealistic strains in Polanski's films have been matched and sometimes overshadowed by bizarre real-life tragedy and scandal: These included the savage murder and mutilation of his pregnant wife, the actress Sharon Tate, and several of her friends by the Charles

Manson cult in 1969, and the charge brought against him in Los Angeles County during the seventies for the statutory rape of a thirteen-year-old girl, causing him to flee to Paris in 1977 to avoid imprisonment. After a brief period of relative inactivity and decline, Polanski has recently regained critical interest with his perverse thriller *Frantic* (1988). Even greater critical interest has focused on his current film project, *Bitter Moon,* which is scheduled to be completed and released as this book goes to press. Based on the controversial French novel *Lunes de Fiel* by Pascal Bruckner, *Bitter Moon* deals with subject matter that is much closer and more complexly related to Polanski's central psychosexual and thematic concerns than has been evident in his last few films. It remains to be seen whether this film will answer those critics who feel that Polanski's best work is already behind him.

Herbert Eagle, in his chapter on Polanski, has provided an original, in-depth analysis of Polanski's comparatively brief Polish period. Eagle then imaginatively links the discoveries made in his close readings of *Two Men and a Wardrobe* and *Knife in the Water* to those made in his equally probing and perceptive readings of four of Polanski's most challenging and complex films made in the West: *Repulsion, Rosemary's Baby, Macbeth,* and *Chinatown.*

István Szabó (1938–) emerged as one of the leading figures in Hungarian cinema during the sixties and seventies, though his international reputation at that time was somewhat overshadowed by the greater acclaim accorded his countryman Miklós Jancsó. In addition to making two award-winning short films, Szabó completed six sophisticated and stylistically varied feature films during this period: *The Age of Daydreaming* (*Álmodozások kora,* 1964), *Father* (*Apa,* 1966), *Love Film* (*Szerelmes film,* 1970), *25 Firemen's Street* (*Tuzoltó utca 25,* 1973), *Budapest Tales* (*Budapesti mesék,* 1976), and *Confidence* (*Bizalom,* 1979). It was not until the eighties, however, that Szabó achieved significant international recognition and critical success through his artistic direction of films co-produced with the West. His Hungarian-West German co-production *Mephisto* (1981) won many international awards, including the Academy Award for best foreign film. His next film, *Colonel Redl* (1985), a Hungarian-West German-Austrian co-production, won the prestigious Jury Prize at Cannes. His critically acclaimed film *Hanussen,* another Hungarian-West German co-production, was completed in 1988 and forms, along with *Mephisto* and *Colonel Redl,* what David Paul discusses in his chapter as Szabó's "Central European trilogy." In his most recent film, *Meeting Venus* (1991), Szabó has directed his first film made entirely without Hungarian financial support. Produced by Enigma in Great Britain, the film expresses, as David Paul perceptively demonstrates, a further expansion of themes found in Szabó's Central European trilogy.

In his expert tracing of Szabó's career and film works, David Paul draws upon his intimate knowledge of Hungarian and Central and East European cinema and his recent extensive personal interviews with Szabó and with several of Szabó's most intimate artistic collaborators. Paul offers an especially perceptive analysis of Szabó's evolution as a director primarily immersed in Hungarian sociocultural realities to one who expresses in his most recent films an acute consciousness of Central European history and a profound sensitivity to that region's social complexes.

Dušan Makavejev (1932–) was a leading figure in Yugoslavia's *new film* (*novi film*) movement of the 1960s, and the one who achieved the greatest international recognition. His richly inventive and sometimes wild and surrealistic sexual and social film satires include: *Man Is Not a Bird* (*Čovek nije tica*, 1965), *Love Affair, or the Tragedy of a Switchboard Operator* (*Ljubavni slučaj ili tragedija službenice PTT*, 1967), *Innocence Unprotected* (*Nevinost bez zaštite*, 1968), and *WR: Mysteries of the Organism* (*WR: Misterije Organizma*, 1971). *WR: Mysteries of the Organism* created a storm of controversy in Yugoslavia, leading to its domestic banning and to Makavejev's emigration to the West. Ironically, however, his first film made in the West, *Sweet Movie* (1974), suffered a fate not very different from that of *WR* in Yugoslavia. Many critics vociferously condemned the film, and it was censured and banned in several countries as pornographic. Seven years passed before Makavejev made his critically and commercially successful comeback film, the Swedish-produced *Montenegro* (1981), followed by the Australian-produced *The Coca-Cola Kid*, and the U.S.-Yugoslav co-production *Manifesto* (1988).

While there exists an impressive critical literature concerning selected films directed by Makavejev (especially dealing with his most acclaimed film, *WR: Mysteries of the Organism*), this book presents the first systematic critical discussion of Makavejev's entire body of film work produced to date. The most significant turning point in his film career occurred during the seven-year period between the making of *Sweet Movie* and the making of *Montenegro*. Beginning with *Montenegro*, Makavejev, partly in response to commercially oriented genre and narrative expectations, began to write and direct films that were relatively more conventional in structure and that abandoned earlier experiments in discontinuous narrative structures and multiple levels of montage association. He did not, however, abandon his personal artistic control over his films nor his predilection for bizarre plots, surrealistic images, and sharp social and political satire.

The present volume offers fresh and original perspectives on the careers and artistic contributions of five internationally significant filmmakers who, each in his own highly individual way, have successfully (although not without pain and some failure) challenged and breached the boundaries that for nearly five decades separated "East" and "West." It is hoped that the present volume increases understanding of the diverse pathways and creative challenges, as well as the limitations, pitfalls, and artistic compromises, that may be encountered in the process of cross-cultural financial and artistic film collaboration.

Five Filmmakers

One Tarkovsky

Vida T. Johnson and Graham Petrie

Even before the destruction of the Iron Curtain, the Soviet Union and its Eastern European "satellites" were not one monolithic entity where filmmakers struggled on similar terms against the ideological and political controls of rigid government-run cinema bureaucracies. Whereas some of their Eastern European counterparts could readily travel to and work in the West, this path, with rare exceptions, was either closed to Soviet artists from the late 1960s until the era of *glasnost* (mid-1980s) or took the form of a one-way ticket as a result of either defection or expulsion. While a significant number of well-known dissident writers followed one or the other of these paths to the West in the conservative "period of stagnation" of the 1970s—the most famous being Alexander Solzhenitsyn—no major filmmaker emigrated during that period. Filmmakers who traveled to the West for brief visits to festivals were either party functionaries or the few talented recipients of foreign awards, such as Andrei Tarkovsky. Moreover, Soviet-Western film co-productions were a relative rarity.

The gargantuan Soviet film industry was much larger, more tightly controlled, and more insular than its East European counterparts, and the directors who worked in it had little opportunity to interact creatively with their Western colleagues. Now that all political, ideological, bureaucratic, and even economic barriers have been lifted, the floundering Soviet cinema industry is desperately playing a self-conscious game of catch-up with the West, regrettably often imitating the worst of Hollywood's commercialism; it is now commonly recognized that the curtain of iron has been replaced by one of gold.

Perhaps it is best that Andrei Tarkovsky, who during his whole creative life struggled against both ideological and commercial tyranny and fought to place cinema on a par with such "high" arts as literature and painting, did not live to see its current turmoil at home. Unfortunately, he also did not have the bittersweet pleasure of seeing the downfall of the bureaucrats who had made his life miserable, or of accepting the 1990 Lenin Prize for his "outstanding contribution to the development of the art of cinema, for his innovative films, which help to affirm universal human values and humanistic ideas."[1] Tarkovsky had become a "nonperson" after his 1984 defection, but, as a direct result of *glasnost,* he was finally given the public recognition which had eluded him in life. At home, as well as abroad, he is now widely seen as the best Soviet filmmaker of his generation, with Sergei Paradzhanov as his closest competitor. A steady stream of generally laudatory articles on his life and work has appeared in the most influential cinema and literary journals; a complete retrospective of his films was held in Dom Kino (The House of Cinema), the headquarters of the Filmmakers' Union, in April 1987, and repeated at the International Moscow Film Festival in July 1987; and his films continue to be regularly screened both in major Russian cities and in provincial towns.

A "myth" of Tarkovsky as a suffering genius, martyr, and prophet has been nurtured in both the Soviet Union and the West, shaped, to some degree, by the director's own messianic tendencies and persecution complex—he did, after all, title his diary *Martyrology* in Russian—but also by his long-standing and well-deserved reputation as an uncompromising artist willing to battle the conservative cinema bureaucracy. His untimely death of cancer at the age of fifty-four, only two years after his defection, has further assured his canonization, with his admirers at home fully convinced that the cancer was caused by his stressful struggles with the Soviet bureaucracy.

While steering clear of political and sentimental clichés, we will try to identify the nature of Tarkovsky's contribution to cinema. We will compare his life and work in the East and the West by looking objectively at the kinds of problems he faced in making films in both places, and by analyzing and comparing his Soviet and Western productions. Finally, we will hypothesize about what Tarkovsky's future as an artist might have been either in the West, which he had come to call home, or in Russia, to which he would have inevitably returned as so many dissident artists have recently done.

A Martyr, or "The Darling of Goskino"?

Tarkovsky was the only major contemporary Soviet filmmaker to defect, ironically, on the very eve of *glasnost.* How and why did he do it? The "how" seems deceptively easy: Tarkovsky had been living for more than a year in Italy working on the Soviet-Italian-French co-production *Nostalghia.* After the film was completed, in a June 15, 1983, letter to Filip Yermash, the chairman of Goskino (the State Committee on Cinema) and the official head of the government-run cinema industry, Tarkovsky asked for permission to continue work in the West for three years. He cited as his reason the fact that in twenty-two years at home he had only been allowed to make five feature films, and had never received any Soviet recognition or prize for his films. While affirming his devotion to his country as a Soviet artist, he encapsulated the history of all five of his Russian films, maintaining that none of them had received the kind of distribution and critical attention they deserved. He complained that his first film, *Ivan's Childhood* (1962), had been shown (perhaps, he speculated, in deliberate mockery of its subject) at children's matinees in Moscow and had not been given a proper release at home despite its success abroad. *Andrei Roublev* (1966) was shelved for six years, which left him without work. *Solaris* (1972), the film he considered his least successful, was the only one to receive a normal, first-category distribution (despite some forty-eight requested changes); his other films, however, were classed in the second category, and both *Mirror* (1975) and *Stalker* (1979) were not even printed in the number of copies required for that category. Both films suffered a similar fate, he claimed: silence on the part of the press, apart from two or three insulting articles, written to order. Although he considered his latest film, *Nostalghia,* to be very patriotic, it too had come under attack; and the Soviet member of the Cannes Festival jury made "superhuman efforts" to deny it a prize.[2]

When the Soviet authorities ignored his repeated requests to extend his visa (apparently requiring him to follow official procedures and first return to Moscow!), he announced at a press conference on July 10, 1984 (in Milan), his intention to stay in the West. Tarkovsky underscored that he was not a political dissident, and that his reasons for staying were artistic freedom and economic necessity. From our personal interviews with Tarkovsky intimates and even hints in his diary, it is clear that he had been considering this action for a number of years. Several immediate factors contributed to his defection at this time, but now he had both motive and opportunity. He was smarting from what he considered an organized Soviet conspiracy to deny *Nostalghia* the Grand Prix at Cannes in 1983, through the agency of jury member Sergei Bondarchuk, a highly placed, conservative director.[3] He was also, however, busily negotiating projects in the West and had signed a contract with Anna-Lena Wibom of the Swedish Film Institute to make a film based on *The Witch,* a script he had been working on since at least 1981. In the fall of 1983 he had collaborated with the conductor Claudio Abbado on a new production of Mussorgsky's opera *Boris Godunov,* which opened to great acclaim at the Royal Opera House in London; in addition, he lectured in West Berlin, London, and even the United States. Clearly tantalized by what must have seemed like endless creative possibilities abroad, and realizing that he would never be allowed to film his favorite projects—above all Dostoyevsky's *The Idiot*—in the Soviet Union, he decided to seek political asylum.[4] After sounding out various possibilities elsewhere, the couple decided to stay in Italy, where they were given an apartment by the city of Florence.

What seemed like a wonderful professional opportunity carried a heavy personal toll. When he and his wife Larissa had left the Soviet Union, they had been forced to leave behind their son Andrei, as well as Olga, Larissa's daughter from a previous marriage, and Larissa's mother—held, in typical pre-*glasnost* fashion, as "human hostages" to assure the Tarkovskys' return after *Nostalghia.* Various committees were organized—in Sweden, England, Italy, France, and elsewhere—to publicize their plight and to put pressure on the Soviet government to allow them to leave, but Tarkovsky was re-united with his son (to whom his final film, *The Sacrifice*, is dedicated) only four years later, after his terminal cancer had been diagnosed. It is not difficult to see how in the West, and under the historical revisionism of *glasnost* in the Soviet Union, Tarkovsky was seen as a martyr.

But was Tarkovsky really a tragic victim, endlessly persecuted and re-pressed by an uncaring, monolithic cinema bureaucracy? While family mem-bers, friends, co-workers, and sympathetic film critics often saw him as a victim, some of his peers have called him "the darling of Goskino." Although he was far from being a privileged insider, he was not one of those repressed artists (such as Alexander Askoldov and Kira Muratova) whose films were banned and who were simply not allowed to work, or who, like Sergei Paradzhanov, were tried and imprisoned. Even in the years of "unemploy-ment" that he complains of in his letter to Yermash, he was rarely completely idle: he planned films, wrote scripts (both for himself and others), and even staged a play, *Hamlet*, in 1977. Tarkovsky's own diary (written from 1970 to his death in 1986) exposes an interesting paradox. At first sight it is a litany of seemingly justified complaints against recalcitrant, unimaginative bureaucrats both at his studio, Mosfilm, and at the higher industry level of Goskino. Every step, from submission of the proposal for a film, to the literary and director's scripts, to funding, casting, locations, shooting, and the acceptance of the final film, was fraught with difficulty and delay. He complains too that his films—despite his high international prestige—were not being sent to enough festivals, even when specifically requested by them. Cannes was a particular source of grievance; he was especially bitter that both *Mirror* and *Stalker* were officially withheld from Cannes, even though the latter was shown out of competition by its French distributor. Tarkovsky triumphantly records what he describes as its "resounding" and "tremendous" success in a series of diary entries in mid-May 1980.[5]

These entries, however, were made in *Rome*—hardly the setting in which one would expect to find a persecuted Soviet artist. At the same time as he is recording all the problems listed above, he calmly notes a series of travels—to France, Italy (several times), Switzerland, Sweden, and elsewhere, mostly to show his films and attend film festivals—to an extent that was generally permitted to only the more established party-line directors. Sergei Paradzhanov, sitting in prison for part of this period, must have envied Tarkovsky his "martyrdom" (to be fair, Tarkovsky did attempt, unsuccessfully, to intercede with the government on Paradzhanov's behalf). Fighting the bureaucrats, whether the ideological watchdogs of the East or the financial ones in the West, is, in any case, part of the director's calling, and "difficult" or "noncommercial" directors everywhere have faced similar problems. De-spite all his genuine difficulties, his films were released in a form that satisfied his original artistic intentions and—with the sole exception of *Andrei Roublev*, which "sat on the shelf" from 1967 to 1971—within a reasonably short peri-od after completion. And, if they were not shown at as many festivals as he would have liked, they gathered a large number of prizes abroad—twenty-six by his own count in March 1980.[6]

How are these paradoxes to be interpreted, and how was he able to make not so few but so *many* films under the circumstances? He *did* come under considerable and constant pressure and it is to his credit that, unlike so many of his contemporaries, he held firm on the inevitable requests for cuts and "changes" in the completed film, accepting only those that he felt would not adversely affect the film's integrity. He withstood the heavy psychological and economic strains—bonuses were not given out until the film was accepted, which meant that cast and crew suffered as well—refusing to budge until, surprisingly, more often than not, it was the bureaucrats who finally gave in. If he was not exactly the "darling of Goskino," he certainly earned the grudging respect of a cinema administration impressed by his growing international reputation and perhaps even by his very intransigence. His fame abroad too was a useful safeguard, guaranteeing that his problems would be well publicized. And then there were his extraordinary talent, his all-consuming dedication, his inordinate self-confidence, his desperate stubbornness, and the loyal support of family and co-workers who returned to work with him again and again, fully aware of all the difficulties that were likely to accompany every film.

Ivan's Childhood *(1962)*

Tarkovsky's career got off to a brilliant start: he was the youngest Soviet director to receive a major international prize when he won the Golden Lion in Venice in 1962 for his first feature film, *Ivan's Childhood,* the tragic story of a young war scout.[7] Newsworthy critical and political scandal followed when *Unita,* the hardline Italian Communist party newspaper, attacked the film for being "petit-bourgeois" and no less a cultural arbiter than Jean-Paul Sartre defended in print the young Tarkovsky's "socialist surrealism" and his depiction of a genuinely "Soviet tragedy."[8] Talent, education, and history all conspired to make *Ivan's Childhood* a true turning point in Soviet cinema.

Tarkovsky was fortunate to have become a filmmaker during the cultural and political "thaw" of the late fifties and early sixties. He spent the years 1954 to 1960 at VGIK (the All-Union State Institute of Cinematography) studying under the highly respected director Mikhail Romm. While Romm is known in the West primarily for well-executed standard socialist realist fare, he was a brilliant intellectual and an inspirational teacher who convinced his students that directing could not be taught and encouraged them instead to think independently and develop their individual talents. At the widely attended series of discussions "The Language of Cinema," held in March 1962 at the Filmmakers' Union, it was Mikhail Romm who introduced an unknown film, *Ivan's Childhood,* as an example of a truly new, contemporary cinematic language and exhorted his audience to "remember the name Tarkovsky."[9] The stunned audience recognized the dazzling new film as a breakthrough in "poetic" cinematography with its subjective camerawork, destruction of traditional narrative continuity, creative use of documentary footage, and intermingling of dream and reality.

Tarkovsky's film was not, however, totally unprecedented: after the moribund late-Stalinist period, characterized by grandiose and simplistic socialist realist epics, the liberal "thaw" period saw a flood of films such as Mikhail Kalatozov's highly acclaimed *The Cranes are Flying* (1957), which attempted to present through highly personal and subjective camerawork a more complex view of humans and their relations to each other, and to social and political institutions and historical events. Like *Cranes, Ballad of a Soldier* (1959), and many other films of the time, *Ivan's Childhood* was a "revisionist" war film, eschewing the excessively chauvinistic patriotism and glorification of standard Soviet World War II films. Although the Soviet soldiers are still honorable, brave, and kind, they are also humanly imperfect; and while little sympathy is wasted on the Germans (mostly a sinister offscreen presence), the film's focus is not on fighting and winning the war—although that too is significant—but on its psychological trauma and human toll. There is remarkably little action and the actual fighting is merely hinted at as Tarkovsky draws the viewer into the terrifyingly real and palpable *inner* world of his hero. *Ivan's Childhood* constituted not just the next step in Soviet cinema, but a quantum leap in the development of a new cinematic style.

Tarkovsky's "poetic" tendencies, while clearly encouraged by the general developments in "thaw" films, may also have had another source: the poetry of his father Arseny Tarkovsky. The complex artistic dialogue between father and son, poet and filmmaker, would operate on two levels in many of Tarkovsky's films: as a highly personal conversation of a son with a father whose perception of the natural world, life, and art he shared; and as a self-conscious attempt to transform the language of lyric poetry—with its subjective point of view, elliptical, nonlinear narrative, progression by associative leaps, striking imagery, and strong emotional appeal—into a poetic language of cinema. Tarkovsky himself was to view his first feature film as ending his apprenticeship: He called it his "qualifying examination," which allowed him to work out his ideas about the art of cinema and to test his abilities as a director.[10]

Tarkovsky began formulating his aesthetics of film around the time of *Ivan's Childhood*, in a series of published articles and interviews, and his ideas took final shape as the book *Sculpting in Time*, his "reflections on the cinema." For him, cinema was an art, not a source of escape, entertainment, or commercial profit,[11] and thus should show itself as capable of spiritual and moral investigation as literature, painting, or music. Like the creators of these arts, the filmmaker should be devoted to the search for a higher, even divine, truth: ". . . art must carry man's craving for the ideal, must be an expression of his reaching out toward it; . . . art must give man hope and faith."[12] Art (or, in his case, film) was a means of communication with other people, a source of knowledge of ourselves and of others, an opportunity to understand more fully the world and our place within it, and the inspiration for the moment of transcendence that enables us to intuit something of the meaning and purpose of our existence. We are a long way here, not just from Hollywood, but from the claims even of most "serious" filmmakers, few of whom would be willing to accept a burden of this kind or to express it in such exalted language.

The specific characteristics of film as an art, for Tarkovsky, were its "truthfulness" and its ability to "capture" or "sculpt" time. The common factor here was the ability of film to recreate—though filtered through the subjectivity of the true artist—the direct and authentic reality of both the external and internal world. In particular it could portray *real time* in a way denied to any other art, and could make both viewer and character live through and within that time with an immediacy and intensity impossible elsewhere. The viewer, as this implies, is to be a co-creator and co-participant in the work of art; no longer the passive consumer of predigested entertainment, but challenged to respond and to interpret at every stage.

Though many of these ideas had been formulated, and indeed published, as early as 1964, *Ivan's Childhood* is—certainly in retrospect—considerably less complex and innovative than any of Tarkovsky's later films. Although, in the context of the time, as has been mentioned, it dazzled Soviet audiences deprived of genuine cinematic experimentation for almost three decades, its stylistic flourishes consist mainly of devices—hectic camerawork, tilted angles, heavily atmospheric lighting, and somewhat obtrusive symbolism—that he would rarely use again. It is in Ivan's dreams, where the anguish and horror of his situation are vividly presented to us, that Tarkovsky is both most intensely personal and the film most innovative and moving. Added to the film's script (in collaboration with Andrei Konchalovsky) when Tarkovsky took over the film from another director, and not present in the much more realistic novella by Vladimir Bogomolov that was the film's source, these dreams reveal a strikingly original talent from literally the first image of the film.

In the opening shots we are with Ivan, a twelve-year-old boy marveling at the beauty of the natural world; then, abruptly, he is flying, looking down on a sunlit landscape, and we realize belatedly that we are participating in a dream that ends, horrifyingly, in the sudden death of his mother at the hands of unseen German soldiers. This and the three other dreams that punctuate the film and poignantly reveal the child's lost and irrecoverable happiness display the respect for reality that Tarkovsky always insisted on, eschewing the special effects and visual distortions employed by most other directors to create a dreamlike state; for him this should arise from "unusual and unexpected combinations of, and conflicts between, entirely real elements."[13] The realistic imagery of the dreams, emphasizing the figure of the mother, water, hair, horses, fruit, and trees, recurs again and again in later films and is "made strange" by "unusual and unexpected" spatial and temporal combinations: the changing positions of mother and son in the dream of the well; the negative film and the repeated appearances of the little

1.1. The last "dream." Ivan (Nikolai Burlyaev) and the dead tree. *Ivan's Childhood.* Artificial Eye.

girl—probably his sister who, like his parents, was killed by the Germans—as he rides with her on a truck and offers her an apple. The final dream, in which Ivan plays with his sister and other children on the beach, appears almost totally "real"—except that by now we recognize the "dream" signals: the mother, water, bright sunlight, a lyrical musical leitmotif.

This dream, like all the others except the apple dream, presents a moment of remembered happiness that ends abruptly in death, this time of Ivan himself rather than his mother. In purely narrative terms the scene is redundant, for we know already that Ivan has been killed by the Germans. It offers, however, the kind of epiphany with which Tarkovsky ended all his other films, giving a glimpse of peace and harmony that briefly—and not always naturalistically—reconciles the suffering and the tensions experienced elsewhere in the film. Here, unusually, the sense of harmony is almost immediately snatched away as the film ends with Ivan running headlong toward the tree that symbolizes his death and the screen turns to black with brutal finality.

Although, with the exception of the dreams, most of the film's narrative is presented in a straightforward, chronological manner, Tarkovsky begins to experiment with the pattern of "retrospective understanding" that is taken to greater lengths in later work. We are given no immediate clue that the opening scene is a dream; once we have grasped that, we are disoriented once more as Ivan wakes up and makes his way through a war-torn landscape with no explanation as to how he got there and why. It is only several scenes into the film that we finally discover that he is a child-scout, risking his life to gain information about the German positions. Only halfway through are we told explicitly about the deaths of the other members of his family that explain his fanatical hatred of the Germans and the destruction of his childhood (though the dreams make the traumatic death of the mother evident early on). Often scenes follow each other with little or no indication as to how much time has elapsed between them and with no attempt to provide establishing shots to orient us as to setting. The reason why Ivan, having been forbidden to continue working as a scout, is nevertheless allowed to leave on a last expedition is never given and has to be inferred by the viewer. This purposeful narrative ambiguity and lack of clear causality constituted Tarkovsky's first real challenge to socialist realism, which had no room for either stylistic or thematic ambivalence in its demand for the "portrayal of reality in its revolutionary development." Thus, despite the fact that, of all Tarkovsky films, *Ivan's Childhood* garnered the most favorable reviews in the Soviet Union, it did not escape criticism either in the press or in the industry.

The film's tortuous path through the studio bureaucracy foreshadowed the difficulties Tarkovsky was to encounter in obtaining approval for all his films. *Ivan's Childhood* was subjected to examination at thirteen separate meetings of artistic councils[14]—groups of established figures from the literary and film worlds—attached to the creative working teams within the studio or found at the studio's upper administrative levels. It was here that Tarkovsky began his other apprenticeship—in the art of self-defense: standing firm on his artistic decisions and battling the bureaucrats, who, as he makes clear in his diary, were present at every step of the film's life. Besides the artistic councils, there were script-editorial boards which approved every stage of the script's progress. Not only did each stage of the film have to be approved, first within the director's creative "team," and then at the studio level, but all the major steps—approval of treatment and script and film acceptance—also had to be repeated in the governmental body on cinema, Goskino. However, these were not all monolithic bureaucratic bodies composed of political hard-liners. Tarkovsky was to find real support as well as antagonism at many levels of the studio and Goskino apparatus. With the help of important directors, his teacher Mikhail Romm, and Grigory Kozintsev, cultural figures such as the composer Dmitry Shostakovich and Yevgeny Surkov, the editor of the influential cinema journal *Iskusstvo kino,* and the relentless support of both his wives, his friends, and his co-workers, Tarkovsky kept fighting and winning, ensuring that, at least in the Soviet Union, his films would be screened in a form that he found aesthetically acceptable.

It is ironic that, for all his resistance to "interference" with his work in the Soviet Union, Tarkovsky had few qualms about cutting his films for foreign distribution, noting quite calmly in his diary that Columbia wanted to shorten *Andrei Roublev* by fifteen or twenty minutes, and "I can certainly do so, starting with the balloon flight."[15] And this was the film which Tarkovsky had extremely grudgingly agreed to cut twice in a prolonged battle with the Soviet bureaucracy, first by fifteen and then by five minutes, practically counting the frames in each shot to be cut! When a third round of cuts was requested, he refused—which helped keep the film shelved for more than five years. He was likewise happy to shorten *Solaris* by twelve minutes for French distribution, cutting the film himself while in Paris, though he was furious about its unauthorized "butchering" by the Italians. Where foreign distribution was concerned, he perhaps knew too well that he had no control over his films, while at home, where his *real* audience was to be found, he would inevitably stand on principle.

Andrei Roublev *(completed 1966; released 1971)*

If in the life of every artist there is a critical event that defines the future shape of both his professional and private life, for Tarkovsky this was *Andrei Roublev,* an ambitious, almost three-and-a-half-hour epic about medieval Russia and its greatest icon painter. As for most directors, a first "hit" placed much pressure on him to create a striking second film, which may explain its ambitious thematics and scope, as well as his dogged five-year struggle (1966–1971) to have it released as his original, untampered-with creation. Irma Rausch, his first wife (from whom he was divorced in 1970), spoke in interview of this period as a time of growing self-confidence and conviction to create only what he felt was "right." From conception to release the film was to take over ten years (1961–1971), and perhaps this film, rather than *Ivan's Childhood,* was to shape the mature person and artist. It is worthwhile, therefore, to look at its history as exemplary both of the workings of the Soviet film bureaucracy and of Tarkovsky's struggles to assert himself against it.

Two seemingly diametrically opposed views of *Andrei Roublev's* significance are offered by the two Russian critics who "discovered" Tarkovsky, knew him well personally, and followed his career closely from its inception. Both Neya Zorkaya and Maya Turovskaya agree that Tarkovsky's life and career were dramatically changed, with Zorkaya believing that the fight over the film with the cinema administration used up his time, energy, and health, preventing him from creating at the height of his powers, and making the bright, eccentric young man hard, suspicious, and embittered.[16] Turovskaya posits that the struggle strengthened him, firming his resolve and making him forever uncompromising in questions of art.[17] Moreover, she offers what will surely be a very controversial view: that Tarkovsky was by nature a "slow" creator and would probably not have made a significantly greater number of films even without all his bureaucratic tangles. There are clearly both positive and negative repercussions of the *Roublev* saga, for it helped to create the controversial Tarkovsky "persona," marking the beginning of a Tarkovsky "cult" both in the Soviet Union and abroad and ensuring that he would receive grudging respect even from those bureaucrats trying to stifle his creativity. It was, perhaps, at this time too that Tarkovsky began to see himself as a martyr and a prophet, sharing the long-held view among Russian intellectuals that an artist must suffer for his art and that his best creations result from a struggle against dogma and authorities.

The history of the making of *Andrei Roublev* not only plays a crucial role in Tarkovsky's career but also exemplifies, though perhaps to an extreme degree, what it meant to make films in the Soviet government-controlled cinema industry. In what was to become his standard operating procedure, he did not wait to complete his first film before he submitted, in 1961, a proposal (*zayavka*) to the studio for a film on the life of the most famous Russian medieval icon painter, Andrei Roublev. The contract was signed in 1962 and a film treatment was approved in December 1963.[18] He received permission to start work in April 1964, at the same time that the completed literary script for the film, titled *Andrei Roublev*, was published in the influential film journal *Iskusstvo kino*. Lively interest and discussion followed among historians, art specialists, critics, and ordinary readers, and the fame of the film began to spread before a single frame had been shot. A year elapsed before the actual Goskino order was handed down for the start of production (April 1965), with a one-year deadline for completion of shooting. The long pre-production period reflects the cinema administration's ambiguous, halfhearted support for the film: the budget was cut several times from the original 1.6 million rubles down to 1 million, which necessitated major cuts in what, in fact, was, as the co-scriptwriter Andrei Konchalovsky admits, an unwieldy and "unprofessional" script.[19] Shooting went on until November 1965, when it was interrupted by snow, forcing a return to the location in April and May 1966 and resulting in a budget overrun of 300,000 rubles. Rather than being congratulated on bringing in such a complex film with a comparatively modest overrun, Tarkovsky and his production manager, Tamara Ogorodnikova, received official letters of reprimand.[20]

As a result of the deletions and other changes during shooting, *Andrei Roublev* ended up being a very different film from the script that had been approved, published, and widely discussed. The first cut of the film was ready at the end of July 1966.[21] It was called *The Passion According to Andrei* and ran three hours and twenty-five minutes. The director of the Mosfilm archive, Tatyana Vinokurova, records that the film was accepted "with high marks" as a "talented and significant work of art,"[22] and on August 25, 1966, the permission (*akt*) for its release was written but—apparently and crucially—not *signed*. It was to be over five years before the film reached Soviet screens.

When *Andrei Roublev* was submitted for approval to Goskino, the next stage of the cinema hierarchy, it was immediately criticized for its length (5,642 meters) and graphic depiction of cruelty, blood, and violence, and suggestions were made for cuts. In a November 1966 letter to Alexei Romanov, the chairman of Goskino, Tarkovsky reported that thirty-seven changes had been made, which represented a cut of 390 meters, or some fifteen minutes. He also complained that the endless discussions and requests for changes on an "already accepted film" had made the final editing process extremely difficult and insisted that further cuts would seriously damage the film's artistic integrity.[23] Nevertheless, some of the most controversial scenes remained: the on-screen slitting of a man's throat; a horse falling down a staircase and then being finished off with a spear; blindings; and torture.

On December 24, 1966, a highly inflammatory article titled "And the Cow Burned . . ." appeared in a Moscow local daily newspaper, *Vechernyaya Moskva.* A documentary crew had come on location to shoot the making of the film and had captured what was one of the most gruesome scenes of the Tartar raid on Vladimir: the burning of a cow. Although later Tarkovsky was to keep repeating that the cow was covered with asbestos before being set on fire, the article became an excuse to galvanize the film's opposition, who pronounced it "anti-historical, anti-Russian, cruel, and harmful."[24] Clearly trying to forestall further attacks "in connection with cruelty to animals," Tarkovsky agreed in a letter to Romanov on December 27, 1966, to make a few more cuts in the "naturalistic" scenes, primarily the real on-screen killing of a horse and the "imitated" beating death of a dog.[25]

A premiere was held for the film industry at Dom Kino either at the end of 1966, according to Turovskaya, or the beginning of 1967, according to Ogorodnikova, with the audience variously reported as being "in ecstasy" and "stunned," but also critical, especially of the film's "naturalism." In February 1967 Tarkovsky complained to Romanov that, despite the success of the premiere, he and his film were increasingly subject to "malicious and unprincipled attacks," a form of "persecution" (which he feels began after *Ivan's Childhood!*); he still did not have the signed "akt" of the film's acceptance, even though Romanov had agreed on the final cut.[26] More requests for cuts and changes, which Tarkovsky stigmatized as "barbaric," were now made; one of the more brilliant suggestions—for an already completed film—was that he should "spruce" up the ragged Russian peasants of medieval times by dressing them better. The director refused to cut any further and the film existed in a kind of administrative limbo for almost five years, discussed at the highest levels of Mosfilm, Goskino, and even at a large gathering of the Central Committee of the Communist party.

During these years *Andrei Roublev* was to become probably the most famous film *not* released in the Soviet Union, and much of its fame was to come from abroad. In 1967 the film was requested for the Cannes Festival, where a Soviet film retrospective was planned in conjunction with the fiftieth anniversary of the Russian Revolution, but the official response was that the film was not yet edited. In 1969, at a very high-level meeting between P. N. Demichev, the Communist party *apparatchik* for culture, Alexei Romanov, the head of Goskino, and Lev Kulidzhanov, the head of the Filmmakers' Union, agreement was reached to release the film, both in domestic general distribution and for sale abroad.[27] There was a "second premiere" for the film industry at Dom Kino in 1969, the film was sold to a company representing Columbia for foreign distribution, and it seemed that *Andrei Roublev* would finally open. It was requested once more for the Cannes Festival in 1969, and, after the festival organizers had rejected all the other Soviet films offered them, an unofficial, out-of-competition screening was permitted. The film was greeted with great enthusiasm and was presented with the prestigious International Critics' Prize, much to the discomfiture of the Soviet authorities, who then made strenuous efforts to prevent its planned opening in Paris and refused to screen it at the 1969 Moscow Film Festival, despite numerous requests by foreign journalists. Resisting the pressure brought to bear on him, the distributor who had, perfectly legally, obtained the French rights eventually opened the film in Paris, where it was much debated and discussed. According to Yermash, its success abroad created problems at home, and renewed notoriety kept the film shelved for another two years.

Although Tarkovsky, his second wife Larissa, and influential supporters in the artistic world continued to keep up pressure on both the cinematic and the political bureaucracy,[28] it seems clear that it was Tarkovsky's firm resolve not to compromise that was responsible first for holding up the film and then for bringing about its release. The one thing he was unwilling to do was to cut the film any further, and, as diary entries for 1970 and 1971 make clear, that was still the prerequisite demanded of him. As it turned out, the cinema administration's intransigence and the fairly transparent attempt to "break" Tarkovsky had the unintended effect of merely strengthening his resolve and growing self-confidence. But another, perhaps even more important reason may have kept *Andrei Roublev* shelved for five years: the changing political climate of the late 1960s. Tarkovsky's innovative and challenging film fell foul of the increasing conservatism, the political and thus also artistic orthodoxy, which were to mark the Brezhnev era.

If one compares typescripts of artistic council meetings for *Ivan's Childhood* and *Andrei Roublev,* one finds Tarkovsky's immediate "boss," V. Surin, the director of the Mosfilm studio, seemingly deferring to the director on the first film: He states that Tarkovsky had the last word and could choose whether or not to accept the suggested changes and cuts. (Although the director *did* officially have to accept changes before they could be made, many directors were, of course, pressured into accepting alterations.) By contrast, in the Mosfilm artistic council meeting of May 31, 1967, which considered *Andrei Roublev* as well as Konchalovsky's *The Story of Asya Klyachina,* Surin himself now reminded everyone that although the directors had their "own strong, clear position and boundaries which they do not consider possible to cross," the films were not "Tarkovsky's or Konchalovsky's but Mosfilm's" and they "could not deal with them as they pleased. This is our collective matter."[29] Surin had just finished reading an anonymous attack on *Roublev* provided by Romanov at Goskino, and he was clearly on the defensive. He suggested finally that Tarkovsky's creative unit invite the directors Romm and Gerasimov to have a talk with Tarkovsky in the hopes of getting him to agree to further changes and to get Goskino off the studio's back. At this meeting Tarkovsky's fellow directors at Mosfilm defended the film, refuting the unfounded accusations, and further questioned an ominous pattern of film rejections by Goskino, which was occurring not only with their own productions but also at Lenfilm and the various republic studios, such as Gruziafilm.[30] Eldar Ryazanov, who was later to direct some of the best Soviet comedies, noted with alarm that a "whole series of films were placed on the shelf, as in days long ago."[31] Characteristically, Tarkovsky himself saw Goskino's actions in purely personal terms, failing to recognize—as his fellow directors had done—that *Andrei Roublev* fell victim to much broader political and ideological repression.

Andrei Roublev was to have its real and final "premiere" at the very end of 1971. The London *Times* (December 21, 1971) reported that it opened for general release on December 20 to "large but subdued crowds" and was ignored by the newspapers.[32] A few days after the film's release, however, an article attacking it came out in the widely read daily *Komsomolskaya pravda* (December 25, 1971) ensuring that the long-awaited film would enjoy a *succès de scandale* unmatched by any other Soviet film of the time. Writing in 1976, Neya Zorkaya stated that *Andrei Roublev* had not come off the repertóry in Moscow since it opened—which means for five years![33]

The vituperative attacks on the film were provoked not only by its unacceptable portrayal of a violent and barbaric medieval Russia but also by the film's structural complexity. The problems of narrative logic and continuity referred to in *Ivan's Childhood* are intensified to some extent in this film, partly as a result of changes between the written script and the final visualization (especially where particulars of time and place are concerned) and partly because of Tarkovsky's growing conviction that an emotional or intuitive response to his films was far superior to a logical, rational one. For a Western viewer these difficulties are compounded by the unfamiliar setting of medieval Russia and a painter-hero who is barely known even to educated Westerners. Though the eight main episodes of the film are dated, they are seldom specifically located, apart from casual references in the dialogue that are not always translated in the subtitles (this defect, to be sure, is hardly Tarkovsky's fault). To some extent this resulted from the excision during shooting, for budgetary reasons, of scenes that would have made the continuity rather clearer, but Tarkovsky seems elsewhere to be making considerable demands on his audience. The scene of the blinding of the stone masons on the order of the grand duke (in the episode titled "The Last Judgment") is introduced so obscurely as a flashback that even competent critics have failed to recognize that this is what it is. Other flashbacks—the false reconciliation of the grand duke and his brother, and Roublev's memory in "The Bell" of a meeting with his former friend Kirill—are also introduced very elliptically.

If scenes like these are perhaps unnecessarily confusing, throughout the film Tarkovsky seems to insist that his audience watch, listen, think, and assess with quite unusual intensity if they are to understand and respond fully to his work. The overall structure is that of a series of journeys, covering

1.2. and 1.3. Two artist/inventors—the balloonist and Boriska, the bellmaker (Nikolai Burlyaev). *Andrei Roublev.* Artificial Eye.

ta period of twenty-three years, that at first seem to follow no particular narrative pattern. We have a prologue featuring a balloonist that is never linked into the story of the film, then a series of meetings and conversations—the three monk/painters Roublev, Kirill, and Daniil with peasants and a buffoon; Kirill and the painter Theophanes; Kirill and Roublev; Roublev and Theophanes; Roublev and a group of pagans conducting erotic/mystical rituals; Roublev and Daniil; Roublev and his patron, the grand duke—that seem perversely unwilling to follow the cause-effect structure that we apply to our normal experience of film narrative. Violent and brutal incidents, such as the arrest and mistreatment of the buffoon and the blinding of a group of stone masons, culminate in "The Raid" of episode six, in which a Tartar army aided by a renegade Russian nobleman (the grand duke's brother) attacks and loots the city of Vladimir and massacres most of its inhabitants; and it is not until this episode that it becomes clear that it is

1.4. The three monk/painters set off to look for work. Roublev (Anatoly Solonitsyn) in the middle. *Andrei Roublev.* Artificial Eye.

the *theme* of the film that matters, not its *plot*. Roublev, who has sought in the previous episodes to maintain and defend his faith in human goodness and the value of his art, upon witnessing the destruction of Vladimir now loses his trust in both, resolves to give up painting, and takes a vow of silence. For the remainder of the film, what matters is whether or not he will recover this faith (as, in fact, he does). A structure of this kind, dealing with inner experience rather than the overcoming of physical obstacles in order to attain a clearly defined material goal, is definitely alien to the expectations of most filmgoers, Western or otherwise.

Despite this, however, and perhaps paradoxically, *Andrei Roublev* is a powerfully physical film—so much so that many viewers recoil in horror from the tactile intensity of the raid on Vladimir or the blinding of the masons (both toned down in the successive cuts that the film underwent before its final release). The Tartar attack is a piece of virtuoso filmmaking that forces us to confront the cold-blooded cruelty that results from the possession of total power over defenseless victims and reflects Tarkovsky's desire to present the harsh realities of the historical past as well as their contemporary relevance. This episode is balanced near the end by one equally energetic and kinetic, but directed toward a positive aim: the casting of the bell that, in its display of human energies united in the service of a creative rather than a destructive or self-seeking endeavor, inspires Roublev to recover his lost faith and idealism. And throughout the film as a whole, Tarkovsky emphasizes the physical reality of the natural world—rain, snow, flooded ground, rivers, forests, trees, fire, galloping horses, barking dogs, the harsh cawing of crows, the birdsong that is heard, in chilling counterpoint, as the blinded masons crawl and stagger helplessly in the forest.

The total impression left by the film, despite scenes of frantic activity, is of a stately and majestically inexorable advance toward Roublev's recovery

1.5. Two opposing views of art: Theophanes (Nikolai Sergeyev) and Roublev. *Andrei Roublev.* Artificial Eye.

of faith both in human beings and in his art, together with the triumphant revelation of the lasting value of that art in the color sequences of the historical Roublev paintings that (almost) close the film: The final shot is of the necessary counterpoise to art, nature, as four horses graze peacefully on the banks of a river. The unhurried pacing of the film and its use of several extended sequence shots lasting two minutes or more force us—as does the structure of the film as a whole—to live through a pattern of time that is not so much imposed by the director but, as Tarkovsky would argue, the result of respecting the natural rhythms, the "inherent quality" of what is being filmed.

The film's thematics also lead on from *Ivan's Childhood* and begin to consolidate the patterns to which Tarkovsky would return, in one form or another, and with varying degrees of emphasis, in all his subsequent films. War and the suffering of innocent victims, contrasted with the beauty and serenity of nature, provides one obvious link, but *Andrei Roublev* develops in particular the theme of art and the artist (touched on briefly in *Ivan* when the boy comments bitterly on the Germans' destruction of their own artistic heritage) and the importance of faith and spirituality. Various types of creators are presented in the film: Besides the painters Roublev, Theophanes, Daniil, and Kirill, we encounter an inventor (the balloonist), a jester (the buffoon), craftsmen (the stone masons), and an inventor/craftsman (Boriska, the creator of the bell).

The four painters are distinguished by their attitudes toward their art, themselves, and their public. Theophanes, Daniil, and Kirill are all "traditionalists," content to continue in an already established style and to use their art to frighten and terrify their audience into what church and state consider acceptable moral behavior. Kirill additionally is vain, jealous, and untalented, and concerned more with personal fame than with the value of his art. Roublev, by contrast, is completely unworldly: he sees himself as the servant of a higher power and his art as a means of guiding people toward an understanding of their own innate goodness by presenting a vision of a just and kindly God. His faith in humankind and in the truth of his vision is steadily undermined, however, by the brutality and cruelty that he sees all around him, culminating in the combined Tartar and Russian attack on Vladimir. It is only restored when he witnesses another artist, Boriska, overcoming his own self-doubt and the initial skepticism and resistance of others and achieving his goal of casting the bell. Boriska's faith in his vision leads him to lie—claiming that his father had passed his secret on to him when in fact he had not—to bully and intimidate his workers (even ordering one of them to be whipped) and drive both them and himself to the point of exhaustion. Yet these acts seem justified in one who has the instincts of a true creator (and may even be necessary attributes, as Tarkovsky must have sensed, of any artist—such as a film director—who has to combine and exploit the talents of others in order to achieve his goal). At the end Roublev suggests that he and Boriska should work together—"You will cast bells and I will paint"—implying that the ideal artist will combine the worldly and the unworldly, the spiritual and the practical, to achieve his or her vision.

Roublev and his companions, and Boriska too, are dependent on patrons (as, again, is the film director) if they are to find work. This can lead, if the artist has genuine integrity and independence, to conflicts with the established power structure both of church and state. The irreverent buffoon is arrested and has half his tongue cut out; the stone masons who refuse to follow the grand duke's instructions and attempt to work for his better-paying brother instead are attacked and blinded; Boriska realizes that he could suffer drastic punishment if he fails to make true his boast of being able to cast the bell. Though it is unwise to see the film—as many early Western critics did—as being an "allegory" of Tarkovsky's own problems (many of which did not really begin until *after* this film was completed), his depiction of the dangers faced by the artist would hardly have been lost on a Soviet audience, many of whom had endured a quarter-century of Stalinism.

Solaris *(1972) and* Mirror *(1975)*

While *Andrei Roublev* was still "shelved" and Tarkovsky clearly in disfavor, he failed to get approval for an autobiographical film about his mother (which was later to become *Mirror*). Instead, he turned to what was officially considered the relatively "light" and "innocuous" science-fiction genre, with an adaptation of Stanislaw Lem's novel *Solaris*—which was in fact far from "light" and to whose complex philosophical and moral thematics Tarkovsky was strongly attracted. Despite what were to become routine problems—constant reductions of an approved budget to around half the original estimate and the inevitable request for a considerable number of changes or cuts—*Solaris* was released without significant compromise on Tarkovsky's part. As was to become his usual practice, he yielded on relatively trivial details: he shortened Hari's resurrection scene which, according to the actress Natalia Bondarchuk, he had deliberately filmed at excessive length in order to give the censors something to focus on and distract them from more important matters (shades of the Hollywood Production Code of the 1930s!), while resisting anything he felt might be truly damaging. The "crazy list" of thirty-five suggestions (almost none of which he accepted) is mockingly enumerated and commented on in his diary for January 12–13, 1972.[34] Mostly they ask for more clarity and explicitness, a stronger "futuristic" element, and a "positive" ending; at their most pathetic they insist on knowing whether the future society is Communist, socialist, or capitalist and show a total inability to understand the film by demanding that Hari should not become human. Rather to Tarkovsky's surprise, the bureaucracy caved in very quickly this time, and the film was rapidly approved and given a normal release. Could this perhaps have later made him suspicious of it and caused him constantly to refer to it as his least-successful film? At the time, he was certainly fully committed to it and making it was in no way a compromise with the cinema administration, as has sometimes been suggested.

His genuine involvement in the film is attested to by the strongly autobiographical elements he introduces into it, which he was to work out further in *Mirror,* whose (revamped) script was finally approved some five years after its initial submission. This daring, self-revealing, and stylistically innovative work shocked even the more perceptive of his fellow directors, finding strong opponents at the Mosfilm studio as well as in the new head of Goskino, Filip Yermash, who refused to release it or send it to Cannes, despite a personal request for it from the festival's director. After minor cuts, however, *Mirror* was released without significant further delay, although the bureaucracy's displeasure with this "difficult," "elitist" work was demonstrated by relegating it to the third category of distribution (a small number of prints, usually shown in small, out-of-the-way cinemas and preferably at inconvenient times). It was later upgraded to the second, rather more accessible, category. Despite the obstacles deliberately placed in the way of audiences, the film ran to full houses for several months from six a.m. to midnight, according to Tarkovsky's second wife, Larissa, and Alexander Misharin, the film's co-scriptwriter. By now Tarkovsky had developed a serious following among a surprisingly broad spectrum of viewers, who, by word of mouth, knew how to find the screenings.

Despite the many real bureaucratic obstacles placed in his way, the seemingly halfhearted and usually unsuccessful attempts to "control" Tarkovsky or censor his films reflect his growing "clout" as an internationally recognized director whose films were frequently awarded festival prizes. A kind of love-hate relationship existed between Goskino, especially its new chairman, Yermash, and Tarkovsky, for, though his films were ideologically and stylistically quite far from the acceptable socialist realist norms of Soviet cinema at the time, he could bring both prestige and hard currency to the Soviet cinema industry. *Mirror*, for example, was sold to the French (to Gaumont's Daniel Toscan du Plantier) for an unheard-of sum of $200,000—an outlandish figure proposed in order to *discourage* the sale of a film Yermash found particularly distasteful! But even du Plantier balked at paying extortion—the *further* $200,000 demanded for permission to screen it at Cannes.[35] For his part, while at home he was very outspoken in defense of his films, Tarkovsky was quite circumspect in foreign public appearances, staying clear of political discussions of any sort, obviously quite aware that a false step might keep him from going abroad the next time. As previously noted, even when he finally announced his decision to stay in the West, he did not call himself a dissident, stressing, as always, that he was an artist and had nothing to do with politics.

Although *Solaris* and *Mirror* are superficially very different—the first based on a well-known science-fiction novel and the second an extremely personal and largely autobiographical work—they share strong similarities in style and theme that make it useful to examine them together. Repeatedly thwarted in his initial attempts to film *Mirror*, Tarkovsky seems to have incorporated some of his ideas into *Solaris* instead, which is in many respects very different from its literary source. Where Lem's novel is set totally in space—in a research station orbiting the planet Solaris, whose all-encompassing ocean appears to have mysterious and disturbing powers that give form to man's deepest fears and desires—Tarkovsky places the first half-hour of his film on earth, celebrating the world of nature that his scientist/astronaut hero, Kris Kelvin, may be about to leave behind forever. As in the earlier films, the camera lingers on images of water (rain, a pond), trees, fruit, grass, water weeds, a horse, a dog; and we hear the sound of wind, birds, and insects—none of them present in the cold sterility of the space station, though the scientists there attempt to reproduce and remember them in various ways. Here too action is retarded, even neglected, as nothing much "happens" except that we receive some background information on Kris's mission—to investigate the disappearance of an astronaut and the appearance of strange "visitors" on Solaris; we also gain some insight into his uncomfortable relationship with his father—a plot line completely absent in the original novel. As in *Roublev*, the pacing is slow and measured throughout and shots lasting two, three, or even four minutes are relatively frequent.

Once Kris reaches the station, our narrative expectations—that he will solve the mystery there—are confounded. At first, suspense is created by the physical disarray of the station; strange sounds and fleeting, barely seen figures; the discovery of the suicide of one of the three remaining scientists; and the emotional turmoil of the others—all leading the viewer to expect that something frightening is about to happen and that Kris will have to fight some unknown forces of evil. But when Hari, a woman he loved in the past, appears as his own personal "visitor" (created as an identical but nonhuman replica by the power of the sentient Solaris ocean), the plot is

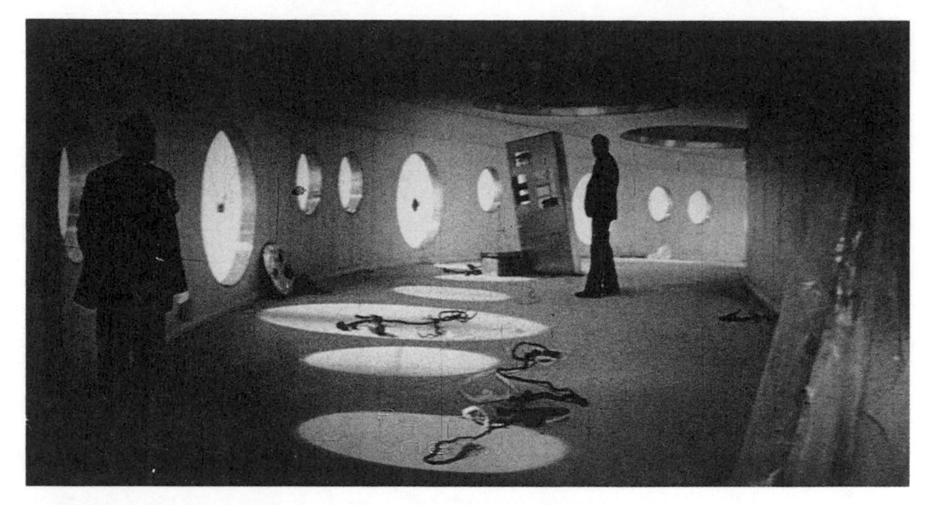

1.6. The outer corridor of the space station. *Solaris.* Contemporary Films.

completely derailed. Instead, as in *Roublev,* Tarkovsky begins an exploration of an inner journey as Kris moves toward self-knowledge, the recovery of the capacity to love, and atonement for his feelings of guilty inadequacy toward his father, his (apparently) dead mother, and, most of all, Hari herself, the wife (or lover) whom he drove to suicide by his emotional coldness some years previously. As the film proceeds, the narrative continuities of time, space, and logical development increasingly fracture and fragment as we enter more fully into Kris's consciousness. The more Kris attempts to rid himself of Hari and physically destroy her, the more she returns in increasingly "human" form, capable of a love and devotion to which he can find no adequate response. Meanwhile, important stages of the plot are assumed to have taken place and are mentioned fleetingly in retrospect: Hari's conversation with Dr. Sartorius in which she learns the truth about her previous existence on earth; or Kris's sending of an encephalogram to the ocean in an attempt to rid himself and the other scientists of their unwelcome "visitors."

Toward the end of the film Kris undergoes a series of hallucinations that both pick up on the imagery of the dreams in *Ivan's Childhood* and prefigure a major theme of Tarkovsky's next film, *Mirror.* Once again the mother is a central figure, but now distant and reproachful rather than warm and loving; she is physically identified and associated with Hari and appears in a setting that strangely combines features of the space station and of the father's dacha at the beginning of the film. As in *Ivan's Childhood,* the dreams seem intended to explain something crucial about the hero's psychology: perhaps in this case that, unable to win the love of a beautiful but coolly remote mother, he has found it impossible to trust and open himself to the love of any other woman.

As the dream ends, he discovers that he has lost Hari once more: she

1.7. Questions of identity: Kris (Donatas Banionis) and Hari (Natalia Bondarchuk). *Solaris.* Contemporary Films.

has committed suicide again, but this time because he *does* love her and this is the only solution to the dilemma they are faced with. She can exist only on the space station, while his natural home is to be found on earth. Kris then decides to return home, but the film's conclusion resolves none of the questions of plot that it initially appeared to be concerned with; instead we have a scene that defies logical explanation and yet is metaphorically "right" in every way. Kris is simultaneously back on earth, reconciled at last with his father, and yet still on Solaris, with the father's dacha and its immediate surroundings situated on one of the newly created islands in the swirling Solaris ocean, which have been formed in response to the encephalogram he had sent earlier.

By this stage of his career Tarkovsky had begun to establish a reputation as the creator of visually powerful and beautiful films that increasingly refused to work in terms of conventional narrative logic and whose meaning was conveyed through dreams and visual metaphors as much as through action and dialogue. The largely autobiographical *Mirror* takes this stylistic process even further, operating within a framework that purposefully mingles present-day action, dreams, memories of childhood and the past, and documentary footage of major historical events from the mid-1930s to around 1960. In the present-day action the narrator Alexei (whose face is never shown, and whose reclining body and hand are seen only toward the end of the film, on what appears to be his deathbed) talks to his estranged wife Natalia about their marital problems and the future of their twelve-year-old son Ignat. He dreams of and remembers his childhood as a five-year-old boy in the 1930s, living in a dacha with his mother, sister, and (in dreams only) father, and remembers/recreates scenes from his mother's life in the 1930s and from his own early adolescence during World War II. Interspersed

1.8. Natalia (Margarita Terekhova as the wife) contemplates her own image, ignoring her husband/narrator Alexei. *Mirror.* Artificial Eye.

with these is newsreel footage from the Spanish Civil War, World War II, and the Chinese-Soviet conflicts of the 1950s (among others); some of these newsreels and memories are accompanied by voice-over readings by Tarkovsky's father Arseny of his own poetry.

Obviously this is a complicated structure, made more complex by the way in which Tarkovsky moves freely between past and present, dream and reality, and by the fact that the roles of Alexei's mother Maria (Masha) as a young woman in the 1930s and 1940s and of his wife Natalia are played by the same actress, Margarita Terekhova. The mother is also seen as an old woman (played by Tarkovsky's own mother), and the roles of the twelve-year-old Alexei (Alyosha) and the twelve-year-old Ignat, his son, are played by the same boy. Although Tarkovsky provides clues for the attentive viewer so that we can distinguish between the various characters and time frames, these are not immediately obvious or even consistent. The present-day scenes are in color and certain obvious dreams are in black and white, sometimes additionally signaled by a verbal clue in the dialogue or voice-over of the preceding scene and by the use of slow motion—but one dream at least is in color. Memories are generally in color: the young Alexei receiving military instruction at a shooting range—a scene that is in turn

1.9. Masha (Margarita Terekhova as the young mother) at the opening of the film, in an image recreated from Tarkovsky's own childhood. *Mirror.* Artificial Eye.

complicated by the fact that, though Alexei is present, the focus is on another boy, a war orphan whose behavior brings him into conflict with the instructor; or Alexei accompanying his mother on a humiliating visit to a well-to-do neighbor during the war, where she attempts to sell her earrings in order to buy food for her children. The powerful scene in a state printing house during the 1930s which evokes so vividly Stalinist terror when the mother thinks she may have made a crucial proofreading error[36] is, however, in black and white and may even represent his mother's memory rather than his own.[37]

Visual and verbal clues also help us to distinguish between the young mother in the past and the wife in the present. Sometimes they are referred to by name (rarely given in the American subtitles, unfortunately); usually when the woman's hair is up at the beginning of a scene she is the mother, and when it is down, she is the wife. As each scene proceeds, it quickly becomes evident which time frame we are in. Yet a good deal of work has to be done by the audience in order to put the various clues together and, as usual, important narrative information is either presented elliptically or retarded to a relatively late stage of the story. Not only does Tarkovsky expect us to view his films "actively," he also seems to want us to see them repeatedly, each time making some new discovery or connection.

Certain scenes, moreover, introduce dreamlike elements into what begins as a realistic situation. Ignat, left alone in their apartment by his mother, has a strange encounter with two women who appear as if from nowhere and vanish equally mysteriously (yet their existence is testified to by the heat mark on the table of a cup and saucer from which one of them had been drinking). During this scene his grandmother (Alexei's mother as an old woman) appears at the door, but neither she nor her grandson appear to recognize each other! The two women later appear, again without explanation, discussing with a doctor the reasons for the illness of the sick and possibly dying narrator. During a dream/memory the five-year-old Alexei approaches his mother, who turns out not to be the youthful woman we expect but her older, future self. These paradoxes come together in the final scene, in which past and present fuse and overlap: The old mother of the present-day action walks with the five-year-old Alexei and his sister in the setting of the dacha in the 1930s as her younger self stands in the distance watching. Once again the conflicts and tensions of the rest of the film are resolved metaphorically in a moment of peaceful harmony and reconciliation.

As his diary entries from 1970 onward make clear, Tarkovsky was becoming increasingly concerned with the lack of faith and spirituality in the modern world and the triumph of materialism and technology (with its concomitant pollution and ravaging of the natural environment and the ever-present danger of nuclear disaster). These concerns are first voiced directly in *Solaris,* where the father's dacha seems an oasis of natural beauty in a futuristic world represented by the visually and aurally ugly city into which the former astronaut Berton drives early in the film, while Kris Kelvin, the film's hero, has to learn that "knowledge is valid only when it is based on morality." Soulless technology is represented in the film by the coldly remote scientist Dr. Sartorius and, at first, by Kris himself, though, under Hari's influence and the example of her willingness to sacrifice herself for his sake, he learns—or relearns—the necessity for love and moral conscience.

The more general theme of the film is combined with a typically personal one in Kris's relationship with his parents, which has no counterpart in Lem's book and reflects Tarkovsky's own "tortured, complicated, unspoken" feelings about his own father and mother, confided to his diary at exactly the time he was preparing this film.[38] Unusually, the father is given equal importance with the mother;[39] his relationship with Kris at the beginning of the film is clearly tense and uneasy and, at the end, as a changed and contrite Kris returns (or appears to return) home, the son kneels before his father in a posture that deliberately echoes Rembrandt's "Return of the Prodigal Son" (in the Hermitage, Leningrad). The reasons for their estrangement are never made clear, though the father reproaches him before he leaves on his mission, saying that men of his (cold, rationalistic, unemotional) temperament are "dangerous" in space. The mother, who is presumably dead, appears only in a photograph in the dacha, in a video Kris takes with him to the space station, and in the hallucinations that he experiences when he falls ill toward the end of the film. Calmly eating an apple, she reproaches him for neglecting and offending her, tells him he lives a strange life, and—speaking to her adult son as if he were still a child[40]—asks how he got so dirty before proceeding to wash his arm. Kris meanwhile gazes at her helplessly and tearfully, unable to do little more than sigh, "Mama!" In contrast to the reconciliation with the father, the estrangement from the mother is not resolved.

The visual identification between wife (Hari) and mother that occurs at the beginning of this hallucination is carried over into *Mirror*, where both women are played by the same actress and the narrator comments more than once that his wife reminds him of his mother. Mark Le Fanu's sentimental picture of Tarkovsky's relationship with his parents (". . . he continued to revere both with an intensity and honor attested to by numerous homages in his work") seriously distorts the true situation, especially where his mother is concerned.[41] It is also significant that, though the mother of *Mirror* is beautiful and obviously adored, she is also cool, aloof, and, where her small children are concerned, unemotional, never even touching the five-year-old boy. Alexei, the hero/narrator of this film, also seems to feel a great sense of guilt and a need for atonement and reconciliation—though this seems to extend more to his childhood and past than to his present relationship with his estranged wife and the son to whom he refers at one point with open sarcasm as a "booby." His dreams of himself at the age of five emphasize feelings of exclusion—from a sexual encounter between his parents in which the mother appears eerie and frightening, or running toward and entering the now deserted dacha of his childhood. The color memories (and the one color dream) of the dacha, however, certainly emphasize warmth and security, perhaps to contrast more strongly with his obviously unsatisfactory present where even his relationship with his (now aged) mother appears to have deteriorated badly—as his wife sarcastically points out at one stage. In an early phone conversation with his mother, he sounds very like Kris Kelvin, asking plaintively why they fight all the time and begging her to forgive him. Perhaps Alexei too feels he has never been able to win his mother's full affection and has transferred his dissatisfaction into the marital warfare he conducts with his wife.

Throughout the film Masha (the mother) is associated with the feminine, maternal element of water, sometimes naturalistically (standing or running in the rain, taking a shower, walking near a river), sometimes in a strange and dreamlike fashion (as when rain suddenly streams down the wall behind her at the end of the "earring" scene). In significant contrast, Natalia, the narrator's wife, who is in conflict with her husband over their son and toward whom he expresses open antagonism, is always seen indoors and is never directly associated with or touched by water (at best she watches rain falling outside). Water is also the dominant natural element in Tarkovsky's final Russian film, *Stalker*, once again based on a science-fiction work, this time by Arkady and Boris Strugatsky; but here, rather than having positive (purifying, redemptive) associations, the water tends to be stagnant, swampy, and filled with the debris of a decaying civilization.

Wider themes of war and the disruptions and sufferings it causes also enter *Mirror*, partly in the newsreel sequences and also in the fictional plot (the earring scene, or the children's brief but joyful reunion with their father on leave during the war). In this respect Tarkovsky is creating an autobiography of his own generation as much as of himself and, of all his films, this is the one that sparked the deepest and most intense responses in the Soviet audience. Although we are never told the narrator's profession, he may well be a poet, and poetry (by Tarkovsky's father), paintings (especially those of Leonardo da Vinci), classical music (especially by Bach), and references to Russia's cultural and historical mission—in the letter by Pushkin to Chaadayev that Ignat reads aloud during his meeting with the mysterious women in his mother's apartment—are important connected motifs which create both a highly personal and a broadly cultural context in which Tarkovsky the artist envisions himself.

Stalker *(1979) and* Nostalghia *(1983)*

Stalker is no less "oneiric" than *Mirror*, but it achieves its effects in a rather different way. *Mirror* collapses the distinctions between past and present, dream, memory, and reality so thoroughly that the viewer finally surrenders to the rhythms, associative patterns, and logic of a dream rather than trying to insist that everything "make sense." *Stalker* (a futuristic allegory) follows—or seems to follow—a straightforward chronology as "Writer" and "Professor" are led by their guide "Stalker" into the mysterious "Zone" toward the "Room" in which their deepest wishes can be realized. The heavily guarded and fenced-off Zone itself has been seen by many critics—especially in the West—as a rather transparent metaphor for the Soviet Union and even the former Eastern bloc as a whole: the word "Zone" refers in colloquial Russian to the network of labor camps and Stalker himself (who has served a term in prison) has the shaven head and ragged clothing of a typical "zek" (inmate). Here Tarkovsky seems to be employing the "Aesopian" language of parable and allusion so common in East European cinema of the 1960s and 1970s. As usual, however, with Tarkovsky, any possible political interpretation quickly becomes secondary to his moral and philosophical concerns.

As with the structurally very similar *Solaris*, the external quest and the otherworldly dangers hinted at in the early dialogue transform halfway through the film into an interior voyage of self-discovery on the part of all three characters. There are no flashbacks or obvious dreams, though one scene, as the three men rest near a swamp, creates thoroughly dreamlike distortions of time and space. Yet, especially once the men enter the Zone, the setting becomes truly hallucinatory and time and space appear to lose all meaning. Their clearly visible goal cannot be approached in a straight

1.10. Professor (Nikolai Grinko) and Writer (Anatoly Solonitsyn) in the Zone. *Stalker.* Contemporary Films.

line but only by means of interminable detours, while scenes in totally different locations follow one another with no indication of how they relate spatially, how the men got there, or how long it took them. (Tarkovsky said in interviews that he had wanted to give the impression that the whole film consisted of a single shot.) In truly dreamlike fashion they keep returning inexorably to a setting they had long since left behind them—most notably a tiled wall that is seen on three separate occasions—and uninterrupted conversations continue over shots that show the characters positioned in ways that are totally discontinuous from one shot to the next. When, as occasionally happens, the men separate from one another, time seems to operate differently for each of them, as when Stalker and Writer "lose" Professor and then find him back at the tiled wall, beside a burning fire that had not existed earlier.

Tarkovsky makes us share the strangeness of the characters' experience by forcing us to share their sense of time. The average shot length of the film is almost one minute (in *Mirror* it was thirty seconds) and many shots last well over three or four minutes—the longest, six minutes fifty seconds, takes place in a room close to their destination[42] that contains a mysteriously still-functioning telephone. In the long, slowly paced shots, with the camera either following the characters or, as in this case, moving almost imperceptibly toward them, nothing *happens,* except arguments, conver-

1.11. The "negative" ending. The three men sit outside the Room. *Stalker.* Contemporary Films.

sations, monologues, and the puzzled and frightened reactions of the men toward their potentially dangerous surroundings—but the sense of the alien is very powerfully conveyed. The main activities in the film occur near the beginning as the men cross the patrolled and fenced-off area that separates the Zone from the dingy, sordid, polluted setting that is all we ever see in the film of "ordinary" (and almost transparently Soviet) life. As the film proceeds, the action slows to almost complete immobility and the resolution of the film occurs as the men sit and do nothing, refusing to cross the threshold of the Room.

This "negative" ending, however, is followed by a "positive" one that suggests that, despite the apparent failure of their expedition, the men have indeed changed and learned something and that the miraculous powers of the Zone can affect and influence everyday reality. Stalker's crippled daughter "Monkey" (whose illness is attributed to his constant excursions into the Zone) performs an act of telekinesis, moving two glasses and a jar across a table by the power of thought, and providing—in the subdued beauty of the images and the grave intensity of the child's gaze—an "epiphany" that compensates for the sense of failure and despair that might otherwise permeate the film.

The nineteenth-century Slavophile concept that Russia possesses a particular spiritual integrity lacking in the materialistic and decadent West—

1.12. The "positive" ending. Stalker's daughter (Natasha Abramova) performs her miracle of telekinesis. *Stalker.* Contemporary Films.

referred to in *Mirror* through the Pushkin quote concerning Russia's "special destiny"—held considerable attraction for Tarkovsky and is central to both *Stalker* and *Nostalghia. Stalker,* he wrote in his diary, "is about the existence of God in man, and about the death of spirituality as a result of our possessing false knowledge."[43] Stalker himself is a figure straight out of the Russian literary tradition (specifically Dostoyevsky): one of the "yurodivy" (as Writer patronizingly refers to him) or "holy fools," who may be physically weak, even cowardly, and are despised and considered crazy by others, yet are spiritually and morally strong. He constantly emphasizes the need for faith, despite the hostility or indifference of his two companions, the pragmatic and rationalistic Professor (a more sympathetic version of Sartorius in *Solaris*) and the skeptical, self-despising Writer, who claims he is going to the Zone to recover his lost inspiration. More bitter and cynical than Roublev, Writer has lost all faith in the value of his art and his ability to satisfy the needs of his audience: He is mocking, sarcastic, and even violent toward the meek and self-effacing Stalker. Yet it is not art as such that he despises, for he speaks feelingly about its power when used, as it should be, to create "images of absolute truth" (echoing a phrase used by Tarkovsky himself in *Sculpting in Time*);[44] his despair results from his realization that he is too egotistical and self-centered to achieve this any longer.

Both Writer and Professor are finally unwilling or unable to formulate a wish or to enter the Room itself; Stalker sees this as a defeat and laments to his wife on his return that no one needs either himself or the Room for no one believes any longer. Yet both men have in fact changed. Professor, who came to the Zone armed with a bomb with which he intended to destroy the Room (so that it could not be used by others for their own selfish ends), changes his mind, moved by Stalker's plea that to destroy the Room means to destroy hope, and throws the bomb away. Though Writer makes no similarly dramatic gesture, he seems to have learned some degree of charity and forgiveness, putting his arm protectively around Stalker as they sit together on the threshold of the Room and behaving in a subdued and thoughtful manner on their return home.

The Hungarian critics Kovács and Szilágyi[45] suggest another grouping for the film's characters, with the wife representing the ethical principle, Stalker the spiritual, and their daughter the mystical. Stalker's wife tries to dissuade him from his expedition, warning that he may end up in jail once more; when she fails to do so, she berates him, blaming him for their daughter's crippled condition, and curses the day she met him. Yet she is welcoming and comforting on his return and attempts to console him when he laments what he sees as his failure to convince his companions. In a monologue that follows[46] she expresses her loyalty and devotion to her husband and insists that, despite all their problems, they have always been happy: if there were no sorrow in their lives, there would be no happiness either. In her love, loyalty, forgiveness, and self-sacrifice she represents, like Hari in *Solaris,* the female virtues that Tarkovsky valued most highly, embodied preferably in someone who combines the functions of both wife and mother. In a self-administered questionnaire about his tastes in music, film, literature, and so on, entered in his diary for January 3, 1974, he asked himself, "What is a woman's driving-force?" and answered "submission, humiliation, in the name of love." The sacristan's comments to Eugenia near the beginning of *Nostalghia* echo this viewpoint.

By the time he made *Stalker,* his last film in the Soviet Union, Tarkovsky's reputation assured him total creative control over scripts, sets, and actors. When he asked his artistic council, which was supposed to decide such matters, to choose between his wife Larissa and the actress Alyssa Freindlikh for the role of Stalker's wife, they left the decision to him, the "great director."[47] In addition, and most astonishingly, he was allowed to reshoot practically the whole film—something that he would certainly never have been able to do in the West. The film was plagued with personnel problems (the firing of the cameraman and set designer) and technical problems of apparently out-of-date film stock that had then been incompetently developed at the Mosfilm labs. Initially, Tarkovsky seemed to have used these problems as an excuse to close down production on a film with whose script he was unhappy and take the opportunity to rewrite it.

What becomes clear from the often conflicting accounts of *Stalker*'s convoluted history is that Tarkovsky was in total control on the set, as he had been ever since *Andrei Roublev.* In his otherwise self-serving memoir of

Tarkovsky, Filip Yermash justifiably calls *Stalker* "an unprecedented case": the closed-down film was given an official transfer from the 1977 production year to 1978, on the pretext that it was undergoing a "change of genre" from "science fiction" to "a moral-philosophical parable," and it was also expanded to a two-part film, thus allowing for additional funds.[48] In this film many of Tarkovsky's problems were of his own making, yet the cinema administration, despite the usual obstacles and even threats to shut down production, nonetheless supported him in the end and allowed him to make another successful film.

In the light of this seemingly privileged treatment, why should Tarkovsky have voiced such constant unhappiness with his situation in the Soviet Union? Throughout the 1970s some of his favorite projects, most notably his desire to film Dostoyevsky's *The Idiot,* had been blocked. He felt, despite working conditions that, in many respects, would have made most Western directors drool with envy, that he was under constant harassment from the authorities and was not really free to choose his own projects and bring them to fruition. (Du Plantier, for example, describes how Goskino made it extremely difficult for Tarkovsky even to see his foreign distributors!) These feelings intensified over a period of several years as he began to work on a planned co-production with RAI, the Italian state television company that was eagerly soliciting films from foreign directors (such as the Hungarian Miklós Jancsó).

The idea of an Italian film seems to have arisen out of his long-standing friendship with Tonino Guerra (Antonioni's regular scriptwriter). Their first collaboration in 1976 was a script of what was essentially a collection of Tarkovsky's personal impressions, called *Journey through Italy,* to be produced for Italian television. But 1977 and 1978 were taken up with the shooting and re-shooting of *Stalker,* and only in 1979 was Tarkovsky able to go to Italy and revive his collaboration with Guerra. In addition to *Journey through Italy,* this time they developed an outline for a fiction film called *The End of the World,* about a man who locks himself and his family (wife, daughter, and son) in their house to await the world's end, spending forty years there, until they arc discovered and released by the police. Simultaneously with the filming and editing of the TV documentary, now called *Tempo di Viaggio* (*Time of Travel*), Tarkovsky and Guerra were working out the film that was shortly to be titled *Nostalghia*—about a Russian writer visiting Italy who dreams of home, refuses to appreciate Italy's beautiful sights (including his lovely female translator), and meets the father and son from *The End of the World. Tempo di Viaggio* itself emerged as a kind of preliminary sketch for *Nostalghia,* with Tarkovsky examining potential locations for the film—and usually rejecting them because they were "too beautiful"—and discussing with Guerra his ideas on art, literature, and film.

The actual negotiations between RAI and Sovinfilm for the feature film *Nostalghia* dragged on through 1980 and 1981 and were recorded in painful detail by Tarkovsky in his diary. The Italian company drove a hard commercial bargain, cutting the budget and production time and almost scuttling the film until Daniel Toscan du Plantier stepped in with financing from Gaumont/Italy. Meanwhile, the unenthusiastic Soviet bureaucrats dragged their feet, "losing" telexes confirming RAI's interest and then treating their representatives very shabbily once contracts were about to be signed. Interestingly, some of Tarkovsky's complaints about RAI's financial restrictions recorded in his diary echo similar gripes about Mosfilm and Goskino! Eventually he agreed to all RAI's conditions (though, on the plus side, he was amazed to be offered ten times more film stock than he had used for *Stalker*). In March 1982 he was in Italy working in circumstances quite different from those he was used to at home, without his "family" of longtime actors (his favorite actor, Anatoly Solonitsyn, was too ill to travel) and co-workers and even without his wife (who was only allowed to join him later).

Moreover, Tarkovsky spoke little Italian at this stage and had to communicate with most of the actors and crew through an interpreter, although, according to Oleg Yankovsky—the only Russian actor in the film—he had improved considerably by the end of filming. For someone used to working in a family-like atmosphere with actors and technicians with whom he had developed a mutual trust and understanding, this must have been initially very frustrating, and there is evidence that the early stages of filming were quite tense, at least where the crew were concerned. On the set his closest working relationship—as had been true in the Soviet Union and as was also to be the case with *The Sacrifice*—was with his cinematographer, Giuseppe Lanci. Despite his eccentricities and high-strung temperament and the heavy physical and psychological demands he placed on his actors, his leading actors in the West, Erland Josephson (in both *Nostalghia* and *The Sacrifice*) and Susan Fleetwood (*The Sacrifice*)—the language problem notwithstanding—found him fascinating, congenial to work with, and even genuinely inspirational, echoing similar sentiments we heard repeatedly from Tarkovsky's Russian actors: Nikolai Burlyaev (*Ivan's Childhood* and *Andrei Roublev*), Natalia Bondarchuk (*Solaris*), Alexander Kaidanovsky (*Stalker*), and Oleg Yankovsky (*Mirror* and *Nostalghia*).

While Tarkovsky seemed to have successfully transferred his style of working with actors and crew, he was to face what for him would turn out to be quite difficult and unfamiliar working conditions imposed by a "commercial" production—even if, as Daniel Toscan du Plantier pointed out, *Nostalghia* was essentially thought of as a low-budget "prestige" enterprise rather than something that might bring a large financial return.[49] Although the film did not go significantly over budget, Tarkovsky worked very slowly. He was reluctant to observe a strict shooting schedule and to accept that he could no longer—as he could in the Soviet Union—suspend production for days, or even weeks, keeping a well-paid cast and crew hanging around or expecting them to work unreasonable hours while he wrestled with some recalcitrant creative problem—something that was to plague his next Western production as well. He was also unhappy at not being able to start to edit the film during shooting, in order to correct "mistakes," as had been his habit in the Soviet Union.

Tarkovsky took great pains, both in interviews and in *Sculpting in Time*, to point out that he was dealing with a specifically *Russian* theme in *Nostalghia:* "I wanted to make a film about Russian nostalgia—about the particular state of mind which assails Russians who are far from their native land. I wanted the film to be about the fatal attachment of Russians to their national roots, their past, their culture, their native places, their families and friends; an attachment which they carry with them all their lives, regardless of where destiny may fling them."[50] He also stressed the deeply personal nature of the film: "The protagonist virtually becomes my alter ego, embodying all my emotions, psychology, and nature. He's a mirror image of me. I have never made a film which mirrors my own states of mind with so much violence, and liberates my inner world in such depth." He had made similar statements about the cathartic nature of *Mirror*, which allowed him to make peace with childhood memories and dreams.[51] "When I saw the finished product I felt uneasy, as when one sees oneself in a mirror, or when one has the impression of going beyond one's own intentions."[52]

The film deals with someone like Tarkovsky himself, living physically in Italy but emotionally and spiritually in Russia; though he feels profoundly alien in the Italian setting, he knows that he could never be truly free if he returned to his homeland.[53] Andrei Gorchakov is a musicologist, researching the career of a Russian composer called Sosnovsky (based on the historical Maximilian Berezovsky, an eighteenth-century Ukrainian serf composer) who had lived for some time in Italy and with whom he feels a strong identity. He is accompanied by his beautiful translator Eugenia, who is clearly attracted to him, but whose increasingly obvious advances he ignores, preferring to indulge in reveries of his wife and family in Russia. He encounters a reputed madman, Domenico, who had locked himself and his family away for seven years to await the end of the world, and who now hopes to save humankind from self-destruction by carrying a lighted candle across St. Catherine's Pool, the therapeutic baths in the town Andrei is visiting that at one time were associated with the virtues of the saint herself. As Domenico is prevented from accomplishing his mission by the skeptical townspeople, he asks Andrei to carry it out for him; Andrei takes the candle but refrains from committing himself further. Eugenia, exasperated by Andrei's indifference to her, returns to Rome but informs Andrei that Domenico is about to stage a demonstration there and is asking if Andrei has carried out the task assigned to him. Domenico burns himself alive in public as Andrei, who had been about to leave, returns to the pool and, on a third attempt, succeeds in carrying the candle across; he then collapses, however, and perhaps dies. The final shot of the film is a typical "epiphany" in which Andrei is seen sitting in a landscape that incorporates his Russian home setting into the ruins of an Italian cathedral seen earlier in the film.

The thematic continuities with *Stalker* in particular are very clear. Domenico is only nominally Italian; in essence he is another "yurodivy" like Stalker, who rejects all social conventions: he is poor and badly dressed, mocked and humiliated by others who cannot comprehend his inspired ravings and simply consider him to be mad. Yet he possesses true spiritual insights and wishes only to help and save others. Although Domenico clearly speaks for Tarkovsky in claiming that it is the "so-called healthy" (the pragmatists, the rationalists, the materialists) who have brought the world to the verge of ruin, and that we have "taken a wrong turning" and "must go back to the main foundations of life," his call goes unheeded and he performs what is in essence a futile (yet perhaps necessary) sacrifice in front of an indifferent and unresponsive crowd. The grimly farcical element is underlined by the malfunctioning record player that emits a distorted version of Beethoven's "Ode to Joy" to accompany his action.

Andrei is essentially Domenico's double, completing his task for him and seeming to gain some spiritual resolution of his own problems as a result. If this seems a rather different matter from "saving the world," the solution may perhaps be found in the long diary entry for September 7, 1970, in which Tarkovsky seems to anticipate some of the major themes of this film: "Thank God," he writes, "for people who burn themselves alive in front of an impassive, wordless crowd," and also, "Everyone can be saved only if each saves himself."[54] The theme of the double, which is hinted at in a long scene between the two men in Domenico's bizarrely furnished (or unfurnished) house, is made explicit in a dream sequence where Andrei, looking at his reflection in a wardrobe mirror in the middle of a rubbish-strewn street, finds his own image replaced by that of Domenico (and also finds himself articulating, in Russian, thoughts that clearly belong to the other man). Moreover, each man owns a seemingly identical dog and the same child plays the role of each man's son.

For most of the film, however, Andrei is less concerned with carrying out Domenico's request than with attempting to resolve his own problems of homesickness. The film opens in black and white on a Russian landscape, inhabited by the figures (two women, a girl, a boy, and a horse—in later scenes a dog and a house will be seen) who will constantly haunt Andrei's reveries. Throughout the film Russia represents what for Tarkovsky are the eternal values of earth, maternity, family, home, patience, and spirituality, while Italy stands for a decaying and "sickeningly beautiful" culture whose superficial attractiveness masks a declining faith and a surrender to transient and destructive material values. Apart from Piero della Franscesca's "Madonna of Childbirth," seen early in the film—an emblem of the "Russian" values that Italy once possessed but has now lost—we see little but ruins, decay, and debris in the Italian landscape. The oddly static Russian scenes, in which the characters are virtually immobile or move only in slow motion, convey a sense of permanence that contrasts with the transience associated with Italy.

Andrei's problematic nonrelationship with Eugenia is perhaps best understood within this context. Like Italy itself, she represents the beauty of the past devoid of its spirituality (her physical resemblance to figures from Renaissance painting has often been pointed out). She is also, as the sacristan tells her, a woman who, in her search for personal happiness, has

1.13. The Russian landscape, home, and family of Andrei's dreams and reveries. *Nostalghia.* Artificial Eye.

neglected her "natural" destiny of motherhood and submissiveness and cannot even bring herself to kneel in church. Andrei's rejection of her is thus not simply indifference to, or fear of, the sexuality that she so vividly embodies, but stems from his search for spiritual fulfillment, which he associates (together with beauty) with his wife in the past and with Domenico in the present. Realizing that she cannot compete with both these rivals, Eugenia finally leaves and returns to her lover in Rome—a menacing and sinister figure whose obvious criminal connections seem to confirm Andrei's wisdom in rejecting someone who, for all her beauty, is inescapably linked with the materialism and corruption of modern society.[55]

Even so, however, Andrei's boorishly imperceptive treatment of her and his grudging and fleeting acknowledgment of her attractiveness (she looks beautiful, he admits at one point, adding cautiously "in this light") contribute to the sense of thick-skinned self-absorption that makes him the least sympathetic of Tarkovsky's heroes. As a result, the hysterical tirade in which Eugenia's patience snaps and she accuses him of being cowardly, inhibited, and boring—"too much of a saint" to be interested in a normal woman—probably has most viewers nodding in agreement rather than seeing her as a dangerous temptress who distracts him from the true path that he must follow. If this is not perhaps exactly what Tarkovsky intended, he does present the character's limitations in other ways, associating Andrei almost entirely with enclosed spaces and repetitive actions and suggesting that he uses his imaginative identification with Sosnovsky as an excuse for remaining in his own moral limbo, committing himself neither to one state of existence or the other: Sosnovsky was miserable in Italy and miserable at home; why then should things be any different for Andrei—or indeed for both Andreis, the character and the filmmaker?

Although Andrei's memories of his home are associated with many of the elements that signal "dreams" in other Tarkovsky films—dripping water, barking dogs, black-and-white film, slow motion—they are rarely literally dreams, for they occur during waking moments and should more strictly be defined as reveries. (The "wardrobe" dream, on the other hand, occurs after Andrei appears to have dozed off.) A more radical innovation occurs in a scene in Andrei's hotel bedroom, where the change from waking reality to dream is signaled entirely by variations in the lighting as the camera moves slowly toward the bed in a single, uninterrupted shot. The two states in fact appear to coexist for a time as the indisputably real dog from Andrei's past pads into the room from the bathroom and settles down beside his bed (knocking over an equally real glass). This is then followed by a more recognizable black-and-white dream in which Andrei's wife and Eugenia embrace, suggesting obviously enough his wish not to have to choose between them, and then a shot of Andrei's wife apparently levitating (a favorite Tarkovsky motif) above his hotel bed, implying that no real choice exists after all.

The visual beauty and subtlety of this scene are intensified by the sound of rain outside, with the pouring water reflected on the bedroom wall. As with both *Mirror* and *Stalker,* water is a central motif in this film: rain falls outside Andrei's room and *inside* Domenico's, where water lies on the floor and his (and also Andrei's?) dog settles down in a posture reminiscent of the very similar dog that appears in the swamp scene in *Stalker.* The thermal baths are a central physical and symbolic location; when Andrei crosses them with the candle they have been drained and only a few puddles are left. Various types of debris have been retrieved during the cleaning, indicating the decay and debasement of a setting once associated with the miraculous powers of a saint. Again, as with *Stalker,* water covers relics of a more spiritual past—the angel in the flooded cathedral through whose ruins Andrei wades drunkenly, reciting poems by Tarkovsky's father (a scene that may not literally be a dream but is certainly dreamlike). Here he perhaps meets a modern angel, a little girl called "Angela"—children, however victimized they may be by the adult world, are almost the only symbols of hope in Tarkovsky's later work. (Another angel appears in an early reverie, walking in the distance past his Russian house.)

The steady increase in shot length found in *Stalker* also continues in this film. The opening, post-credits shot lasts almost four minutes, establishing a pattern right away, and many shots in Andrei's room, in Domenico's room, and at the pool last anywhere from two-and-a-half to five minutes. The climactic scene of Andrei carrying the candle across the pool lasts eight minutes forty-five seconds, fully capturing the character's slow and agonized progress and forcing the audience to share every moment and every step. Yet, although the pain and intensity are acutely experienced, the

1.14. Domenico's dog in the flooded interior of Domenico's house, with Andrei (Oleg Yankovsky) in the background. *Nostalghia.* Artificial Eye.

prolongation of the shot carries its own dangers in foregrounding its virtuosity—possibly prompting irrelevant speculations as to how Tarkovsky succeeded in ensuring that the candle finally stayed lit and how many takes were needed to achieve this—rather than allowing us to concentrate on what the shot conveys.

The Sacrifice *(1986)*

While *Nostalghia* was being screened at Cannes, Tarkovsky signed a contract for *The Witch* (which was to become *The Sacrifice*) with the Swedish Film Institute; additional financing was provided by the French producer Anatole Dauman and the British TV company Channel 4—all of them with a solid record for supporting low-budget "art" films and respecting the artistic integrity of the director. Nevertheless, as with the initial stages of *Nostalghia,* shooting did not always go smoothly. Tarkovsky seems to have found it particularly difficult to understand that he had to observe work schedules, that his technical personnel did not want to stay up all night and then get up at two a.m. to shoot, and that he could not, as Susan Fleetwood put it, "order out the Red Army" when he needed another hundred or so extras for a particular scene, but had first to arrange and pay for them. He petulantly and unfairly accused the Swedes in his diary of being "lazy and slow and only interested in observing rules and regulations," adding loftily that "where artistic work is concerned, timetable considerations don't enter into it."[56] Though this was finally sorted out, a more serious problem arose when his producer, Anna-Lena Wibom, insisted on applying the clause in his contract that limited the length of the film to two hours ten minutes. Tarkovsky claimed that the "natural" length of the completed film was two hours thirty minutes and, after acrimonious discussion, he had his way. Just as in the Soviet Union, Tarkovsky once again fought for the cause of art and won out against what he perceived—unjustly in this case—to be its natural enemies: the "bureaucrats."

Despite the many financial problems involved in setting up both the Soviet-Italian co-production and his first completely Western film, Tarkovsky was at no stage under any particular pressure to prove himself commercially. The Western backers understood what was involved in a "Tarkovsky" film and had no illusions about huge financial success; they hoped, rather, to impose and stick to a reasonable budget that would eventually be recouped, even if over a period of several years. Though there were also problems during shooting (as described above), they did not interfere substantially with the concept or execution of the films, which were shot and released very much as he had intended them to be. With both films, moreover, the subject was one he had been mulling over for several years and, despite the alien setting, he was not surrounded completely by strangers. On *Nostalghia* his scriptwriter Tonino Guerra was a longtime friend; he had worked with Oleg Yankovsky (who played the main role) on *Mirror;* and his wife Larissa is credited as assistant director. On *The Sacrifice* he continued the close collaboration with Erland Josephson (who had been new in *Nostalghia*), and developed, after initial misunderstandings, an extremely warm relationship with his cinematographer Sven Nykvist. Despite his irritated sniping at the Swedes in his diary, he soon found himself once again in a tight familial atmosphere, where, as Susan Fleetwood described it, everyone recognized that "he was a bloody nuisance most of the time, but he was still wonderful."[57] In Michal Leszczylowski's documentary of the shooting of *The Sacrifice,* the crew obviously shared Tarkovsky's distress when a camera malfunctioned during the single long take of the burning of his main set, Alexander's house, and were willing to work hard on rebuilding it and reshooting the scene.

What is amazing is that, despite the great differences between filmmaking in the Soviet Union and the West, Tarkovsky needed to change very little during his brief Western career. His international fame as a creator of complex, difficult, but strikingly original films assured him of funding from small, noncommercial producers. More importantly, his unchanging vision of the world and art's role in it, and the sheer power of his charismatic and stubborn personality, allowed him to continue making *his* kind of films. Doubtless it would never even have occurred to him to alter or compromise either style or theme to make his "Western" work more accessible to a wider audience, as so many other filmmakers in similar situations have done.

Instead, he produced two films as deeply personal and even autobiographical as *Mirror,* which enlarged even further the challenging stylistic experimentation of that film and of *Stalker.* The first of these films, *Nostalghia,* in no way marks a break between his Russian and his non-Russian films; instead it can in many ways be seen as the middle section of a triptych, preceded by *Stalker* and followed by *The Sacrifice.*

Like *Nostalghia, The Sacrifice* is based on a story that Tarkovsky had been thinking about before he left the Soviet Union.[58] *The Witch* was about a man terminally ill with cancer, who is instructed by a soothsayer to spend a night with a "witch." The man is miraculously cured, and then, at the witch's bidding, he leaves his "splendid mansion and respected life happily and [goes] off with her, with nothing but the old coat on his back."[59] Before filming began, however, Tarkovsky had combined this plot with another, apocalyptic theme that was clearly derived from the "Domenico" story of *Nostalghia* and had assigned the main role of what was now *The Sacrifice* to Erland Josephson, who had played Domenico. The result is a degree of intellectual confusion that damages the film, for, if it is not immediately evident how Andrei can resolve (even if only metaphorically) his personal problems by carrying out an action that is intended by Domenico to save humankind, it is even less clear how Alexander can save humankind by making a vow to God that is fulfilled by sleeping with a witch.

The film that finally evolved begins on the birthday of Alexander, a former actor who is now a lecturer and critic. He plants a dead tree on the seashore and tells his seven-year-old son (who is recovering from a throat operation and cannot speak) a legend indicating that, if the tree is watered every day, it will come back to life. Later he has a vision of an imminent, probably postnuclear war disaster, and shortly afterward planes fly low over his house and a TV broadcast indicates that a war is about to break out. His wife Adelaide becomes hysterical, but turns for help not to her husband but to a family friend (and doctor), Victor, who is clearly her lover. Alone in his study, Alexander prays to God to avert the disaster and promises that, if this happens, he will take a vow of silence, renounce his family, and destroy his beloved home. He then has a dream that crystallizes his fear of losing his son, and is visited by Otto, the local postman, who is something of a philosopher and mystic. Otto tells him that Maria, one of the family's servants, is a "good" witch and, if Alexander goes to her house and sleeps with her, the catastrophe will not happen. Though he is initally skeptical, Alexander leaves on Otto's bicycle and goes to Maria; she seems not to understand the purpose of his visit but takes pity on his obvious distress and sleeps with him. After another vision of disaster, Alexander wakes in his room to find everything as it was the previous day, with no evidence or talk of the threatened war. (Although this is what *appears* to happen up to this point, there is a strong possibility that much of it—starting perhaps with the TV broadcast or with Otto's visit to Alexander—is dreamed by Alexander himself.) He then begins secret preparations to burn down his house as Victor and Adelaide quarrel outside and then go off with Marta

(Adelaide's grown-up daughter) and the housemaid Julia to look for the boy, "Little Man." When they return, Alexander has already set the house on fire; Maria too arrives, as do Otto (on his bicycle) and an ambulance. After some resistance, Alexander enters the ambulance and is driven away; the house then collapses in ruins. Maria rides off on the bicycle and is seen near the shore, where "Little Man" is carrying buckets of water toward the dead tree. The ambulance drives past as the boy begins to water the tree and Maria rides away. The child is seen lying at the foot of the tree as he speaks for the first time in the film: "In the beginning was the Word? . . . Why is that, Papa?" The film ends with a dedication to Tarkovsky's son Andrei.

Once again Tarkovsky was extremely fortunate in having enlightened backers for a complex and far from "popular" theme of this kind. With the help of Bergman's brilliant cameraman Sven Nykvist, he was able to push even further than in *Nostalghia* in creating an ambiguous intermediate state between reality and dream in which much—perhaps even most—of the film's action takes place. As in the previous film, this state is indicated by subtle variations of color and lighting rather than by the more obtrusive switching to black and white of the earlier work (a switch of this kind does occur, however, in Alexander's anxiety dream about his son). After the credit sequence (superimposed on Leonardo da Vinci's "Adoration of the Magi," which is later seen in reproduction in Alexander's study) the film begins outdoors in full color. Inside the house, however, the effect is closer to black and white, with color systematically drained—but not totally removed—from the image to create a metallic, glistening effect that suits the coldly artificial relationships between most of the characters.[60] This effect persists throughout the central action of the film, sometimes, as in Alexander's visit to Maria, becoming almost indistinguishable from black and white; full color returns after this visit and remains till the end of the film.

In most of Tarkovsky's previous films the switching between black and white and color had usually indicated a move from one state of reality to another—from the real to dream, reverie, or imagination; or from the mundane to the mystical, supernatural, or transcendent. Now, however, Tarkovsky seems to want us to experience the central "action" of the film as simultaneously real *and* nonreal, just as the images themselves are simultaneously color *and* black and white.

It is perhaps rather futile, then, to attempt to decide which of the apparent events in the film really happen and which are dreams—and also at which point the dream or dreams begin. Tarkovsky himself was happy to suggest that the threat of nuclear war was merely ". . . the fruits of a sick imagination"[61] on the part of the obviously depressed and anxious Alexander, and it is possible to interpret all the major "events" of the film—Otto's visit to Alexander's study, Alexander's visit to Maria, the miraculous reversal and elimination of the seemingly imminent nuclear catastrophe—as at one and the same time real *and* imaginary. The various clues that Tarkovsky scatters around are systematically incompatible with one another

1.15. The alienated family. From left to right, Victor (Sven Wollter), Alexander (Erland Josephson), Marta (Filippa Franzén), Adelaide (Susan Fleetwood). *The Sacrifice.* Artificial Eye.

and, taken together, suit neither a "realistic" nor an "it was all—or mostly—a dream" explanation.

If this is so, Tarkovsky has moved a step beyond his habitual tolerance for differing interpretations of his films by individual members of the audience[62] and his consistent belief that audiences should *experience* rather than analyze his films and respond to them with dreamlike rather than rational logic. Interpretation is no longer a question of *either* A or B, but both A *and* B; and the already strongly oneiric qualities of *Mirror, Stalker,* and *Nostalghia* are pushed to an extreme that defies differentiation between one state of reality and another. In a dream, all explanations coexist together and perhaps this is the case too here. Yet, even if it ultimately does not matter what "happens" in the film, there is no ambiguity in the moral statement that Tarkovsky—speaking through Alexander—is making: humans have violated nature and have built a civilization based on power and fear; our scientific discoveries are put to evil use and "savages" are more spiritual than we are; and we have created a dreadful imbalance between our material and our spiritual development. If sin is that which is unnecessary, our whole civilization is built on sin.

Although—contrary to what is sometimes still believed to be the case—he did *not* know while shooting *The Sacrifice* that he was fatally ill (his cancer was diagnosed after shooting was completed but before the editing was finished—see the moving entry in his diary for December 15, 1985),[63] he was often ill and unhappy in his last years and tormented by his separation

1.16. The apocalyptic vision of Alexander's dreams. *The Sacrifice*. Artificial Eye.

from his native land and his son. It is not surprising that some of this unhappiness should spill over into the character of Alexander—a sad and lonely cuckold whose only strong emotional relationship is with his small son—who becomes, much more directly even than Andrei or Domenico, the spokesman for many of his own private and public concerns. Yet Alexander berates himself for talking rather than acting, and perhaps Tarkovsky himself is speaking *too* openly and directly to us here. It is possible that, in some subconscious way, he was "aware" of his impending death. He certainly referred several times in his diary to a "prophecy" by Boris Pasternak that he would make only seven films, which he seemed to take quite seriously (*The Sacrifice* was his seventh feature film). At any rate, both in the film and in the chapter on it in the expanded edition of *Sculpting in Time* that he completed shortly before his death, he seems concerned to "explain" his meaning in a way that contrasts sharply with his earlier contention that meaning resulted from a collaboration between artist and audience. Chapter IX of *Sculpting* tells us what *The Sacrifice* "means" far more directly than his discussion of any of his other films; he also urges his audience to interpret the symbols in it (such as the dead tree) after years of insisting that there were no "symbols" in his films.

Paradoxically, then, his last two films combine an increasingly tantalizing ambiguity in the imagery and narrative structure with an increasing *lack* of ambiguity in the dialogue and articulation of ideas. The formal experimentation with ever-increasing length of shot is also pushed even further in *The Sacrifice,* resulting in one shot of nine minutes twenty-six seconds (the opening, post-credits shot, the longest in his work) and many of between four and eight minutes, including the notorious six-minute fifty-second shot of the burning of the house. Beautiful as many of these shots are, it sometimes appears that the action is beginning to exist for the sake of the shot, rather than the other way round, and occasionally logical discrepancies such as the unexplained and far too rapid appearance of the ambulance (in the script it was given more time to appear) are ignored.

Yet, with all its flaws, the film is far from negligible and is in most respects fully worthy of its creator. It is possibly the most visually impressive of Tarkovsky's films where the photography is concerned and, for all its didacticism, it reaches conclusions that are both moving and simple: love, hope, and faith in God can rescue humanity from its rush toward self-destruction. Instead of attempting to dominate (and in the process, destroy) the natural world, we should return to a spirit of reverence and harmony within it: only thus can potential or real catastrophes be averted and our life take its proper place within the unbroken cycle of the natural world. The final shot of the film brings together all of these concerns in an unashamed and unaffected affirmation both of human potential (as embodied in the music of Bach) when inspired by love and faith, and of the respect for nature and the trust in humanity symbolized by the dead tree that "Little Man" will lovingly nurture back to life.

An Unchanging Artist

If critics have sometimes expressed disappointment with Tarkovsky's last two films, their status on what one might call the "second level" of his work (*Mirror, Andrei Roublev,* and *Stalker* occupying the first) does not result from his being forced to compromise his artistic integrity, to work with uncongenial or imposed material, or allow the finished film to be altered and mutilated by others. They are true in every respect to the stylistic and thematic concerns that occupied him throughout his career and can be seen, as was suggested earlier, to have particularly close links with *Stalker* in presenting a society apparently bent on self-destruction because it has lost all links with nature, its own past, and any sense of a spiritual or moral dimension to its behavior. Stalker himself leads on to Domenico in *Nostalghia* and Alexander in *The Sacrifice* as a "holy fool" whose words are greeted with scorn or incomprehension by those they are intended to save, while Writer's aimlessness, self-contempt, and sense of entrapment are echoed, to at least some extent, by Andrei and Victor in the later films. *Stalker,* Tarkovsky's last film in the Soviet Union, was already marked by an increasing stylistic preoccupation with lengthy shots and depiction of real time as well as his growing tendency to preach, to warn humanity with his apocalyptic visions (he lectured on "The Apocalypse" at St. James's Church, Piccadilly, London, in January 1984). If one can speak of a "break" in Tarkovsky's work, it occurred *not* when he came to the West but probably during the filming of *Stalker,* between its first and second versions, when, as Yermash relates, a "science-fiction" film became "a moral-philosophical parable."

Why didn't Tarkovsky's work change in the West? We have already pointed out his good fortune (resulting from a well-deserved international reputation) in attracting producers who believed in the uniqueness of his talent and fully expected him to continue making his idiosyncratic, fascinating, and definitely "noncommercial" films. Unable or unwilling to acclimatize himself to Western life and culture (Konchalovsky talks of his living in an insulated cocoon), Tarkovsky pursued his artistic vision with the same singlemindedness as he had done in the Soviet Union. It is important to note also that he was working on two projects which had mainly been conceived *before* his emigration. He was able, to a surprising degree, and, at times, over much resistance, to recreate the relatively unconstrained working conditions he had enjoyed while shooting his films in the Soviet Union, and was even able, with *The Sacrifice,* to determine the length of the film's final cut. He certainly knew how to fight the "bureaucrats"! He genuinely inspired some of his most crucial co-workers with the depth and originality of his ideas and the intriguing intensity of his "Russian temperament": Erland Josephson, Susan Fleetwood, and Sven Nykvist are among those who speak of him with respect and deep affection. As a result, he was able to reproduce, especially on the set of *The Sacrifice,* the supportive family-like atmosphere of his Russian productions. In our interviews with his co-workers in both the East and the West we were struck by the similarities in their descriptions of what it meant to work with Tarkovsky: all had learned something from him, had high regard for his work and expressed their willingness, even eagerness, to work with him again. Finally, Tarkovsky saw himself as a Solzhenitsyn figure, a "prophet" in cinema. Rejecting what he saw as the moral and spiritual bankruptcy of contemporary technological societies, whether in the East or the West, he proceeded to "preach" the same message but simply to a new audience. Having been an outsider, an "internal émigré," a "visionary," and a "martyr" in the Soviet Union, he found that role quite "natural"—perhaps even congenial—in the West as well.

Whether Tarkovsky would have changed or whether he would have been able to continue making his noncommercial films is something we, of course, will never be able to say with any certainty. His producer on *The Sacrifice,* Anna-Lena Wibom, feels that Tarkovsky would have had a very difficult time making an adjustment to "real" filmmaking in the West, not the state-subsidized kind he had in the Soviet Union, or, for that matter, at the Swedish Film Institute. Andrei Konchalovsky, however, who knew Tarkovsky well and had himself made the transition from the Soviet Union to the West, offers perhaps the most "informed" opinion on the subject, suggesting that he would always have found producers for his kind of films. Tarkovsky's busy schedule at the time of his death supports this contention: he was negotiating another long-cherished film project, *Hoffmaniana,* and another opera, *The Flying Dutchman* (for the Royal Opera House), and was planning more films—*The Life of St. Anthony,* an almost totally silent *Hamlet,* and even a film based on the New Testament. The fact that Tarkovsky's production of Mussorgsky's opera *Boris Godunov* has been revived three times in London alone, placed on the repertory of the Kirov Theater in Leningrad, and performed again in the fall of 1991 with Claudio Abbado conducting the Vienna Opera attests to the enduring nature of Tarkovsky's talent and his ability to continue attracting a Western as well as a Russian audience. Since his death, his fame has steadily increased, as demonstrated by the many retrospectives of his films in the Soviet Union, Europe, and North America; the release of a new, uncut version of *Solaris* in the United States; and the posthumous award of the Lenin Prize in the Soviet Union for *The Passion According to Andrei,* his first "banned" version of *Andrei Roublev,* finally released in 1988. These developments, together with the undoubted quality of the films themselves, will continue to fuel the "myth" of Tarkovsky as man and artist and will assure him a prominent place in the history of cinema, transcending the artificial—and now obsolete—boundaries of "East" and "West."

NOTES

The authors would like to thank the following persons and institutions: all our interviewees—family, friends and co-workers—in the Soviet Union, Great Britain, France, and Sweden who kindly shared with us their knowledge of Tarkovsky both as a man and as a filmmaker; Pam Engel of Artificial Eye and Kitty Cooper of Contemporary Films, Tarkovsky's distributors in Britain, for allowing us to see and use the 35mm prints of the films for making frame enlargements; Elaine Burrows of the National Film Archive for providing facilities and Jim Adams of the British Film Institute for filming and printing the frame enlargements. To complete the research for this project Vida Johnson received financial support from the American Philosophical Society, the Jasper and Marion Whiting Foundation, and Tufts University, and Graham Petrie received an Arts Research Board Grant from McMaster University.

N.B. All comments by Tarkovsky's co-workers and family that are not credited to written sources are taken from personal interviews conducted by the authors in 1988, 1989, 1990, and 1991.

1. Vida Johnson's translation from a page-1 story in the influential Moscow paper *Literaturnaya gazeta,* April 25, 1990. All further translations from the Russian are by her.

2. The letter is printed as an appendix to the French edition of *Sculpting in Time* (*Le temps scellé*) (Paris: Cahiers du Cinéma, 1989, pp. 232–35) but does not appear in the English edition. Perhaps understandably, Tarkovsky exaggerates some of the injustices done to him here, and he is characteristically imprecise about dates and figures: in his diary (*Time within Time: The Diaries 1970–1986,* pp. 49–50), for example, he lists thirty-five requested changes to *Solaris,* rather than forty-eight. In later years he seemed to become almost paranoid about the lengths to which the Soviet authorities might go in persecuting him, even fearing forced repatriation (Konchalovsky interview, June 1991).

It might also be mentioned here that, though Tarkovsky's films were often withheld from the official theater repertoire, they were quite widely screened at film clubs and workers' institutes. Tarkovsky would often introduce these screenings and noted in his diary the lively discussions that followed.

3. Daniel Toscan du Plantier, former general manager of Gaumont Films and Tarkovsky's primary patron in the West, questioned the conspiracy theory, pointing out that the *Palme d'Or* at Cannes tends to be awarded to films with more commercial potential than *Nostalghia* (interview, March 1990).

4. *The Idiot* and other works by Dostoyevsky, along with Bulgakov's *The Master and Margarita* and books by Tolstoy and Thomas Mann, occur repeatedly in the lists of favorite projects that he constantly entered in his diary.

5. His diary from 1970–1986 was published as *Time within Time: The Diaries 1970–1986* by Seagull, Calcutta, in 1991. It had already appeared, with a partly different selection of extracts, in German, under the more accurate title of *Martyrolog* (Frankfurt a. Main/Berlin: Limes, 1989).

6. Ibid., pp. 237–39.

7. In the late 1950s at the State Institute of Cinema, Tarkovsky worked on two collaborative films, *The Killers* (*Ubiytsy*—an adaptation of a story by Ernest Hemingway) and *There Will Be No Leave Today* (*Segodnya uvolneniya ne budet*), an unlikely action story, a "docudrama" based on a real postwar incident. His first solo performance was his diploma film, *The Steamroller and the Violin* (*Katok i skripka,* 1960), which combined relatively conventional thematics (the friendship between a simple worker and a small boy who is a talented violinist) with some of the self-conscious stylistic bravura (extreme and unusual angles and complex montage) that would be repeated in *Ivan's Childhood,* but disappear thereafter. This film also introduces, although lightheartedly, the all-important theme of art and the role of the artist as well as Tarkovsky's favorite water imagery.

8. Jean-Paul Sartre, *Les lettres françaises,* December 26–January 1, 1964.

9. Neya Zorkaya, "Zametki k portretu Andreya Tarkovskogo" ("Remarks toward a Portrait of Andrei Tarkovsky"), *Kino panorama* Vol. II, Moscow (1977): 144.

10. *Sculpting in Time* (2nd revised edition, London: Faber and Faber, 1989), pp. 15, 27. First published in German and in English in 1986. Hereafter cited as *Sculpting.*

11. His diary also constantly returns to similar themes: ". . . I am categorically against entertainment in cinema: it is as degrading for the author as it is for the audience." (From the record of a talk on *Mirror* on April 29, 1975, printed in *Time within Time,* p. 367.) In an entry for May 2, 1982 (pp. 323–24), after viewing what he considered a typically "commercial" production, he commented: "Monstrous. Money, money, money . . . Nothing real, nothing true. No beauty, no truth, no sincerity, nothing. All that matters is to make a profit . . . It's impossible to watch . . . Anything is possible, anything is allowed, provided that 'anything' can be sold" (ellipses in the original). The film he refers to is identified only as *Possession,* probably the French film of that title directed by the Polish exile Andrzej Zulawski, who had produced some distinguished work—notably *The Third Part of the Night* (1971)—before leaving his native country, and has enjoyed an uneven career in France since. If this is so, Zulawski's fate highlights—and justifies—even further Tarkovsky's intransigence in refusing to make "commercial" concessions.

12. *Sculpting,* p. 192.

13. Ibid., p. 72.

14. Interview with Liudmila Feiginova, Tarkovsky's editor, October 1989.

15. *Time within Time,* p. 74 (April 6, 1973).

16. Interview with Neya Zorkaya, July 1990.

17. Interview with Maya Turovskaya, July 1990.

18. Maya Turovskaya, *Tarkovsky: Cinema as Poetry* (London: Faber and Faber, 1989), p. 46.

19. Interview, June 1991.

20. Interview with Tamara Ogorodnikova, September 1989.

21. Ibid.

22. Tatyana Vinokurova, "Khozhdeniye po mukam 'Andreya Rubleva'" ("The Tormented Path of *Andrei Roublev*"), *Iskusstvo kino* no. 10 (1989): 63–76.

23. Ibid., p. 65.

24. The quotation is from Filip Yermash's somewhat self-serving and unconvincing attempt (published after Tarkovsky's death) to prove that, in his capacity as head of Goskino for much of Tarkovsky's career, he had really sought to *help* rather than obstruct the director: "On byl khudozhnik" ("He Was an Artist"), *Sovietskaya kultura,* September 9, 1989, p. 10, and September 12, 1989, p. 4.

25. Vinokurova, p. 65. Maya Turovskaya notes that there were three variants of the film: the original 5,642 meters, a second of 5,250 meters, and a final, release print of 5,076 meters (p. 48).

26. Ibid., pp. 66–68.

27. Yermash, p. 10.

28. *Time within Time,* pp. 23–24 (September 21, 1970).

29. Vinokurova, p. 75.

30. Ibid., pp. 69–75.

31. Ibid., p. 74.

32. Turovskaya gives October 19, 1971, as the release date and Le Fanu copies her, but Zorkaya and Yermash support Tarkovsky's own diary entry, which notes that the film was released on the "eve" of the New Year (which in Russia need not literally mean December 31).

33. Neya Zorkaya, in *Problemy sovremennogo kino* (Moscow: Iskusstvo, 1976), p. 65.

34. *Time within Time,* pp. 49–50.

35. Interview with Daniel Toscan du Plantier, March 1990.

36. Never revealed openly to the audience, but based on an actual incident in which Stalin's name was misspelled as "sralin" (based on the Russian verb "to shit").

37. It could also be Andrei's recreation of a scene related to him by his mother (he would only have been around five at the time). A similar ambiguity attaches to the earlier scene of the mother sitting on the fence, in which the young Andrei is actually shown asleep. These and other problems are discussed more fully in our recently completed book on Tarkovsky.

38. *Time within Time,* p. 19 (September 12, 1970).

39. Ivan's father is mentioned (by the officers) but never appears in the boy's dreams. In Tarkovsky's diploma film, *The Steamroller and the Violin* (1960), the absent father is replaced by a father-figure, the competent, kindly, and protective steamroller driver.

40. "It's patently clear that I have a complex about my parents. I don't feel adult when I'm with them. And I don't think they consider me adult either" (*Time within Time,* p. 19 [September 12, 1970]).

41. *The Cinema of Andrei Tarkovsky* (London: The British Film Institute, 1987), p. 16. Our own interviews with Tarkovsky's sister, his first wife, Irma Rausch, and others confirm a considerably less idyllic relationship.

42. They never actually enter the "room" itself, which is situated nearby.

43. *Time within Time,* p. 159 (December 23, 1978).

44. "An artistic discovery occurs each time as a new and unique image of the world, a hieroglyphic of absolute truth" (*Sculpting,* p. 37).

45. Bálint András Kovács and Akos Szilágyi, *Les Mondes d'Andrei Tarkovski,* trans. (from Hungarian) by Veronique Charaire (Lausanne: L'Age d'Homme, 1987).

46. Initially filmed as being spoken to Writer and Professor in the bar on their return, but transferred during the editing to the apparent setting of Stalker's house—similar enough to the bar to be mistaken for it by most members of the audience. (Information provided in interviews with the film's editor, Liudmila Feiginova, and its cameraman, Alexander Knyazhinsky.)

47. July 1990 interview with film critic Maya Turovskaya, who sat in on that meeting.

48. Yermash, p. 4.

49. Tony Mitchell gives a budget figure of 500,000 pounds ("Tarkovsky in Italy," *Sight & Sound,* Winter [1982/3]: pp. 54–56). Daniel Toscan du Plantier, speaking from memory, offered a roughly similar figure, adding that Tarkovsky himself was paid around $100,000—the normal amount for a small-scale film of this kind. According to the latter, Tarkovsky tried (unsuccessfully) to dispense with an assistant director and claim the extra salary for himself. His wife Larissa is officially listed as an assistant in the credits.

50. *Sculpting,* p. 202.

51. Ibid., p. 128.

52. Tony Mitchell, "Andrei Tarkovsky and *Nostalghia.*" *Film Criticism* VIII, 3 (1984): 5 (quoting interview in *Corriere della Sera*).

53. In a letter by Sosnovsky (see below) that is read during the film, the composer recounts a dream in which he had to stage an opera for his landlord/owner at home in Russia, the first act of which was set in a park full of men forced, under threat of severe punishment, to pose as naked statues. The metaphorical significance is clear enough. (In his 1984 production of *Boris Godunov* at Covent Garden Tarkovsky used "living statues" of this kind for the Polish scenes in Act III.)

54. *Time within Time,* pp. 16–17.

55. The Russian critic Neya Zorkaya drew attention to some of these ideas in conversation with the authors.

56. *Time within Time,* p. 342 (March 6, 1985).

57. Interview with Susan Fleetwood, May 1988.

58. *Sculpting,* p. 217.

59. Ibid., p. 220.

60. The fifty or so shots in the night scenes in the film were created by making two dupe negatives, one color and one black and white, from a color negative and then marrying these in the optical printer, progressively eliminating certain colors until the desired effect was achieved (interview with Sven Nykvist, May 1988). The result, then, is literally both black and white and color at once.

61. Ibid., p. 223.

62. See, for example, his comments on audience reaction and interpretation in *Sculpting,* pp. 168–69.

63. *Time within Time,* p. 349.

Two Forman

Peter Hames

Jan Němec's observation that Miloš Forman is now an American filmmaker rather than a Czech one[1] recalls the Polish view of the American Polanski as more businessman than artist. It crystallizes the traditional European/American split between art and commerce. Similarly, Forman decided to move in the direction of orthodox narrative after audiences had difficulty with the form of his first American feature, *Taking Off* (1970). Feeling that he could never be 100 percent creative outside of his own culture, he deliberately set himself the task of working within American themes, forms, and traditions.

Forman was not the first Czech filmmaker to work in the American industry, but he was the first to make a successful transition. Gustav Machatý, director of the "notorious" *Ecstasy* (*Extase,* 1933), featuring Hedy Lamarr, was signed to an MGM contract in the thirties and forties but only made four films, effectively ending a promising international career. The Jewish writer/director/actor Hugo Haas, who fled Czechoslovakia after his filming of Karel Čapek's antifascist *The White Sickness* (*Bílá nemoc,* 1938), was also condemned largely to obscurity. He did, however, pioneer the area of B movie authorship by writing, directing, and starring in a whole series of films in the fifties, including *Pick Up* and *Girl on the Bridge.*

Following the Warsaw Pact invasion of Czechoslovakia in 1968, a number of Czech and Slovak directors left the country, most notably Forman's colleague, Ivan Passer (*Born to Win, Cutter's Way*), and Ján Kadár, the Oscar-winning director of *The Shop on Main Street* (*Obchod na korze,* 1965), who made *Lies My Father Told Me* in Canada and *The Angel Levine* and *Freedom Road* in the United States. None of them made successful artistic transitions and, although Passer has made more films than Forman, his output has been remarkably uneven.

Excluding British directors such as Ridley Scott and Peter Yates, very few European filmmakers have made a transfer to Hollywood in the post-World War II period. In contrast, the Hollywood of the thirties and forties saw the arrival of Lubitsch, Wilder, Lang, Siodmak, Curtiz, Koster, Sirk, Renoir, Hitchcock, Saville, and many others among directors alone. With the exception of the Hungarian-trained cinematographers Vilmos Zsigmond and Laszlo Kovacs, both of whom fled the Soviet suppression of the Hungarian Revolution, there has been no postwar equivalent. Apart from Forman, the only director to achieve a major American success has been Polanski, with *Rosemary's Baby* and *Chinatown*. Yet Polanski's career was different. Not only did he make only one feature in Poland, but the majority of his films in exile have also been British and French rather than American-based.

The clean break between Forman's work in Czechoslovakia and the United States suggests obvious parallels with the careers of Fritz Lang and Alfred Hitchcock, and inevitable comparisons between the "Czech Forman" and the "American Forman." Yet while Lang and Hitchcock worked in commercial industries before going to Hollywood, the contexts for Forman's work differed much more radically. In Czechoslovakia, he worked in a nationalized industry that, in the sixties, allowed the development of a cinema based on notions of art that were frequently oppositional in character. The commercial assumptions of the American industry differed much more from Forman's experience than they did from Lang's or Hitchcock's. Similarly, the contrast between the personal and intimate approach of his Czech films and the frequently literary origins of his American work is much more pointed.

While there are certainly continuities between Forman's Czech and American work, there is little point in pursuing a simple auteurist approach to his films. More important is the recognition of the work of a filmmaker working in fundamentally different contexts and of the ways in which these contexts have shaped his films. In the United States, it can be argued that Forman has been an émigré filmmaker seeking to identify himself with a new culture. In Czechoslovakia, he was very much part of an existing culture and, as a central figure in the Czech *new wave* of the sixties, committed to the process of social and political change of which it formed part.

In considering the work of Forman as a whole, auteurist assumptions of some kind are inevitable and to some extent justified by a degree of control over his own work. However, while it will be apparent that his work shares common themes and approaches, these continuities are not necessary criteria of value. A historical and critical approach will be adopted to Forman's ten completed features in which issues of context, objective, and form are all seen as important factors.

Before discussing Forman's work in Czechoslovakia, it is worth recalling that he was born in 1932 and lived through five different regimes—the prewar republic, the Nazi occupation, the briefly reinstituted postwar republic, Stalinism, and the reform communism of the sixties. Both his parents died in a concentration camp during the war. His adult experience coincided almost precisely with the worst years of Stalinism and the period of hope engendered by the reform movement of the sixties.

The Communist takeover of 1948, while undemocratic and reliant on Soviet power, also enjoyed a measure of public support. In the last free elections of 1946, the Communist party had gained a third of the votes, which was not too different from the support for the British Conservative party in the eighties. There was talk of a specific Czechoslovak way to socialism, but such ideas were soon suppressed in favor of a rigorous application of the Stalinist model. This was typified not only by the wholesale imprisonment of political opponents but, also, most blatantly, by the arrest and trial of the Communist leadership itself in the early fifties. This led to the execution of no less than eleven members of the ruling elite, including the general secretary, Rudolf Slánský. As party secretary from 1953, Antonín Novotný supervised the final stages of the purges, combining his office with that of president from 1957 till the onset of the Prague Spring in 1968.

When Krushchev made his speech denouncing Stalin in 1957, the responses in Czechoslovakia were predictably mild compared with the Hungarian Revolution and the unrest in Poland and East Germany. However, it was from this time that the movement for change could be dated. As Ota Šik, architect of the economic reforms of 1968, put it: ". . . I could not be satisfied with the ingenuous argument that the 'cult of Stalin' was the root of all evil. I had to decide—either to leave the Communist party or to stay in order, by long-term, patient, and systematic work, to help change the system."[2] For reform Communists, 1968 provided the opportunity to realize ideals suppressed by years of Stalinism; for others it signified a recognition of the bankruptcy of the system as such.

Czechoslovakia has a long film history, and between the wars averaged twenty to thirty features a year. Apart from Machatý and Haas, other filmmakers to attract international attention in the thirties included Martin Frič (*Janošík*); Josef Rovenský (*The River* [*Řeka*]); Karel Lamač, who frequently worked with the best-known star of the period, Anny Ondra; Alexander Hammid, the avant-garde and documentary filmmaker who later worked with Maya Deren in New York; and the comedy team of Jan Werich and Jiří Voskovec. After World War II, the industry was nationalized in 1945 and the Prague Film School (FAMU) was established in 1947, both before the Communist takeover. Despite the postwar achievements of directors such as Kadár, Jiří Weiss, Jiří Krejčík, and the animators Jiří Trnka and Karel Zeman, it was FAMU that provided the new generation of directors who spearheaded the international success of Czech and Slovak cinema in the sixties. The first generation of directors, which included Vojtěch Jasný and Karel Kachyňa, began to make films in the late fifties, to be followed by the *new wave* proper in 1963–64. The leading figures of the *new wave* were Forman, Věra Chytilová, Jiří Menzel, Evald Schorm, Jaromil Jireš, Pavel Juráček, and Ivan Passer, although Forman had graduated much earlier (as a scriptwriter) in 1956. All were united by a desire to tell the "truth" and by an interest in experimenting with different forms. Most important, they were opposed to the falsifications of socialist realism, with its obligatory content and routinized narrative. As Forman himself put it, the Zhdanovist aesthetics that dominated in the fifties ". . . monstrously overemphasized the idea of a work of art, while calamitously underemphasizing its contents and form. The country's culture was, in practice, degraded to the status of a special branch of education and propaganda."[3] The films of the *new wave* ranged from the more orthodox narratives of Schorm via the poetic lyricism of Jireš and Menzel to the avant-garde experiments of Chytilová. The films of Forman and Passer were characterized by a kind of improvisatory realism, drawing on both Italian neorealism and cinéma vérité.

Forman speaks of an early childhood commitment to theater after attending the last performance of a provincial repertory theater after the Nazis decreed the closure of all theaters in Czechoslovakia. Later, while still at boarding school, he was involved in a production of Voskovec's and Werich's prewar play, *Ballad of Rags* (*Ballada z hadrů*) at the E. F. Burian theater in Prague at a time when it was still banned. A production that used jazz orchestra and modern dance, it suggests that Forman's American production of *Hair* was not such a new departure as some may have thought. After failing to get into drama school, he studied scriptwriting at FAMU, later working with the film and theater director Alfred Radok as an assistant on the film *Grandpa Automobile* (*Dědeček automobil,* 1956) and in the Laterna Magika theater. A multimedia success at the Brussels Exposition of 1958 (and again at Montreal in 1967), the stage production of *Laterna Magika* was quite the reverse of Forman's first films. According to Forman, "Laterna used multiple projections, cinemascope, a 'live' stage, and stereophonic music, so it was really a kind of cybernetic machine one had to keep one's eyes on all the time."[4]

Forman worked on two other films, Martin Frič's *Leave It to Me* (*Nechte to na mně,* 1955) and Ivo Novák's *Puppies* (*Štěnata,* 1957), for which he wrote the original script. Yet it was again through theater that he came to make his first film, *Talent Competition* (*Konkurs,* 1963). While working in Brussels, he had shared an apartment with Jan Roháč, Vladimír Svitáček, and Jiří Šlitr of the Semafor Theatre. All of them admired the work of Voskovec's and Werich's Liberated Theatre and wished it had been recorded on film. It was a theater with frequent political overtones based on the liquidation of traditional artistic genres and drew its influences from dada, circus, and silent-film comedy. Apart from their film work, Voskovec's and Werich's stage productions followed in regular sequence from the appearance of their *Vest Pocket Revue* of 1927 through to the enforced closure of the theater in 1938. Although different in a number of respects, the Semafor Theater played a similar role in the culture of the fifties and sixties (and beyond), and out of that grew a project for recording its work. The film never materialized, but *Talent Competition* emerged from a plan to film auditions for the Semafor.

The film started as an amateur project filmed on 16mm with a camera borrowed from Miroslav Ondříček, who was director of photography on virtually all of Forman's subsequent films. With the encouragement of one of the production groups at the Barrandov film studios, they developed a story line to accompany the original "cinéma vérité" footage. The envisaged short film turned out to be too long, and they got the money to develop

2.1. At the audition. *Talent Competition.* BFI Stills, Posters and Designs. Photo by Jaromír Komárek.

the project as a feature by adding a second medium-length film, *If There Were No Music* (*Kdyby ty muziky nebyly*). This largely accidental merging of "cinéma vérité" observation with simple narrative elements provided the genesis of a style that was to form the basis for all of Forman's Czech films, in particular *Black Peter* (*Černy Petr,* 1963) and *Loves of a Blonde* (*Lásky jedné plavovlásky,* 1965). The two sections of the film adopt very much the same strategy. *Talent Competition* focuses on the subject of auditions at the Semafor and *If There Were No Music* on the annual brass band competition at Kolín. Both derive their force from the cinéma vérité material but both employ simple narrative elements to maintain progression. While the stories do not add much to the film, a full-scale cinéma vérité approach would have been unlikely at the time.

The strength of the film lies in its witty, ironic, and sympathetic observation of its subjects. Much the most powerful element is its presentation of the teenage hopefuls of *Talent Competition.* The famous scene (repeated in Forman's first American film, *Taking Off*) where different girls sing the same song, each image and face cut to different phrases, manages to be funny, cruel, and beautiful all at the same time. The film's qualities lie less in the satisfaction to be gained from overall form than in the authentic atmosphere of rehearsal, the revelation of individual hopes and fears, and, in the case of *Talent Competition,* the tuneless vitality of its youthful performers. Jiří Suchý and Jiří Šlitr, the stars of the Semafor, perform and conduct the auditions but play very much a subsidiary role, the focus having changed from theater and show business to the everyday. Nonetheless, even in this early film, Forman shows a willingness to manipulate his observed material, with evidence of lyricism (the morning motorcycle ride in *If There Were No Music*), the use of frozen images, and the cutting of shots to satirical effect.

While *Talent Competition* gave birth to a style, it also featured many of the actors and nonactors who were to appear in later films. Jan Vostrčil, conductor of one of the brass bands, was to play the father in *Black Peter* and one of the leading firemen in *The Firemen's Ball* (*Hoří, má panenko!,* 1967); Vladimír Pucholt, the defaulting band member, is in *Black Peter* and *Loves of a Blonde;* and Věra Křesadlová, the singer who dries up (and the future Mrs. Forman), had leading parts in Ivan Passer's *Intimate Lighting* (*Intimní osvětlení,* 1965), Jiří Menzel's *Larks on a String* (*Skřivánci na niti,* 1969), and Jaroslav Papoušek's *The Best Age* (*Nejkrásnejší věk,* 1968).

The style of Forman's Czech films was also a group style that owed much to his regular collaborators, Ivan Passer, Jaroslav Papoušek, and Miroslav Ondříček. Passer and Papoušek collaborated on all three of Forman's subsequent films and Papoušek, trained as a sculptor, contributed the original story for *Black Peter.* Ondříček worked on *Loves of a Blonde, The Firemen's Ball,* and Passer's first feature, *Intimate Lighting.* Papoušek also worked with Passer on *Intimate Lighting* before taking solo writer/director credit for *The Best Age.* Made after Forman and Passer had left for the United States, *The Best Age* was superficially similar to their earlier work but more consciously structured, an approach that Papoušek continued through his Homolka series of the early seventies. Significantly, the latter were considered too abrasive by the "normalized" regime and withdrawn from circulation. Speaking of his collaboration with Forman and Passer, Papoušek said, "I never had the feeling that the boys were expert filmmakers while I was only a sculptor who got in the way. Nor did I feel that they contributed more than I. Each of us was an equal among equals."[5]

Despite the strong similarities between the films directed by Forman, Passer, and Papoušek, there are important differences. If we recognize Forman as the dominant influence on the films he directed, we should also recognize their collaborative nature. Forman himself noted the change in working conditions when he went to the United States. Despite the fact that, in the early seventies, the role of the director was not as readily credited or identified as in Czechoslovakia, he found himself regarded much more as the final arbiter.[6] The informally collaborative approach to filmmaking could not be continued.

Forman's subsequent Czech features are generally regarded, certainly in Czechoslovakia, as superior to his American work. The vicious humor of *The Firemen's Ball* and the revelatory qualities of *Black Peter* and *Loves of a*

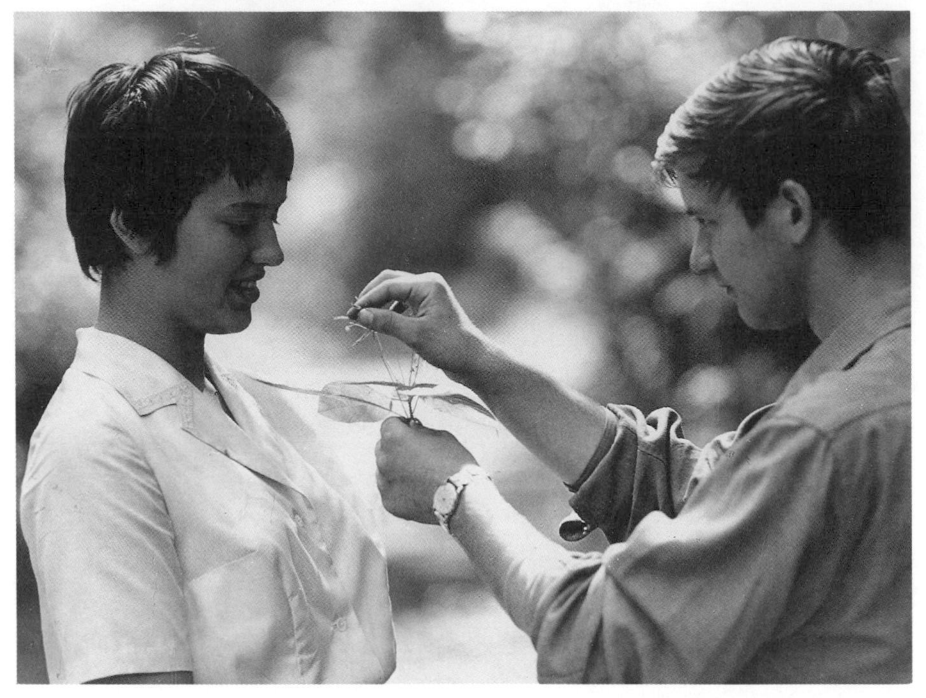

2.2. Pavla (Pavla Martínková) and Petr (Ladislav Jakim). *Black Peter.* BFI Stills, Posters and Designs. Photo by Jaromír Komárek.

Blonde were not to be repeated. While all three films grew from the same context and impulses, *Black Peter* and *Loves of a Blonde* are most closely linked to the style of *Talent Competition.*

Both share a background that can be described as working class, their heroes respectively a boy, Petr, who begins work in a grocery store, and a girl, Andula, who works in a shoe factory. Neither has prospects, ambitions, or wider horizons, and their only outlets are romance and music. Yet despite their negative life situations, they show a resilience that suggests they are survivors. Their portrayal is the opposite of the socialist realist stereotype with its idealization, political motivation, and utopian vision. Initially attacked by Stalinist critics, Forman's films were eventually adopted by the more liberal wing of the Communist party as a new development in socialist art. It is easy to see how the films could be considered too negative for release in the USSR and "progressive" in the West.

Neither film has a developed narrative, and both are composed largely in terms of set pieces with elliptical links. Forman said at the time that his screenplays were constructed in terms of what interested him.

> . . . I never worried much about whether a story is logical or not. Still, a certain logic does crop up at certain moments, in certain situations and scenes. If one adds up all these "interesting" moments, they don't have the weight of

2.3. Čenda (Vladimír Pucholt) in the center. *Black Peter.* BFI Stills, Posters and Designs.

a "classic" logical construction; but they do have the advantage of a certain nonsense with its own strict rules, depending on the behavior of the characters involved.[7]

Although they are comedies, they find space and opportunity for a fair degree of social and political criticism. In *Black Peter,* this is fairly general—lack of motivation, petty thievery, sexism—and achieves its effects principally through the portrayal of characters locked in a situation from which there appears to be no escape. In *Loves of a Blonde,* the criticism moves beyond its down-at-heel surroundings and the aging couple who have worked all their lives to end up dozing in front of a television set. One of the main themes concerns the fate of young girls condemned to live and work in the provinces in order to meet the needs of the economic plan. There is no concern for their social needs, and the temporary import of soldiers for a dance (they turn out to be middle-aged reservists) is presented as a major breakthrough in bureaucratic thinking. The film's sharp portrait of authority is supplemented by a superb sequence in which the girls are treated to a lecture on morality by the warden of their hostel. It is a brilliant portrayal of hypocrisy, acquiescence, and fake democracy.

The nominal focus of the films is on "boy meets girl" relationships, but these are scarcely notable in themselves. They are portrayed with an authenticity and casual cruelty nearer to life than Hollywood (or socialist

2.4. Andula (Hana Brejchová) on the right. *Loves of a Blonde.* BFI Stills, Posters and Designs.

realist) convention, but the films focus much more effectively on the relations between generations. In *Black Peter,* Petr is constantly harangued by a shirt-sleeved father who marches to and fro mouthing platitudes about work, a career, and motivation. At the end of the film, there is a frozen shot of his father clasping his head in exasperation. His last words to his son are, "Do you have any idea what you are talking about, do you have any idea at all?" While this can be interpreted as a final comment on the theme of conventional wisdom, something still remains of Forman's original (and more political) conception. This was of a man who had lived through six different regimes but was unable to explain the complexities of his Central European fate to his son. In the second half of *Loves of a Blonde,* the focus changes from that of the girl pursuing her lover to Prague to a developed character study of his parents, the mother's worries about the neighbors and Andula's presumed pregnancy, and their depressed lifestyle. Indeed, in both films it is the older generation that is shown to have suffered the realities of life's injustice.

The films echo the sense of unobtrusive observation that characterized Ermanno Olmi's *The Job* (*Il Posto,* 1961) and *The Engagement* (*I Fidanzati,* 1962), while sharing some of the more abrasive observation of the British "kitchen sink" school.[8]

In *Loves of a Blonde,* the dance hall scene is particularly successful both for its comic timing and in its dramatization of relations between the sexes and generations. It is here that three middle-aged reservists try to pick up three teenage girls, the hopes and fears of different generations shown with Forman's characteristic mixture of humor, cruelty, and sympathy. But it is the formal mechanisms of comedy, the reversals and the timing, that are foregrounded. In a less obvious sense, sensitivity and timing are the distinguishing features of the films in general.

Forman's Czech films have the appearance of "cinéma vérité" and of improvisation, but they are in fact highly organized. As Antonín Liehm has pointed out,[9] Forman's films were quite rigorously scripted despite the lack of orthodox dramatic construction, and working with nonprofessionals required more rather than less thorough preparation. While clearly fascinated by the unique qualities that nonactors could bring to their parts, Forman knew that they had to be selected with extreme care. He also got impressive results from mixing the work of professional and nonprofessional by his use of Vladimír Pucholt, who was an actor, in a substantial part in *Black Peter* and in the central role of Míla, Andula's lover, in *Loves of a Blonde.* Speaking of his experience in casting Vladimír Menšík as one of the three reservists in the dance hall scene in *Loves of a Blonde,* he referred to it as "a fantastic experiment" in which the actor gave form to the work of the nonprofessionals and his own performance gained in depth and authenticity.[10]

The script is rarely improvised, although the last scene in *Loves of a Blonde,* where Míla is invited into his parents' bed to protect him from the temptations of Andula in the next room, is an exception. Here his "actors" were Pucholt, Josef Šebánek, the uncle of his cameraman's wife, and Milada Ježková, whom Passer and Papoušek had found on a Prague streetcar.

In order to ". . . capture those fleeting moments that will never come again,"[11] Forman is concerned to respect the integrity of his actors' performances, to give maximum space for interaction, to keep the camera subservient, and to avoid directorial flourishes (he is *not* a Hitchcock or a Scorsese). It is interesting to note the difference between Ondříček's work on *Loves of a Blonde* and Jan Němec's *Martyrs of Love* (*Mučedníci lásky,* 1966), the first a documentary gray with imperceptible camera movement, the second an exercise in high contrast and fantasy. The images in *Black Peter* and *Loves of a Blonde,* particularly viewed from a twenty-five-year perspective, have acquired a marvelous documentary patina normally associated with still photography, unrepeatable faces captured at a particular point in history.

While drawing on the style of *Black Peter* and *Loves of a Blonde, The Firemen's Ball* (*Hoří, má panenko!*—literally, *It's Burning, My Love!*) is a more self-conscious work, a continuous allegory on both the state of society and, more specifically, of the Communist party. While Forman's comments at the time were purposefully inexplicit, he has recently spoken of the fact that not only did the nation learn to read between the lines, but writers and artists also learned to write between the lines.[12] All films with any claim to honesty were inflected with the realities of life under Stalinism.

In its absence of central characters, *The Firemen's Ball* adopts a more

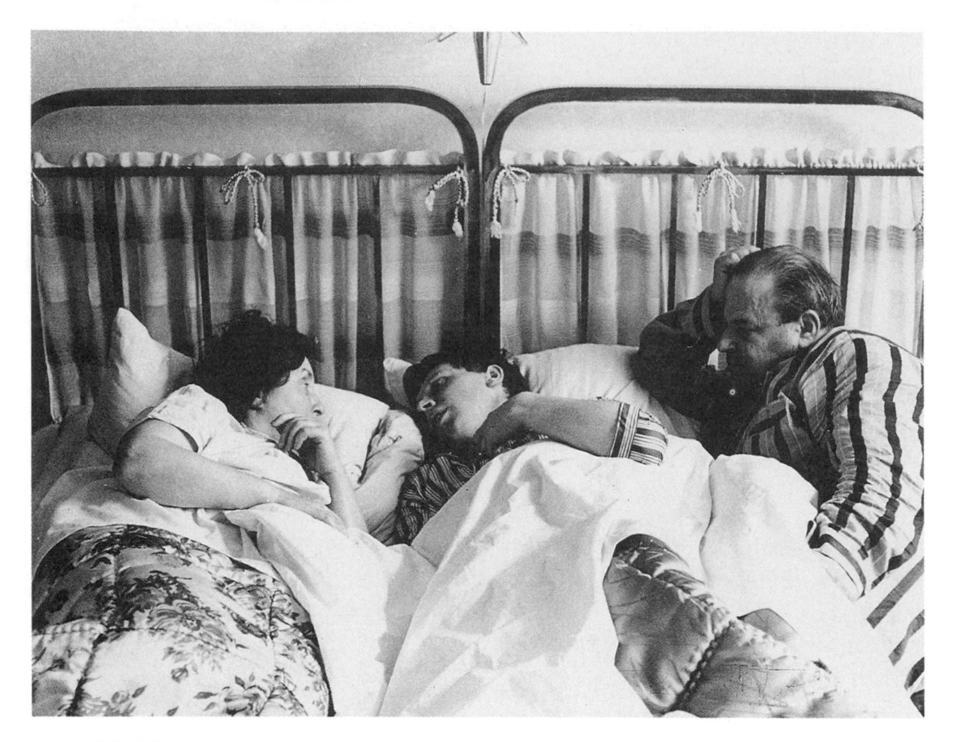

2.5. Mila's mother (Milada Jezková), Mila (Vladimír Pucholt), and Mila's father (Josef Šebanek). *Loves of a Blonde.* BFI Stills, Posters and Designs. Photo by Jaromír Komárek.

radical form. While the hero and heroine of *Black Peter* and *Loves of a Blonde* were often instrumental, a means of getting things moving from observation to observation, they also provided a sense of identification. The absence of identification in *The Firemen's Ball* makes it a more distanced, harder, and more cruel vision of society. "I think this is quite all right, because when I'm dealing with somebody who is weaker than I, I cannot be completely cruel; but if I'm attacking someone who is a hundred times more powerful, then malice and even a certain amount of cruelty are quite appropriate."[13]

The group as hero (in this case the firemen's committee) has some notable precedents. Eisenstein experimented with the mass as hero in *Strike* (*Stachka,* 1924) and *The Battleship Potemkin* (*Bronenosets Potemkin,* 1925) while, in the thirties, Jean Renoir worked more successfully with group heroes and villains in films such as *La Marseillaise* (1938) and *La Règle du Jeu* (1939). Forman's film can be presented as a negative version of the group as hero or, specifically, the Party as hero. While the firemen's committee can more appropriately be regarded as incompetent, shortsighted, and well meaning rather than malicious, there is plenty of scope for reading political meanings between the lines.

Two of the key sequences in *Black Peter* and *Loves of a Blonde* take place at dances, and *The Firemen's Ball* extends the device to the whole film. The

2.6. Committee members. Josef Šebánek in the center. *The Firemen's Ball.* BFI Stills, Posters and Designs.

dance floor functions both as an extended metaphor and, as in the earlier films, an arena for dramatizing human relations. The action centers on an annual firemen's ball in which a dance, a beauty competition, and a raffle are promised. The first half of the film, with its familiar mixture of affectionate/cruel observation and classic comic influences, recalls the earlier films, but the second half moves to a bitter and negative conclusion.

The narrative concentrates on two main developments, the progressive theft of the raffle prizes and the committee's abortive attempts to organize the beauty contest. The contest ends in chaos when the fire siren goes off, the fire brigade fails to put out the fire, and an old man is left homeless. The firemen then hold a collection of raffle tickets for him, but by this time they are worthless because all the prizes have been stolen. Even the ceremonial hatchet preserved for their aging president (who is dying of cancer) has been stolen. The film ends with two old men climbing on to a bedstead set in a snow-covered landscape, one the man whose home has been burned down, the other a fireman left to make sure none of his belongings are stolen. Beside them is a discarded crucifix in a wastebasket.

Although filmed on location, Ondříček has spoken of how the central set was constructed to create a warm atmosphere, with costumes to complement it. Within this, the amateur cast interacted and behaved in an

2.7. *The Firemen's Ball.* BFI Stills, Posters and Designs.

entirely natural way. Ondříček described it as a unique experience, and a number of the crew stayed on to marry local people.[14] But while it is true that most of the cast remain natural, the principal players (most of whom appeared in *Black Peter* or *Loves of a Blonde*) appear much more mannered and are given more pointed dialogue. A vicious and acute social comedy, its tone alienated not only the Stalinist bureaucracy but also co-producer Carlo Ponti, who withdrew his investment, and American and European distributors. As one of the leaders of the Prague surrealist group, Vratislav Effenberger, wrote, Forman's humor was "vicious, dangerous, concealed, and explosive," striking at the ". . . spiritual wretchedness out of which, essentially, spring various kinds of fascism and Stalinism . . . ."[15]

While the film does not restrict its attack to the firemen's committee, it makes some fairly specific political points. In the closing stages of the film, a fireman is caught returning one of the stolen prizes and is accused of putting his "honesty" before the reputation of the brigade. This was taken as a reference to the current debate within the party on the degree to which the truth about the political trials of the fifties should be revealed. In other scenes the mismatch between official platitudes and human reality is clearly pointed. In 1969, *The Firemen's Ball* was listed as one of the films to be banned "forever" but, with unplanned irony, it was rereleased the summer before the "velvet revolution" of 1989.

With *The Firemen's Ball,* Forman was quite widely criticized for making fun of ordinary people. He commented: "I'm always fascinated by this formulation 'He's mocking the simple man.' I wish someone would accuse me of mocking a complicated man. I've even invented a theory to prove that my heroes are really very 'complicated' people, not simple and ordinary at all."[16] Nonetheless, there is a sense in which, intentional or otherwise, the characters in *The Firemen's Ball* are more grotesque, more like visual caricatures, than in the earlier films. The film is almost a hymn to the diversity of facial and bodily appearance, with conventional good looks difficult to find. He was criticized for laughing at the teenage beauty contestants forced to parade up and down behind closed doors. But, since the majority of them have been coerced, Forman is criticizing the behavior and fantasies of the committee, not the delusions of the contestants. If the audience ends up uneasy and embarrassed, it is in the final analysis, Liehm suggests, because the characters are too close to the audience in their behavior, thinking, and attitudes.[17]

In different contexts, both the novelist Josef Škvorecký and František Daniel, former dean of FAMU, have linked Forman's work to the cynical-humanist traditions of Czech comedy. For Škvorecký, it is a tradition that extends from Jaroslav Hašek (*The Good Soldier Švejk*) and Bohumil Hrabal (*Closely Watched Trains*) to his own work (*The Cowards*).[18] Daniel, describing Hašek's novel as the bible of the Czech nation, said that *Švejk* was a film that Forman felt almost obliged to make.[19] In the spring of 1968, he had plans to make a film of *The Cowards.*

This comic and essentially ironic tradition has been seen as the reverse side of Kafka. In a famous essay written in 1963, the philosopher Karel Kosík imagines the hero of Kafka's *The Trial,* Josef K., passing Josef Švejk on Charles Bridge. This provided the springboard for a reflection on the work of two contemporary writers living in the same city. "While Kafka depicted the world of human reification and showed that man must experience and live through all types of alienation to be human, Hašek showed man transcending reification, irreducible to an object, to reified products or relations. One posited a negative, the other a positive scale of humanism."[20]

While the comic tradition that is in many ways a defining characteristic of Czech cinema derived equally from cabaret and theater (not least Voskovec and Werich), the impact of Hašek's *Švejk* was enormous. First published in 1921–1923, it had gone through ten editions by 1936 and five feature films based on *Švejk* had appeared by 1931. Initially based on Hašek's experience of the Austrian army in 1915, its anarchistic and apparently idiotic hero was clearly a Czech making fun of his Austrian masters. But beyond that, it is a marvelous defense of the little man who refuses to succumb to petty tyranny and oppression.

When Škvorecký's *The Cowards* was first published in 1958 (it was banned and reissued in 1963), it was seen by some as doing for the Second World War what Hašek had done for the first. His heroes were concerned with their own lives, with girls and with jazz, rather than the delights of Nazi ideology or the sacred cause of liberation.

Hrabal's first published works, *Pearls from the Deep* (1963) and *The Crazies*

(1964), were far from the forms of the conventional novel. He had worked in a great variety of jobs, in the process meeting many of the gossips, misfits, and dropouts who feature in his stories. Hrabal focuses on the individuality of his characters, which is always at variance with the transience of ideologies.

From a formal perspective, all three writers are in some sense subversive. Hašek was considered illiterate and uncouth, and his improvisatory form condemned. Škvorecký offended through his use of slang, and Hrabal opted for virtually plotless dialogues. Despite important differences, they share a concern for the lives and language of ordinary people, asserting their value, common sense, and humor when faced with the simplified visions of dominant powers.

In both *Black Peter* and *Loves of a Blonde*, there is not only an improvisatory style and authentic dialogue but also a focus on young people whose interest is not work and "socialism" but love and music. The marvelous gallery of characters and portraits from everyday life derives, like those of Hašek and Hrabal, from a lived experience and an acute observation of the absurd and the incongruous.

What Forman and his fellow filmmakers of the *new wave* shared was a common culture that embraced the broader comic tradition. The freedom to experiment that arose in the sixties also brought their films closer to the spirit of Hašek than the films actually derived from his work. The loose and episodic narrative structures, the characters who verge on Josef Lada's caricatures for *Švejk*, the individuality and the resilience, are all factors held in common.

Forman had already begun work on his first American film during the Prague Spring, and *Taking Off*, finally completed in 1971, is the film closest to his Czech films. Although using professional actors, it is constructed with a similarly loose narrative that serves principally as a pretext for its key scenes. Yet again, the nominal story—a young girl appears to run away from home—gives way to an analysis of the lives of the parents, who appear to have much more serious problems than their errant daughter.

Forman originally wrote the script in 1968 in collaboration with Buñuel's regular collaborator, Jean-Claude Carrière, but May in Paris and August in Prague intervened. The film was eventually made after further work with the writers John Klein and John Guare. By this time, of course, Forman's American experience was added, an ironic view of the idiosyncracies of East Village culture with its runaway teenagers, hippies, and Hell's Angels as well as a perceptive view of the conformity of middle-class America. Just as Forman nearly went to jail when Carlo Ponti withdrew his investment in *The Firemen's Ball*, he had a second traumatic encounter with the realities of capitalist filmmaking. The title of his *Show* article was self-explanatory—"How I Came to America to Make a Film and Wound Up Owing Paramount $140,000."[21]

Taking Off begins with a reprise of the auditions that were the subject of *Talent Competition*. The songs are different, the girls are American, but there is the same montage of unrepeatable faces. "Some are pretty; more are not. Some have talent; most do not. But what they all have in common is a great deal of courage and, above everything else, a desperate desire to succeed."[22] However, the competition is used in a slightly different way: first as an ironic counterpoint to the situation of the couple whose daughter has disappeared (she is at the audition) and, second, as a kind of chorus commenting on the action as it progresses.

The daughter's disappearances are fundamentally innocent, to the auditions, and later, after a row with her parents, to her boyfriend. The parents, on the other hand, embark on a voyage of self-discovery through their encounter with the alternative culture. After Jeannie Tyne's second disappearance, her father Larry (Buck Henry) meets up with the attractive, middle-aged Ann, whose daughter has run off with two Hell's Angels. Through her, he and his wife, Lynn (Lynn Carlin), become members of the Society for the Parents of Fugitive Children (SPFC). Encounters with Black Power and Hell's Angels progress to a night at a motel where a couple of sleazy men try to pick up the drunken Lynn, an evening at SPFC where the cream of middle-class America learn to smoke joints in order to understand their children better, to a game of strip poker in the Tyne household. Jeannie, who is sleeping peacefully upstairs, emerges to find her father naked on the sitting-room table singing an aria from *La Traviata.* The gulf between the generations is compounded when her hippie boyfriend is invited to tea. An affluent rock musician who accepts the "contradictions" of making money, he is treated to Larry's rendition of *Stranger in Paradise.* The younger generation looks on in disbelief at an alien culture.

As with *Black Peter* and *Loves of a Blonde, Taking Off* begins with the younger generation and ends up with its focus on the parents, with the difference that they are now middle aged rather than old. "I've never worried about the middle aged, because I was naive enough to think they were strong and had all the power, so that they didn't deserve anybody's sympathy. It was only now that I discovered that no generation had a monopoly on feeling helpless and impotent."[23]

There are some marvelously observed scenes of insecurity and self-confrontation. As a girl sings, "I was born into a world full of angels and kings . . . ," the parents look at their missing daughter's bedroom, the reassuring collection of ceramic cats, discover the evidence of her smoking, that their portrait of her is already four years old. When Larry and Ann are brought together in the search for Ann's daughter, the discussion of SPFC is the occasion for the socializing of the parents. The possibility for continuing the quest promises an incipient date in an increasingly routine lifestyle.

There is little concern with narrative motivation, the links between scenes being established by simple devices such as a telephone call or an invitation to dinner. The motel scene leads directly to the SPFC convention, the only linking a rather strange cut forward to the convention, then back again to the motel. Similarly, the montage of early morning New York street scenes accompanied by Dvořák's *Stabat Mater* is virtually unmotivated. The

2.8. *Taking Off.* BFI Stills, Posters and Designs.

use of the audition as Greek chorus sometimes functions predictably (e.g., "Lessons in Love Are Free" as the well-dressed Ann pursues her errant daughter plus two Hell's Angels through the streets). At other times, it is used for purely formal effect; for instance, when the chords from an electric organ are intercut with Larry's session with the antismoking hypnotist or the clapping of "He's Got the Whole World in His Hands" is synchronized with Lynn's hand clapping during the game of strip poker.

Silent comedy references abound, from classic drunk sequences to Allen Garfield (the sleazy man at the hotel) losing his trousers. The pursuit of Ann's daughter develops into a double chase sequence with the Hell's Angels after Larry and Ann chasing her daughter and the unpaid taxi driver chasing her. Eventually, Ann and Larry end up on a roof, the Hell's Angels steal the taxi, and the taxi driver is abandoned. Apart from the sheer comedy of joint passing and puckered lips at the SPFC convention, the faces when listening to officialdom recall the impassive reaction of the participants at *The Firemen's Ball* when requested to return the raffle prizes or the girls listening to the moral homilies of their warden in *Loves of a Blonde.*

Taking Off is Forman's lightest and most entertaining film. While he uses the structures of his Czech films and relatively unknown actors, he does not, understandably, share the same immersion in its subject matter. It is less bitter, more affectionate, and clearly allied to the generation of flower power. An official American entry at Cannes, it won the Special Jury

Prize and was well received by the critics, from *Variety* to the *New York Times,* from *Newsweek* to *Rolling Stone.* Writing in the London *Times,* Dilys Powell complimented Forman on what she described as an extraordinarily successful transition to the American scene and for taking his narrative style and gift for observation with him.[24] Yet this was the last film in which he used the "Forman style." Feeling partly that he was repeating himself and responding to the fact that American audiences had difficulties with his unconventional narrative, he deliberately moved toward a more conventional form. A pity, because many would argue that his films lose a great deal of force in the process, and there are many American directors, from Altman to Hopper, from Scorsese to Coppola, who have shown a less disciplined approach to narrative.

The close links between *Taking Off* and Forman's Czech films are worth considering in greater detail. Jeannie Tyne's expression of bewilderment as she looks at her singing parents parallels the exchange between Petr and his father in *Black Peter,* and both *Taking Off* and *Loves of a Blonde* begin with girls singing to the camera. They have stories that serve only as a pretext for social observation, with conventional narrative development virtually ignored or elided. The episodic construction of *Loves of a Blonde* and *Taking Off* reveals a number of close parallels.

Links between scenes are rarely the result of direct motivation and geographical connections are entirely subservient to thematic ones. Typical of these implicit links is the scene in *Loves of a Blonde* where the girls vote "unanimously" in favor of the woman warden's advice at the Union of Young Czechoslovaks. The phrase "any abstentions?" is answered by a shot of Andula waiting for a lift to Prague. In *Taking Off,* when Larry calls home and discovers that Jeannie has been spotted in upstate New York, there is only a brief shot of him and Lynn in the car before they are seen in the upstate police station.

Scenes vary in length and location according to their themes and interest. An early scene in *Loves of a Blonde* shows Andula meeting a forest guard against a snow-covered background. It has no narrative connection with anything else and only has a thematic link with the first scenes. However, it does have a visual impact and arguably a poetic one. In *Taking Off,* Larry's visit to the psychiatrist is also outside of any narrative context. In contrast, other scenes receive an extended treatment quite unrelated to their narrative roles—notably the dance scene in *Loves of a Blonde* and the SPFC meeting in *Taking Off.* Both provide an opportunity for observing the wider social context that becomes the whole subject of *The Firemen's Ball.* However, whereas the dance scene serves as a springboard for later developments, the SPFC meeting functions almost as a climax.

Both *Loves of a Blonde* and *Taking Off* focus on the parents. This is very obvious in the case of *Taking Off,* where the story of Jeannie Tyne is basically a pretext for an examination of the parents' reactions. In this sense, the film is more focused and consistent than *Loves of a Blonde.* There, Forman begins with a focus on Andula, only to shift attention to the three soldiers, and subsequently Míla's parents, with no satisfying narrative resolution to the quest for her lover.

It is difficult to imagine any American film in which the climactic scene is an improvised episode with three people squabbling over the bedclothes. *Taking Off* has its card-playing equivalent but, with some concession to the audience, it *is* a game of strip poker and does include the central characters. Although closer to the American ideal of the well-made film, Forman is still working within the Czech tradition of comic improvisation and casual authenticity. *Taking Off* is some way from the tightly woven narratives and carefully structured high points of classical Hollywood film.

As Kristin Thompson has pointed out, the norms governing the construction of classical Hollywood style were not those of the novel and drama as such, but their late nineteenth-century variants.[25] From this perspective, it seems a pity that non-American directors find themselves unable to extend those norms and are constrained, perhaps more than native-born directors, to conform to them in order to work.

It is tempting to see Forman's move away from his Czech style as a sellout to commercialism. Yet it is important to recognize that he had no offers for a number of years after *Taking Off* and it was better to compromise than to make no films at all. Furthermore, unconventional topics such as *One Flew Over the Cuckoo's Nest* and *Amadeus* would never have reached the audiences they did had they been treated in a less conventional and "popular" manner.

What might have seemed at one time like a personal decision can be viewed more and more as a kind of imperative. A recent conference on East European filmmakers working in the West identified the problem of American narrative mentality as one of its central issues.[26] In 1991, a conference for East European film and television program makers held in London informed them of the need for the simple dramatic story if they were to gain access to Western markets. But, as one Czech director commented later with a sense of exasperation, theirs was a tradition based on the primacy of the image.

When Forman made *One Flew Over the Cuckoo's Nest* (1975), neither he nor his producers expected the success they achieved. Kirk Douglas originally suggested the project when Forman was still in Czechoslovakia, but the copy of the novel he sent never arrived. Ten years later (in 1973) the book finally reached Forman via the new owner of the rights, Michael Douglas.

In adapting the novel, Forman, unaware of its near-mythical status with American counterculture, eliminated the psychedelic aspects of Ken Kesey's original. Although filmed in a psychiatric hospital in Oregon, he described it as a "political" film about America, but one whose observations could well be applied elsewhere. He also described the novel as "a Czech book."[27] In another context, Jiří Menzel, the director of *Larks on a String* and the Oscar-winning *Closely Watched Trains* (*Ostře sledované vlaky*), described *One Flew Over the Cuckoo's Nest* as part of the history of Czech cinema. Had it been shown in Czechoslovakia, it would certainly have received a political interpretation. It was a project that clearly appealed to the Czech love of creating and reading between the lines.

Although one should guard against viewing it as "a Czech film"—it was, after all, made for an American audience—it was clearly intended as allegory and not as a specific analysis of the treatment of insanity in the United States. It is more transparently political than *The Firemen's Ball,* and it is instructive to compare it with one of the more overtly political Czech *new wave* films, Jan Němec's *The Party and the Guests* (*O slavnosti a hostech,* 1966).

The Party and the Guests tells the story of a group of bourgeois picnickers who voluntarily attend a banquet in honor of the birthday of a political leader. As they are escorted to the celebration by members of the secret police, the film analyzes the process by which they learn to adjust and accommodate themselves to oppression by a dominant power. At the center of the system is the leader himself, whose sadism only occasionally emerges from his show of affability. Beneath him is his psychotic "adopted son," Rudolf, whose purpose is to ensure "order," to make sure that everyone sits in the right place, to hunt down the guest who leaves without permission. At the end of the film, the screen turns black and we hear the barking of dogs and the fake gaiety of fairground music.

In *One Flew Over the Cuckoo's Nest,* the asylum is run by reasonable men in suits (the doctors), with a hierarchy of white and black assistants, all dressed identically in white with either ties or bow ties. Nurse Ratched (Louise Fletcher) is in charge of the ward with a brief to maintain order and routine and to keep the inmates from disruptive activity. The film focuses on a group of male voluntary inmates, people who seem to be there because they fear the outside world and, in particular, the opposite sex. R. P. McMurphy (Jack Nicholson), the criminal who has himself committed for an easier life, is the "sane" man who penetrates this closed world, in the process promoting the self-confidence, independence, and initiative of his fellow inmates. Before he escapes (like one of the principal characters in *The Party and the Guests*), or encourages others to escape, he must be silenced and rendered harmless by electric shock treatment. Just as one of the "guests" in *The Party and the Guests* satisfies his desire for democracy with the return of a stolen cigarette lighter, so one of the inmates of *One Flew Over the Cuckoo's Nest* is pacified by being allowed to keep his own cigarettes. Just as the guests are not allowed to change places, so the inmates are not allowed to break order by watching the World Series. When order is restored and pills are administered, the bland tones of a string orchestra playing *Charmaine* echo through the ward (a parallel with the music that accompanies the end of *The Party and the Guests*). The volume cannot be turned down because the music is "for everyone." There could not be a more powerful indictment of the mechanics of power and conformity, of a system that cloaks its power in the trappings of concern for the well-being of others.

This could, of course, be presented as a demonstration of the virtues

2.9. Jack Nicholson as R. P. McMurphy. *One Flew Over the Cuckoo's Nest.* BFI Stills, Posters and Designs.

of individualism vs. collectivity, of capitalism vs. socialism. Yet while the film is undoubtedly anti-Stalinist, it is also, according to Forman's own account, a political film about the United States. One is reminded of Václav Havel's observations that the distortions of Western and Eastern European societies differed only in degree, of his demand that social change be effected by "living in truth."[28] One is reminded also of the Marxist philosopher Karel Kosík's observations on praxis—that change is effected through the sum of individual action, through reproduction enacted on a day-to-day basis.[29] The Czech-born British dramatist Tom Stoppard has a key speech in his television film *Professional Foul* (1977) given over to the theme of the interdependence of individual and collective rights.[30] Viewed from a Central European perspective, McMurphy's actions can be seen as something more than individualism: as a sense of individual worth being a prerequisite for collective action.

Apart from the sin of individualism, the film has also been accused of racism and sexism. It is easy to see why. The black orderlies are the inmates' first level of communication with the "repressive" system; the "positive" hero, R. P. McMurphy, is a man committed for statutory rape; and Nurse Ratched is the classic castrating female. The film is constructed in terms of the sexual confrontation of McMurphy and Ratched, a conflict in no way minimized by the performances of Jack Nicholson and Louise Fletcher. All this is in the novel, of course, and there is a sixties flavor to the whole enterprise. Yet this is also a simplistic perception.

The black ward orderlies are at the base of the system, not at the top, and while one of them shares Nurse Ratched's attitudes toward the patients, the night watchman joins in with their subversive midnight orgy. If their position in the power structure is intended to mirror their position in society, then it is largely accurate. Furthermore, it is Chief Bromden, the deaf and dumb Indian, the archetype of the cigar store, who is McMurphy's greatest ally and ultimately achieves what McMurphy fails to do—escape. When the Chief finally breaks his silence in a key dialogue exchange with McMurphy, he talks of his father, a man who refused to conform, who was destroyed because "they" got at him (just as "they" are getting at McMurphy). The escape of Chief Bromden, representative of the most repressed and invisible section of society, is surely evidence enough for Forman's identification with the powerless.

The charge of sexism is more substantial. The conflict between Ratched and McMurphy is between a woman in power, desexualized and controlled, and a man who "fights and fucks" too much. His sexuality is presented as natural and "sane"; she as unnatural and repressed. Six actresses, including Anne Bancroft, Ellen Burstyn, and Geraldine Page, apparently rejected the part of Ratched, and Forman was clearly aware of the problems. By casting Louise Fletcher, he sought to avoid both the caricature of the original and the charge of misogyny. The women smuggled into the asylum are clearly "available," but in this respect are no better or worse than McMurphy himself.

Like Makavejev's *WR: Mysteries of the Organism* (*WR: Misterije organizma*, 1971), the film shares a Reichian concern with the benefits of sexual liberation. It is sexual self-confidence that seems to offer a cure for both the victims and the protagonists of totalitarian systems. Nurse Ratched is certainly repressed and works out her own problems on the patients, probing and reinforcing their sexual anxieties. Equally, Billy Bibbit's sexual initiation offers the possibility of health and the threat of repression leads to his suicide. While there is no logical necessity for the role of the nurse to be female, the film clearly gains from its male/female opposition. The film's only example of a woman in power shows her to be vindictive, unnatural, and duplicitous. But the short haircuts, suits, and uniforms of the asylum establishment would also meet the Reichian criteria of unnatural behavior.

Despite Forman's references to politics and allegory, he was opposed to his actors digging too deep for motivation and interpretation. Characters would then become too transparent and predictable, losing a certain mystery. "What is great about McMurphy's character is his unpredictability, you don't see through him. Is he really sane or insane—you don't know." Of McMurphy's rebellion, he said, "I think it's true of any altruism that it's based on very egotistical motives. . . . The main drama is beyond his consciousness. . . ."[31] With reference to Ratched, he argues that few people

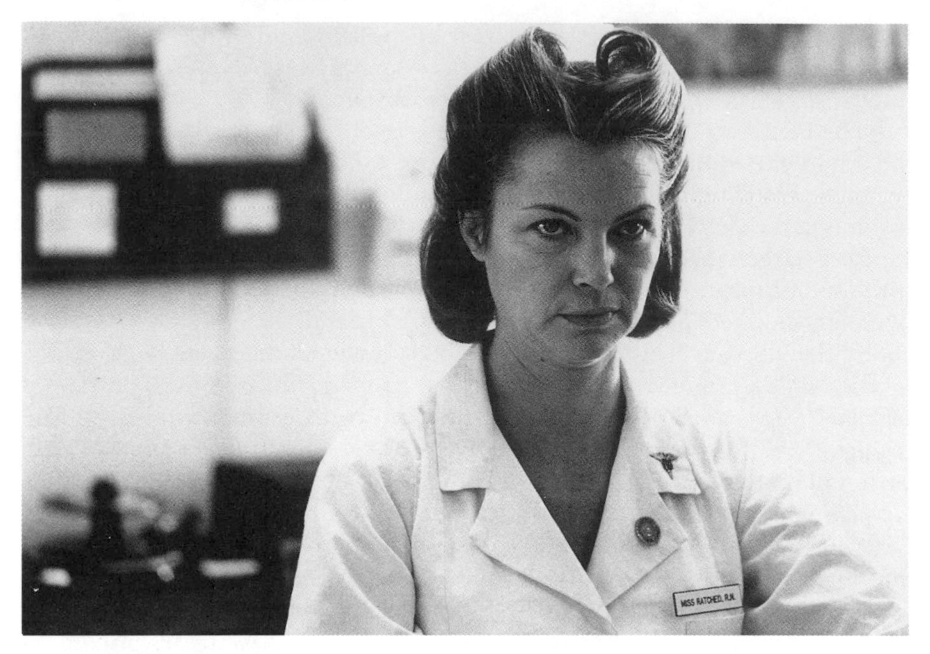

2.10. Louise Fletcher as Nurse Ratched. *One Flew Over the Cuckoo's Nest.* BFI Stills, Posters and Designs.

believe themselves to be evil and even Nixon and Stalin probably thought they were doing their best. "She [Nurse Ratched] believes deeply that she is doing right. And that is where the real drama begins for me. . . . If you stand up to people who know they are doing wrong, they will back down because they don't have belief behind them. But people who believe that they are doing good—they can break your neck."[32] It is possible to compare Nurse Ratched to a party activist in Czechoslovakia in the fifties. The combination of idealism and intolerance is a heady mixture. But Forman's target is fanaticism and conformity as such, to be found as much in the United States as in Central Europe.

Structurally, *One Flew Over the Cuckoo's Nest* is the first of Forman's films to conform to the conventions of classical narrative, a story that begins with the arrival of McMurphy at the asylum and ends with his death, that progresses toward a climax in which he attempts to murder Ratched, Billy commits suicide, and Chief Bromden escapes. Similarly, the confrontation between McMurphy and Ratched and the alliance between McMurphy and Bromden are carefully plotted through the exchange of looks and the orchestration of narrative progression.

The film has fifteen major characters, and the many scenes in the asylum depend on the kinds of group interaction that Forman had developed in his earlier films. He was always ready to improvise, to change the emphasis in accordance with how things developed. The search for "realism" was reflected in a desire to reveal the inside through the surface. "And that involves not destroying the surface but leaving the reality as it is. . . . nothing should strain your credibility."[33] His disagreement with cinematographer Haskell Wexler related to his desire for "invisible" photography, a set where the lighting was just switched on and off, his use of improvisation, and personal direction of the cameramen.[34]

It is precisely this kind of approach that encouraged some critics to view the film as being literally about problems of mental health. The film simultaneously pursues the objectives of coherence (through the use of classical narrative) and ambiguity (in its use of actors). It is a strategy that allows the film's allegory to work on a number of levels—to adopt Max Brod on Kafka, the symbol can refer to a nation, a class, an individual, or an epoch. It is even possible to interpret the conflict between McMurphy and Ratched as a struggle for the "repossession of the phallus."[35] It is the film's uncertainties and ambiguities that allow it to work on an audience, avoiding an easy response to standard polemics.

After winning all four major Oscars with one classic of American counterculture, it is not surprising that Forman should have been attracted by *Hair,* with its celebration of love and its rejection of war, conformity, and the draft. The stage show had originally impressed him in the autumn of 1968. Even then, he had fantasies of producing it on stage in Prague and ambitions to make a film. The problem with the film version of *Hair* (1979) is that the original was very much of its time (a revival two years before Forman's film had been a failure) and the film never really escapes the pitfalls of nostalgia. Added to this was the problem of form. The original had no story, but it had meanings and associations requiring the reinvention of a particular context. Despite its critical success, *Hair* also marks the definitive break between the Czech Forman and the American, the "auteur" and the director of presold subjects. Beginning with *Hair,* his films lack the degree of intimacy and observation but, above all, the authenticity that had always characterized his work. On the other hand, there are carefully considered attempts to reach a wide and predominantly young audience with subjects he believes to be important.

The framing narrative of *Hair* seems to have been constructed with precisely that audience in mind. Claude Bukowski (John Savage) is the son of an Oklahoman farmer and is called up to serve in Vietnam. En route to the Army, he meets up with a group of hippies in Central Park and samples the virtues of an alternative lifestyle. He falls in love with a rich society girl, Sheila (Beverly d'Angelo), and is saved from the draft when the spokesman for the hippies, Berger (Treat Williams), changes places with him so that he can have a last meeting with her. Berger dies in Vietnam in his place and the film ends with a close-up of his tombstone. Demonstrators flood onto the White House lawn.

The film has many of the ingredients of the teen musical, with chases on horseback, car chases, and conflicts with parents and officialdom. These are probably not accidental. Quite apart from its budget, *Hair* is a much

2.12. Debbie Allen as Sarah in *Ragtime.* BFI Stills, Posters and Designs.

the confines of its genre, something of an achievement. Its social and political conflicts are presented with a good deal of perception, with a convincing portrait of the interplay between white and black cultures as well as the lives and roles of Irish and Jewish immigrants. Stanford White, Vice President Sherman, and Booker T. Washington are featured as characters while the newsreel scenes at the beginning and live scenes at the end focus on contextual subjects from the original—the heatwave, Houdini, Theodore Roosevelt, J. P. Morgan, and so on. Forman originally filmed scenes featuring the character of the pioneer feminist Emma Goldman, but they were cut by De Laurentiis.

Forman's use of old Hollywood stars provides its own kind of cultural resonance with parts for James Cagney as the police chief (a part considerably expanded for the film), Pat O'Brien as a defense attorney, Donald O'Connor as a performer and dance instructor, and Bessie Love as an old woman. The period reconstruction has a Hollywood flavor—the New Rochelle household recalling the domesticity of the Smith residence in Minnelli's *Meet Me in St. Louis,* nightclub scenes recalling musicals set in the era. This media resonance is enhanced by Coalhouse Walker's playing his piano in movie houses and Tateh's rise to fame as the film director Baron Ashkenazy.

Yet Forman evokes the grace and history of Hollywood only to show another reality—the prejudice and intolerance that leads to an abandoned black baby, the story of sadism and murder involving Stanford White, the suppression of a black man who doesn't know his place, the casual thought-

2.13. James Cagney as Rhinelander Waldo in *Ragtime.* BFI Stills, Posters and Designs.

lessness that leads to his girlfriend's death, the ruthlessness of police chief Rhinelander Waldo and others, their actions determined by the logic of a system of power.

Although it is Forman's first film to feature violent action (save for the conclusion of *One Flew Over the Cuckoo's Nest*), cinematic flourishes never come between him and his actors. The scenes at New Rochelle provide some beautifully balanced ensemble playing, and there are subtle performances from Howard Rollins as Coalhouse Walker, James Olson as Father, and Mary Steenburgen as Mother.

David Thomson wrote of *Ragtime* that it ". . . teems with kindness: it is like looking down into a steerage full of eager faces."[36] But underneath the attractions of the New World lie the other realities. Far from being an exercise in liberal rhetoric, the film shows how, from Father to Booker T., such rhetoric has proved inadequate. As Coalhouse says to the latter, "You speak like an angel. It's too bad we're living on the earth." In an uncharacteristically dramatic montage sequence, as police marksmen line up for the kill, we hear his last words, "Lord, why did you put the rage in my heart"—a man who could have lived had he learned "how to be a nigger." The growth of urban terrorism is shown not as the excesses of evil men but a result of the pressures exerted, a spectrum ranging from the crude racism of the Irish fireman, Coghlan, to the powers of the police, to the intelligent hypocrisy of Waldo, to the well-meaning but patronizing views of the white liberal. Father learns and shows courage but, in the end, loses his wife and recognizes the inadequacies of his lifestyle. The heroes of *One Flew Over the Cuckoo's Nest, Hair,* and *Ragtime* all die victims of the system, a system whose agents are rarely evil but instruments of a power they do not understand.

Apart from working with Miroslav Ondříček on *Taking Off, Hair,* and *Ragtime,* Forman always sought to help fellow exiles. The actors Pavel Landovský and Jan Tříska, for instance, had small parts in *Ragtime.* It was not surprising that, when the opportunity occurred to film Peter Shaffer's play, *Amadeus,* in Prague, he should have put together a strong Czech team. Apart from Ondříček and the art director, Karel Černý, who had worked on his Czech films, he also worked with Theodor Pištěk (costumes), Josef Svoboda (opera production), and Zdeněk Mahler (dramatist and Mozart expert as well as author of Evald Schorm's banned film *Seventh Day, Eighth Night* [*Sedmý den, osmá noc*]). The film directors, František Vláčil and Jan Schmidt, also did second unit work.

Amadeus was an enormous success—and not merely with the arguably unrepresentative members of the Academy of Motion Picture Arts and Sciences (it won eight Oscars). As usual, there were complaints. Those from the musical world had some substance. Peter Shaffer's original play is an elaboration on motifs from Mozart's life—his suspicion that the court composer, Salieri, had tried to poison him, the anonymous commission to compose a requiem mass by a wealthy musician (who wanted to pass it off as his own), and relations with his father, the theme of *Don Giovanni.* Putting them together, he came up with the theme of a relatively talentless Salieri, insanely jealous of Mozart, hounding him to death by impersonating his dead father, the alleged commissioner of the mass. The claims that he poisoned Mozart are presented as Salieri's own, a belated attempt to achieve notoriety. It can be argued that to present this as fact is a willful distortion and that, while the theatricality of the original maintains an awareness of dramatic license, the detailed historical reconstruction of the film reinforces it as history.

The charges of being unfair to Shaffer are less easily substantiated, since he and Forman worked together on the screenplay for four and a half months and conceived it as a joint work. Certain scenes have been lengthened with considerable wit and humor while other expansions serve the needs of the narrative. The story is told in flashback as Salieri confesses to a priest, thus heightening the theme of Salieri's conflict with God through Mozart. The part of Mozart's father, who did not appear in the original, is developed in the film, in the early stages wearing the mask later adopted by the anonymous caller (Salieri) when commissioning the fatal requiem mass. Otherwise, the major change is in the opening up of the play, filming against a background of real theaters and castles, reconstructions of the operas, and a liberal use of Mozart's music. Since the emphasis here is on authenticity, the film can hardly be accused of "Americanizing" its subject.

2.14. Tom Hulce as Mozart. *Amadeus.* BFI Stills, Posters and Designs.

But it does take the film more in the direction of the biopic and it becomes less a tale of obsession and more historical biography with an unusual slant.

The film is not as powerful as its theatrical original simply because *Amadeus* was conceived as theater and not as film. It reveals neither the "authentic" Shaffer nor the "authentic" Forman. What Forman does do—and it is no mean achievement—is to take a play designed for an elite audience, combine it with music normally viewed as elite, and present both in a popular and entertaining format. The film did wonders for the sales of Mozart's music and a great deal to cross over the increasingly rigid barriers between so-called high and low art.

Mozart is presented as an artist, albeit a vulgar one. In the scatological introduction to his character that so shocks Salieri, the dialogue makes more or less explicit reference to the theme of his *Leck' mich am Arsch* (*Kiss My Ass*). He taxes the patience of his audience with *The Marriage of Figaro,* but the adaptation of Beaumarchais's forbidden and "low" play is also an assault on convention and censorship. The play is said by the emperor to increase the antagonism between social classes and to be, therefore, potentially subversive. Mozart, attacking the existing conventions, asks who would not rather "listen to his hairdresser" than to tales of gods who "shit marble."

The portrayal of the Hapsburg court, while it is in itself part of Czech history (Bohemia was under Hapsburg rule), has its contemporary "Czech" dimension. The operations of censorship and its concern with the suppression of dissident ideas are shown as absurd. Should operas be in Italian or German, or based on French plays, or include ballet? Whatever the case, it is always best to play it safe. Salieri is a classic portrait of the dissimulating intellectual who flourishes under totalitarianism. A man of considerable intelligence and ability, he sees the absurdities but always agrees with the views of the powerful, distancing himself with moderate but insignificant qualifications. He manipulates the situation for the destruction of Mozart in an atmosphere that is ideal for intrigue. One is reminded of Forman's account of the withdrawal of his Czech passport (he became an American citizen in 1975). He always thought it was the fault of the Communist party but later discovered it was due to the influence of filmmakers jealous of his success. At any rate, the portrait of the court had a clear resonance for Czechoslovakia in the years of normalization.

While giving full rein to his rapscallion Mozart (Tom Hulce), Forman keeps his actors in a precise balance, with a wonderfully modulated performance from F. Murray Abraham as Salieri. The casting of Elizabeth Berridge (looking every bit like the pregnant hippie from *Hair*) as Mozart's wife, Constanze, works very well. According to Forman, the multiplicity of accents accurately reflects the cosmopolitanism of Vienna at the time, even if it breaks the film convention that all historical characters should speak with English accents. As usual, Forman's leading actors were relatively unknown and, as with *Hair*, he looked for actors who were also musicians, specifically rejecting the view of the artist as superman as "alienating and false."[37]

Despite filling the Tyl theater in Prague with thousands of candles, or producing snow-covered streets and thoroughfares with dancing bears, Forman does not overplay the local color. The vengeful masked figure stalking through the streets toward the end never falls into the trap of Gothic indulgence. Everything is kept subordinate to the theme. Commenting on the ease with which the Czech extras wore their historical costume, Peter Shaffer said that it was like participating in history.[38] The focus on Mozart and Salieri in the play is extended in the film to allow space for the music, which plays a dramatic role in the film and becomes a third major character—the source of conflict and the living evidence of God's laughter.

The theme of the film, and also of the play, is the extraordinary relationship between Mozart and Salieri, a meditation on the contradictions between Mozart's "divine" music and his obscene behavior, between Mozart's poverty and Salieri's position and wealth, between Salieri as Mozart's greatest admirer and his deadliest enemy. Forman was fascinated by the task of understanding and explaining these opposed beings. Salieri's own preoccupation with his "mediocrity" is seen by Forman as self-defined and purely a function of his jealousy.[39]

Amadeus is certainly the best feature film on a classical music theme, and it is music that primarily distinguishes it from the play. Shaffer, once a music critic, had been unable to find a satisfactory way of using music in the stage version, but the film provided an opportunity. Apart from the attempts to reconstruct the operas as closely as possible to contemporary

2.15. *Amadeus.* BFI Stills, Posters and Designs.

performance,[40] there are two scenes (Mozart's dictation of the *Requiem,* and Salieri's account of the adagio from the *Serenade for Wind Instruments*) that attempt a genuine insight into the realities of composition. All this is integrated with the developing drama, but the film mercifully avoids the excesses of the conventional musical biopic. Judging from the contradictions between the surviving images of Mozart, Forman concluded that he was probably unremarkable in appearance. In this and other respects, Tom Hulce's Mozart is a far cry from Cornel Wilde's Chopin, Dirk Bogarde's Liszt, and Richard Chamberlain's Tchaikovsky.

It is interesting to reflect a little on the high-culture/low-culture debate around *Amadeus.* Gilbert Adair commends Forman for making a genuine adaptation, an eighteenth-century cartoon leavened with "showbiz raciness," in which Mozart conducts his orchestra like a dance band leader.[41] Entertainingly and appositely, he describes Mozart as an amalgam of the three Marx Brothers (Harpo for his appearance, Groucho for his lechery, and Chico for musical virtuosity). The conflict between Mozart and Salieri is seen as closer to that of the Roadrunner and Wily Coyote than the grander heights of Shakespearean tragedy.

George Lellis sees the film as fundamentally ambivalent about its own status as high culture, relating its subversive qualities to Mozart's and Salieri's presentation as gay stereotypes, albeit disguised by the absence of conventional models of masculinity.[42] More crucially, they also differ from the conventional romantic image (Wilde/Bogarde/Chamberlain) which is not without its own contradictions. The degree to which the characterizations can be recognized as gay and the relations between the men as homoerotic is, of course, open to debate.

Given Forman's aversion to stereotypes and love of ambiguity, there is no question that his characterizations generate a liberating force. He has sought to represent Mozart as a mischievous teenager, opposed to convention and the establishment, his work representing a liveliness and vitality frequently stifled by cultural polarities. In this respect, he crosses the borders of elitism and the high-culture divide that is as much a creation of opponents as proponents.

After moving into the world of cinematic superproduction with *Ragtime* and *Amadeus,* Forman was inadvisedly seduced by the prospect of another historical creation with *Valmont* (1989). He first read Laclos's *Les Liaisons Dangereuses* while at FAMU, considered the possibility of a film, but only got the opportunity following the success of *Amadeus.* He was offered the chance to direct the film version of Christopher Hampton's stage play, *Dangerous Liaisons,* but, in a lapse of business acumen, decided to produce an original version of his own. This was to have disastrous consequences because *Dangerous Liaisons* was rapidly and effectively made by the British director Stephen Frears, beating Forman's film to both the market and the Oscars. The economical Frears, trained in television, seems to have relished the challenge. "I thought for a short time of doing it for one million as a punk version to attack Miloš Forman."[43]

With *Valmont,* Forman returned to France and renewed his association with director/producer Claude Berri, who, in 1968 along with François Truffaut, had helped raise the money to replace Ponti's investment in *The Firemen's Ball.* He originally brought Forman and Jean-Claude Carrière together to work on the script of *Taking Off,* and they were now to renew their collaboration for *Valmont.* In the meantime, Berri had produced Polanski's *Tess* (1980) and directed the enormously successful Pagnol productions, *Jean de Florette* and *Manon des Sources* (1986). Carrière had become one of France's leading screenwriters, working on films as diverse as Wajda's *Danton* and Oshima's *Max, Mon Amour.* Forman had co-scripted Carrière's *La Pince à Ongles* (1968) and provided the story for Berri's *Le Mâle du Siècle* (1975), as well as producing Carrière's *Aide-Mémoire* on Broadway. Forman and Carrière wrote the script over four and a half months in the United States and the film was completed in France.

When Forman saw Hampton's play, he found it did not correspond to his memories of the book but, on rereading it, discovered Hampton was right. Seduced nonetheless by "the characters, the sensuality, the colors and the sounds" and "something indefinable,"[44] he had already fallen in love with his own conception before the offer to direct an adaptation of the play occurred.

The script written by Forman and Carrière was liberally "inspired" by the original and the subject is, in many ways, quite different. Rather than dramatize the action described in the novel's succession of letters, they chose

2.16. Valmont (Colin Firth) and Cécile de Volanges (Fairuza Balk). *Valmont.* BFI Stills, Posters and Designs.

to portray what might have happened before the letters were written, using only a few lines of dialogue from the original book. The script is also unusual in that it was written in English by Forman and Carrière, for neither of whom is English a first language. As with *Taking Off,* Forman used other collaborators, in this case Anne Gyory and the émigré writer Jan Novák, to negotiate Czech nuances.

Apart from its cavalier approach to the original, *Valmont* differs in almost every respect from Frears's *Dangerous Liaisons. Valmont* has a simple but stylish script, little-known actors, a slow and relaxed pace, and is about characters who are fundamentally innocent. In contrast, *Dangerous Liaisons* has a theatrical script, star performances, a rapid pace, and is about decadent and cynical characters. Forman sees Laclos's novel as concerned with contradictions while Frears sees it as obsessed with cynicism and manipulation. Forman's gay and teasing Mme de Merteuil (Annette Bening) is portrayed by Glenn Close in *Dangerous Liaisons* as an updated (or backdated) equivalent to Phyllis Dietrichson in *Double Indemnity.*[45]

Forman did not remember the characters of the original novel as evil and presents them as victims rather than manipulators of their emotions. In portraying Merteuil and Valmont as under thirty, he was true to the novel and, in his view, this was another reason for their failure to see the consequences of their actions. Merteuil's revenge derives from her egoism and narcissism, while Valmont is presented as the embodiment of contradictions, at different times both honest and duplicitous, both lover and libertine. However, Forman's focus is as much on the two young lovers, Cécile and Danceny, who have all the simplicity and charm of the teenage characters in *Black Peter, Loves of a Blonde,* and *Taking Off.* Their farcical trips and slides recall the comic tradition that was never far from the surface of his earlier films.

The film probably represents Forman's views on sexual relations rather than those of Laclos and is full of humorous and amorous banter and a good deal of mutual attraction. Merteuil and Valmont (Colin Firth) show a naive enthusiasm for their amorous exploits. There is also a genuine play in the relationship between Valmont and Cécile (Fairuza Balk), although the emphasis on her girlish charm and stockinged feet is sometimes a little cute. In the final scene, Cécile marries her intended, Monsieur Gercourt—in this version of the story, a lover who has spurned Merteuil. Already pregnant with Valmont's child, she appears none the worse for her ordeal.

The subject of Laclos's novel was, of course, the life and loves of the French aristocracy and, in particular, the treatment of women. Cécile is raised in a convent, innocent of men and of the world outside. She finally emerges to be married to a man she has never seen, who will treat her as his private property. It is little wonder that enforced innocence followed by marriages of convenience should lead to double standards. Merteuil quite explicitly avoids remarriage so that no one should ever have any rights over her. Following Rousseau, the system was seen by Laclos to go against nature and to pervert the course of love. It was a society that encouraged "petits maîtres" like Valmont to which a Mme de Merteuil might seem a justified answer. Some contemporary critics thought the characters of Merteuil and Valmont exaggerated. In showing them as victims, Forman exposes the machinations of the system as such rather than an evil rooted in individuals. While the subject is historically specific, it still has a contemporary relevance.

Carrière and Forman have fashioned an elegant comedy of manners with precisely stylized performances in which even the timbre of the voices has been carefully orchestrated. The wit is deliberate—these aristocrats certainly have a "discreet charm"—and even the death of Valmont, which takes place offscreen, becomes another example of life's tragedies, part of an unending tragicomedy. In the end, the comic observation is closer to the character and wit of a Marivaux than any portrayal of good vs. evil.

Valmont is Forman's most sophisticated and carefully plotted narrative, with an elaborate pattern of verbal and visual repetition. The dialogue is in constant play with silence and a carefully modulated music score, which was partly prerecorded and played on set to create the mood of the piece. Although Forman's main focus is still on his characters, *Valmont* is a beautifully designed film in which camerawork and editing are given unaccustomed prominence.

A large-budget film, 70 percent of *Valmont* was shot on location in real chateaux. The images derive from Fragonard and Watteau, and Christopher Palmer's score is supplemented by a sensitive use of music ranging from

2.17. Mme de Tourvel (Meg Tilly). *Valmont.* BFI Stills, Posters and Designs.

Grétry and Couperin to Philidor and Galippi. The costumes were again by Theodor Pištěk.[46]

Forman changed the setting to the early eighteenth century, partly because of costume, partly because he wanted to show the contradictions of the time without taking a position for or against the aristocracy. He does this effectively by showing the physical gulf between the aristocracy and ordinary people, the extended spaces of the chateaux contrasting with the crowded cacophony of the market place. Again, as in *Amadeus,* the characters are at ease in their surroundings and their leisured lifestyle, the chateaux never becoming mere local color or an excuse for grandiose ceremony. As Jean-Loup Bourget points out, this is a lived-in space and a far cry from the posed tableaux of a *Barry Lyndon* or *Draughtsman's Contract.* The characters do not just cross the space, but meet, run, gallop, and swim in it.[47] But despite the subtlety of its social criticism, Forman is clearly fascinated by his aristocrats, the colors, the sounds, and the indefinable. An elaborately simple film, it is his nearest approach to an "art" movie; and one suspects that, had it been in French with English subtitles, it would have been treated rather better by American and English critics.

In considering Miloš Forman's films overall, it is possible to find continuities of both theme and approach. However, from a pure auteurist approach, it is clear that his early and more personal films were very much the result of collaboration with Passer and Papoušek and that his later films are interactions with work that originated elsewhere: Kesey, Rado, Ragni, and MacDermot, Doctorow, Shaffer, and Laclos. On the other hand, this is the norm for mainstream cinema and there are many respects in which he does function as an auteur. He directs subjects he wants to and locks himself away with his writers for months on end, shaping his films as much as an Alfred Hitchcock. His preference for working with Ondříček, aside from friendship, relates to a particular style and method of working.

There are many ways in which his use of actors has remained consistent. The style of his Czech films was always subservient to the revelation of the truths revealed through observing the personalities, performances, and interrelations of his largely nonprofessional casts. His concern with authenticity extends from using actors who could sing and dance in *Hair* to actors who were credible as musicians in *Amadeus.* With the exception of Nicholson in *One Flew Over the Cuckoo's Nest,* he has consistently avoided star actors or known faces, preferring a believable, realist surface and a balance of performances. Basically, the techniques are the same: the avoidance of preconceived notions of character, the pursuit of ambiguity, the use of improvisation in rehearsal, a concern with ensemble playing, and an emphasis on what can be revealed in the scene rather than through the elaboration of narrative.

There are thematic consistencies in his work: the problems of young people in a repressive society (*Black Peter, Loves of a Blonde, Hair*), the generation gap (*Black Peter, Loves of a Blonde, Taking Off*), attacks on systems of power and manipulation (*The Firemen's Ball, One Flew Over the Cuckoo's Nest, Hair, Ragtime, Amadeus*), the individual as protagonist in a group revolt (*One Flew Over the Cuckoo's Nest, Hair, Ragtime*).

However, the American films differ quite radically from the Czech ones. The Czech films are concerned with resistence, survival, and the exposure of contemporary society. In the American films, apart from *Taking Off,* his characters fight against the system, but one constructed in the past. Also, despite their unorthodoxy and the importance of subsidiary characters, heroes such as McMurphy, Berger, Coalhouse Walker, and Mozart all stand out as being in some way admirable. In his Czech films, the nice characters simply survivc.

The focus on the individual in Forman's American films can be seen as a feature of his move toward classical narrative and as part of the American ideology of individual worth. Liehm wrote on *One Flew Over the Cuckoo's Nest:* "The stream of tragicomic irony is broken at the very end of *Cuckoo's Nest,* for the first time in Forman's career giving way to a 'positive' ending with a 'positive' hero. . . . Had the film ended with an accent on melancholy ambiguity, it would have lost its American credibility."[48] However, it can be argued that Forman's move toward classical narrative is contradicted by his emphasis on the scene; he may have moved toward classical narrative but he has never been fully consumed by it.

It is worth noting that many of the most political Czech films of the sixties focused on the group rather than on individuals. As well as *The Firemen's Ball,* these included *The Party and the Guests, Larks on a String,* and

All My Good Countrymen (*Všichni dobří rodáci,* 1968). When the films do focus on individuals (e.g., Schorm's *Return of the Prodigal Son* [*Návrat ztraceného syna,* 1966]), they are often shown as powerless and alienated. No doubt this was due to a need to express the reactions of society as a whole to the realities of Stalinism and the distortions of socialist realism. Maybe it is genuinely impossible to make films with such a group identity in Hollywood, but Forman's films have more of it than most.

A few years ago, the Hungarian film *The Princess* (*Adj király katonát!,* 1982), directed by Pál Erdöss, a story of the life and loves of a working-class girl, showed its characters watching *Loves of a Blonde* in a cinema, an obvious homage to Forman's early work. In 1991, the British director Ken Loach selected *Loves of a Blonde* as his favorite film for a season at London's National Film Theatre. With the possible exception of *One Flew Over the Cuckoo's Nest,* it is difficult to imagine Forman's American films attaining a similar resonance among filmmakers.

Loach is a director whose style has remained close to that of early Forman. In the mid-sixties he made two historic drama documentaries for British television with *Up the Junction* (1965) and *Cathy Come Home* (1966), but the film most clearly reminiscent of Forman is his *Looks and Smiles* (1981). Both *The Princess* and *Looks and Smiles* focus on the lives of ordinary people, observe the unique qualities and value of everyday life, and use a particular style to achieve it. They express the lives of their respective societies in a way that no film by Forman ever looks at his adopted society.

The essentialist debates that characterized discussion of film form in the seventies are thankfully behind us. Nobody now seriously confuses *The Sound of Music* with George Eliot, nor is deconstruction necessarily privileged over naturalism. The Czech *new wave,* of which Forman's films were part, showed how a variety of forms came together to reject the artificialities and simplifications of the bureaucratic state. The films were also fundamentally linked to their own time and context. Forman's Czech films spoke from and of a particular society and it was highly unlikely that their forms and concerns could be easily transplanted elsewhere (despite the success of *Taking Off*). Forman, quite apart from the exigencies of the commercial industry, simply found himself unable to work in the same way in a foreign culture.

The naturalist form of early Forman and of Ken Loach is wonderfully revealing but, of course, it only reaches a fraction of the audience that saw *Amadeus. Loves of a Blonde* and *Looks and Smiles* are marvelous films, but they caused little public debate compared with the response to *One Flew Over the Cuckoo's Nest.* There is surely a place for both, and if Forman chose to adapt to his new society through literature and mainstream success, then that is a choice dictated by history and exile.

Forman's films do not have a clear political message and he has, at various times, been described as socialist, revisionist, and individualist. As Josef Škvorecký has suggested: "Forman's vision is deeply rooted in the anti-ideological, realistic and humanist tradition of such cynics of Czech literature as Jaroslav Hašek and Bohumil Hrabal."[49] Faced with the fall of liberal democracy, the Nazi occupation, and the corruption of the Communist utopia, it is not easy to adopt any political position claiming a monopoly of truth.

In his interviews with Liehm, Forman seems anxious to underplay the political significance of his work. While admitting the political content of some of his films, he argues: "Politics and social interpretation—they're just one facet of our lives. And I don't go out of my way to look for material that will deal with them."[50] On the other hand, *The Firemen's Ball* was clearly political, and Forman described *One Flew Over the Cuckoo's Nest* as a "political" film about the United States. "At a certain moment you abandon the deference of the visitor and you begin to look around you, to see what, where and how things touch directly on your life."[51]

While accepting that Forman's attraction to different subjects is not purely political, it is surprising how often his films have an overt political dimension. Leaving aside *Black Peter, Loves of a Blonde,* and, to some extent, *Taking Off,* which show the inadequacies, compromises, and contradictions in society, political themes tend to be close to the surface. If *The Firemen's Ball* is a satire about Stalinism and the bureaucratic state, *One Flew Over the Cuckoo's Nest* is about the everyday adaptation to structures of power and ideology. It is interesting that its allegory is aimed firstly at the United States and only secondarily "elsewhere." *Hair* rejects militarism, conformity, and the values of everyday capitalism. *Ragtime* attacks institutionalized racism. *Valmont* shows distortions in sexual relations linked to structures of male domination. Even *Amadeus* has a hero who is impoverished and foul-mouthed, whose music is frequently seen as subversive.

But does it all add up to a coherent political stance? Forman once described his attraction to stories about ". . . the individual's helplessness against the Establishment."[52] Since he said that before *One Flew Over the Cuckoo's Nest,* it is striking how easily the idea can be applied to his later films. In one way or another, his American films demand the recognition of human rights, freedom of speech, justice, and social, racial, and sexual equality. What they do not do is to suggest the overthrow of capitalism as a means of achieving this—which returns us to the Cold War and the politics of Czechoslovakia.

Many Western socialists have tended to view criticisms of the Soviet Union and Eastern Europe as synonymous with right-wing ideology. The repression exerted in the name of "socialism" was quietly ignored in favor of less problematic causes. As two anonymous Czech socialists described the situation to John Keane:

> One of the surest ways of guaranteeing that the socialist idea comes to grief is to ignore the absurdity and barbarity committed in its name. . . . Everyone knows in our countries that socialism is a keyword of the Party-dominated state. This state seeks to entomb us, its subjects, within a pyramid of fictitious ideological clichés designed to silence everybody and to ensure their conformity to the state.[53]

In Czechoslovakia before the "velvet revolution," many leading intellectuals were concerned with the resurrection of civil society as an alternative to state absolutism. From their perspective, the roots of democracy were to be found outside of the single party state. The Czech equivalent of Forman's "liberal rhetoric" was one of the factors that gave birth to Civic Forum and hastened the end of totalitarianism.

Forman's art is predicated on the notion that challenges to justice and democracy know no frontiers, that no social system or organization has a monopoly of truth. While recognizing the realities of class and racial conflict, his essentially moral stance places him in the tradition of Masaryk and Havel. While it is a Czech tradition, it is also based on a bitter experience of the primacy of politics. If Forman emphasizes humanity and dramatizes the plight of the powerless, this finds its counterpart in Havel's demand for a "moral reconstitution" of society, ". . . a radical renewal of the relationship of human beings to . . . the 'human order,' which no political order can replace."[54]

NOTES

I would like to thank Eva Kačerová and the Czechoslovak Film Archive for arranging screenings of *Talent Competition* and *Valmont*, when the latter was unavailable for screening in Great Britain.

1. Jan Němec, interviewed in the film, *The Kids from FAMU* (Paul Pawlikowski, 1990), BBC Television.
2. Ota Šik, *The Third Way: Marxist-Leninist Theory and Modern Industrial Society*, trans. Marian Šling (London: Wildwood House, 1976), p. 9.
3. Miloš Forman, "Chill Wind on the New Wave." *Saturday Review*, December 23, 1967, p. 11.
4. Miloš Forman, interviewed in Antonín J. Liehm, *The Miloš Forman Stories*, trans. Jeanne Němcová (New York: International Arts and Sciences Press, 1975), p. 28.
5. Jaroslav Papoušek, quoted in Josef Škvorecký, *All the Bright Young Men and Women*, trans. Michael Schonberg (Toronto: Peter Martin Associates, 1971), p. 93.
6. Forman, in Liehm, *The Miloš Forman Stories*, p. 140.
7. Ibid., pp. 108–109.
8. The British "New Wave" (Tony Richardson, Karel Reisz, Lindsay Anderson) had other links with Czech cinema. Reisz was, of course, born in Czechoslovakia. Anderson, who supervised the English subtitles for *The Shop on Main Street*, also had a walk-on part in Němec's *Martyrs of Love* (1966). Forman was particularly impressed by Anderson's *This Sporting Life* (1963). Ondříček photographed Anderson's three films *The White Bus* (1966), *If . . .* (1968), and *O Lucky Man!* (1973). The principal contemporary exponent of the British "realist" tradition, Ken Loach, was clearly influenced by Forman's early work.
9. Antonín J. Liehm, "Miloš Forman: The Style and the Man," in David W. Paul (ed.), *Politics, Art, and Commitment in the East European Cinema* (London: Macmillan, 1983), p. 216.
10. Forman, in Liehm, *The Miloš Forman Stories*, p. 64.
11. Ibid., p. 138.
12. Forman, interviewed in *The Kids from FAMU*.
13. Forman, in Liehm, *The Miloš Forman Stories*, p. 86.

14. Miroslav Ondříček, interviewed in *The Kids from FAMU.*

15. Vratislav Effenberger, quoted in Škvorecký, *All the Bright Young Men and Women,* p. 91.

16. Forman, in Liehm, *The Miloš Forman Stories,* p. 84.

17. Liehm, "Miloš Forman: The Style and the Man," p. 217.

18. Josef Škvorecký, "Miloš Forman," in Christopher Lyon (ed.), *International Dictionary of Films and Filmmakers: Vol. 2. Directors/Filmmakers* (London: Firethorn Press, 1984), p. 195.

19. František Daniel, "The Czech Difference," in Paul (ed.), *Politics, Art, and Commitment in the East European Cinema,* pp. 54–55.

20. Karel Kosík, "Hašek and Kafka," trans. Karel Kovanda, *Telos* no. 23 (Spring 1975): 88.

21. Forman, "How I Came to America to Make a Film and Wound Up Owing Paramount $140,000," *Show,* February 1970.

22. Forman, John Guare, Jean-Claude Carrière, and John Klein, *Taking Off* (screenplay) (New York: New American Library, 1971), p. 61.

23. Forman, in Liehm, *The Miloš Forman Stories,* p. 112.

24. Dilys Powell, *The Golden Screen: Fifty Years of Films,* ed. George Perry (London: Pavilion Books, 1989), pp. 236–37.

25. Kristin Thompson, "The Formation of the Classical Style, 1909–28," in David Bordwell, Janet Staiger, Kristin Thompson, *The Classical Hollywood Cinema: Film Style and Mode of Production to 1960* (London: Routledge and Kegan Paul, 1985), pp. 157–240.

26. See Graham Petrie and Ruth Dwyer (eds.), *Before the Wall Came Down: Soviet and East European Filmmakers Working in the West* (Lanham, MD: University Press of America, 1990), pp. 45–47.

27. Forman, interviewed by Larry Sturhahn, "One Flew Over the Cuckoo's Nest," *Filmmakers Newsletter,* December 1975, p. 26.

28. Václav Havel, "The Power of the Powerless," trans. Paul Wilson, in John Keane (ed.), *The Power of the Powerless: Citizens against the State in Central-Eastern Europe* (London: Hutchinson, 1985).

29. Karel Kosík, *The Dialectics of the Concrete: A Study of Problems of Man and World,* trans. Karel Kovanda and James Schmidt (Dordrecht and Boston: Reidel, 1976).

30. Tom Stoppard, *Professional Foul,* in *Squaring the Circle with Every Good Boy Deserves Favour and Professional Foul* (London: Faber, 1984), pp. 173–74.

31. Forman, quoted in Richard Combs, "Sentimental Journey," *Sight and Sound* 46 (Summer 1977): 153.

32. Forman, interviewed by Sturhahn, p. 31.

33. Ibid., p. 26.

34. Ibid., pp. 26–27. See also Antonín J. Liehm, "Forman Talks Cuckoo," *Take One* 5 (August 1976): 20.

35. Reynold Humphries and Genevieve Buzzoni, "One Flew Over the Cuckoo's Nest," *Framework* 2, 5 (Winter 1976–77): 23–24. Humphries and Buzzoni argue that McMurphy is the father-figure who rescues the children from the castrating mother. Arguing that the film is sexist, individualist, and anti-intellectual, they conclude that it is ". . . a dangerous and criminally irresponsible movie."

36. David Thomson, "Redtime," *Film Comment* 18, 1 (January–February 1982): 12.

37. Forman, interviewed by Michel Ciment, *Positif* no. 285 (November 1984): 24.

38. Peter Shaffer, "Making the Screen Speak," *Film Comment* 20, 5 (September–October 1984): 57.

39. Forman, interviewed by Ciment, *Positif* no. 285.

40. Where possible the performances were based on surviving documents and designs. *The Magic Flute* was based on a production from 1815.

41. Gilbert Adair, "What's Opera, Doc?," *Sight and Sound* 54, 2 (Spring 1985): 142–43.

42. George Lellis, "A Dissenting View of Miloš Forman's *Amadeus,*" in Petrie and Dwyer (eds.), *Before the Wall Came Down,* pp. 49–60.

43. Stephen Frears, interviewed by Jonathan Hacker and David Price, "What's on at the Pictures," *Weekend Guardian* (London), May 11–12, 1991, p. 13.

44. Forman, interviewed by Ciment, *Positif* no. 346 (December 1989): 5.

45. The differences are well documented in Ciment's interviews with Forman (*Positif* no. 346) and Frears (*Positif* no. 338, pp. 6–9).

46. Pištěk subsequently designed the uniforms for President Havel's palace guard.

47. Jean-Loup Bourget, "École de Gaspillage (*Valmont*)," *Positif* no. 346 (December 1989): 3.

48. Liehm, "Miloš Forman: The Style and the Man," p. 221.

49. Josef Škvorecký, "Miloš Forman," in Christopher Lyon (ed.), *International Dictionary of Films and Filmmakers: Vol. 2. Directors/Filmmakers,* p. 195.

50. Forman, in Liehm, *The Miloš Forman Stories,* p. 147.

51. Forman, in Liehm, "Forman Talks Cuckoo," p. 20.

52. Forman, in Liehm, *The Miloš Forman Stories,* p. 148.

53. John Keane, *Democracy and Civil Society: On the Predicaments of European Socialism, the Prospects for Democracy, and the Problem of Controlling Social and Political Power* (London: Verso 1988), p. 197.

54. Havel, "The Power of the Powerless," in Keane (ed.), *The Power of the Powerless: Citizens against the State in Central-Eastern Europe,* p. 92.

Three Polanski

Herbert Eagle

Of all of the directors who have worked in East Central Europe and in the West, Roman Polanski is, on the face of it, the most enigmatic. In the body of his work over more than three decades, there appears to be no explicit position on the major political, social, and ideological issues which characterized the Cold War and the period of Soviet domination over Eastern Europe. Indeed, a viewer who watched virtually any of his feature-length films (without knowledge of who the director was) would be unlikely to conclude that the film had anything to do with Poland. Even *Knife in the Water* (*Nóż w wodzie,* 1962), with dialogue in Polish and some specific references to life in Poland, seems easily transposable to any postindustrial society.

Of course, to a significant degree it is precisely the tendency toward universality, generalization, and allegory that has made Polanski's films so culturally transportable and has led both to critical and to popular success in a number of European countries and the United States. If we consider for a moment other directors who have achieved this kind of international recognition over roughly the same time period (for example, Ingmar Bergman or Federico Fellini), we note in their work pronounced individual tendencies with respect to philosophical issues and the treatment of human psychology. It is thematic features of this kind, in addition to the filmmakers' characteristic style, which have led to the designation auteur in referring to filmmakers such as Bergman and Fellini. They are the clear authors of a body of work not only in terms of artistic structures but also in the realm of ideas.

The term "auteur" is not so often used in Polanski's case. The body of his work does not seem to have the same kind of coherence in the realm of ideas, although certain stylistic tendencies are more easily noted. Representations of his philosophy, when they are asserted, rely as much on the tragic and bizarre circumstances of his personal life as they do on his films. There is good reason for the impression that Polanski as a filmmaker is an author to a lesser degree than a Bergman, a Fellini, a Tarkovsky, or a Makavejev. First of all, the origins of Polanski's filmscripts have nearly always been collaborative, either written together with others (Jakub Goldberg and

Jerzy Skolimowski for his most important films in Poland, Gérard Brach for most of his films which were not adaptations) or closely following in sequence of events and dialogue the literary works on which they were based (this is the case for the films *Rosemary's Baby, Macbeth,* and *Tess*). Polanski has most definitely inflected these works, however, and this inflection has been most palpable in the realm of the films' visual imagery.

Polanski's concern with visual realization of a theme, emotion, or idea is not only apparent in the films themselves (it is the visual aspect of his films which is always their most striking feature), but is also well attested in a multitude of interviews and comments by co-workers. But to begin with the position that Polanski approaches film as a craftsman, as an artist obsessed with techniques and their effects, is not to deny the powerful thematic dimensions of his films. Indeed, style and structure must be considered the key to his equally obsessive thematic concerns. *What* Polanski chooses to heighten visually and *how* he achieves this heightening have to do directly with his most enduring preoccupations. And many of his films have been so compelling because those preoccupations are broadly shared by audiences across international and cultural boundaries: the predominance of pain in the world; the interchangeability of victim and victimizer; our easy acquiescence to evil for personal gain or pleasure; the rape of innocents (both figuratively and literally).

The above themes relate directly to the political, social, and cultural structures that govern life in the modern world, and to the history of the twentieth century. That is not to say that these sad dimensions of human experience are not present in all centuries, but they fly in the face of the positivistic rationalism and utopian idealism that were a legacy of the nineteenth century. The tragedies that underlie the core of Polanski's films are real and they defy reason in certain respects. That they relate to his personal biography would also seem unquestionable, but the connection is most clearly to experiences that his life shares with the lives of people in East Central Europe more generally: the Holocaust and the period of authoritarian rule that followed it. As I will point out in what follows, the two hugely tragic and bizarre events of Polanski's later life (the murder of his pregnant wife Sharon Tate and three of his friends by the Charles Manson gang in 1969 and his statutory rape of a thirteen-year-old girl in 1979) did not affect the nature of Polanski's films in a substantial way. The most pronounced tendencies in his work (structural, stylistic, and thematic) were set before 1969, and although there are new developments in his films of the 1970s and 1980s, these represent further elaboration of characteristics already present.

My approach in this chapter is based directly on the films of Polanski themselves. I will not attempt to psychoanalyze this very complex and highly problematic personality; indeed, I do not have the competence to do so. I would argue, in addition, that a reading of Polanski's personal psychology is not a necessary factor for understanding the appeal and effect of his films. Clearly, Polanski's films strike chords inside the viewer, whether or not the viewer knows anything about Polanski's personal biography. What is important is that viewers, in general, share Polanski's experiences, needs, and drives to some degree (experiences, for example, of abandonment, rejection, violation, and oppression; needs for safety, solace, and meaning; drives for subjectivity, power, and dominance). Nor are Polanski's *conscious intentions* a major determinant. His strengths as an artist derive from his ability to represent what he feels in a compelling way—whether or not he understands what he feels, whether or not he has any progressive agenda with respect to the underlying causes of his feelings. Clearly, Polanski understands what he feels to some degree, and, in some films, one feels the more explicit presence of what might be termed a "progressive" theme—this is perhaps most clear in *Chinatown* (1974) and *Tess* (1980). But Polanski's films also embody raw drives that he may not fully understand and that are certainly not progressive; this is true in scenes where he creates and we participate in vicarious sexual and physical aggression of the most extreme kind.

Historical factors (not only political history but also, for example, historical aspects of the construction of gender and of the family, and the history of cinema as an art form) are highly relevant to the question of why and how Polanski's films work. But what is most important here is the shared nature of that history. Certainly, not all viewers have lived through particular kinds of experiences as intensely as Roman Polanski has, but we all live in the political, social, ideological, and cultural systems of this century and we all live around its typical events (from the domestic to the national sphere). People who grew up in East Central Europe during the same period as Polanski may share his sensibilities more fully in some respects, but there are (one is tempted to say here, unfortunately) analogous occurrences and situations in other parts of the world. It is for this reason that Polanski's filmic visions crossed the boundaries from Poland to the United States so successfully.

Let me review, then, some of the most relevant circumstances of Polanski's life up to the point when he began making films, as they have been recorded by his biographers, including Polanski himself in his autobiography *Roman.*[1] Roman Polanski was born in Paris in 1933; his father was a Polish Jew, his mother was part Jewish, part Russian. When Polanski's father failed in his attempts to make a career for himself as an artist in Paris, he returned with his family to his native Poland and settled in Krakow, going into business with a brother. After the Nazis overran Poland in 1939, Polanski's family was interned in the Krakow ghetto with the rest of the city's Jews. Barely seven years old, Roman experienced the traumatic effects of this situation on his family and the community. His parents' domestic quarrels were exacerbated by the tensions; he saw how people, by and large, focused on their own survival, even at the expense of others; he was sent through the ghetto fence into the main part of the city to steal food; he witnessed bloody beatings and executions by the Nazis. Everyday life also continued, but shifts from the mundane to the absolutely terrifying were normal (as a filmmaker, Polanski was to become a master at envisioning and embodying such abrupt shifts).

The feelings generated by these kinds of experiences do not fade and many of the experiences themselves are indelibly, one might say photographically, recorded in the brain. I cite two examples here, taken from Polanski's autobiography, because they have fairly clear visual analogues in his films:

> One old crone, at the rear of the column, couldn't keep up. A German officer kept prodding her back into line, but she fell down on all fours, groveling, whining and pleading with him in Yiddish. Suddenly a pistol appeared in the officer's hand. There was a loud bang, and blood came welling out of her back.[2]

> The officer returned, followed by my mother. We thought the inspection was over, but he lingered, smiling faintly, circling the room like a bird of prey, picking up my teddy bear and swinging it by one leg, looking the place over. Suddenly, with the tip of his swagger stick, he reached up and flicked the hatbox off the top of the wardrobe. He picked it up, opened it, and scattered the rolls all over the floor.[3]

As we shall see, very specific visual elements of these memories occur in Polanski's films. In general, violence and blood are common, and they almost always erupt suddenly and unexpectedly.

In 1941, first Polanski's mother and then his father were rounded up and deported to the concentration camps. His father had entrusted the care of Roman to a Polish family in Krakow and had provided some funds for this purpose. For reasons of space (Polanski's cousins had also been placed with this family) and because of fear of discovery, Polanski spent the period 1941–1944 with several different families, until the spring of 1943 in Krakow and in 1943–1944 with an impoverished family in rural Central Poland. Throughout this period, he was treated more as a ward than as an adopted child; when circumstances became dangerous he had to move on and, indeed, spent most of 1944–1945 as a fugitive and a "street child" in Krakow, roaming with gangs of boys, stealing in order to survive. Polanski became a nominal Catholic at this time (his parents had been agnostic, nonpracticing Jews), but without any serious belief and with a distinctly negative reaction to the authoritarian nuns and priests who tried to instruct him. God did not figure seriously in Polanski's childhood world; his presence cannot be felt in the world of Polanski's films either.

The Devil is an entirely different matter. He is embodied explicitly or implicitly in most of Polanski's films, but not because Polanski believes literally in such a supernatural being. Rather, for Polanski, evil is not only an undeniable fact of human existence but a dominant aspect of human behavior. Given his experience, and our recent collective history, it would be hard to argue that the manifestations we associate with the word evil are not objectively equally copresent with what we term good. In this sense, Polanski's philosophy, although rather loosely defined, might be viewed as existential and Manichean. Evil, in his filmic worlds, is inevitable, just as it has seemed to be in his life. Moral impulses are present and are valued, but they are simply overpowered by amoral and immoral drives.

In evaluating Polanski's films, his artistic judgment and his craftmanship are factors just as important as his compelling themes. Artists transform the difficult experiences of their lives in order to transcend them or, at least, survive them. During the war years in Krakow, Polanski escaped from the pain of his daily life by sneaking into the movies, at some personal risk (he could be caught and his Jewishness could be discovered; also, Poles were beaten up by their countrymen for patronizing the German propaganda films). His fascination with and love of the cinema thus began as an antidote to the pain of life. After the war, Polanski was reunited with his father (his mother did not survive the camps), although family life was never reconstituted. Polanski's father remarried, and the young Roman did not get along well with his father or his father's new wife; on the other hand, he was accustomed to fending for himself. Roman was boarded first with other families and then in rented quarters, while his father saw to his education. Returning to school, Polanski was attracted to drawing; his father felt Polanski's talents could be turned toward technical studies. Quite by chance (noticed during a class visit to a radio station which produced Communist-inspired plays for children; Polanski complained about the unnaturalness of the child actors, was jokingly given an on-the-spot audition, and earned a place in the company), Polanski became a child actor, first on the radio, then on the Krakow stage, and ultimately in films. His short stature and childlike looks, and his talent, kept him in demand: At the age of seventeen, he could easily play a child of ten. In Andrzej Wajda's film *A Generation* (*Pokolenie*, 1954), Polanski plays an adolescent who looks to be about fourteen; he was twenty-one.

In 1950, Polanski had transferred from a technical school to Krakow's School of Fine Arts, from which he graduated in 1953. Polanski's training here certainly contributed to his evident concern for visual composition as a filmmaker. Polanski pursued his art studies and his acting career simultanously and hoped to gain admission to the Krakow Drama School; he was rejected, his small size now being seen as a disadvantage (suitable parts would be too few). Polanski's "class origins" (his father had continued to be a small-time businessman) kept him out of the university, but he finally succeeded in 1954, as a result of his acting connections, in gaining admission to the State Film School at Łódź.

During the years of Polanski's education prior to film school, Poland underwent major transformations: the installation of a Communist government under Soviet domination; the rejection of any independent Polish path to socialism; the arrest and imprisonment of Polish party leader Władisław Gomułka as a "bourgeois nationalist"; the ensuing Stalinist purges. Developments within the Polish film industry were conditioned by those events. Prior to World War II, the rich and varied Polish artistic, literary, and theatrical tradition had already been augmented by new experiments in cinema:

avant-garde shorts, cinéma vérité reportage, and lyrical documentaries. Many of the young innovators, in particular Alexander Ford, Antoni Bohdziewicz, Jerzy Bossak, and Stanisław Wohl, spent the war either in the Communist resistance movement within Poland or in the USSR, where they became part of military film units. Because of their solid left-wing credentials, and their experience and talent, these men assumed major positions in the post-World War II film industry. Ford was made head of Film Polski (as the nationalized film industry was called), and later Bohdziewicz, Bossak, and Wohl joined the faculty of the Higher School of Film established at Łódź in 1948.

Although the school was a boon to young filmmakers in many respects (it was equipped to industry standards and its staff included the best veteran directors, cinematographers, etc.), there was a considerable down side to state patronage and funding as well. After a few years of relative artistic freedom following the war, Polish cinema was made to conform to the doctrine of socialist realism which had been developed in the Soviet Union in the 1930s and 1940s.

This imported doctrine of socialist realism entailed "representing reality in its revolutionary development," which amounted to representing historical or contemporary events as the ruling Communist party wanted them represented. The "positive hero" of socialist realist film had to overcome natural obstacles, ideological antagonists, and his or her own lack of developed political consciousness on the way to achieving historical goals: defeating fascism, building socialism, overfulfilling production quotas, solving particular industrial problems, etc. Older "mentor" figures, usually Communist party members, helped the hero, while negative characters actively battled the forces of humanism. Enemies (Nazis, neo-Fascists, collaborators, spies, wreckers, former capitalists, etc.) were defeated, whereas those who blocked the accomplishment of progressive goals through insufficient consciousness could be converted and reformed. Partymindedness was thus an ever-present value. In addition, the films were to be didactic, clear, and optimistic. It would be hard to imagine an official doctrine less conducive to Polanski's tendencies as an artist.

Many other Polish filmmakers opposed socialist realism as well, including, importantly, major figures among the teachers at the Łódź Film School, including its dean, Jerzy Bossak, who became one of Polanski's mentors and supporters. Bossak and other prewar filmmakers associated with Poland's left-leaning avant-garde used their influence at the Łódź Film School and in the Communist film industry in general to promote the careers of promising young filmmakers and support their efforts to stretch the boundaries of the permissible. In Polanski's own words, they "did their best to campaign for artistic originality and freedom, standing up to party hacks and ministry bureaucrats at considerable personal risk."[4]

These factors were important in shaping Polanski's early filmmaking style, not because he followed the tenets of socialist realism, but because he rebelled (as did his talented contemporaries Andrzej Wajda, Andrzej

Munk, Jerzy Kawalerowicz, and Jerzy Skolimowski) against the constraints of this official canon, and did so in directions which were sufficiently tolerated (just barely!) to get his films made. Because socialist realism's unrealistic schematism was offensive to Polish audiences and, after the death of Stalin in 1953, met with increasing resistance from informed film critics as well, an arena was created within the censorship process whereby filmmakers could fight for the integrity of their artistic visions. There were several stages of review and censorship, from the vetting of the initial screenplay to a final viewing and approval of the finished film. Changes could be requested at any stage and they frequently were. Filmmakers could agree to the requested changes or they could propose compromise solutions, meeting the party halfway so to speak, without completely abandoning their own conceptions. Such a strategy could succeed in these years because of the support of Bossak, Wohl, and Bohdziewicz (who during the war had made a documentary of the Warsaw Uprising as a member of the *non*-Communist Resistance).

In 1953, after the young Polanski had appeared onstage in the socialist realist play *Son of the Regiment,* Bohdziewicz hired him to play a small part in a student film, *Three Stories.* While on location, Polanski met a number of the rising stars of Polish cinema: Jerzy Lipman (who later would be his cinematographer on *Knife in the Water*); Andrzej Wajda, to become the most distinguished filmmaker of the postwar decades (and who gave Polanski a role in his first feature film, *A Generation*); and Zbigniew Cybulski, the actor who galvanized Polish audiences for a decade, before his accidental death. A year later, after Lipman and Wajda recruited Polanski for *A Generation* (one of the first films to depart from socialist realism), Bohdziewicz interceded on Polanski's behalf to gain him admission to the Łódź Film School.

Polish society and politics took a liberalizing turn in 1956, with Gomułka's release from prison and his rapid ascension to first party secretary. Under Gomułka, the regime recognized the "errors and distortions" which had occurred during the Stalinist period and indicated that a greater measure of social criticism would be allowed in the arts. The film industry was reorganized into several fairly autonomous production units, each headed by a veteran director. Young documentary filmmakers under Bossak's tutelage made a number of very frank films about poor living conditions and social problems like juvenile delinquency and prostitution. The new cinema, both fictional and documentary, generated considerable debate in the press, including criticism of its supposed pessimism and cynicism. The parameters of acceptable art were thus still being hotly contested, within the party as well as in society as a whole.

During the next two years, a number of important films were made by these units, addressing historical, philosophical, and psychological themes *outside of* a canonical socialist realist framework; these included Wajda's *Kanal* (1957) and *Ashes and Diamonds* (1958) and Munk's *Man on the Track* (1957) and *Eroica* (1958). Another important trend in those years was the theater of the absurd. The alienation conveyed in the plays of Beckett or Ionesco was permitted, in that it could be seen as an indictment of the dead-end values of the capitalist era or, at the very least, as a generalized depiction of the human condition not specific to communism or to Polish society. Jerzy Grotowski produced Ionesco's *The Chairs* in Krakow in 1957, and Sławomir Mrożek's indigenous theater of the absurd began to emerge in the same year. With Gomułka's return to power, the "errors and distortions" of the Stalinist period could also be reflected allegorically in absurdist plays or films. This is the direction which Polanski took in his first films, beginning with *Two Men and a Wardrobe* (1958).

There is one more very important point to be made about Polanski's years at the state film school in Łódź. This training ground for the new generation of Polish filmmakers not only had the benefit of experienced directors, screenwriters, cinematographers, and technical experts as teachers, and a quite respectable level of material support for students' filmmaking projects, it also had intimate connections with the state-sponsored Polish film industry in general, and could thus provide its students with additional professional experience in the form, for example, of "assistant director" assignments with the nation's then leading young filmmakers, among them Andrzej Munk and Andrzej Wajda. Polanski emerged from his film education with a very high level of knowledge and competence, particularly as regards the technical aspects of film style. His considerable experience as an actor made him a more than adequate director of acting as well.

The scope of this chapter does not allow for a detailed consideration of all of Polanski's films (a listing of these can be found in the filmography), nor is such a comprehensive study necessary for gaining an appreciation of Polanski's characteristic stylistic approaches and their relationship to the development of his thematic concerns. Here, I will choose to discuss in some detail the films which I consider Polanski's best: *Two Men and a Wardrobe* (1958), *Knife in the Water* (1962), *Repulsion* (1965), *Rosemary's Baby* (1968), *Macbeth* (1971), and *Chinatown* (1974), with only passing reference to his other films.[5]

Two Men and a Wardrobe

Two Men and a Wardrobe was Polanski's first serious student film, and it won the Bronze Medal for Experimental Film at the Brussels World's Fair. Three short student exercises had preceded it in 1957, all of them involving violent or sexually aggressive imagery. In *The Crime* (*Morderstwo,* 1957–1958), a one-minute film, a man enters a bedroom, opens a pocket knife, stabs a sleeping victim repeatedly, and walks out again. In *The Smile* (*Śmiech,* 1957), two minutes long, a Peeping Tom watches from a hallway window as a naked young woman dries herself from a bath; caught in the act, he walks away, but then returns; only now, instead of the woman, he is confronted by the mirrored reflection of a man brushing his teeth, who grins directly at him. *Breaking Up the Party* (*Rozbijemy zabawe,* 1957) was a longer exercise planned by Polanski to satisfy a *cinéma vérité* documentary requirement. He organized an open-air dance on the school grounds for the students, then used his contacts in Łódź bars to arrange for a gang of hooligans to crash the party and start a fight. "My single camera crew struggled to shoot as much of this concentrated action as they could, barely managing to get enough footage before the dance turned into a shambles,"[6] writes Polanski in his autobiography. All three films are indicative of Polanski's desire to attest to the violence and exploitation which had characterized his own personal experience.

Two Men and a Wardrobe was a much more ambitious project. Polanski submitted a script and a storyboard and succeeded in getting funding to shoot the film on location at Sopot, a resort near Gdansk. Polanski's ability to translate not only evil, exploitation, and alienation but also creativity, playfulness, innocence, and nurturing into powerful and evocative visual images is abundantly evident in this film. The film opens with a shot of waves rolling in on a sandy beach; from beneath the waves, a large, heavy wardrobe emerges and is carried onto the shore by two men, who have also magically appeared from under the sea's surface.

Polanski selects material objects in which symbolic and associative meaning is already embedded; this is a characteristic of his style which continues in his mature works. The large wardrobe is stately, though worn; the full-length mirror on a front panel is not only practical but also capable of serving an aesthetic function. Even as it is moving out of the water, it is reflecting a "seascape" of waves and sky. Also, as soon as it is set down on the sand, it begins to interact with the two men like a faithful pet. As the two men dance and do exercises to limber up, it quietly and modestly reflects them.

Another hallmark of Polanski's cinematic practice also already manifests itself in *Two Men and a Wardrobe:* his shrewd typecasting of actors. Selecting within the limited field of those fellow students at Łódź who collaborated on the film in other respects as well (on the story, as assistant director, as cinematographer), Polanski judiciously matched physical characteristics to roles. The "two men" were played by Jakub ("Kuba") Goldberg, a very short man with an elfin face, and Henryk Kluba, thin, balding, and with a short scruffy beard which Polanski had him grow. The actions and gestures of the two men are delicate, hesitating, and somewhat effeminate (they could be taken for a gay couple). Also, their appearance would, in the Polish context, suggest Jewishness (Goldberg was, in fact, Jewish). Thus, before the action proper has even begun, we understand that these men are outcasts, somehow "other," with religious and spiritual qualities (they were born directly from the sea, walked out from the water). In their humble and common dress, they are also "the meek" in biblical terms. One could, of course, continue to make even more specific historical associations—other additional meanings are possible: they are concentration camp survivors, they are people persecuted by a political regime more generally, e.g., victims of Stalinist purges. None of these specific associations are necessary, but these and many more are possible.

As the men take up the wardrobe and carry it down the beach, the image dissolves to a trolley stop, where they wait patiently with the wardrobe and then try to board a trolley with it. The image is absurd, since the trolley is already packed with people. The two men are naively good-natured, uncomprehending of the ridiculousness of their effort (this strengthens the impression that they have come from some other world). The crowd on the trolley is, however, hardly good-natured; they meet the men with shoves, taunts, and angry gestures (if one looks closely, one can see that Polanski himself and his assistant director, Andrzej Kostenko, play angry passengers).

Our impression of the indifference and the immorality of this all too recognizable urban "world" is reinforced in the next two sequences. The two men encounter a girl whose possible sensitivity is suggested by a caged bird in a pet shop window, at which she is looking when they come upon her (one wonders if Polanski came by his use of cinematic metonymies, characterizing personages by what is *near* or *attached* to them, by studying the Soviet films of Pudovkin). As she walks away down the street (a shadowy urban canyon walled by tenements), the two men put down the wardrobe and run to catch up. They introduce themselves with urbane politeness, which, when combined with their vagabond appearance, evokes Chaplin and the values associated with the Chaplin persona. They gesture toward the wardrobe which they have left a block away. The young woman pauses briefly, but when they dash off happily to retrieve the wardrobe, *she* walks off. In the next sequence, as the men walk along a canal, the camera pans away from them to the top of a small bridge, where two younger men, somewhat inebriated, are standing with arms over each other's shoulders and boisterously laughing. When the camera lowers to waist level, however, we see that one man is deftly using his *other* hand to lift his buddy's wallet from a back pocket.

These sequences constitute a cycle of events, a syntagmatic unit which Polanski then repeats with variations: (1) naively innocent gestures on the part of the men, who merely want their wardrobe to live usefully in the world of the film; (2) the wardrobe demonstrates its usefulness or beauty; (3) rejection and indifference on the part of the people of the film's world, in a group and as individuals; (4) the evil of the world manifest in the shape of a crime. Polanski now repeats this cycle, varying the specific form of each stage and the order of the stages in a manner which escalates both the associative potential of the imagery and its emotional effect. A sequence in which the men try to carry the wardrobe into a small, high-class restaurant, once again to be rudely rejected, is followed by a surprising, even beautiful, image of a fish "flying" through a sky dotted with white puffy clouds. When the camera pulls back, it reveals a dried fish, lying on the mirror of the wardrobe (laid on its back) as a table; the two men are eating a modest lunch. The wardrobe's mirror, reflecting the clouds scudding overhead, had created the image of the flying fish. The wardrobe has again shown itself to be a thing capable of creating beauty and a useful friend (providing a table for lunch).

The two men next take the wardrobe to a hotel, placing it on the sidewalk while they talk to the proprietor about gaining admittance. They are rejected once again, but while they are talking the wardrobe shows its usefulness, as a patron uses its mirror to straighten his tie (the wardrobe is useful, but not essential; when the two men pick the wardrobe up and carry it off, they reveal a street mirror positioned directly behind it—the patron takes one step forward and continues straightening his tie as if nothing has happened).

If the wardrobe has shown its ability both to create art and to be mundanely useful, it subsequently demonstrates a humanistic desire to prevent evil, in a sequence which foregrounds its anthropomorphic qualities. The two men carry the wardrobe past a nearly deserted bandshell, where four young toughs (Kostenko and Polanski play two of the four) are hanging out. There is an endearing shot of a black kitten. One of the hooligans throws the remains of an apple he has been eating at the kitten; another throws a rock. The next shot shows the rock—and a dead black kitten. Kostenko picks up the kitten and shoves it into the face of one of the other gang members. Noticing a pretty young woman standing on the street, the gang begins to sneak up on her, apparently intending to shove the dead kitten in *her* face. It is at this point that the two men and the wardrobe intervene, moving in front of the young woman and positioning the wardrobe's mirror in such a way as to reveal to her what is about to happen. She quickly walks away.

The wrath of the gang now falls on the two men and their wardrobe. Kostenko throws the kitten in the face of the small elfin man (Kuba Goldberg). Now, the "two men" show a courage which we would not have anticipated. Goldberg slaps Kostenko in the face, but is then himself hurled brutally against the wardrobe, whose mirror is smashed. As he slips to the ground, his tall, scruffy companion (Henryk Kluba) quixotically shadowboxes in a circle around the hooligans (he does not hit them). Kostenko watches for a minute, then taps Kluba on the shoulder and unceremoniously knocks him down with a solid punch in the jaw. Then the gang holds Kluba against a fence, while the smallest punk (played by Polanski) beats up the entirely defenseless victim.

Thus, what Propp might call the function "crime in the world manifests itself," our (4) above, is greatly expanded and filled with much greater affect in this variation. A word should be added about casting here. Kostenko was tall and very muscular; handsome, but with high cheekbones and slick-backed hair that gave him a cruel look. Polanski, as usual, looks small and thin. The fact that he administers the beating is significant. He is the weak "punk" who can only prove his "manhood" by attacking those who are weaker and more defenseless than himself. The victim (here one who looks like a potential victim) has become the victimizer. A member of such a gang during his early adolescence in Krakow, Polanski may have been reenacting quite literally a potential for viciousness and cruelty he knew was within himself. Both of these negative qualities in Polanski's personality are attested to by co-workers and by his biographers as are, of course, his innocent, charming, and generous qualities. The duality of good and evil within a single character was to become a constant motif in Polanski's work. And whenever he played a role in his own films, he was either a victim (*The Fat and the Lean, Fearless Vampire Killers, The Tenant*) or a victimizer (*What?, Chinatown*).

The beating is undoubtedly the most disturbing sequence in the film, as Polanski deftly creates out of commonplace images of innocence (the kitten, the pretty young girl, two homeless men) and cruelty (the gang members) a searing portrait of what might more abstractly be called "man's inhumanity to man." In a historical sense, one might also consider it a microcosm of the Holocaust.

The film continues with further images of violence and regimentation. After passing a drunk who is about to fall down the steps leading to the river below, the two men seek refuge in a yard filled with empty barrels, stacked symmetrically. This is a fitting image of a regimented, bureaucratized order, where even the discarded and the abandoned must be routinely organized, cataloged (the fastidiousness of the Nazis in this regard comes to mind). A watchman discovers the men and beats them with a stick, driving them off again.

The two men next pass by a ravine, where one man has just smashed the head of another with a rock. Returning to the sandy beach, they tread past a young boy who is making rudimentary sand castles by inverting his sand-filled pail. The shot widens to show us that he has made perhaps 100 of these—all arranged in neat rows. In the world of the film, even a child's playful imagination is regimented, his creative potential turned into a sterile exercise, devoid of any humanity (the child is also oblivious to the two men and the wardrobe). With no hope for a future, even from this child, the two men carry their wardrobe into the sea. All three disappear into the waves. The film ends as it began, with the waves rolling up onto the empty shore.

Polanski deliberately sought out the well-known Krakow jazz composer Krzysztof Komeda to do the music for *Two Men and a Wardrobe.* His bluesy jazz score is extremely effective, capturing both the sweet playfulness of the men and an aching sadness. Komeda did the music for almost all of the films Polanski made in the next decade (I do not intend to deal, in this chapter, with the musical soundtracks of Polanski's films, a subject deserving a separate study).

Three other short films of Polanski's early "absurdist" period share many characteristics with *Two Men and a Wardrobe:* cyclical patterns of events, developed through variations; images rich in associative possibilities, evoking both general truths about the human condition and more specific commentary on existing political systems; the ever-present themes of exploitation and violence; nostalgia for a lost innocence, kindness, and nurturing. *When Angels Fall* (*Gdy spadaja anioły,* 1959) makes more specific reference to Polish culture and history in developing these themes; *The Fat and the*

Lean (*Le Gros et le maigre,* 1961), made in France, shows the complicity of the victim in his own enslavement, in a manner reminiscent of Beckett's *Waiting for Godot;* in the same vein, *Mammals* (*Ssaki,* 1962), made independently and illegally in Poland, explores not only the ever-present willingness of people to exploit each other but also the essential interchangeability of victim and victimizer. None of these films attracted the notice accorded *Two Men and a Wardrobe,* particularly in Poland. Polanski's mentors did not consider his diploma film as accomplished as *Two Men and a Wardrobe; The Fat and the Lean* was seen only in France at this time; and *Mammals* was reedited secretly in Poland only after *Knife in the Water* had been shot.

Knife in the Water

Knife in the Water (1962), Polanski's first feature-length film, came into much more explicit conflict with the ideological arbiters of culture, both during its long path to realization and after its initial screenings. In 1959, after Polanski had become a member of Bossak's production unit "Kamera," he proposed a brief treatment for the film and received a contract to write the screenplay. This he completed in the summer of 1959, in collaboration with Jerzy Skolimowski. In spite of Bossak's continued support, however, the screenplay was rejected by the Ministry of Culture for lack of social commitment. *Knife in the Water* has a realistic contemporary setting and thus implicitly invited comparison with films aimed at social commentary. However, Polanski's attack on power and authority was quite unlike a typical socialist realist treatment, both in theme and in terms of the film's structure.

Two years later, upon Polanski's return to Poland after an extended stay in France, Bossak sensed some liberalization in cultural policy and urged Polanski to resubmit the film after adding sections which would make its social relevance more explicit. This Polanski did by writing some explicit monologues aimed at social problems. In spite of these minor alterations, the film continues to share many structural features and thematic motifs with Polanski's absurdist shorts, in particular the cyclical repetition, with variations, of a sequence of typical events (or functions, in the Proppian sense). In order to make a structure like this effective over the length of a feature film, Polanski needed interesting story material, incidents which were rich enough to mask the potentially monotonous cyclical repetitions. Also, dialogue was now an important component as well—it needed to have authenticity and wit commensurate with the cleverness of Polanski's visual contructions. Polanski was fortuanate to have, at the stage of writing the screenplay, the collaboration of Skolimowski, who, in fact, is solely credited for the film's dialogues.

The high quality of *Knife in the Water* as a work of art was very indicative of the inspired work Polanski could do with the visual aspects of a film when he had an equally talented co-creator for the narrative verbal elements. This situation was to occur again in Polanski's best films—*Rosemary's Baby* (which closely follows the narrative events of Ira Levin's novel and uses the dialogue from the novel virtually verbatim); *Macbeth (*narrative and dialogue by William Shakespeare, adapted by Polanski and Kenneth Tynan); and *Chinatown* (original screenplay by Robert Towne). Of Polanski's many screenplay collaborations with the Frenchman Gérard Brach (and in spite of Polanski's own greater personal artistic investment in these projects), only *Repulsion* is in the class of Polanski's other films as a work of art, and here, as we shall see, dialogue plays a fairly minimal role.

Polanski wanted his first feature film "to be rigorously cerebral, precisely engineered, almost formalist."[7] Indeed, *Knife in the Water* exhibits the economy of plot characteristic of his absurdist short films and the precise use of space and composition of figures within that space. Polanski has indicated his own very formal conception of the screenplay: "From the first, the story concerned the interplay of antagonistic personalities within a confined space."[8] There are actually three confined spaces: a car in which a married couple is driving to Poland's Mazurian Lakes for a one-day sailing trip; the deck of their small sailboat; and the even smaller and more confining interior of its cabin. The "exterior" sets also constitute a limited set: a narrow muddy road; a dock; the water of the lake, with only the horizon line or thin islands in the background; a grassy-sided canal between two lakes. The repertoire of settings is not much larger than in Polanski's short films.

The three personalities are Andrzej, a sportswriter in his early forties; his considerably younger wife, Krystyna; and a nineteen-year-old hitchhiker to whom they give a lift and whom they then take along on a twenty-four-hour sailing trip (they never even ask him his name—we will call him *the hiker*). In casting the film, Polanski exhibited his typical shrewdness about physical characteristics which reflect personality or essence. For the husband (outwardly self-confident, egotistical, overbearing), he chose Leon Niemczyk, an experienced actor, solidly built, rugged, but with a physique that showed obvious signs of middle age. Polanski had envisioned playing the role of the wise-guy (reckless, charming) hiker himself, but after being talked out of this dual responsibility by Jerzy Bossak, he settled on Zygmunt Malanowicz, a delicately handsome young method actor who took himself a bit too seriously. After the film had been shot, Polanski reclaimed part of this role for himself by redubbing Malanowicz's part with his (Polanski's) voice. For the young wife, Polanski needed a woman who would be erotically charged, but in a very understated way, and whose personal desires would not be openly expressed, manifesting themselves more as a smoldering resentment. For this role, he chose a nonactor, Jolanta Umecka, whose appropriate physique he spotted at a Warsaw swimming pool (the wife spends a good part of the film in a scant bikini). Umecka's voice was also redubbed by someone else during the final editing, with only Niemczyk redubbing his own voice.

In an expansion of the binary oppositions he had used in *The Fat and the Lean* and *Mammals,* Polanski had three separate characters battling to assert their individuality, their desire, and their control. The battle takes the form of games, some of them merely verbal sparring, others leading to physical action of a sexual or aggressive nature. Skolimowski's dialogue is sharp and effective throughout, providing a fitting counterpoint to Polanski's work on blocking, spatial composition, and visual symbolism.

The positioning of the characters within the frame is particularly telling, mirroring the competitions, alliances, and oppositions. One frequently used pattern is a point-of-view shot with one character in the foreground and the other two in the background; alternately, Polanski may place two of the characters in the foreground of the shot, symmetrically placed, with the third character situated in the distance, but between them spatially in the shot.

As the film opens, we are looking at the couple driving—from the hood of the car, as it were. Their images are hazy, however; we cannot make out the details of their faces because the front windshield is reflecting the trees and sky above instead. The image is a surprising one; it suggests the instability and insecurity of the characters, which flares up in the dialogue as soon as the images become clear. Komeda's jazz soundtrack mimics the edginess and energy of the conversations throughout the film. Krystyna is driving, wearing a scoop-necked blouse which provides a hint of sensuality. As we alternate viewing the couple from the front and from the rear (soon to be the position of the hiker, as backseat passenger), it is apparent that they have been arguing. Andrzej does not like his wife's driving and he pulls at the wheel himself to correct her "line." She abruptly stops the car and gets out in order to change places with him. Now Andrzej drives and Krystyna stares sullenly straight ahead. When Andrzej bends over to kiss the back of her neck in a gesture both of desire and of apology, she remains motionless and passive. Suddenly, the figure of the hitchhiker appears in the distance, a small image on the windshield, between the heads of Andrzej and Krystyna, but one which grows larger as the car speeds ahead. Visually, the hiker's role is represented here through spatial symbolism—as a catalyst which will grow in power and cause the couple's relationship to explode.

What is symbolically suggested is immediately realized in dialogue and gesture. Andrzej blows his horn, but does not slow down. The hiker stands his ground in the middle of the road. Finally, Andrzej has to slam on his brakes, sending the car skidding to the side of the road. He leaps from the car and rushes angrily toward the young man, who remarks (sarcastically): "You left your lights on."[9]

"Bastard," replies Andrzej. "Half a mile earlier you would have been a corpse." Already, the hiker has been a catalyst for Andrzej's insulting his wife's driving—and her judgment, as he continues: "No, you would have stopped and offered the shit a ride." Andrzej then, with exaggerated politeness, escorts the hiker, the "gentleman" (*pan* in Polish) he calls him, into the back seat and offers him a pillow, blanket, and cushion for his comfort. Andrzej's motivations may be unclear, but the young hiker's good looks and his boldness suggest that, somehow, sexuality will be an issue.

Within the confined space of the car, Polanski creates a triangular disposition of the characters—either we look from the front of the car, with the young man positioned in the space between and behind Andrzej and Krystyna, or the camera is behind the young man, so that his head is in the foreground, with the other two beyond him in the front seat. The young man is clearly the outsider, but his mediate spatial position suggests his potential for replacing Andrzej. The sparring dialogue, in which each tries to "one up" the other, cements this impression.

When the car reaches the dock, Polanski shifts the geometry to heighten the tension. Krystyna climbs onto the dock, as Andrzej and the hiker watch. The composition points to her as the sexual object over which the two men will duel. Then, in a point-of-view shot taken over the young man's shoulder, we see that he is looking at Krystyna's bare legs as she walks down the dock (and, of course, we are looking at her legs too; thus, Polanski involves the spectator, as voyeur, in the subject position of one or another of the male protagonists.)

All the while, Krystyna is preparing the boat for sailing, while Andrzej stands smoking his pipe and giving her orders. Then the banter continues:

> *Andrzej:* I meant to frighten you.
> *Hiker:* You succeeded.

The young man appears ready to leave.

> *Andrzej:* You weren't going to get out of the way?
> *Hiker:* I knew you would stop.
> *Andrzej:* You're a sucker. But I like you.

The young man now walks all the way down the dock, but Andrzej calls him back again.

> *Hiker:* I knew you would call me back. I can read your mind. You want to continue the game.

Once the trio are off on the sailboat, Polanski again utilizes the spatial composition to reflect the ever-changing shifts in relationships of power. At the outset, Andrzej, as the captain, continues to give orders. He tells the others stories about the tough boatswain who commanded him when he was in the navy ("If he told us to call an oak a willow, we called it a willow"). He is the master; Krystyna and the hiker are his slaves. Andrzej's usual position is at the rudder-end of the sailboat (this is the most common position for the camera as well, just beyond Andrzej so that it captures him in the foreground of the shot). The young man is usually at the front of the boat, responding to Andrzej's orders. Krystyna's position varies: Either she sits beside Andrzej at the rudder, or goes to a mediate position (the ship's cabin area) to carry out some task; or she is isolated on the deck in a very revealing white bikini which barely contains her breasts.

There are many shots in which Krystyna functions as a sexual "spectacle," and (as is true in general in Polanski's films) the viewer is located in the position of voyeur, whether or not the camera position is motivated as

3.1. Krystyna (Jolanta Umecka) adjusts the sail while we look at her in a scanty bikini. The hiker (Zygmunt Malanowicz) is in the background. *Knife in the Water.* Museum of Modern Art/Film Stills Archive.

another character's point of view. In this way, Polanski identifies the viewer as "one who also desires," as essentially similar to the desiring characters, as complicit in the objectification (usually of women) which is taking place. Thus, in many shots, Krystyna functions principally as a sexual object; she lies outstretched along the deck with only the water or a line of trees on an island in the background. Whenever she emerges from the cabin below deck, the camera peers down at her cleavage, frequently in shots from the hiker's point of view; we are inclined toward the view that he might act on the erotic impulses which we also share.

As in Polanski's earlier films, physical props with rich associational possibilities figure centrally as well in the composition and blocking of the film (Krystyna's alluring body could be considered one of those props). I will now turn to these, although the reader should keep in mind that the spatial play with character positions continues as well throughout the film.

Both through verbal means and because of his position in the foreground, Andrzej becomes associated with the sailboat—it is the symbol of his mastery of the world, his virility. When Andrzej is first enticing the hiker to come along, the hiker insists that he likes walking better. His identity as a *hiker* is linked metonymically, via judicious close-ups, to his backpack and his knife, symbolic of his ability to survive in the wilderness. As Andrzej exhibits his knowledge of the sailboat and his skill in handling it, the young

3.2. The phallic knife positioned between the two male antagonists, Andrzej (Leon Niemczyk) and the hiker. *Knife in the Water.* Museum of Modern Art/Film Stills Archive.

man pulls out his large switchblade knife and demonstrates its usefulness in several practical tasks, from slicing bread to hacking through the underbrush as the two men pull the boat through a grassy canal. The phallic symbolism of both the knife and the sailboat is clearly suggested in visual compositions. The boat is seen in long shots, slicing through the water, and Andrzej is often seen manipulating its rudder. When the hiker pulls out his knife, it is from a sheath at his belt. He presses a button, and the knife snaps out directly in front of him.

"Sailing is a kid's game," the hiker tells Andrzej. "When you want to walk straight ahead you need a knife."

When the young man suggests that Andrzej do some of the work while *he* takes the sail, Andrzej lets him try. The hiker cannot control the boat, however, particularly since Andrzej surreptitiously moves the rudder, causing the sails to swing wildly from side to side. Andrzej cynically observes, "You need brains to do this—not muscle."

The young man's ascendancy and perhaps his martyrdom are prefigured (ironically, as it turns out) through the use of easily recognizable Christian symbolism. For example, he is filmed from the very top of the mast as he lies spreadeagled at the point of the sailboat, with a coil of rope resting underneath his head, resembling those golden haloes which surround Christ's head in religious paintings. Told by Andrzej that sailors who whistle are made to climb the mast, he immediately and agilely does so—looking down at the couple from the elevated vantage point he has boldly achieved ("Does he get a prize for this?" Andrzej remarks sarcastically). Later, the young man playfully "walks on water" while hanging on to the sail.

Polanski keeps the viewer's interest, given the limited set of variables, by alternating scenes of relative calm (the trio is having a pleasant time sailing) with scenes of sudden high tension, and later, of confrontation. This is a device of rhythmic composition which the director uses in subsequent films as well. In *Knife in the Water* the first sequence of high tension occurs as Krystyna finishes preparing a pot of soup for lunch and Andrzej lifts it off the stove using a plier-type gripping tool especially designed for this purpose. The young man laughs at it as just one more of Andrzej's unnecessary toys, an indulgence for the wealthy, like the overly large ship's compass fastened to the deck.

"You think it's unnecessary," says Andrzej, holding out the pot with the tool. "See how it works without it."

Without pausing, the young man takes the pot in his two hands and holds it, obviously in great pain, for nearly twenty seconds, until Krystyna tries to take it from him and makes him drop it ("You knocked over the soup," says the hiker sarcastically; the line echoes his earlier "You left your lights on" when he forced Andrzej to brake and lose control of his car).

We anticipate a fight here, but there is none. Instead, Polanski releases the tension by developing the competition in a somewhat lighter comic sequence. The young man now asks to be put ashore, but there is no wind to move the boat. He grabs an oar and begins to paddle earnestly, looking down at the water intently, while Andrzej sits with Krystyna at the rudder. The camera pulls back to show us that the boat is moving slowly—in circles. Andrzej laughs to Krystyna; the young man finally looks up, realizes the trick, and hurls the paddle into the water.

Tension immediately flares again as Andrzej shouts at him: "Jump!"

"I can't swim," says the hiker.

"Jump, I said!" repeats Andrzej even more forcefully.

Krystyna breaks the tension by jumping in after the oar herself. She turns the film toward a lighter playful mode once again, by swimming around and asking Andrzej to inflate a crocodile raft for her. As Andrzej blows up the raft, the young man toys with his knife. The hiker, with his right hand, rapidly moves the sharp blade between the outstretched fingers of his left. When Andrzej warns him not to scratch the deck's surface, he replies that he has a very light touch. Andrzej, as if to show his complete lack of fear, offers his own hand for the game. The hiker begins to move the knife rapidly between Andrzej's fingers, then he lifts his head and looks Andrzej in the eye, smiling and continuing to move the knife in a rapid rhythm. He is clearly flaunting the fact that Andrzej's safety depends on his skill and calmness. Andrzej needs to do something to reverse this momentum, for now the hiker is the "master" and Andrzej is the potential "victim." Andrzej suddenly seizes the hiker's hand (tension rises again) and tells him that he should go below and use the first-aid kit to dress the burns on his hand (this makes Andrzej the solicitous conqueror and the young man his defeated and injured ward).

Next it is the hiker's turn to play a "lighter" joke. When Andrzej joins Krystyna in the water to play with the inflated crocodile, the wind rises up and the hiker loses control of the boat (or at least pretends to do so). Andrzej begins to swim energetically after it, but each time he is about to head it off, it changes directions. Now the boat goes in circles again, but this time it is Andrzej's efforts to catch it which are comically futile. And once again it is Krystyna who intervenes, positioning herself in the water in the right spot to catch the boat.

In *Knife in the Water,* we can thus see the same pattern of repeating functions and "figures" that we noted in *Two Men and a Wardrobe*. Competitive games of various kinds, seemingly playful, mask a struggle for power; Krystyna functions both as the object of desire and as the mediator. The potential for a violent confrontation remains ever-present; we are constantly expecting it and finally it erupts. Trapped in the cabin during a storm, after running aground (Andrzej fails in controlling the sailboat), the trio spends the evening playing pick-up-sticks for "forfeits." Just earlier, the hiker has stolen a glance at Krystyna as she is changing out of her wet bathing suit; now she is positioned spatially between the two men as they play. Andrzej is the experienced one at this game, and he always wins (the sticks are his phallic objects in this sequence). Paying a "forfeit" with his knife, the young man reverses the power momentum by hurling it into the wall opposite. Andrzej retrieves the knife and does even better, sending the knife into the center of a cutting board hanging on the wall. The young man tries to match this, but his throw of the knife is off center.

In the meantime, Krystyna has paid her forfeit with her shoe, removing it suggestively as in a striptease (we know that Krystyna is wearing only these shoes and her bathrobe). The losers then must perform to redeem their forfeits, and it is at this point that the increasing alienation of Andrzej from the other two becomes apparent. Krystyna shyly and self-consciously sings a song; the hiker recites a romantic poem with sincere intonation. Andrzej is self-absorbed, continuing to masterfully pick up sticks while listening to a boxing match on his crystal radio, with earplugs isolating him from the sounds of the others.

The next morning, Krystyna sits bare-legged on the foggy deck at dawn, and the hiker comes up to talk with her. On the face of it, this is an entirely innocent conversation, but its components—early dawn, intimacy, Krystyna's state of partial undress—make of it an erotic encounter. Awakening below, Andrzej seemingly reacts to what *we* have seen. He angrily takes the hiker's knife from the wall and pockets it (a gesture of emasculation of the hiker in the symbolic language which the film has developed). As if to emphasize his own male power further, Andrzej goes on deck and begins to bark out orders to the young man in a tone which completely contradicts the informal friendliness of the previous night. The series of orders seems designed to humiliate the hiker and demonstrate Andrzej's unconditional

3.3. Andrzej prepares to throw the knife. Krystyna is positioned between the two men, as she is throughout this sequence. *Knife in the Water.* Museum of Modern Art/Film Stills Archive.

power: "Bring up the anchor!" "Stow it in the forepeak." "Go down into it." "Find a box there." "There's a rag in the box." "That's not all. Take the pail too." "The deck has to be swabbed!" "This picnic will teach you a lesson!"

Krystyna attempts to be a mediator once again, but Andrzej rebuffs her with another order: "Keep on course toward that buoy!" The confrontation now explodes, and over that quintessential symbol of phallic power, the knife.

Hiker: Where's my knife? What happened to my knife?
Andrzej: Keep calm! Nothing gets lost on my yacht.
Hiker: I didn't say it was lost. Where is it?
Andrzej: In my pocket.
Hiker: Why did you hide it?
Andrzej: Why? Do you think that I'm afraid of you?
Hiker: I don't need a knife to do things.
Andrzej: Come and get it!

Standing in the middle of the deck, Andrzej holds the knife high above his head, almost as a trophy (his rival's castrated phallus, so to speak). As the hiker approaches, Andrzej throws the knife at the mast, intending to impale it there, further demonstrating his masculine mastery. But his toss is errant; the knife hits the mast and falls into the water, as the hiker, diving to his knees, lunges for it in vain. Now it is the hiker's turn to give orders: "Jump!" he shouts at Andrzej. "Jump!"

The two men scuffle and Andrzej shoves the hiker onto the sail, which swings out over the water, thus suspending the hiker in a helpless position (and on that very object which has been the symbol of Andrzej's phallic power). In a clear visual indication of her sympathies, Krystyna rescues the hiker by quickly hauling in the sail. She literally provides the momentum for the punch he throws as he swings back to the deck. But Andrzej (who perhaps was an amateur boxer in his younger days) is unaffected by this blow, and returns a punch squarely to the hiker's jaw, knocking him into the water. He disappears below the waves as the boat speeds on.

Krystyna remembers immediately that the young man cannot swim and that Andrzej is therefore, potentially, his murderer. She dives into the water, and Andrzej somewhat reluctantly follows. Neither of them sees any sign of the hiker in the water or at the nearby buoy (however, as Krystyna finishes searching, *we* see the young man shoot up on the other side of the buoy, gasping for air; he has been deliberately hiding and he obviously *can* swim).

When Krystyna and Andrzej return to the sailboat, it is claer that the power situation has reversed itself. Krystyna insinuates that Andrzej will be proven a coward if he does not report the incident to the police. As Andrzej tries to get rid of the evidence by throwing the hiker's pack overboard, Krytsyna stops him, grappling with him so that the sack's contents spill across the deck. "Phoney! Fathead!" she screams at him. "Trying to save your face. I hate you." Now that Krystyna has called Andrzej's manhood into question, he must respond to reassert it. He jumps into the water and begins to swim toward shore, but Krystyna dismisses his gesture as just another way of showing off. She expects Andrzej will swim back to the boat, but he doesn't. Instead it is the hiker who, moments later, quietly slips onto the deck. He (and we) look toward Krystyna, who is naked, wringing out her wet bathing suit and crying.

If we viewed the hiker as a victim before, our perception of him now changes. He is a *voyeur.* Krystyna notices him and slaps him. "You are just like him," she says. "Only half his age, but weaker and stupider." Krystyna now launches into a long monologue about the difficult life of a student (one of the speeches added to the screenplay to increase its social relevance). In the process, she moves to a position of sympathy, begins to dry the hiker's hair, and finally is seduced by him and seduces him (the erotic scene develops in such a way that it is clear *both* participants desire each other).

Besides being an act of desire, the lovemaking is a rebellion against patriarchal authority (Andrzej's) and thus marks the beginning of Polanski's filmic preoccupations with the politics of gender and sexuality. As the boat approaches the shore, Krystyna bids the hiker farewell without ceremony—their liaison was not a matter of love, only lust and rebellion. Krystyna uses this incident to establish her own power vis-à-vis Andrzej. When she finds him at the dock, she at first gives him no clue that the hiker is alive. Instead she taunts him about his obvious failure to go to the police.

They begin to drive. The shots of Andrzej and Krystyna in the car are now identical to those at the beginning of the film. Krystyna now reveals that the hiker is alive. When Andrzej refuses to believe her (saying she only wants to save him, and thus implying for himself a martyr's role), Krystyna continues: "He's alive. . . . So much so that he made me unfaithful to you." The car reaches a crossroads; in one direction, the sign reads "Police." The car sits motionless. The film ends.

Andrzej has been left with two emasculating alternatives. He can go to the police and place himself at the mercy of the courts, who may imprison him (if he continues to believe that the hiker drowned) or he can admit that he has been cuckolded by the hiker (if he chooses to believe Krystyna's story). He has lost his patriarchal power (a fact which the viewer approves of), but at the same time Krystyna has seized it with perhaps equal cruelty. A moral order has not been achieved—victim and victimizer have merely changed places.

Like Polanski's absurdist shorts, *Knife in the Water* reveals essential patterns in human nature: the need for self-affirmation and the way it is, regrettably, obtained at the expense of others; the master-slave relationship as a basic mode of human interaction; the inherent reversibility of this relationship; and the expression of these power dynamics through the agency of human sexuality. All of these thematic strands continue to be taken up in Polanski's subsequent films.

In spite of its abstract and formal setting and the unspecific nature of its characters in terms of social or political position, some official Polish critics did not like what they saw when the film was released, sensing an attack on the privileged position of the Communist party apparatus, the *nomenklatura* as it is called. Already during its production, there were reports about too much spending and high living on the set (the expensive props—a sailboat and a Mercedes—encouraged this perception). The centrality of an affluent couple to this narrative brought charges that the film was "bourgeois," an affront to the basic concerns of ordinary workers. The film clearly gave primacy to sexual drives and motivations (the psychological) over analysis of class antagonisms (the social), in spite of the generational and economic disparity between the main antagonists. The most disturbing aspects, however, were the absence of any ideologically defined characters and of a clear, didactic message about civic behavior (in spite of Polanski's additions of speeches for the hiker and for Krystyna which referred to the unfulfilled aspirations of youth).

Not only adherents of socialist realism but even the more liberal critics expected a clearer moral for society. And, arguably, the Polish critics were not entirely inaccurate in seeing the film's thematics as lying outside a socialist critical framework (in fact, when Polanski had been unable to get the script approved in Poland he spent some time trying to get the film made in France). The unenthusiastic reception which the film received, coupled with the fact that Communist party First Secretary Gomułka himself condemned it, convinced Polanski that his prospects for making more feature films in his own country were very slim. His drive across the border, on the way from Krakow to Paris, was a matter of finding a way to continue his artistic endeavors. Now funding and box office returns would replace ideological acceptability as the material determinants of Polanski's filmmaking possibilities.

Repulsion

Repulsion (1965) remains today one of Polanski's most important films. It is particularly indicative of the way in which his films' thematic relevance exceeded his own intentions and expectations. Polanski and Gérard Brach were trying to get backing for their first co-authored script *When Katelbach Comes* (in 1966 filmed as *Cul-de-sac*) when they got a commission from Michael Klinger of the Compton Group (a small company which had been specializing in soft-core pornography) to make a horror film. The filmscript for *Repulsion* was written by Polanski and Brach in a few weeks. In Polanski's words, the guiding idea was "a homicidal schizophrenic running amok in her sister's deserted Condon apartment," with the twist that the portrayal of the life surrounding this homicidal milieu would be "as realistic and psychologically credible" as possible.[10]

Polanski and Brach envisioned the main character, Carol Ledoux, as a young woman who was "simultaneously attracted to and repelled by sex"[11] and thus, while otherwise painfully shy, would be given to sudden fits of violence against men who showed sexual interest in her. Indeed, there was considerable critical response to the film which commended its successful portrayal of a pathological paranoid schizophrenic. However, the film remains compelling to a broad audience today precisely because Carol's victimization by men is made so palpably *real* (even when we understand this victimization to be a matter of hallucination in the "story"). What underlies the film's construction is Polanski's sense of the reversibility of aggression, a motif he had handled so well before—the victim can become the victimizer. From the standpoint of sexual politics, this sense is even stronger and more specific in *Repulsion:* the victim *inevitably* will become the victimizer, because, in fighting back, the victim will have to resort to mechanisms of power and violence. In later films, Polanski explores this process on other, more specifically political levels.

The game of power in *Repulsion* is a game of sexual dominance in a much more tangible and explicit way than in *Knife in the Water.* In that film, Krystyna remains in the background (often literally, in terms of the composition), only to assert her own sexual desire and power toward the end of the film. Carol (played by the young Catherine Deneuve) is the principal focus in *Repulsion* from the outset and the main (often the *only*) character in all but a few of the film's sequences. Her status as a victim is suggested via the inclusion of an almost "everyday" documentation of sexual harassment as part of her daily routine, by the organization of an increasingly oppressive stylized *mise-en-scène,* by the use of embodiments of male phallic power, as well as by situating the viewer as a *voyeur* who participates directly in Carol's sexual oppression. (There is a metatextual aspect to this as well: Catherine Deneuve, and young starlets like her, are exploited as sexual objects by the cinema industry; the fact that the Compton Group specialized in soft-core porn is an interesting sidelight in this regard).

Polanski's ability to represent the oppression of women in contemporary Western culture in a compelling way manifests itself strongly in *Repulsion*. This might, on the surface, seem a strange claim to make for a director who was, no doubt, an exploiter of women in his personal life (during his years in London, Polanski was a regular at the Playboy Club; his autobiography reveals a man proud of his many affairs and one-night stands with beautiful and sexy women). On the other hand, Polanski certainly knew what such exploitation looked like from the point of view of the exploited, and at some level he may have felt identity with women, since he himself had been a powerless victim in his childhood. It is worth noting that Polanski as an actor in his own films *played* a woman in his 1959 graduation film *When Angels Fall* and, as Trelkovsky in *The Tenant* (1976), "becomes" the deceased woman who preceded him in his apartment.

Polanski's representation of woman as victim of sexual aggression in *Repulsion* began with the casting: as Carol, a young French-speaking Belgian who lives with her older sister Helen in London and works as a manicurist at a fancy beauty salon, Polanski cast Catherine Deneuve. Deneuve had a classically beautiful face which expressed a certain naiveté, innocence, and purity—also suggested by her very light blonde hair. At the same time, her body had all the attributes of movie sexiness. Thus, before even beginning to act, Deneuve projected the two antagonistic qualities which the film's structure demanded. Here, as in later films, Polanski constructed the role effectively by utilizing an actresses's personal attributes of modesty and reserve (Deneuve, for example, would not do any scenes in the nude; she wears a slip in virtually all of the scenes which require her to exhibit her sexuality, thus even here creating a tension between exhibitionism and modesty). Deneuve's childlike qualities were contrasted with those of Yvonne Furneaux, who played Helen. Furneaux was an established star who played her role in an unequivocally sexy way.

There is innocence on the male side as well, embodied in the character of Colin, a young man who apparently has fallen in love with Carol and is pursuing her with charm and politeness. In this role, Polanski cast Briton Jon Fraser, whose face possesses a boyish innocence and openness. The corruption and destruction of both of these innocents by the end of the film is a pattern which is prevalent in most of Polanski's work. The other two male characters are disposed on a scale of increasing male chauvinism. Michael (Ian Hendry), Helen's married lover, is a good-natured man, relatively considerate, but he does not question his right to a mistress and considers her function mainly one of his sexual gratification. The stockier and older landlord (Patrick Wymark) is a brazen exploiter in more ways than one, sleazy and quite willing to take sexual advantage of a woman who is powerless and in need.

Polanski's establishment of the everyday aspects of the objectification and fetishization of women goes hand in hand, in *Repulsion,* with an involvement of the viewer in this process as *voyeur.* The film's credit sequence has as background an extreme close-up of an eye (Deneuve's) which appears still at the outset, but then moves and blinks as the sequence progresses. Finally, the camera pulls back to reveal Deneuve's pretty but absolutely still face and her motionless hands. Carol is at work at the salon, where she is careful, solicitous, and obedient in the manner of a servant. Leaving work, Carol walks out onto the street and as she crosses an intersection three workmen ogle her body and one of them lurches toward her, accosting her with some unintelligible remark. We, of course, are looking at Carol as well, and a close-up of her face shows hints of her discomfort and her fear. In later street scenes, the camera drops down to street level, for no other apparent reason than to give us a view of Carol's legs.

Colin spots Carol through the window of a restaurant (she is sitting absolutely still before a plate of very dry fish and chips) and tries to invite her to lunch or dinner. Carol declines, saying she has to have dinner with her sister. Finally she accepts a dinner date for the next night (but when that time comes she has obviously forgotten it completely).

From any objective standpoint, of course, we might conclude that Carol simply is not attracted to Colin—period. However, he is so handsome, witty, and earnest in this conversation that we have every expectation (every expectation based on romantic film genres, in particular) that he will overcome her resistance. In the scenes which follow, we continue to be implicated in a pattern of desire which parallels Colin's. Once at the apartment she shares with her sister, Carol takes off her dress and walks around in her slip. Walking into the bathroom, she lifts her leg into the sink and washes it slowly. Her leg is completely exposed in this shot, with her slip hiked up to the very top of her thigh. Carol's stroking of her leg makes the shot particularly sensuous and puts the viewer in a position of objectifying her. When Michael arrives, he more specifically treats the women as a collection of parts, squeezing Helen's bottom and pinching Carol's cheek ("Ah, the beautiful younger sister"). Polanski does not make us feel anything negative about Michael here; Michael is just engaging in typical and accepted male behavior.

Woman as an object in sexual intercourse is foregrounded specifically in certain sequences. Twice Carol cannot sleep because of the moans of her sister as she reaches orgasm. The first time this sequence of sounds occurs, it is prolonged with the moans becoming ever more dramatic (as they might, for example, in a soft-core porno film). After the second time, Carol reacts pointedly to a spot of blood on her sister's bedsheet. At work, Carol hears complaints about men from her co-worker Bridget and, in another scene, a client complains: "There's only one thing they want. . . . They're all the same. They want to be spanked, then given sweets." Also in the realm of typical harassment are the crank calls which Carol receives in the apartment. No one speaks, but heavy breathing can be heard.

If the patterns of everyday treatment of women as sexual objects cast Carol as a potential victim of sexual aggression, Polanski's insistent use of symbolism reinforces this. Upon hearing that Carol's sister is making rabbit for dinner, Colin says, "Poor bunny"—planting the suggestion that the slaughtered rabbit might somehow be identified with a sexually attractive woman. The rabbit's naked (i.e., skinned) body on the plate indeed suggests a nude torso, at the same time that it suggests an enlarged male sexual organ, because of the particular way it is disposed on the plate. In later sequences, it becomes a rather terrifying and disgusting testament to sexuality gone awry. After Helen and Michael leave for a ten-day vacation, Carol removes the plate with the rabbit from the refrigerator (it never was cooked because Colin wanted to eat out that night instead); bloody juices now surround the pale, elongated carcass. She seemingly absentmindedly places the plate on a table, where the rabbit remains, rotting, until the film's bizarre conclusion.

The toothbrush and particularly the razor belonging to Michael also assume a pronounced phallic function from the outset. As she is washing her leg in the sink, Carol notices a razor and a toothbrush in a glass on the washstand under the mirror. She lifts these out very gingerly, as if she is handling something organic. When Carol finds these objects in her glass a second time, she drops both in the trashbin. The razor seemingly refuses to go away, however. Carol finds yet another razor left by Michael after the couple has left for their vacation. She opens this straight-razor and lays it on the shelf; at the finale, it becomes emblematic of her own assumption of phallic power, in particular as it is connected with cutting and with blood.

The first occurrence of blood in the film is in connection with sexual intercourse (the spot on Helen's bedsheet); the second is the pool of bloody liquid on the rabbit-plate. Soon shots of this plate reveal that the straight razor has been placed on it as well. We hear the buzzing of flies on the soundtrack, suggesting death and decay. A related image which simultaneously evokes decay and organic sexual processes is derived from a very mundane household image—a handful of potatoes that have sprouted. Carol and *we* look at these at several stages in the narrative, and each time the image is more disturbing—these potatoes become almost insectlike with their long intertwining tendrils, and are sexually threatening as well.

Mysterious cracks and fissures which open in the apartment wall also take on clear implications of sexual aggression; they echo insistently, establishing a sense that the entire environment is malevolent. On one of her walks, Carol pauses, transfixed by a crack in the pavement, a jagged line drawing as it were, in a Y-shape—schematic rendering of the spot where the legs meet the torso. Later, in the apartment, Carol will stare at a new crack which uncannily matches the one on the sidewalk. The cracks which open in the apartment wall in the second half of the film are huge fissures, such as an earthquake might produce, and their image is always preceded by an abrupt shocking crash on the soundtrack. Not only do the cracks visually suggest sexual violation (a membrane is ruptured), but the sound-

3.4. Carol (Catherine Deneuve) opens the bathroom door to find Michael (Ian Hendry) shaving. She slams it immediately, as if she had seen him naked. *Repulsion.* Museum of Modern Art/Film Stills Archive.

track treatment is identical to what accompanies the film's explicit images of rape when these occur. The importance for Polanski of this image (and others to be discussed below) and its particular visual texture is suggested by the amount of time and effort which went into construction of the "special effects" in *Repulsion.*

Throughout the first half of the film, Carol is the *object* with respect to phallic and vaginal imagery. It is only when she opens the straight razor, and when she places it on the plate with the rabbit, that her potential for seizing phallic power and shedding blood herself emerges. Notwithstanding this "symbolic" foreshadowing, the actual instances of Carol's bloodletting are sudden and shocking. In the first such sequence, Carol is seated in her usual manicurist's position, next to an elderly upper-class woman who is having a mud-treatment while Carol works on her cuticles. Carol stares vacantly at the manicuring clippers in her hand; the subsequent shot shows us the decrepit mud-covered face of the client, which suddenly erupts with a blood-curdling scream, immediately followed by a close-up of blood spurting from her finger. This nightmarelike construction, with its sudden explosion of graphic naturalistic detail, is perfected by Polanski in *Repulsion* and becomes an important part of his arsenal of imagistic devices.

In the next sequence, Carol is returned from her function as a bloody

3.5. Carol reaches for the phallic razor as the landlord (Patrick Wymark) enters the apartment. *Repulsion.* Museum of Modern Art/Film Stills Archive.

avenger to that of a meek victim—she sits in a slip in the employees' dressing room as her friend Bridget tries to comfort her and finally succeeds in getting her to laugh by retelling a scene from Chaplin's *The Gold Rush* (not a scene which is without "tendency," however; in it the other starving miner envisions Charlie as a chicken and wants to eat him). We feel relief until Bridget goes to retrieve Carol's purse for her and the purse falls open to reveal—the rotting severed head of the rabbit! The shocking motif on the soundtrack again accompanies the image to produce a *nightmare* effect (a sequence of unexpected images culminating in a graphic naturalistic detail).

Thus, against a continuing background of actual and symbolic harassment, Carol's dementia emerges. Her victimization has been suggested strongly enough for us to feel a certain sympathy; to a degree we are on her side in the violent acts she perpetrates. Polanski builds tension skillfully by having Carol's madness manifest itself first in small ways which might be overlooked. After seeing Michael in the bathroom shaving, she brushes her hand frantically across the front of her nightgown, as if she is trying to rid herself of some contamination. She responds to Bridget's story of being mistreated by a man by trying to brush some imaginary substance from the chair in which Bridget was sitting. Later, this sort of gesture reappears as a mannerism involving brushing her fingers across her nose in a compulsive manner. It is a visual expression of Carol's sense of being violated or sullied and often follows her encounters with men.

Carol's madness accelerates after Colin offers her a ride home and kisses her without any invitation to do so. Carol abruptly dashes out of the car (she is almost hit by oncoming traffic) and races up to her apartment where she frantically brushes her teeth. Thus, Polanski turns a "stolen kiss" (harmless in terms of the governing male code) into an image of bodily penetration and violation. After Helen and Michael leave on their vacation, Carol is catatonic much of the time. She begins to have more extensive hallucinations; however, many of the images are understood by us to be imaginary *only after* we have experienced them. Their embodiment, for the viewer, is no less graphic and real than any of the other images we see in the film. Since supernatural phenomena as "actual" occurrences within a narrative are a conventional expectation of the horror film, the viewer can never completely dismiss the possibility that the "nightmares" are actually happening. The more mundane and naturalistic the image is the more terrifying it is, since, at least for an instant, we receive the image as a "real" event.

The most mundane image in *Repulsion* is arguably its most awful for the viewer. Alone in the apartment, Carol walks into the bedroom, opens the closet door, and looks at her sister's dresses. As she closes the door, a mirror on its front catches the image of a man lurking on the far side of the room (the nightmare music suddenly erupts as well). The man looks something like the worker who accosted Carol on the street; he could be the "crank" caller, who has found a way into her apartment and now is going to attack and rape her. Carol whirls around, she *and we* see that the room is empty—but the realities of a rape have been conveyed to us emotionally with even greater force than if Polanski had made this a "real" event within the story.

Subsequent events in the apartment are only slightly less terrifying. Although we understand that Carol is sick and that she is only imagining these things, the images themselves are graphic embodiments of what actually occurs when a rapist breaks into an apartment in the middle of the night. Carol "imagines" a light under the door (is it to a closet or does it lead to a neighboring apartment?) and pushes a dresser in front of the door to protect herself. Suddenly, the door begins to open, pushing the dresser aside. A man (the man from the street?) enters and grabs Carol by the hair, pushing her face down onto the bed and raping her as she grips the sheets in terror. In the viewer's perception, the naturalistic image of the rape is not a hallucination; the viewer quickly realizes, however, that, in "the story," it is. The relationship of this scene to other intrusive forms of male behavior is confirmed by Polanski's editing; as Carol is seemingly being raped, the phone rings, and she answers it. It is Colin, pursuing her. She doesn't speak to him.

The hallucinations, the bizarre behavior, and the insistent symbolic details continue to build. The potatoes continue to sprout ever more grotesquely. Inexplicably, Carol fills the bathtub with water and allows it to overflow. To sudden crashes, more deep fissures materialize in the walls, which now become organic and alive as well—Carol's hands leave imprints in them as in soft clay.

The film's riveting finale is built by Polanski through a rapid-fire repetition and intensification of previous motifs—with one significant addition: Carol fights back and her violence not only looks real, it is "actual" within the story. A frustrated Colin arrives at the apartment and when Carol refuses to answer his ringing, he backs up and runs down the hallway into the door repeatedly until he breaks it down (so great is his romantic ardor). He is immediately extremely chagrined and apologetic: "I'm sorry . . . I'm sorry. . . . What's the matter? I had to see you, that's all. I've been so miserable without you. I phoned and phoned. The ringing nearly drove me mad. Is it something I've done? . . . Carol, please tell me."

As Colin was bursting through the door, Carol had picked up a large metal candlestick, which she now holds behind her back. Noticing that a nosy neighbor with a dog is watching the drama unfold, Colin pushes the door closed again. Just as he does this, Carol rushes forward and repeatedly beats him on the head with the candlestick. He falls and we watch Carol's blows from a low angle (Colin's point of view, although he is probably no longer conscious); blood splashes around us—Polanski effectively puts the viewer in the position of the male victim.

Carol's behavior in the aftermath of this murder resembles more the typical moves of the pathological killer in a horror thriller. She boards up the door of the apartment, and deposits Colin's body in the filled bathtub. But she does all of this in a trancelike state and in a very haphazardly sloppy manner. Humming to herself, she sits calmly in the living room chair, doing some sewing and mending. Within the expectations of the horror genre, we are now ready for the next "innocent" victim to arrive. Instead Polanski gives us another, almost systematic, reprise of the prior set of symbolic images—the rotting rabbit; the razor on the plate; the buzzing; another "imaginary" rapist who suddenly appears in Carol's bed as she is about to climb in (he tears her clothes off and lies on top of her as she struggles; this rape is even more graphic than the previous one).

Colin, of course, had not attempted to rape Carol, but his basic assumptions and actions bear some relation to these awful visions—he not only broke through Carol's door into her apartment (a clear violation of her space), but he somehow assumed that his own feelings and desires gave him a right to do so. Carol's next visitor, the landlord, is a much more explicit exploiter of women. He has angrily come to collect the back rent, which Helen had left in an envelope for Carol to bring to him (of course, Carol had not done this). Polanski links the landlord's visit visually to rape. First, the ringing of the doorbell interrupts the most vivid of the "fantasized" rape scenes noted above. The camera cuts quickly to the door and then back to the now empty bed. As it slides back across the room, it reveals Carol lying facedown, nude, on the floor, with only a blanket draped across her buttocks (this is the most explicit shot of physical nudity in the film;

the only time Deneuve does not wear at least a nightgown). As Carol walks down the corridor, the wall grows hands and clutches at her breast. A woman calls on the phone and tells Carol she is a "filthy little tart"; Carol cuts the phone wire with the razor. The doorbell rings again, and when no one comes to answer it, the landlord pushes his way in.

He begins by berating Carol about the unpaid rent and the obvious damage to the apartment, but after Carol hands him the envelope with the money his interest shifts to the young, sexually attractive woman and her obvious disorientation and helplessness. Carol sits on the couch with her legs uncrossed and her slip hiked up almost to her crotch—the camera is positioned directly in front of those legs, Polanski again putting the viewer in the position of "voyeur" and co-exploiter with the landlord. The landlord becomes more solicitous (he notices the rotting rabbit and throws it in the trash) and begins to make sexual advances ("Your sister's gone away, hasn't she? You must be a bit lonely, I expect. There's no need to be alone you know. Poor little girl, all shaking like a poor frightened animal. . . . There's no need to be frightened of me . . . I could be a very good friend to you. You look after me and you can forget about the rent," he says as he lunges onto her and begins to pull up her nightgown). As he tries to kiss her, Carol reaches behind his head and slashes his neck with the razor. In the frenzy of slashing which follows, with blood flowing all over, we are, in part, sympathizing with Carol, acting in self-defense *not only* against this one attacker but against *all* the sexual aggression which has been directed against her in the film, literally and symbolically, and in "nightmares" rendered so naturalistically that they are indistinguishable from reality.

Polanski ends *Repulsion* with a reprise and a coda. A dozen hands now reach out from the elongated corridor walls to grab at Carol. The apartment grows deeper and womblike (to achieve this effect, not only was a wide-angle lens used, but the set itself was rebuilt to change its size and geometry). Carol puts on lipstick, garishly, goes to bed, and is raped by another "imaginary" intruder. Finally, Helen and Michael return and (after further scenes where we anticipate violence; it does not occur) Michael carries the limp Carol down the stairs to an ambulance, as if she were a little girl.

As the camera scours the debris of the empty apartment, Polanski, with his characteristic sense of closure, returns to an unexplicated set of images. The film had begun with a close-up of Carol's eye. Later, the camera had twice panned around the bedroom and settled on a framed family photograph showing two middle-aged couples, with their dog and (presumably) their two daughters, sitting on the patio of an aristocratic home. The younger daughter, perhaps eleven or twelve, is blond, and the camera had previously isolated her. It does this again, now moving in to give us an extreme close-up of her face; it is the young Carol we see with a fixed stare, catatonic and intense. What are we to make of this ending? We might conclude that Carol's obsessive fear of sex and of men has legitimate origin in her childhood. There are two men in the photo, both men in their late forties or fifties—one certainly her father, the other perhaps a relative or a

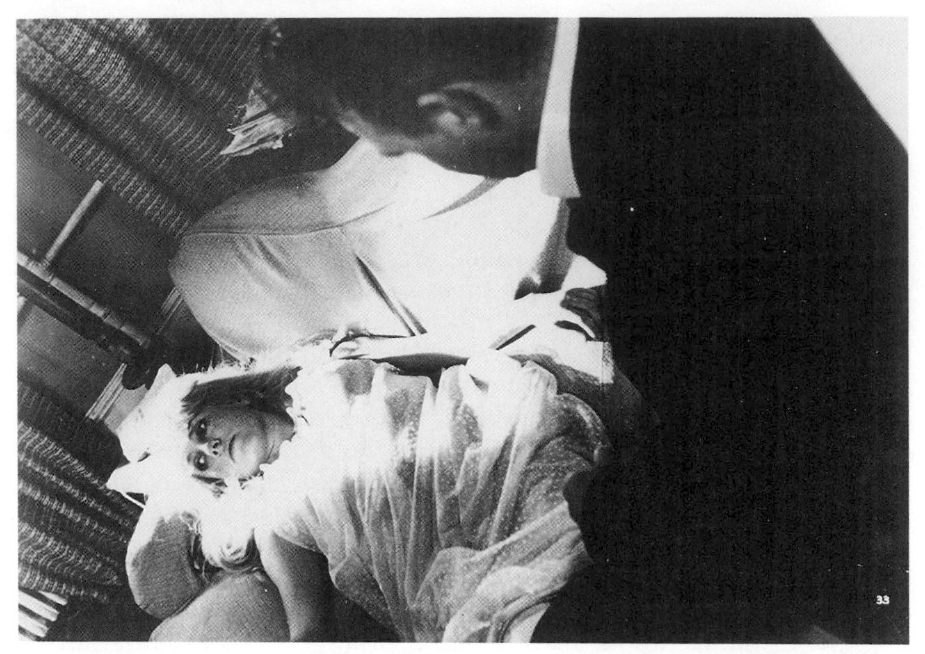

3.6. As the landlord begins his rape of Carol, the spectator is placed in a voyeuristic position by the camera. *Repulsion.* Museum of Modern Art/Film Stills Archive.

close family acquaintance. Is this where the sexual aggression against Carol began? An experience of incest or sexual molestation in childhood is not only suggested here but inscribed in Carol's simultaneously childlike and sexual image throughout the film. The motifs of male dominance, incest, and the rebellion of female victims against male power were to become dominant in Polanski's two most successful and well-known American films, *Rosemary's Baby* and *Chinatown.*

Rosemary's Baby

As soon as he had read Ira Levin's novel, Polanski embraced enthusiastically the proposal that he direct the film version of *Rosemary's Baby* (1968). The story itself had enormous potential for expressing the director's characteristic interests in the banality of evil, its inherent presence in human nature and in human sexuality in particular, the slippery interface between victim and victimizer, and the malevolent power of the patriarchy.

Polanski inherited the project from producer William Castle, who had originally wanted to direct it but was convinced by Paramount executive Robert Evans to place it in Polanski's hands. In turn, Polanski had to agree to bring Ira Levin's highly successful novel to the screen with a minimum of changes.[12] This turned out to be no problem, as Polanski found the dialogue excellent, the narrative pacing crisp, and the potential for visualizing the imagery great. As in *Repulsion,* it was Polanski's tendency to make the supernatural as realistic as possible. That Levin's novel dealt with the supernatural would be well known to many viewers, even those who had only heard of the novel or seen the pre-film press clippings ("Pray for Rosemary's Baby"), which insinuated the presence of *real* demonic forces in the narrative. Hence, the existence of supernatural agents *per se* could not in itself be the central question which the plot would resolve. Polanski constructed and filmed the "supernatural" events in such a way that they had possible plausible explanations and thus made Rosemary's efforts to convince anyone else of her suspicions difficult.

When Rosemary Woodhouse and her husband Guy are contemplating renting an apartment at the elegant Bramford building, they are taken on a tour by the building's manager. The apartment is large but dark and cluttered (still containing the furniture of its now deceased former occupant), and a large bureau has been recently shifted to bar access to a closet. When Guy and the manager push the bureau back to its former spot and open the closet, they find linen and a vacuum cleaner. There is, of course, nothing particularly unusual about a piece of furniture having been shifted, for whatever reason. However, Polanski films the corridor, with the massive wooden monolith of the bureau looming before us and blocking further access, in such a way as to make it appear sinister.

Hutch (an old friend of Rosemary's) tells the couple of the Bramford's history of grisly murders and of rumors of witchcraft. While this story is being told, Hutch is serving (and then all three characters are eating) a juicy leg of lamb. Polanski matches the eating of the lamb to the moment when Hutch is telling of the notorious Trent sisters, who murdered and ate children. By using this visual detail (which Polanski himself added; lamb is not served for dinner in the novel), the director evokes such associations as "lamb of God" and thus suggests a "black" ritual in which the typical Christian symbolism is perversely inverted.

This is Polanski's dominant narrative strategy in the early part of the film; he mixes perfectly mundane events and everyday characters with symbolic details (most of them, in fact, taken from the novel) of an ominous nature. Thus, for example, the Woodhouse's neighbors (whose apartment adjoins theirs, the two having at one time been a large ten-room apartment), Roman and Minnie Castevet, are an eccentric but friendly old couple. Roman Castevet (Polanski did not choose the character's first name, it is in the novel) is very grandfatherly and solicitious, with an old-world gentility and charm; Minnie is excessively nosy, with a grating New York accent, but she too seems very good-hearted. In the building's laundry room, Rosemary meets a young woman, Terry, a former down-and-out drug addict, taken off the streets and rehabilitated by the Castevets, with whom she now lives. They talk, among other things, of their dislike of the spooky basement, and Terry shows Rosemary a good luck charm given her by the Castevets: a lovely silver filigree sphere on a silver chain, the sphere containing a green substance which gives off an unpleasantly pungent odor. Polanski gives us a close-up of the amulet, thus using this commonplace cinematic convention to put us on alert as to the sphere's future significance in the plot and/or the symbolic meanings it may acquire (this is the same kind of treatment he gave to the knife and the razor in the films we have discussed above). When, in the next sequence, Terry "commits suicide" (the police's conclusion; she left a note) by jumping from the Castevets' window, we are given a close-up of her head and torso, lying in a particularly large pool of blood (another visual image created in the film, at variance with the description in the novel). Roman and Minnie may seem to us a bit too perfunctory in their grief, and when they later give Rosemary the silver talisman as a present, we suspect they may be witches.

Thus, the central questions for the viewer become: Will Rosemary realize the danger she is in and act to defend herself? Will she be able to convince others that there is an evil conspiracy afoot? Will she be able to save herself and (later) her baby? Polanski manages to prolong tension with regard to all of these questions, in part by placing the genuinely sinister images *inside* Rosemary's dreams (essentially the strategy of Levin's novel as well). Thus, she herself is uncertain of the reality of witchcraft, and she is in a weak position trying to convince others that she is in danger on the basis of "nightmares."

Polanski's visual versions of Rosemary's dreams are even more fragmentary than the novel's corresponding texts, and thus more surreal. The dreams contain imagery central to the film's semantics on a number of planes (in particular, the conflation of religion and violation). After eating part of a chocolate mousse brought over by Minnie (Minnie calls it her chocolate "mouse," a typical malapropism for her), Rosemary becomes dizzy and Guy puts her to bed. Polanski's realization of the important dream which follows is vaguer and its visual elements more shocking than Levin's corresponding verbal description.

Rosemary is on a bed, floating on the sea. She sits on the deck of a ship, bare-breasted. But suddenly she has a bikini on and she is on a cruise ship with some of her friends and man who looks like Jack Kennedy. Next she is lying in a small boat and someone is pulling off her clothes. Someone pulls off her wedding band. She is lying on a painter's scaffold, being raised toward the ceiling of the Sistine Chapel. Hutch shouts to her in the midst of a typhoon, although he seems to be in an oil field (there is a rig behind him). On the deck of the ship again, Rosemary walks naked toward a black sailor at the wheel. She is ordered by him to go below deck. In a dark chamber, Rosemary passes a burning church in the distance. She lies naked on a bed, surrounded by other naked people (*we* recognize Roman, Minnie, the building manager, other neighbors, and Guy in this group). Roman bisects her body with a brush dipped in red and draws symbols on it. When Guy protests that Rosemary is awake, Minnie assures him that this is impossible after Rosemary has eaten the chocolate "mouse." Rosemary complains of being bitten by a mouse. A woman descends a stairway; she looks like Jacqueline Kennedy. She tells Rosemary that she should have her legs tied down in case of convulsions. Rosemary agrees and two men tie her legs to the bedposts with sheets. Roman's ritual painting having been completed, Guy's face appears over Rosemary, but it is very hairy (with something of a "werewolf" quality). A scaley, reptilian hand slides down Rosemary's side, along her hips, down her legs. Now she sees over her, not Guy's face, but the piercing eyes and animal-like face of a Devil. As the Devil is having intercourse with Rosemary, she looks passive and uninvolved. The Pope appears before her in his mitre and she asks him if she can be forgiven. "Oh, absolutely," says the Pope. "You have been bitten by a mouse. We wouldn't want you to jeopardize your health."

This dream could obviously be subjected to "Freudian" analysis. Its details come from recent experience (Guy and Rosemary had intended to have sex that night and "make a baby"; the apartment's basement is dark and forbidding; Minnie's chocolate "mouse" tasted unpleasant; Rosemary has recently watched the Pope's visit to Yankee Stadium on TV, etc.). Its latent content could be seen as deriving from a Catholic girl's guilt at recognizing her own sexual desires. Were Rosemary to tell this dream to a professional, she would be assured of its non-supernatural nature. Guy even gives her an explanation for the long scratches on her flanks: he made love to her after she had passed out in order not to miss their baby-making opportunity. He, too, was drunk (they had had cocktails and wine), was overly rough, and had forgotten to trim his finger nails.

But this is only one way the audience makes sense of the dream. Because the dream imagery is photographically actual (unlike a description in a novel), the viewer is more inclined to believe that these events actually occurred—that Guy must have joined the coven of witches and that his explanations are only a cover-up. The underlying meaning of the scene in the novel also comes across more viscerally—we have seen what looks like an actual rape. It was a rape of a wife by her husband. *Rosemary's Baby* has underlying semantics which bring it very close indeed to *Repulsion,* another probable reason for the novel's immediate appeal to Polanski.

The mystery aspects of the plot of *Rosemary's Baby* become quite involved, too involved to be described here in detail. Another important character is introduced, Dr. Sapirstein, an extremely competent Jewish pediatrician, recommended by the Castevets and trusted by Guy, who assures Rosemary that the very unusual and painful aspects of her pregnancy are normal. We ultimately manage to figure out that Guy has "sold his soul to the Devil" in exchange for the promise of a successful career as an actor (he has all kinds of good fortune, at the expense of another actor who inexplicably goes blind, *after* the night of the strange dream). When Hutch finds a book on witchcraft and tries to get it to Rosemary, he falls into a coma and eventually dies.

At Hutch's funeral, Rosemary is given the book, which Hutch had left for her with the message "it is an anagram." Playing with various possibilities, using the letters from her Scrabble game, Rosemary discovers that the letters in Roman Castavet rearrange to spell the name Steven Marcato, the son of

3.7. Rosemary (Mia Farrow), knife in hand, approaches the cradle of her child Adrian, son of the Devil. *Rosemary's Baby.* Museum of Modern Art/Film Stills Archive.

Adrian Marcato, a warlock who lived in the Bramford at the turn of the century. Indeed, Roman is exactly the age that Steven would be. Finally, Rosemary is firmly convinced that her awful suspicions of witchcraft are correct. The plot's initial questions resolved, Polanski turns us toward two more potentially horrific ones: Will the witches obtain Rosemary's baby and sacrifice it in a bloody ritual, as Rosemary fears? What will the baby be like? (These were the questions which the pre-publicity campaign suggested with the admonition: "Pray for Rosemary's baby.") Rosemary is sedated by Dr. Sapirstein, after trying to escape from the coven (this is another sequence which visually resembles a rape); she goes into labor, but we never see the baby. Later, Sapirstein and Guy tell her that the baby died, but that she is fine and will be able to have others. Rosemary's solicitous neighbors help her during her convalescence, but she grows suspicious about what they are doing with the milk she expresses using a breast pump, and she hears a baby's cries from the other side of the partition.

At the film's climax, Rosemary arises from her sickbed, grabs a large kitchen knife, and makes her way through a hidden passage in the closet into the Castavets' apartment. There she encounters a party in progress (in its symbolism, as we shall see, it is a comic "black" inversion of the Adoration of the Magi). Roman is kindly as ever, asking her if she will not consent to

3.8. Rosemary, who wears miniskirts throughout the early part of the film—making her look both childlike and sexually desirable—is shown here with husband Guy (John Cassavetes) and neighbor Terry (Angela Dorian). *Rosemary's Baby.* Museum of Modern Art/Film Stills Archive.

be a real mother to her baby. Rosemary approaches the dark blue cradle, knife in hand, and together with her we get a momentary (almost subliminal) glimpse of the baby's intense animal-like yellow eyes. Rosemary is horrified, but she cannot kill her baby. Overcome by the adoration being lavished on the child by all the guests, some of whom have come from other parts of the world, she tacitly consents to be the child's mother and begins to rock the cradle—as the film ends and its lullaby theme comes up on the soundtrack.

In realizing the film version of *Rosemary's Baby,* Polanski exhibits the same shrewdness in typecasting and skill with visual symbolism we have noted in his earlier films (only here he did not have to invent the symbolism, most of which was explicitly given in the novel.) The young Mia Farrow had a distinct air of girlish innocence and incipient sexuality. Polanski enhanced this by dressing her in miniskirts, and progressively raising the hemline during the first part of the film. This made Rosemary appear increasingly childlike and manipulable, but at the same time increasingly an object of (our) sexual interest. The simultaneous escalation of both sexuality and innocence was crucial to the film's thematic development. Polanski also utilized his own relationship with the actress to advantage; Farrow, not yet a star, took Polanski's acting instructions willingly and eagerly, an attitude which paralleled her tendency to accept the advice and control of the older male characters in the narrative.

The principal male characters are typecast in just the opposite direction. John Cassavetes (as Guy), a director in his own right, continually clashed with Polanski about how things should be done, and his mood of egoistic assertiveness transferred to his constant controlling intonation whenever his character and Farrow's Rosemary disagreed. Sidney Blackmer brought to the role of Roman Castevet a deep voice, friendly but strong, piercing eyes, and a habit of taking lengthy pauses in his speech—as if weighing the effect of each word. Ralph Bellamy (Dr. Sapirstein) brought with him the scientific authority associated with his prior roles in film and television. Finally, Ruth Gordon's Minnie had all of the controlling instincts of a New York middle-class matron—nagging, cajoling, but always determined to be right and to get her own way.

The film's symbolism is oriented toward a demonic characterization of both the setting and the protagonists. Besides the cavernous corridors and hallways and the frequent shadows (Polanski did not physically alter the sets as he did in *Repulsion*, but achieved similar effects cinematographically), Polanski foregrounded the color red, in particular emphasizing its association with blood. Beginning with the bloody lamb roast at Hutch's dinner and the large red pool of blood around Terry's body, Polanski gives us other "red" liquids. When the Woodhouses first visit the Castevets, Roman serves them as cocktails "vodka blush," and their expression when they drink it suggests that it might be flavored with something odd (Roman wears a red shirt in this scene as well). Guy's invitation to Rosemary ("Let's make a baby") is accompanied by a bouquet of red roses. After she becomes pregnant, Rosemary loves red, too. She wears red often, cuts and eats nearly raw steak, and, while preparing dinner, absentmindedly chews a raw chicken liver she has just removed. Rosemary learns from her reading that witches use babies' blood in their rituals, an additional link between the color and her pregnancy. When, at the film's finale, Rosemary picks up a kitchen knife and intends to use it, perhaps on her own demonic child, her joining of the fellowship of blood is prefigured. The symbolism of blood is consistently linked to actual associations of a woman's blood with her sexual initiation and her reproductive potential.

White is also evident as an important symbolic color, used to link Rosemary's pregnancy to death. Ira Levin's choice of his character's name is particularly apt, inasmuch as "rose" is a mixture of red and white (the reason for "Mary" becomes explicit at the film's finale). White is the color of the organic potion which Minnie Castevet (on Dr. Sapirstein's orders) makes for Rosemary while she is pregnant. Soon Rosemary begins to look almost as chalky as the drink, with dark circles around her eyes emphasizing the whiteness of her face and making her look distinctly skeletal.

There is a great deal of symbolism which is explicitly sexual or religious, and these two levels are clearly linked to the film's major themes. As noted above, Rosemary's skirts become progressively more revealing, and there are a number of shots in which we see her from the waist down—reduced to eroticized parts with the viewer placed in "voyeuristic" positions as in *Repulsion.* It is after one such sequence that she says to Guy: "Let's make love." What follows is one of the film's erotic sequences—Rosemary and Guy take off their clothes as we watch; in her case the scene has a "striptease" effect. (This scene was erotic enough that Cassavetes objected to doing "a skin flick" and kept his jockey shorts on; Farrow allowed her body to be completely visible in this sequence, as in the later dream sequence.) Polanski clearly wanted Rosemary's body objectified, her sexual allure explicit, and wanted to draw the audience into voyeuristic complicity.

After Guy brings Rosemary roses and arranges a seductive evening, he objectifies her doubly—not only as sexual object, but also as a biological machine for making a baby, one which he intends to give away for his own personal gain. The sexual and economic aspects of woman as fetish and as commodity are simultaneously represented here. The rape dream is particularly graphic with its linkage of sex and bondage. Rosemary has her legs tied down (evoking both sadistic sex and delivery room procedures) and is clawed by an evil man who rapes her. Her expression during intercourse shows no pleasure at all. Yet she does feel guilt, as evidenced by the presence of the Pope in her dream; her religion has taught her that she is the sinner. The rapist is the Devil in the film's supernatural plot, but he is the husband in terms of underlying meanings. When Rosemary says to Guy, "I dreamed someone was raping me," he admits to having intercourse with her while she slept: "It was fun . . . in a necrophile way." Again, sex, pregnancy, and death are linked. Rosemary is deeply offended that Guy could not wait until morning. His use of her as a sexual object and as a procreation machine could not be clearer.

Rosemary's pregnancy is also turned visually into a sadistic assault on her body. It causes her to become emaciated; she has terrible pain in her stomach, like a wire being tightened, she says. Not only Dr. Sapirstein and Guy, but also the young and handsome Dr. Hill from whom she seeks help, restrain her physically and imprison her. The scene of her labor resembles another rape. The coven of witches holds her down on the bed as Dr. Sapirstein injects a sedative with a needle (which we see in close-up).

Polanski not only seeks to implicate us personally, by allowing us to view Farrow's body and its simulated sex acts, and experience pleasure in this, but he also explicitly accuses religion of complicity in the objectification of women (here we recall Polanski's Catholic reeducation in Poland). Nuns and the Pope appear in Rosemary's dreams and do not protest her victimization. When Rosemary is enraptured by the Pope's visit to Yankee Stadium on television, Roman Castevet calls attention to it as a form of idolatry (he, of course, can easily recognize this, since he is the high priest of another religion, so to speak). Rosemary, with her hair cropped very short (she gets a fashionable haircut from Vidal Sasson) and in her maternity dresses, begins to resemble a pregnant nun; a disturbing visual amalgam of thematic motifs.

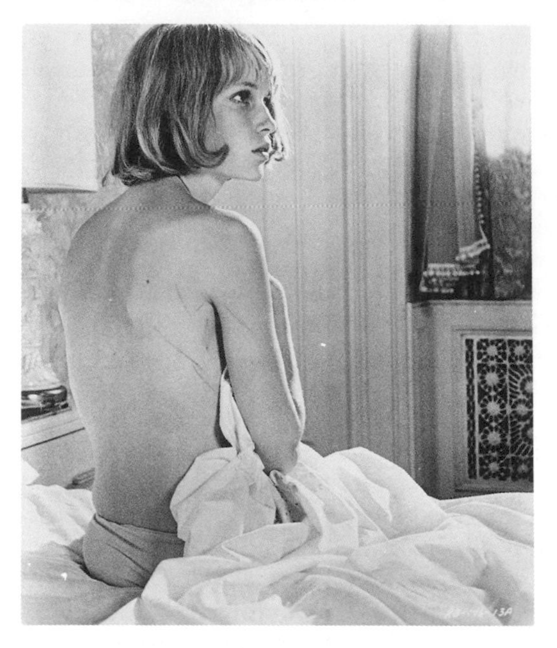

3.9. The morning after the nightmare, Rosemary's body shows scratches inflicted by her rapist (the Devil or her husband). *Rosemary's Baby.* Museum of Modern Art/Film Stills Archive.

The music which accompanies the increasingly diabolical events is discordant—but its melodic origins are religious chants and church choir hymns (Rosemary also hears this music when she looks at a crèche in a department store Christmas display).

Rosemary deciphers verbal clues the way a cabalist would play with numerical values of letters to discover hidden meanings in the Bible. In addition to spelling out Roman Castevet, she plays with the title of the book Hutch bequeathed to her ("All of the Witches") to spell out various cryptic messages, including "Comes with the Fall," a phrase which announces a Second Coming not of grace but of sin. As noted above, the film's final sequence is a complete parody of the birth of Christ and the Adoration of the Magi. As the baby lies in the draped cradle, complete with sign of the inverted cross, the modestly dressed witches stir around the Castevets' drawing room like so many admiring shepherds. Emissaries from abroad include a Japanese tourist who is continually snapping pictures and one Giran Stavropolis, a Greek who resembles an aristocratic vampire and a doting relative from the old country at the same time. To Rosemary's awful cry when she sees the baby—"What have you done to its eyes?"—Roman Castevet replies: "Satan is his father, not Guy. His name is Adrian. He shall redeem the despised and wreak vengeance in the name of the burned and the tortured! God is dead. Satan lives. The year is one." Everything here echoes very closely the Christian texts, even down to their commitment to the downtrodden. The difference between the Kingdom of Good and the Kingdom of Evil is purely illusory. As in much of Polanski's previous work, all human beings are complicit in evil.

Although one cannot credit Polanski alone with these thematic implications in *Rosemary's Baby* (since certain aspects of these themes are Ira Levin's as well), they certainly were in accord with the director's own sentiments and he realized them in a masterful way. His probing of the inherent evils of existence focuses more explictly here on the institutions of the patriarchy (within the family) and the church. This dimension of exposing the hypocrisy of "political" institutions (in the broadest sense of that term) continues in *Macbeth* and *Chinatown*.

Macbeth

Macbeth (1971) is perhaps Polanski's most underappreciated film. Critics made much of Polanski's "bloody" version of Shakespeare's play, seeing it as a cathartic rendering of the director's own personal nightmares and thus as a somewhat spurious distortion of Shakespeare's original. From others came complaints about Polanski's abbreviations of speeches, omissions of scenes, and rearrangement of the order of particular monologues; symptoms, they felt, of a diminution of the play's intellectual content. None of these observations are entirely unfounded, but these aspects of Polanski's approach should be examined in the light of the structural strategies he had employed in earlier films. Polanski saw *Macbeth*'s world as one where evil triumphs because of the inevitable weakness of human beings and the institutions that prey on that weakness—a continuing thematic approach present in *all* his films. Also, Polanski had used violence, unexpected and graphic, from the very beginning of his career. The director's skill and control are even more remarkable in view of his personal circumstances—it was only a year after Polanski's pregnant wife Sharon Tate and three of his friends had been murdered by the Manson gang.

Polanski places Shakespeare's play in a meticulously naturalistic setting (for example, King Duncan's retinue, as guests of Macbeth, sleep in a dirt-floor courtyard among piles of hay and animals.) In accord with his previous pattern of placing the horrible and the supernatural in the context of the mundane, Polanski attempted to capture a primitiveness and brutality corresponding to the realities of twelfth-century Scotland. Madness, murder, the unfeeling slaughter of human beings—all of these are undeniably key elements of Shakespeare's play. This Polanski appreciated viscerally and personally, not only because of the recent murder of his wife and friends, but as a result of his childhood experiences in Krakow. He knew this violence, murder, and blood to be *real* parts of the world and he felt that their depiction (although running counter to the theatrical conventions of Shakespeare's time) would enhance the work's effect as a cinematic piece. In all, there is much less blood and gore in Polanski's film than in many contemporaneous American films, but critics reacted to such an egregiously emotional and primitive handling of what was the property of intellectual high culture, usually distanced from such direct affectual devices. The strong reaction to these moments of violence is, in part, testimony to their effectiveness within Polanski's design for the film.

The director certainly felt the cinematic work to be his own creation, based on Shakespeare's masterpiece. By omitting nearly one-third of Shakespeare's verbal text and by introducing via visual action new themes and motifs not present in Shakespeare's story, Polanski and his co-scenarist Kenneth Tynan[13] behaved as Polanski had previously in working with scripts written by others. In his own view, Polanski restructured *Macbeth* in order to make it more effective cinematically; the only constraint on him was that he could not alter the *words* of the characters' speeches. He *could*, however, inflect their meanings by omissions or rearrangements, and by placing them in unusual visual contexts. And this he did throughout.

Of course, Polanski bends *Macbeth* to his own purposes, toward his own characteristic themes: the underlying evil of the world and the apparent role of fate in guaranteeing that evil; the rape of innocence and the inevitable collaboration of the innocent in their own destruction. That the world is an evil place, governed by violence and crudity, is the background impression given by Polanski's mise-en-scène. The opening shot looks toward a sunrise over low hills, but the yellow light quickly fades over grey mud flats. The first image to break into this dull emptiness is a twisted serpentine rod; it draws a circle in the mud and three witches (Shakespeare's "weird sisters"), one wielding the stick, plunge down and dig a hole in the mud into which they place first a knife, then a noose, and finally a human arm severed just below the elbow. The knife is placed in the severed hand by the oldest of the witches, a withered crone who has no eyes or eye sockets. After anointing this burial with spit and a vial of blood, the witches depart across the mud flat.

The imagery of the opening brands the witches as agents of violence and murder (the crooked staff, the knife, the noose, the severed limb), an implication only vaguely present in Shakespeare's lines which they recite ("When shall we three meet again? / In thunder, lightening, or in rain? / When the hurly burly's done, / When the battle's lost and won"). Brutality immediately springs from the supernatural to the film's *natural* world. Before the noble King Duncan has recited his first words, we hear,through a dense fog which renders all invisible, the clang of swords, neighing of horses, and screams. As the smoke lifts, one of Duncan's soldiers moves among the fallen on the mud flats. Finding a man who is still alive, he immediately bludgeons him with a crushing blow of a mace into his back. Only then does Duncan appear in his crown to hear, from another bloodied soldier, a report on the victorious outcome against the Norwegians and the traitorous Thane of Cawdor. In the film, the everyday violence of warfare and execution is never out of sight for very long.

Polanski made every effort to convey authenticity in background detail, costumes, and actions. He filmed in three actual castles and filled their courtyards with typical work activities and games. These included, notably, the cruel sport of bear-baiting. Women and children join in tormenting a caged bear with sticks before it is to be torn apart by hounds for the amusement of the spectators. As we have seen, this realism is particularly important in all of Polanski's embodiments of the world as evil. He wants

3.10. During the opening sequence of *Macbeth*, a severed arm is buried by the three witches, the oldest a crone with no eyes. *Macbeth.* Museum of Modern Art/Film Stills Archive.

to impress upon the viewer that evil of supernatural and apocalyptic proportions exists everywhere in the quotidian world we inhabit. Except in the sequences marked explicitly as supernatural, stylization is avoided. Polanski's decision to render the greater part of all of the play's soliloquies in voice-over narration (which we hear as we follow the facial expressions of the protagonists and watch the action with them, from their viewpoint) is also motivated by a desire not to disrupt realism by having the characters so clearly address the audience. Instead, we interpret these soliloquies as the protagonists' inner thoughts, even when they occasionally switch to actual speech for a few lines (as if the speaker was musing to himself or herself). In sharp contrast to this realistic treatment are the supernatural sequences, where characters react to and talk to ghosts as if they actually see them.

Throughout the film, Polanski's choice of visual imagery has clear function, as do the action sequences added in their entirety by the director. Whereas the Thane of Cawdor is only referred to in Shakespeare's play, Polanski builds an important series of images around him. Duncan encounters him captured and bleeding, tied to a sledge. With his sword, Duncan removes from around the neck of this robustly handsome and muscular man a heavy chain necklace and amulet—the noble vestment of a thane. The very weight and crudeness of this sign of nobility serve, in every subsequent occurence, to remind us of the basis of political power in violence. Later, a sequence of the execution of the Thane of Cawdor is added by Polanski. Defiantly he stands before the castle wall, a metal collar around his neck, fastened to chains running to four soldiers who stand symmetrically around him. The emphasis on the muscularity and the upright stature of the rebellious nobleman is reminiscent of Sergei Eisenstein's treatment of the execution of the noble Kolichev family in *Ivan the Terrible* (a film from which, as we shall see, Polanski may have borrowed a number of visual motifs).

For his execution, the thane mounts a scaffolding on the castle walls and leaps to his death after boldly proclaiming "Long live the king." His metal-collared neck snaps with an audible crack as the chain breaks his fall. Thus does Polanski amplify and illustrate Shakespeare's lines referring to Cawdor's execution: "Nothing in his life / Became him like the leaving of it, he died / As one that had been studied in his death, / To throw away the dearest thing he ow'd / As 'twere a careless trifle." When Macbeth is later presented with the chain necklace and amulet which Cawdor wore, we appreciate in Macbeth the same potential for courage and the steel nerves we saw in the former thane. Macbeth's acceptance of violence and his ability to withstand violence are a part of the hero's dual personality, a part which his symbolic linkage to the former Thane of Cawdor underscores. Even the very first shot of Macbeth in the film shows a grave, shadowed, even tormented face in the foreground of the shot, while in the background we see traitors being hanged.

All of the play's violence is rendered visually and realistically by Polanski. There is no question that this technique makes the murders in *Macbeth* palpable and emotionally wrenching, rather than merely an abstract reference to evil (arguably, the murders in a traditional stage production, already familiar to the audience, lose much of the ability to produce *affect*). When Macbeth kills Duncan, he pulls back the king's covers, trembling and hesitating. Only when Duncan suddenly awakens does Macbeth spring into action, stabbing him six or seven times in a nearly sexual frenzy of blows to the chest and stomach as he straddles Duncan's body. Finally, Macbeth places the point of the dagger against the flesh of Duncan's neck. Although we do not see the blade point thrusting into the neck (a rapid cut away to Duncan's falling crown ensues instead), the image of steel against actual flesh is perhaps the most horrific moment in the sequence. It recalls a similar close-up on the neck of Kolichev the Wise as it is about to be severed in Eisenstein's film.

Most of the subsequent murders are treated in a similarly graphic way. Either we see bodies stabbed and the resulting spurts of blood, or we see shots of slaughter or dismemberment (this is the case with Duncan's grooms, decapitated by Macbeth, and with Lady Macduff's children, butchered by Macbeth's murderous band). The ultimate act is the most graphic. When Macbeth is beheaded by Macduff at the end of their battle, his head falls from a parapet as his truncated neck spurts a stream of blood. Polanski's graphic depiction of the *actual* violence is not heavily stylized (slow motion and superimpositions are reserved, instead, for the dreams and hallucinations). The graphic shots of Macduff's slaughtered children make his speech upon learning of their deaths even more heartrending because we have seen the brutality of those murders.

If Macbeth and Lady Macbeth are marked by an acceptance of violence and cruelty, there is a softer side of the protagonists as well, and this vulnerablity (cf. Lady Macbeth's reference to "th' milk of human kindness" in her husband's personality) Polanski embodies by visual means as well—youth, nakedness, softness of gesture. In particular, in her first sequence, when the young, beautiful Lady Macbeth, with her flowing auburn hair and pale blue dress, receives a letter from Macbeth telling her of the witches' prophecy and its partial fulfillment, Lady Macbeth's girlish pride in and love for her husband is emphasized. She strokes the hair of her pet dogs as she thinks admiringly of her husband, and Macbeth himself embraces these dogs in the joyous scene of his arrival at Inverness Castle.

In casting the roles of Macbeth and Lady Macbeth, Polanski chose young actors (Jon Finch and Francesca Annis) with particularly delicate features. Annis's long hair and fair complexion, the pitch of her voice and her studied gestures, evoke the displays of the "flower children" of the 1960s. In the early sequences, Lady Macbeth's cruelest admonitions to her husband (e.g., ". . . bear welcome in your eye, / Your hand, your tongue: look like th' innocent flower, / But be the serpent under 't . . .") are delivered as the young couple are seen in intimate embrace and tender kisses. Visually, these could be sweet nothings whispered by lovers. Innocence and evil are fused—one carried by visual imagery, the other by verbal text.

Polanski alternates the modes of innocence and violence by cross-cutting between them. This motivates most of his displacements of Shakespeare's scenes and speeches. Cinema makes possible a much more frequent and dramatic confrontation between scenes taking place in different locales at the same time. Polanski takes advantage of this to create juxtapositions which the need for set changes would render very difficult on stage. Thus, Lady Macbeth's almost childish joy at Inverness while she reads of the witches' prophecy in Macbeth's letter is cross-cut with Macbeth's expression of envy and hatred as he hears, at Dunsinane Castle, Duncan pronounce his son Malcolm "Prince of Cumberland" and heir to the throne.

In Shakespeare's play, it is Macbeth who is tormented by his conscience, both before and after the murder of Duncan. Lady Macbeth is much tougher and more resolute; she reenters Duncan's chamber to place the daggers in the hands of his grooms, whom she has previously drugged (Macbeth cannot bring himself to reenter the chamber). She replies to Macbeth's anguished cry that "all great Neptune's oceans" cannot wash the blood from his hands with the straightforward: "A little water clears us of this deed: / How easy it is then!" In contrast, there is an almost childlike innocence in Polanski's representation of Lady Macbeth's acceptance of violence, as if she does not appreciate its meaning (here a connection with

3.11. Departing from convention, Polanski portrayed Macbeth (Jon Finch) and Lady Macbeth (Francesca Annis) as relatively young lovers. *Macbeth.* Museum of Modern Art/Film Stills Archive.

the young women in Manson's cult group does suggest itself). Indeed, Polanski's portrayal of Lady Macbeth's childlike quality, completely at odds with the violence of the actions she encourages, motivates the sudden change in her personality at the end of the play (her madness) more convincingly than does Shakespeare's text.

Once Macbeth and Lady Macbeth have committed the murder of Duncan, its logic (to ensure that not only Macbeth but his *seed* as well will be kings) necessitates the further killings of Banquo and of Macduff's family. The villany of Macbeth and his lady is balanced, however, by the evocation of an essential human innocence. No matter how criminal their acts, they now seem victims of an inevitable fate which they cannot escape. After Macbeth had been tortmented by Banquo's ghost, Lady Macbeth attempts to soothe him, caressing his face as she speaks to him in a soft voice. He, in turn, kisses her cheek tenderly and strokes her face. The gestural language designed by Polanski in these scenes is appropriate for innocent victims rather than murderers.

The theme of nudity also links Lady Macbeth with the victims of the murders ordered by her husband. Before the murder of her family, Lady Macduff is talking jestingly with her young son (a boy of about ten) as she pours water over him in a tub. The male frontal nudity of this boy drew objections from the critics, but Polanski uses it to embody the boy's non-threatening pluck—his genitals are small and vulnerable, unprotected by pubic hair. This image increases the pathos of his courageous resistance to his murderer, who answers a kick in the shins by stabbing the boy in the chest. After this, the camera follows the fleeing Lady Macduff past a scene where a screaming maidservant is being raped by soldiers; Lady Macduff opens a door and we see the naked, bloody bodies of her other children. Only a shot of the burning of Macduff's castle at Fife separates this nakedness and murder from Lady Macbeth's sleepwalking scene. Polanski insisted on Lady Macbeth's nakedness in this scene in order to link her directly with the previous victims, to show her as a pathetic innocent, her long auburn hair only partially covering her breasts. As she seeks to remove the imagined blood from her hands, rubbing them together frantically, her nakedness appears completely asexual, that of an innocent child. Polanski also prepared this moment by inserting an earlier sequence (with no dialogue) in which Lady Macbeth sees a bloodspot appear on her hand and reacts in a crazed manner which evokes the madness of Ophelia. After the childlike Lady Macbeth is put to bed by her maidservant and doctor, she appears again only after her suicide—as a corpse lying defenseless and uncovered in the courtyard while Macbeth fights for his own life.

Macbeth's most famous of speeches ("Out, out brief candle . . ."), on hearing of Lady Macbeth's death by her own hand, is thus given greater meaning by Polanski. The closing lines (". . . it is a tale/Told by an idiot, full of sound and fury,/Signifying nothing") stands here for the absurdity, not only of ambition, but of guilt and innocence itself, in a universe governed by an idiotic random evil which is indifferent to all of these categories.

Polanski's Macbeth may have been inspired by Eisenstein's Ivan the Terrible, a noble ruler who declines into tyranny and must wrestle with his conscience. In parallel to Eisenstein's treatment, Polanski creates a laudatory scene of the coronation of Macbeth as visual counterpoint to Banquo's soliloquy at the end of Act III (which essentially voices Banquo's *suspicions!*). Humble and barefooted, a "pure" looking Macbeth, who resembles Eisenstein's young Ivan, stands on a rock and then is hoisted aloft on a shield as in his hands are placed the orb and sword (the symmetrical placement of these props parallels the orb and sceptre given to Ivan). In spite of his evil deeds, Macbeth retains throughout Polanski's film a certain aura of courage and nobility with which Shakespeare endows him only in the last act. Polanski's treatment emphasizes Macbeth's nobility through the addition of sequences nowhere envisioned in Shakespeare's text. In addition to the above-described coronation, Polanski has Macbeth "think" his soliloquies in noble poses from the tower of his castle, as he watches the movements of his enemies below. His constant sense of his own impending doom ennobles him—he looks into a dying sunrise, the red light reflected in his face, as he solemnly invites the night to "Scarf up the tender eye of pitiful Day."

Polanski elaborates the supernatural aspects of the play's story

3.12. Macbeth strikes a characteristically noble pose as he prepares to spare the life of Macduff (Terrence Bayler). *Macbeth.* Museum of Modern Art/Film Stills Archive.

substantially: expanding the power of each of the weird sisters' appearances through visual imagery, increasing the duration of scenes involving ghosts and apparitions, and creating riveting hallucinations, recalling in their "nightmare logic" the visions in *Repulsion* and *Rosemary's Baby.*

Macbeth's encounter with Banquo's ghost at the banquet (Macbeth knows that his men have already killed Banquo) is filmed with Polanski's particular skill at embodying horror. Invited to sit at a place which appears to him to be filled, Macbeth watches as its occupant, Banquo, turns toward him smiling (the background noise of boisterous revelry goes silent at this point). Macbeth drops his golden chalice (echoing the dropping of his golden crown in an earler dream). Looking again at Banquo, he sees a face all bloodied. As he orders the ghost away, the bloodied Banquo marches steadfastly toward him, now with his eye sockets replaced by vacant flesh ("Thou hast no speculation in those eyes,/Which thou dost glare with"). Macbeth huddles helplessly on the floor, as Lady Macbeth and Ross attempt to create a plausible excuse for his sudden seizure.

Polanski's masterpiece of surreal visions in this film is, however, the sequence of Macbeth's second visit to the weird sisters. Now in the cave he encounters not three, but a coven of nearly twenty naked women, including the eyeless crone, whose stomach protrudes from her skinny frame and sunken chest. The breasts of many of the other middle-aged crones are large and pendulous. Hardly erotic, these masses of flesh threaten to engulf Macbeth in the crowded space of the shot. After the witches have thrown all manner of human and animal body parts into their steaming cauldron,

Macbeth drinks the ugly potion from a golden chalice (an action which is, in itself, a metaphor for his deeds and their aim) and sees an extended vision. First, he sees his own reflection in the cauldron's liquid, suddenly grown limpid, warning him: ". . . beware Macduff,/Beware the Thane of Fife." Then this head grows small and tumbles to infinity in the depth of the shot. Macbeth now sees a newborn babe, and a sequence of two young boys, dressed in noble attire, and then in chain-and-mail armor, who prophesy: ". . . none of woman born/Shall harm Macbeth." Polanski chooses these images to foreshadow the story's future events—the naked newborn babe could be Macduff (". . . from his mother's womb/Untimely ripp'd"), the two boys Banquo's progeny. Next a suit of armor appears—and when Macbeth strikes it with a sword it collapses in a heap. From above the visor of the helmet, a snake crawls—this snake is a metaphorical vision of Macbeth's enemies ("We have scotched the snake, but not killed it").

Then a laughing Malcolm and Donalbain (Duncan's sons) appear to tell Macbeth: "Macbeth shall never vanquish'd be, until/Great Birnam wood to high Dunsinane hill/Shall come against him." They say this mockingly, as if there lies in this a hidden joke of which Macbeth is the butt. The figure of Macbeth himself (as a character in his own nightmarish vision) asks: ". . . shall Banquo's issue ever/Reign in this kingdom?" Pushing through the forest, Macbeth encounters Banquo in royal vestments, seated upon a throne. His crown reflects a light which blinds Macbeth. Banquo shows him a mirror, in which is an image of another Banquo in different royal garb, holding a mirror with yet a third Banquo, and so on, until a final mirror in the series reveals a laughing young Fleance with a crown; then another mirror returns us to the bloodied image of Banquo, laughing jovially at Macbeth. Macbeth swings his sword at this Banquo, but only succeeds in smashing the mirror. Macbeth awakens as water drips on his face in the now empty cave.

Careful examination of this hallucination reveals the way in which it echoes not only the images Shakespeare's lines suggest but also many other visual motifs developed by Polanski in the earlier sections of the film. The dream is a fitting embodiment of Polanski's vision of a world closed and inevitable, in which every detail can be foretold.

Polanski's two most significant changes in the plot of his *Macbeth* also serve to characterize the entire world of twelfth-century Scotland as dominated by evil and treachery. These involve the development of an entirely new subplot about the activities of the nobleman Ross and a change in the play's optimistic *coda* to an extremely pessimistic one. In Shakespeare's version, Ross is a nobleman who initially is Macbeth's vassal, but who is so outraged by Macbeth's villainy that he eventually goes over to the side of Malcolm and Macduff (in this role, he is the most prominent of a number of noblemen who do the same). Purely through brief visual scenes (Polanski *could not* add dialogue), Polanski changes Ross's role entirely—in what is certainly a powerful display of his mastery at creating visual meaning.

First, Polanski makes Ross a background figure in the sequence wherein the murderers sent by Macbeth kill Banquo and attempt to kill Fleance. The fact that Ross observes this scene and does not intervene to prevent the murder clearly implies that as Macbeth's henchman he has come to make sure the murderers do their job properly. As Fleance flees, Banquo—in his last act before he is killed with a blow to the back—shoots an arrow into Ross's horse to prevent him from pursuing Fleance, who rides off. In the next sequence (the murderers' return and their reporting to Macbeth), Ross exchanges knowing glances with his sovereign and then leads the murderers away, under guard, and has them thrown into the dungeon.

These two scenes completely alter our understanding of Ross's visit to Lady Macduff. In Shakespeare's original he comes to tell her of her husband's flight to England to join Malcolm and to explain to her the necessity of this flight; that is, in Shakespeare's version, he is clearly already taking sides against Macbeth out of conscience. Without altering the lines themselves, Polanski makes Ross's speech hypocritical, his visit merely serving the purpose of allaying Lady Macduff's fears. Polanski then shows us Ross riding *out* of the castle just as the murderous party arrives through the same gate. Visually, it is clear that Ross is part of the group sent by Macbeth to carry out this deed. Polanski adds another sequence to show that Ross's later desertion to Malcolm's side is motivated by opportunism and envy, not by conscience. When Lennox flees Macbeth's camp, he throws to Ross his chain necklace and amulet, the symbol of his rank as thane. Ross brings this to Macbeth and Macbeth condemns this flight before the other nobles; holding the amulet, he hesitates in front of Ross, and then places the amulet around the neck of *another* nobleman. We understand Ross's subsequent actions as motivated by his anger at Macbeth for not making *him* a thane (in Shakespeare's version, he is already Thane of Ross).

At the film's finale, Polanski has *Ross* proclaim Malcolm "king of Scotland" (in Shakespeare's original these lines are Macduff's). Immediately afterward, as we see Macbeth's head raised high above the crowd on a pike, the film cuts to a final sequence entirely of Polanski's invention (and, of course, entirely without words). Instead of Shakespeare's coda, a speech from the new King Malcolm announcing an end to tyranny, the return of exiles, and the reestablishment of "honor" and "measure," Polanski gives us a sequence in the rain and fog, at the witches' cave—with the same dissonant sound track which accompanied this milieu earlier. We watch as a lone horseman arrives (as Macbeth did earlier) and walks through the rocks toward the cave. By a close-up of his face and his limp, we recognize Donalbain, Malcolm's younger brother. The film ends as his horse stands alone, waiting for his return from the cave. The implication: Donalbain will hear from the witches a prophecy about his own future power and will thereafter plot the murder of his older brother Malcolm. Because of the evil inside men, and the institutions created to embody that evil, history will repeat itself.

In his version of *Macbeth,* Polanski made the inevitability of evil in the world a consequence of the drive toward partriarchal power. Donalbain must be expected to strive for such power (inasmuch as he is the powerless younger brother), just as Macbeth did. No matter how sensitive or courageous a man is, he is *bound* to become evil as a result of the rules and customs of the patriarchy. Lady Macbeth herself is caught up in the inevitable logic of the system, her delicacy and beauty notwithstanding. She comes to identify completely with her husband's power and is destroyed as a result.

Chinatown

Polanski's expansion of his contemplations of evil to the social and political spheres led to what was to be his most masterful film, *Chinatown* (1974). Two principal factors made the Robert Towne filmscript so ideal for Polanski. First of all, his personal themes of the persecution of the innocent, the victim become the victimizer, and the all-pervasive nature of evil are wedded in this film to a genre (the *film noir* thriller) already richly equipped to represent them. Polanski's insights brought out many meanings inherent in the genre, but not critically examined until after *Chinatown*. Secondly, the film is exceptionally well crafted on all levels—from Robert Towne's intricate yet precisely logical plot and his witty dialogue, to Polanski's conceptions of mise-en-scène and his development of symbolic motifs, to the outstanding acting of Jack Nicholson (detective Jake Gittes), Faye Dunaway (Evelyn Mulwray, the rich "femme fatale"), John Huston (Noah Cross, her wealthy entrepreneur father), and an excellent supporting cast.

In order to understand the intricate workings of Polanski's *Chinatown*, it is necessary to examine the structures (setting, characters, plot) which the genre made available to him. The *film noir* thriller had been a popular genre for over two decades when Polanski made *Chinatown*. Its conventions were well known, and these genre conventions shaped expectations on both the formal and the semantic levels. The elements of Robert Towne's filmscript and of Polanski's direction accorded with these expectations in many respects, but also involved some shocking turns. These were not so much "against the grain" of the genre as they were revealing of its essential meanings.

The traditional *film noir*, as represented, for example, by *Double Indemnity* (1944), *The Big Sleep* (1946), and *Out of the Past* (1948), already possessed typical characters and character-functions upon which Polanski could build. Centering the narrative was the private-eye figure (with Phillip Marlowe the most well-known embodiment of the type)—courageous, smart, independent, and ultimately more committed to discovering the truth and defending the victims of evil than in earning his meager remuneration from his employers. He could be described as a knight in not very shining armor; a man with a personal commitment to fight evil, although his profession, demeanor, and dress do not suggest knightly virtue. In spite of these positive attributes, the private eye is not a saint. Because he is in the employ of someone richer and more powerful, he can be manipulated to serve evil causes. Also, in his battle against what he perceives to be evil, he may become the victimizer of others. And most importantly, he can be and usually is blinded by love or lust, seduced by the *femme fatale*. He may redeem himself and her as well (*The Big Sleep*), or he may succumb to her evil, in which case he typically perishes with her (*Out of the Past*). In this latter version, which I will term the "tragic" *film noir*, the private eye is a quintessentially Polanskian hero, trapped in a world of evil which he cannot escape, try though he may. In these plots, he is in many respects a victim, but he is just as clearly also a victimizer, an accomplice of evil.

Also of critical importance in the genre is the private eye's function as narrator. In many of the films in the genre the private eye comments on much of the action as it is occurring in voice-over narration (usually motivated by framing the narrative as a recollection of events from the past). In this way, the private eye, in some measure, controls our interpretation of events. Even where there is no voice-over narration, the viewer generally follows in the private eye's footsteps, sees and hears what he sees and hears, and is logically inclined toward similar conclusions. However—and this might be seen as particularly important in terms of Polanski's interaction with the genre's conventions—the private eye is *mistaken* in central aspects of his hypothesis. In the tragic version of the genre, in particular, the evil forces at work in the *film noir* world destroy him.

The *femme fatale* is a character who is trapped in this world of evil, who finds herself "under the thumb" of a more powerful authoritarian figure whom she is trying to escape. The question of her true nature is generally one of the two major mysteries of the plot (the other relating to a crime for economic motives) and is often the most compelling. Because she is enmeshed with the evil figures in the narrative, in particular the *patriarchal* figure (usually a significantly older husband or lover), the private eye assumes she is guilty, although perhaps only as an unwitting accomplice. Her sexual allure dazzles him and us (hence, the term *femme fatale*); he falls in love with her or, at least, becomes erotically involved; and he wants to save or rescue her from her criminal surroundings and her evil cohorts. For example, in *The Big Sleep*, Phillip Marlowe (Humphrey Bogart) saves Vivian Rutledge (Lauren Bacall) from the clutches of the powerful gangster Eddie Mars. When she turns out to be "redeemable," the private eye not only redeems her, but also will marry her (thus assimilating her to the more domestic version of the patriarchal order).

In the genre's later years, the tragic variant is more common—the *femme fatale* is irredeemable, genuinely evil or inextricably (from a psychological or material standpoint) invested in evil. In this variant, she is killed at the film's climax and the private eye, not infrequently, dies with her and because of her. In spite of her negative qualities, her role in the narrative is usually the most dynamic. Visually, she appears with an impressive array of properties—seductively dressed, her hair or bare shoulders gleaming (often enhanced through backlighting), witty, resourceful, brave. She is the one who *really* understands what is going on, and has often planned the very intricate set of deceptive events (Lawrence Kasdan's *Body Heat* is a good example of this feature). However, even where she is ultimately proven to be the source of evil, there are things about her that appear innocent, and we *desire* her to be innocent because, visually, from our position as *voyeurs,* she is an object of erotic attraction as well.

The patriarchal male character is a man of power, wealth, and influence—and almost always markedly older than the *femme fatale.* He is her husband or her lover, possibly her employer, but always in a position to exercise power over her. In addition, he also has financial power over the private eye (he frequently is his employer, too), the system of law enforcement, or even government bodies. From the point of view of the *femme fatale,* the *film noir* narrative is the story of *her* rebellion against this power. Because the private eye also stands in the position of the "little man," the defender of moral values and the public good against the abuse of power, he can identify with the heroine's rebellion and generally participates in it in some way. In the "happy" resolution of the plot, these two characters do indeed defeat the patriarchal figure (he is killed) and the evil he represents. In the tragic version as well, the patriarchal figure is usually killed; however, the *femme fatale* proves *not* to be interested in the love or patronage of the private eye—she has embarked on a quest for *independent* power, through criminal means, and has used the private eye for her own ends. Although he is torn because of his love for her, the private eye ultimately comes down on the side of morality. He opposes the *femme fatale* and is forced to kill her, often at the same moment that she kills him.

The general social milieu of the action in the *film noir* thriller embraces both the lower and the upper classes. Individuals involved in the crimes may come from the former group, but those who control and profit from the criminal activity tend to be upper class in their lifestyle, influence, and status (even if they are explicitly gangsters). In terms of class values, the private eye is usually middle class, able to appreciate the struggles of the working-class milieu from which he came, but also proud of having risen above those origins. Thus, the private eye has an antagonistic attitude toward the wealthy, even when they are his employers.

Mise-en-scène is a central element of the genre, so much so that it takes its name from its "look." In its traditional form (during the period 1944–1954), it features urban settings, frequently shot at night, with high contrast between black and white. The visual atmosphere is claustrophobic, not only because of the darkness, but also because of the narrow streets and tall buildings in exterior shots, and the small cluttered rooms used as interiors. Shadows play a major role as do the architectonics of the set. Bands of black and white subdivide the space, segment it in such a way as to dominate with patterns and make discerning other details often difficult. Faces, particularly that of the *femme fatale,* are often seen half in light and half in shadow, as if to suggest duplicity. Polanski retained some of these stylistic elements, while replacing others in ways which expanded the semantic implications of spatial patterns.

Dramatic changes in the look of the genre are evident from the outset.

The credit sequence is in a nostalgic tint of black-and-white film stock, but it is also in wide-screen panavision, an epic format seemingly antithetical to the disjointed, claustrophobic look of the classical genre. The first images are also in black and white; they are still photographs which are being flipped before our eyes to the rhythm of offscreen moans of emotional pain (these are very unattractive photos of a man and woman, partially clad, in various stages of having sex in the woods). The moans, it turns out, come from Curly, a working-class client, a fisherman, who has hired Jake Gittes, a private eye specializing in "matrimonial work," to follow his wife. After ushering Curly out of his office, Jake receives another prospective client, "Evelyn Mulwray" (this Evelyn is an imposter, as we learn only later), who wants to have her influential husband, Hollis Mulwray, head of the Los Angeles Department of Water and Power, followed.

The office of Jake Gittes contains clutter typical for the genre, and horizontal lines created by venetian blinds and the shadows they cast. The cinemascope format is utilized by Polanski to enhance the claustrophobic effect, as only parts of the figures of Gittes, "Mulwray," and Gittes's assistants Walsh and Duffy are visible, their images truncated by the long and narrow ratio of the film's frame dimensions. The sense that characters are crushed in interior compositions in *Chinatown* is balanced by a quite opposite impression when Gittes gazes out at the dry expanse of the Los Angeles River's bed, the land in the Northwest Valley, or the Pacific Ocean coastline (these images occur as Gittes carries out his investigations). Here one does feel the open possibilities of nature, and perhaps even associates them with the biblical panoramas linked, in the viewers' experience, to the cinemascope format.

Towne's narrative for *Chinatown* involves a criminal plot, the intricacies of which the viewer is unlikely to decipher until the end of the film (if then); the typical complexity of the genre's narrative is present in most extreme form. The private eye, like the viewer, does not figure out the motivations for the crimes until the end. Jake Gittes begins to tail Hollis Mulwray, and photographs him with a pretty girl less than half his age, who Mulwray has lodged at the El Macondo Apartments (we and Gittes conclude that this young woman is his mistress). Gittes's scandalous photos of the couple end up in the local newspapers. As Gittes, in his office, is telling his assistants an off-color joke, the attractive and confident figure of the *real* Evelyn Mulwray appears behind him—Gittes is ultimately embarrassed not only because he has told an inappropriate joke in mixed company but also because he was taken in by an imposter. Furthermore, Evelyn Mulwray's lawyer serves him with a lawsuit for slander.

Gittes does some more snooping at the office of Ross Yelburton (Mulwray's second in command at the Water Department) and then goes to Mulwray's home where Evelyn offers to drop the lawsuit. The private eye could let matters end here, but his sense of honor and manhood will not let him ("I'm not supposed to be the one who is caught with his pants

3.13. With the Pacific shoreline in the background, Jake Gittes (Jack Nicholson) tries to convince Police Lieutenant Escobar (Perry Lopez) that water is being deliberately dumped into the ocean. *Chinatown.* Museum of Modern Art/Film Stills Archive.

down"). When Gittes goes to a reservoir looking for Hollis Mulwray, he learns that Mulwray's body has just been found; Mulwray seemingly slipped in one of the spillway channels and fell to his death.

At this point in the narrative, Gittes begins to act to protect Evelyn, to whom he seems attracted, supporting her statements to the suspicious police. In the course of his snooping, Gittes has discovered that water is being dumped from the reservoir channels into the ocean, an unusual practice at a time when Los Angeles is suffering through a drought. Gittes goes to see Noah Cross, Evelyn's wealthy father and Hollis Mulwray's former business partner; Cross gives him no information but hires him to find the girl whom Hollis was with (Evelyn had already hired Gittes; Cross offers him double the rate). Ultimately, Gittes pieces together the components of an intricate conspiracy (and the viewer is with him every step of the way). The drought is being worsened by deliberate actions of Yelburton, who is a hireling of Noah Cross. By terrorizing the orange grove farmers of the valley and poisoning their wells, Noah Cross is forcing them to sell their land. The buyers (unbeknownst to themselves) are the inhabitants of the Mar Vista Old Age Home, owned by Noah Cross—so that the land will revert to him upon the deaths of these very aged people. The dam which Yelburton and

Cross are urging the inhabitants of Los Angeles to fund with a bond issue will ultimately bring water to Cross's soon-to-be acquired real estate empire, which he plans to develop and have incorporated into Los Angeles.

Jake Gittes allies himself with Evelyn Mulwray to defeat these villains. But when Evelyn, after a mysterious phone call, leaves the bed in which they have just made love, asking *him* please to trust her and wait, Jake cannot resist his private eye instincts to follow her to a house where, seemingly, Evelyn and her Chinese American butler Kan have imprisoned the young woman he earlier saw with Hollis. The young woman is visibly upset and Evelyn and Kan apparently are giving her drugs to sedate her. Jake is now convinced that he has been played for a fool and that it was a jealous Evelyn who murdered Hollis and is now holding his mistress captive to prevent her from talking. When he confronts Evelyn, she claims that the young woman is her sister, upset because she just learned of Hollis's death.

Before Jake can take further action, he falls into the hands of his former police buddy Lt. Escobar because a woman named Ida Sessions (the impersonator of Evelyn Mulwray) has been found murdered, with Jake Gittes's phone number written on her wall. Gittes promises to bring his client Evelyn in for questioning. He goes to her home and finds that she has already packed for a trip. In an artificial tidepool in the Mulwrays' garden, Jake finds a pair of broken glasses, which he takes to belong to Hollis. Here he pieces together an important clue. The autopsy had revealed salt water in Hollis's lungs and the water of the reservoir was, of course, fresh. Jake realizes that the Japanese American gardener has been complaining about something being "bad for the *grass*" (not "bad for the glass" as Jake had previously heard it). This is, of course, the salt water of the tidepool! This confirms Jake's suspicions (and ours). He goes to the house where Evelyn is holding the young girl Catherine captive, confronts her with the evidence, and calls the police. The film now reaches its most climactic moment:

> *Jake:* Don't tell me she's your sister. You don't have a sister.
> *Evelyn* (haltingly): She's my daughter.
> [Jake slaps her brutally.]
> *Evelyn:* She's my sister.
> [Jake slaps her again.]
> *Evelyn:* She's my daughter.

Jake's next slap knocks Evelyn down onto the couch. She looks up at him in tears.

> *Evelyn:* She's my sister and my daughter. Do you get it now, Mr. Gittes, or is it too hard for you?

The viewer and Gittes are both shocked and shamed by the discovery of the film's underlying incest plot, just at the moment of greatest antipathy toward Evelyn as a duplicitous *femme fatale*. Later Evelyn adds: "By the way, those aren't Hollis's glasses. He didn't wear bifocals." (We may remember that Noah Cross *does*.)

From this moment on, Jake is committed to saving Evelyn and her daughter Catherine from the clutches of Noah Cross and bringing him to justice. But, unfortunately, in the fateful hours during which he did not trust Evelyn he has already set in motion the events which will lead to her death and Noah Cross's possession of his daughter and granddaughter Catherine. Once the incest plot is revealed, the viewer recalls many hints and clues which were previously ignored. When Jake Gittes first came to see Evelyn, she had told him that the matter was "very personal. It couldn't be more personal." Later, she is upset when Gittes learns that her middle name is Cross. When Gittes met Noah Cross, the latter warned him: "You may think that you know what you're dealing with, but believe me you don't. Just find the girl, Mr. Gitts [sic], just find the girl." When, after making love, Gittes remarks to Evelyn that he met Noah Cross, Evelyn instinctively covers her breasts with her arms in a defensive gesture, as she stutters: "You met . . . my father. My father is very dangerous, very crazy." Likewise, when she first tells Gittes that Catherine is her sister, she can barely force the words out of her mouth.

It is through the use of pervasive symbolism that Polanski makes the multiple dimensions of patriarchal evil in *Chinatown* manifest. While investigating at the dam after Hollis's murder, Gittes is caught by two thugs in Yelburton's employ, Claude Mulvihill, a corrupt former sheriff, and a little man with a thick accent, played by Polanski himself. The Polanski character places the tip of his switchblade inside Gittes's nostril ("You're a very nosy fellow. Do you know what happens to nosy fellows? They lose their noses. I'll cut it off and feed it to my goldfish"), and with a flick of his wrist, he slices through Gittes's nose and blood pours down. Throughout the rest of the film, Gittes carries the mark of this symbolic castration, first as a comically large white bandage on his nose and then as a raw area with a very prominent row of stitches.

Another prefiguring motif relates Gittes to Hollis Mulwray and to Evelyn. Many times in the film we are presented with two circles alongside each other, not infrequently as the lenses of glasses or binoculars. However, most often one of these circles or lenses is damaged or smashed. As investigators, Hollis peers through glasses, Gittes through binoculars. They are trying to learn the truth about the water, as we are. One side of Gittes's sunglasses are smashed when he gets into a fight with angry farmers, as is one headlight of his car. Later, he smashes one of the taillights on Evelyn's car so that he can follow her more easily. Just before they make love, Evelyn caresses Gittes's nose, cleaning it with peroxide. At the same time, he notices a black spot on the brown iris of one of her eyes. "A birthmark," she says. It is as if both characters already carry the mark of their inevitable disempowerment, of their inevitable infection by evil (one might even imagine Evelyn to have this birth defect as a result of incest in previous generations).

Polanski also uses visual and verbal motifs to give the incest theme biblical and apocalyptic reverberations. In the early sequences, Hollis Mulwray, head of Water and Power, moves between the dry land of the Los Angeles

3.14. The thug with the foreign accent (Roman Polanski) prepares to slit Jake's nose; his cohort Mulvihill (Roy Jensen) holds Jake's arms. *Chinatown.* Museum of Modern Art/Film Stills Archive.

River bed and the Pacific Ocean. He is the one who has brought water to the land and made it fertile. He is also fascinated by tidepools, as Noah Cross tells Gittes, "He [Mulwray] used to say: 'That's where life began.'" Throughout the film he is associated with water. At a public hearing, he speaks against building another dam like the Vanderlip Dam, a dam that was built against his advice and that broke and resulted in many deaths. With the image of Franklin Roosevelt behind him (an image also associated elsewhere with Gittes), he declares: "I won't make the same mistake twice. I won't build it." Like the Old Testament God, the Good God of Creation, he promises that there will not be another Deluge.

When Duffy photographs Hollis in a heated dispute with Noah Cross, in which the only word he can make out is "Applecore," we have a hint that Noah is indeed symbolically Hollis's antagonist—the God of Evil. His name associates him with the Deluge, and "Applecore" suggests the core of evil in original sin (the apple eaten by Eve). In fact, what Duffy misheard as "Applecore" was "Albacore," the name of Noah Cross's yacht club. This club has as its insignia a black flag with a schematic, skeletal design of a fish somewhat suggestive of a pirate's skull and crossbones. Polanski places a fish image in the mise-en-scène repeatedly, not only on this flag. A fish is mounted in Yelburton's office as is the club's flag. When Gittes goes to see Noah Cross, they eat a lunch of broiled fish, served with the heads on

(Noah Cross likes them this way). At the Mar Vista Home, the Albacore flag appears as part of a quilt being made by Emma Dill, an octogenarian "owner" of vast land tracts in the valley. The fish insignia is very schematic, and thus may also recall for us the symbol used by the early Christians. But Polanski suggests to us that religion (Judaism/Christianity) is only a corrupt front for the patriarchy (Noah—Cross), and, literally in his film, an emblem for a Kingdom of the Dead (Jacob Lamar Crabbe, one of the other owners, has already appeared in the obituary column; Emma Dill tells Gittes that the Mar Vista Home is an official charity of the Albacore Club).

By using biblical symbolism, Polanski suggests the inevitability of evil in human civilization as presently constituted. Even victims are complicit. *EVE*lyn Mulwray is linked by her name to original sin; "Jake" (Jacob) Gittes to a patriarch who obtained his birthright through deception. Jake thinks he is working to establish good in the world, but, in reality, his own *need* of power guarantees the triumph of evil.

The events which lead to the finale are explicitly set up by Jake. He tells the police to meet him in Chinatown, at an address where Evelyn, Catherine, and Kan are to meet Curley, who will take them to Mexico in his boat. Gittes, in the meantime, calls Noah Cross and lures him to the Mulwray house in order to confront him with the evidence. There is no *rational* need for Gittes to do this until after Evelyn and Catherine have safely escaped, but his desire for personal power over Noah impels him to act immediately. Instead, after Cross has admitted to the crime, his henchman Mulvihill "gets the drop" on Gittes. Cross wants to be taken to the girl, and Gittes complies, knowing that the police will be there, too. When they arrive in Chinatown, Gittes tries to explain, but an angry Lt. Escobar will not listen. Evelyn (saying "He owns the police") vows that Noah will never get Catherine; she pulls a gun and when Noah continues toward her she shoots him. Evelyn attempts to flee in a car with Catherine, and the police begin to fire at her. Gittes, in the meantime, is helplessly handcuffed to the steering wheel of the police car. A police sergeant fires. Evelyn's car comes to a sudden halt, its horn blaring. The police rush up to find Evelyn's body slumped over the steering wheel; turning her over, they see that one of her eyes has been blown out, leaving only a bloody socket (Polanski conceived and insisted upon this ending; in Towne's original filmscript, Gittes saves Evelyn). Catherine's screams rend the air and this shocking image is immediately followed by another even more disturbing. Noah Cross (who has suffered only a flesh wound) engulfs his distraught granddaughter Catherine in a spiderlike embrace and begins taking her away—even as she continues to scream.

The viewer can imagine an apocalyptically evil and all-powerful Noah Cross who will copulate with his daughters and granddaughters forever—a hyperbolic extension of the biblical Noah who repopulated the world after the flood.

"How is this possible?" mutters a stunned and completely powerless Gittes.

"It's Chinatown," says Duffy. "Forget it, Jake." The camera slowly cranes back and up to reveal the street filling with curious onlookers, equally disempowered residents of Chinatown.

Polanski uses the Chinatown references to develop a motif of ethnic oppression within the film (there is a sense of class oppression as well). All of Evelyn Mulwray's servants are Asian Americans, and she herself, in the bedroom scene, is made up and photographed in such a way as to look vaguely Asian. Catherine Mulwray speaks to her protector Hollis in Spanish (she was raised in Mexico, where Hollis took her after Evelyn, fifteen at the time, gave birth to her). A young boy from whom Hollis, and later Gittes, get information in the Los Angeles River bed is Chicano. Curley's family is Italian American, and Jake Gittes himself at first feigns being Jewish (and then being an anti-Semitic bigot) in his efforts to get information and access to the Mar Vista Home. Noah Cross, on the other hand, is clearly a WASP, and his inability to pronounce Gittes's name (he calls him Mr. Gitts, throughout) is indicative of his disdain for people with other than Anglo-Saxon names.

In the film Chinatown is not only the mysterious place where evil befalls people; it is also the home of the oppressed and powerless. It is where Jake Gittes had his police beat and from which he hoped to escape. It is also the place where he had earlier confronted and been defeated by evil. When Noah Cross had told him he didn't really understand what was going on, Gittes had replied: "That's what the D.A. told me in Chinatown." Gittes later tells Evelyn Mulwray: "You can't always tell what's going on there. I was trying to keep someone from being hurt. I ended up making sure she was hurt."

"Dead," says Evelyn. Gittes nods. Gittes is fated to repeat his mistake and cause the death of another woman he loves.

Thus, Polanski in *Chinatown* addresses the terrible evils of the patriarchy in the context of American culture specifically, expanding the thematic range of a quintessentially American genre. Noah Cross is the epitome of an inhumane capitalist. When Jake asks him, after he admits to the crime, what a man as rich as he is could possibly gain, Cross replies: "The future, Mr. Gitts, the future." Cross wants all of the power, all of the money, all of the daughters—and seemingly will go on this way forever. He is a patriarch grown to grotesque proportions. As a film, *Chinatown* stands as one of the bleakest assessments of American culture ever made. Polanski successfully fuses his own personal themes of oppression, alienation, and corruption with a very specific agenda of American social and cultural problems: economic oppression, ethnic prejudice, and, most centrally, sexual abuse and incest.

Conclusion

Chinatown is also a fitting place to conclude our detailed consideration of the films which marked Polanski's success in "crossing the borders" from Poland to the West. His own personal obsessions as an artist could be mapped

3.15. Evelyn Mulwray (Faye Dunaway), looking vaguely Asian, lies in bed with Jake after the two have made love. *Chinatown.* Museum of Modern Art/ Film Stills Archive.

onto larger social and political issues which applied to Western culture as much as to East Central European culture. Polanski's individual sense of abandonment and oppression was transferred to the situation of others who were victims of the culture and the system—women in particular. His later films—in particular *The Tenant* (*Le Locataire,* 1976), and *Tess* (1980)—continued to address issues of class, ethnicity, and gender in compelling fashion. Trelkovsky, the tragicomic hero of *The Tenant,* is victimized because he is "other" (a Polish immigrant living in France) and he is soft and meek; he internalizes his own victimization and begins to take on the identity of the woman who inhabited his apartment before him; ultimately he commits suicide as she did. As in *Repulsion,* the slide from ordinary, everyday discrimination and oppression into harrowing persecution and torture is gradual—as Trelkovsky slips into madness. Although the violent events are motivated as hallucinations, the possibility that they are actually occurring torments orchestrated by supernatural characters remains present. Even more unsettling is the fact that some of the hallucinations visually echo aspects of the harassment and persecution suffered by Jews in Poland before and during the Second World War (Polanski himself played Trelkovsky; the applause he receives from other residents of the apartment building as he throws himself from an upper story window—not once but twice—might be seen as a metaphor for Polanski's filmmaking acrobatics itself).

In *Tess,* Polanski remained faithful to the narrative lines of Thomas

Hardy's *Tess of the d'Urbervilles,* again using visual imagery to heighten the sense of class and gender oppression. In *Frantic* (1987), a skillfully made thriller, Polanski once again created a Kafkaesque world where a foreigner (this time an American doctor attending a convention in Paris) is plunged into a conspiratorial world he cannot understand. The doctor doesn't speak French, and when his wife (who does) is kidnapped, the doctor's efforts to find her are hampered by unfeeling bureaucrats and by his own limited ability to communicate. Only an alliance with a young woman who is a drug courier enables him finally to defeat the terrorists and rescue his wife. He is successful in no small measure because of the young woman's courage and daring; without wanting it or even realizing it, he has fallen in love with her, but he cannot save her from death. *Bitter Moon,* to be released as this book goes to press, promises to return Polanski to the psychological complexity of love and the role which power plays in the structure of human passion. The film promises to probe the victim-victimizer dynamic as a deeply embedded aspect of sexuality as it is currently constructed in human culture.

Thus, Polanski has been able to extrapolate and generalize his own experiences under Fascist and later Stalinist regimes and relate them to patterns of personal sexual behavior. The implicit linking of the personal and the sociopolitical in a generalized or allegorical setting has given his work international appeal. No less important in enabling Polanski's films to cross borders is his skill as a visual artist, his ability to embody our worst fears and anxieties in riveting visual images and in narrative structures that build tension and make the shocking finales particularly effective. Finally, whether out of compulsion or courage or a combination of the two, Polanski was willing and able to represent moments of pure horror, to call evil by its name and to force us to peer unflinchingly at its face.

NOTES

1. Polanski and his principal biographers are in basic agreement about the facts I present here. See Roman Polanski, *Roman* (New York: William Morrow, 1984); Barbara Leaming, *Polanski, a Biography: The Filmmaker as Voyeur* (New York: Simon and Schuster, 1981); Thomas Kiernan, *The Roman Polanski Story* (New York: Delilah/ Grove, 1980). Interpretations of these facts at times differ considerably.

2. Polanski, *Roman,* p. 26.

3. Ibid., p. 27.

4. Ibid., p. 104.

5. The analyses I present here are essentially my own, although in certain respects my conclusions are in agreement with those of other authors cited in the bibliography. My own views were influenced by the emphasis on voyeurism in Barbara Leaming's *Polanski, A Biography* and by the analysis of gender issues in Virginia Wright Wexman's *Roman Polanski* (Boston: Twayne, 1985). A number of particular observations on stylistic and structural matters are also very close to the terms of Wexman's highly perceptive analysis. Her corroboration of insights which I had arrived at independently (in most cases) was a welcome confirmation of their likely validity.

6. Polanski, *Roman,* p. 145.
7. Ibid., p. 156.
8. Ibid., p. 157.
9. For the most part, my citations of dialogue follow the film's subtitles, although in some cases I may have changed the wording to render it in better colloquial English.
10. Polanski, *Roman,* p. 207.
11. Ibid., p. 208.
12. Wexman, *Roman Polanski,* p. 63.
13. Polanski describes working with Tynan in a manner similar to his collaborations with Brach. They developed the ideas together. Thus, in what follows, the attribution of particular innovations to Polanski may more correctly be stated as belonging to Polanski and Tynan.

Four Szabó

David Paul

István Szabó is a consummate Hungarian who has successfully broadened his film audience over the years without losing his cultural identity. Szabó began directing international co-productions in the 1980s after nearly two decades' work with the Hungarian State Film Company, MAFILM. His first co-production was a triumph—*Mephisto* (1981), the result of a collaboration between MAFILM and Manfred Durniok of Berlin. Further co-productions followed—*Colonel Redl* (*Oberst Redl/Redl ezredes,* 1984) and *Hanussen* (1988). In 1991 Szabó completed his first English-language film, *Meeting Venus,* shot in Budapest but produced solely by Enigma of London. Unlike the other directors who are the subjects of this book, Szabó has continued to reside in his native country and shuns all thought of emigration.

The evolution of Szabó's films follows a pattern consistent with the increasing internationalization of his career. His earliest features, from *The Age of Daydreaming* (*Álmodozások kora,* 1964) through *Love Film* (*Szerelmes film,* 1970), present distinctly Hungarian stories, albeit with hints of a broader message. The films from Szabó's second period, from *25 Firemen's Street* (*Tűzoltó utca 25,* 1973) through *Confidence* (*Bizalom,* 1979), show Szabó reaching for more universal themes while still working within recognizably Hungarian settings. His films during the 1980s take a step further; the setting moves to Nazi Germany in *Mephisto* and ranges broadly across Central Europe in *Colonel Redl* and *Hanussen.* These three films constitute a "Central European trilogy" that makes a complex statement about the cultural affinity of that region the Germans call *Mitteleuropa.*

In *Meeting Venus,* Szabó extended his reach further. *Meeting Venus,* a contemporary story about a multinational opera production, is a comedy about human cooperation and the creative impulse. It is also a parable about the new Europe in the process of redefining its identity as a multinational community.

Szabó is a disciplined artist who chooses his projects deliberately and embarks on new ventures wtih caution. He thoroughly researches the contexts of his stories and thinks their implications through. Szabó wrote all of

4.1. István Szabó. HUNGAROFILM.

his early screenplays himself; today he works with other screenwriters but continues to initiate the stories and co-authors the scripts. His work is consistently driven by probing questions about personal identity, community, and security.

Szabó's Life and Times

István Szabó was born in Budapest to Jewish parents one year before the outbreak of the Second World War. To this day he carries memories of hiding in cellars during the siege of Budapest in the winter of 1944–1945, when Soviet troops fought in door-to-door combat against the last German holdouts. Szabó and his parents had escaped the Holocaust, thanks to the help of family friends. Just as the war ended, however, the elder Szabó died of natural causes.

István Szabó's father was a physician, carrying on a family tradition that can be traced back to the late eighteenth century, when the first Dr. Szabó practiced medicine in Pest. Young István grew up expecting to do the same, and today he expresses regret that he could not have become both a film director and a physician.[1]

At the age of sixteen, Szabó performed in a student play. He enjoyed the experience but didn't feel he was cut out to be an actor. Then he read a book about the cinema by Béla Balázs, the great Hungarian film pioneer and theorist; Szabó started going to the movie house every day, and thoughts about film filled his head. Eventually he applied to the Budapest Academy of Theater and Film Art and was accepted. He graduated in 1961.

Young Szabó did not need a wild imagination to invent stories; his life experiences were replete with material. As he grew up, Hungary stumbled through postwar recovery and plunged into revolution. He had not reached puberty when his country first experienced the horror of Stalinism. He was eighteen when a popular revolt was crushed by Soviet tanks, and in his early twenties when the regime took its first cautious steps toward de-Stalinization. Thus in his youth, Szabó saw his world change radically several times. Heroes rose and fell and rose again; myths were destroyed and recreated; truth became falsehood and falsehood, truth.

Artists in socialist Hungary, as elsewhere in the Soviet bloc, lived lives that reflected the ironies and contradictions of the Communist system. Once established in their professions, they enjoyed modestly comfortable incomes and other benefits regardless of whether their work was commercially successful. In return, they were expected not to offend their rulers. In time, those who felt called to address society's realities through their work learned through trial and error how to expand the boundaries of what was permitted.[2]

Szabó was particularly sensitive to those ironies and contradictions. However, he was—and is—a cautious and personally conservative man; he examined reality from a critical position, but he chose not to challenge the political authorities head-on. Szabó therefore shied away from the kind of projects that some of his more daring Hungarian cohorts championed during the 1960s and 1970s—for example, Károly Makk's five-year effort to film *Love* (*Szerelem*, 1970) and Pál Gábor's startling *Angi Vera* (1978), two films that probed the open sores of Stalinism. Szabó's approach to social criticism was more indirect; rather than examining specific evils in contemporary life, he took on the broader problem of the individual caught up in the perverse dynamics of history.

> **Every film I've made is about the same thing—it's about the individual's search for security.**
>
> **—István Szabó, 1985**

Throughout Szabó's career, consistency of theme and growth of stylistic confidence have marked his filmmaking. His numerous awards have included major honors received in Budapest, Moscow, Berlin, Cannes, and Hollywood. Few directors have won major prizes for films as different, for example, as *Mephisto* and *Father* (*Apa*, 1966). And yet, these two works, like all of his others, speak to the subject that has obsessed István Szabó throughout his career: the individual's search for identity and security in a world dominated by powerful forces militating against personal security.

Szabó was the youngest of the Hungarian directors whose *new wave* created an international stir in the mid-1960s, and despite the fact that some of his most interesting work was produced during the 1970s, his reputation then was still eclipsed by that of his elder colleague Miklós Jancsó. Following the critical success of *Confidence* and especially of *Mephisto*, however, Szabó came to be widely regarded as Hungary's foremost director, and the judgment held throughout the 1980s. This was no trivial honor among a group of award-winning Hungarians who now included Márta Mészáros, Károly Makk, Pál Gábor, Zsolt Kézdi-Kovács, Gyula Gazdag, and others.

As a young director, Szabó borrowed from other artists, especially those of the French *new wave*. He also admired Ingmar Bergman, Luis Buñuel, and Akira Kurosawa, and drew to some extent upon their ideas, especially those of Bergman.[3] Szabó's early shorts and his first two features clearly show the influence of the French, especially François Truffaut: They are clean, straightforward, and simply narrated. However, by his third feature, *Love Film,* Szabó had grown bolder and more experimental, playing with time sequence and manipulating a complex set of symbolic images.

Szabó continued to explore new narrative forms in an artful series of short films without dialogue under the overall title of *Budapest, Why I Love It* (*Budapest, amiért szeretem,* 1971). These were followed by *25 Firemen's Street,* which is built on a rich, collagelike effect, and *Budapest Tales* (*Budapesti mesék,* 1976), an allegory whose simplicity belies the story's profundity.

Then, beginning with *Confidence,* Szabó returned to more conventional narrative lines. This is not to say that his style ceased to develop, nor that it became undistinguished. Rather, Szabó since 1979 has settled into forms that rely on greater realism while allowing room for complex, and sometimes subtle, symbol systems.

True to the overwhelming trend in his country's filmmaking traditions, Szabó tells predominantly dramatic stories rather than comedies. (*Meeting Venus* marked his first effort at a comedy.) His films are never without wit and irony, however. There is playful banter among the young friends in *The Age of Daydreaming.* There are visual jokes and humorous juxtapositions in *Budapest, Why I Love It.* And there are lines of witty dialogue almost hidden within the tragedy of *Hanussen*—rewards to the viewer who pays close attention.

Szabó's career has consistently centered on film directing. In 1990, however, he served as artistic producer for *The Book of Esther* (*Eszterkönyv*), a film directed by Krisztina Deák. This he appears to have done as a personal favor to Deák, who is the wife of András Bálint, Szabó's close friend and erstwhile on-screen alter ego. Szabó has done a limited amount of work on television plays and directed a stage production only once, at the Paris Opera. About stage directing he expresses some distaste, preferring the more natural tones of cinematic dialogue—in which talk is talk and whispers are whispers—to the "shouting," as he characterizes it, of stage dialogue.[4]

We can distinguish among three phases of Szabó's work to 1990. These encompass his early films, from his days at the Budapest Academy through *Love Film;* a second group of works, from *Budapest, Why I Love It* through *Budapest Tales;* and, counting *Confidence* as a transitional piece, his Hungarian-German co-productions, *Mephisto, Colonel Redl,* and *Hanussen. Meeting Venus* suggested the beginning of a fourth phase, but it remains to be seen just where Szabó's work takes him in the 1990s.

Szabó's Early Period

Like most young directors, István Szabó cut his teeth on short films before he tackled feature-length stories. It took only three years, however, from his diploma film to the completion of his first feature.

SHORT FILMS

In Szabó's diploma film, *Concert* (*Koncert,* 1961), three young men pedal an odd three-seater vehicle along the embankment of the Danube, pushing a grand piano ahead of them. They stop near a cluster of people sunbathing along the bank, and one of the boys plays a jazz number. A young woman looks up and smiles, but most of the others appear annoyed. The boys, discouraged, pedal away. The camera rolls and tilts; the embankment seems to shift and jump. As it straightens out again, a large, wood-framed mirror appears beyond the wall separating the embankment from the street above. Eventually, we see a girl carrying the mirror. The boys get off their vehicle and follow her, leaving the piano behind.

Another man approaches the abandoned piano. He plays a scale and then a pop tune. A young woman plays a single note repeatedly. An elderly man plays Chopin beautifully. A composer performs his own piece, contemporary and dissonant. An older man picks out a one-finger version of the Marseillaise.

Suddenly rain begins to pour down, and all scamper for cover. As the people huddle against the embankment wall, they become concerned about the piano. One by one they take off an article of clothing, dash to the piano, and lay their clothing over it. Soon it is covered and protected from the drenching. Eventually, the rain stops. The three original boys return and pedal the piano away again.

Concert is a subtle and precocious piece about responsibility, the fickleness of youth, and the variety in human expression. The story line is simple and clean, notwithstanding a little youthful cinematic ostentation in the tilting and rolling of the camera. Confidence and discipline are evident in the filming.

Szabó's next work, *Variations on a Theme* (*Variációk egy témára,* 1961), is the first of two films he directed at the Béla Balázs Studio, where many young Hungarian film artists get their first chance at professional work. *Variations on a Theme* is divided into three segments.

The first, *Objectively,* is a collage of documentary clips. There are scenes of a past war—a cavalry attack, the agony of life in the trenches—played against gay baroque music. Next, armed troops march in formation and give Nazi salutes. Bombs fall on a city and buildings crumble as a voice-over narrates casualty statistics from World War II. Soldiers return home to cities in rubble. A battlefield is strewn with corpses.

In the second segment, *Shocked,* eerie background music plays as the camera pans artifacts in a military museum—machine guns, gas masks, uniforms. There is no dialogue, only distant sounds of warfare. Fathers are explaining the weapons on display to their small sons; the boys' eyes are wide, and the fathers' faces glow with the thrill of battle memories.

The third segment, *As a Shriek,* opens with shots of wounded men in a military hospital and then cuts to an open-air café along the Danube. People are drinking and conversing; a lone saxophonist plays. From a distance comes the faint sound of troops marching. The café patrons continue drinking, comb their hair, smoke cigarettes. The marching sound grows ever louder, until it drowns out the jazz. Now it is almost deafening, and still the people are indifferent. Finally, one man snaps off his sunglasses and looks about worriedly.

There is no mistaking the message. *Variations on a Theme* is a cry against war, a call to contemporary citizens not to glorify the battlefield, and a plea to heed the warning signs of militarism.

Szabó's third short, *You* (*Te,* 1963), is a visual love poem. If Robert Browning had been a film director, he might have dedicated a similar piece to his celebrated wife. After a quick collage of female portraits through the ages, from Nefertiti to Goya, the film focuses on a contemporary woman in her early twenties (Cecilia Esztergályos). We see her naked, then in a summer dress eating ice cream and walking through the streets. She smiles; she boards a bus; she waves from a rooftop to a friend below. She walks pensively down a stairway. She trips gaily up the same stairs; she dashes downstairs and outside. Snatches of dialogue reveal the deeper side of the girl's character. She relates a dream; she wonders if her beau is serious when he tells her he loves her.

You, a small film in every sense, is lovely in its simplicity. Its soft visual texture is a quality that will characterize Szabó films for the next sixteen years.

In 1967, following his second feature, Szabó made another short film, *Piety* (*Kegyelet*), a documentary essay that carries forward Szabó's earlier thoughts about war. Like *Variations on a Theme, Piety* is divided into three segments. The first, ironically accompanied by a Strauss waltz, shows groups of people in a cemetery carrying bouquets. It is All Souls' Day, and the mood of those paying tribute, as they move through the cemetery in family groups, is rather more gay than mournful.

The second segment shows another crowd of people gathered together outdoors. A sad, jazz version of "Let My People Go" plays on the soundtrack. The camera closes in on a cloth Star of David, then another, and more—all being sewn onto coat sleeves. Off to the side is a small boy with a toy gun. Now the entire crowd mills about cheerfully, all wearing Stars of David on their sleeves. Finally, they are herded along a street by soldiers. It is not real—it is only a film being shot.

The third segment opens with clips of Budapest's bridges, destroyed and drooping pathetically into the water. Workmen with heavy equipment are cleaning up and beginning the long task of rebuilding. There are further scenes of devastation around the city, and again the beginnings of reconstruction. In the final sequence, the bridges are ceremoniously reopened, pedestrians cross the old Chain Bridge, and boats glide along the river below. Downriver, the foundations for a new bridge can be seen.

This affecting piece was constructed partly from existing documentary footage and partly from Szabó's own shots. A more mature work than *Variations on a Theme,* it is all the more powerful for its soft-spoken irony. Szabó seems to be wondering how seriously his world takes the tragedies of the past; do we so easily forget history? The second segment, on the Jews, was shot on the set of *Father.* By including it in *Pięty,* Szabó allowed himself a rare reflection on the subject of the Jews.[5]

EARLY FEATURE FILMS

Szabó's first three feature films constitute an informal trilogy. They tell personal stories about young people becoming adults, struggling for self-identity, falling in love, and exploring the boundary between truth and fantasy. Between these early features and Szabó's short films there are clear parallels, both thematic and stylistic. The idea of community recurs, as it will through all of Szabó's films, and the problem of personal identity comes clearly into focus. Stylistically, the soft tones of *You* and *Piety* dominate. With the completion of *Love Film* in 1970, Szabó succeeded in blending his lyricism with a playful juggling of narrative time.

While making these films, Szabó developed a close relationship with András Bálint, whose quiet, reflective acting style accurately conveyed the mood Szabó sought. Bálint starred in all three films from this first Szabó period, and he played the most important male roles in Szabó's next two features, *25 Firemen's Street* and *Budapest Tales.* Eventually, Szabó would look for other faces and different acting styles, but his friendship with Bálint continues to this day.[6]

> **My first films were like diaries about the experiences of my generation.**
>
> **—István Szabó, 1991**

The Age of Daydreaming (1964) examines the postwar generation with its youthful idealism and ambition. Four newly graduated communications engineers, three men and a woman, set out to redress the failings of their elders by collaborating on work they consider significant and innovative. Teaching their elders turns out to be difficult, however, and the youngsters must face the reality of their own subordinacy. Those whose work they would improve upon are not impressed by their ideas.

The young friends drift apart and are brought together only when one of them, Laci (Béla Asztalos), dies. The survivors mourn not only the loss of their friend but the abandonment of their ideals as well.

If this sounds familiar to American audiences of the 1980s, it must be said that *Daydreaming* is not just an early version of *The Big Chill. Daydreaming*'s subtext contains a precocious comment on the power of television, coming in the same year as Marshall McLuhan's *Understanding Media.*[7] In

4.2. Éva and János. True love or an illusion? *The Age of Daydreaming.* HUNGAROFILM.

the opening scene, the four friends are watching a TV program while an attractive young law graduate tells of her plans for the future, mirroring the idealism of the engineers. János (András Bálint) later meets the young woman, Éva (Ilona Béres), still enchanted by the magical images he has already seen of her. Their love affair, however, turns out to be just as illusory and transient as TV pictures.

The look and feel of *Daydreaming* mimic Truffaut. Like the Frenchman's works, *Daydreaming* is sadly ironic yet colored by a subtle wit. It is also a personal film, following Truffaut's focus on the director's own generation. The characters were drawn from people Szabó knew, and the style is documentary-like. According to Hungarian film historian Judit Pintér, younger audiences loved *Daydreaming* because it captured some of the vital currents running through their subculture. This was a generation that grew up under Stalinism and experienced the tragedy of 1956, young adults who were ashamed of their elders for submitting once again to ideas and standards that had been discredited. They were of course attracted to the fads and fashions of the West—which were now, for the first time, penetrating the barriers the Stalinists had erected against them.[8]

By modeling his first feature film on Truffaut, Szabó picked up on his cohorts' fascination with Western popular culture, and by telling a story about young people with ideas of their own, he addressed the theme of generational conflict (no less important in Hungary than in the West during the sixties). Audiences were quick to read into *The Age of Daydreaming* a parable with political implications. For this, Szabó came under official criticism, but fortunately, no sanctions were imposed upon his work.[9]

Daydreaming received a mixed reception abroad, winning an award at the 1965 Locarno festival but causing little excitement elsewhere. More than a decade later American critic Karen Jaehne, writing a generally laudatory article on Szabó's films, branded *Daydreaming* a poor imitation of *new-wave* styles—"*cinéma-manqué* rather than *-vérité*."[10] Still, as Jaehne was quick to add, this first effort introduced a number of motifs and images Szabó would develop in future stories—the "image of the missing father, role of the inspirational woman who remains a dream, dreams themselves trying to realize themselves, persecution, the social role of the doctor, Hungarians [in] exile."[11]

In retrospect, Szabó himself now feels that the documentary style of *Daydreaming* lacked the power to tell all he wished to say.[12] Nevertheless, with *Daydreaming,* István Szabó emerged as Hungary's leading cinematic spokesman for his generation—a role he carried further, and with greater aplomb, in *Father.*

In style and tone, *Father* (1966) can be recognized as the work of *Daydreaming*'s director. *Father,* however, is a far more polished and mature film.

The father in this story, like the director's own, died of natural causes immediately after World War II. Because so many real-life fathers had died in the war, *Father* could be the story of any Central European boy after 1945. Szabó created a purely personal story, but he was conscious of its wider relevance. Years later, he described *Father* as "a psychological sketch of our childhood."[13]

The film assumes the point of view of the young protagonist, Takó. As Takó grows up, memories of his dead father blend with the boy's fantasies. The man was a doctor; Takó imagines him to have been a brilliant surgeon whose daring techniques saved lives. In Takó's mind, his father becomes all that the changing social order identifies with heroism—a valiant partisan, an enlightened atheist, a face on May Day placards—despite evidence that the real father was someone else.

These emotionally charged myths guide the development of Takó's self-identity. Because his father loved bicycling, Takó takes it up. Even as a university student, Takó seeks to emulate the fantasy father when, during the 1956 revolt, he runs through the echoing sounds of gunfire to procure a Hungarian flag—something, he is sure, his father would have done.

And here we see something that tells us exactly what Szabó is getting at. When Takó returns to the classroom with his hard-won flag, he finds the room filled with Hungarian flags. Takó's action is everybody's deed. Szabó repeats this subtle but startling technique a few scenes later. Returning to a watchmaker's to retrieve his father's wristwatch, broken during Takó's "heroic" quest for the flag, he sees a drawer full of watches, each of them as unremarkable as his.

Later, in another variation of these universalizing metaphors, Takó resolves to swim across the wide Danube. He dives in and swims, and just

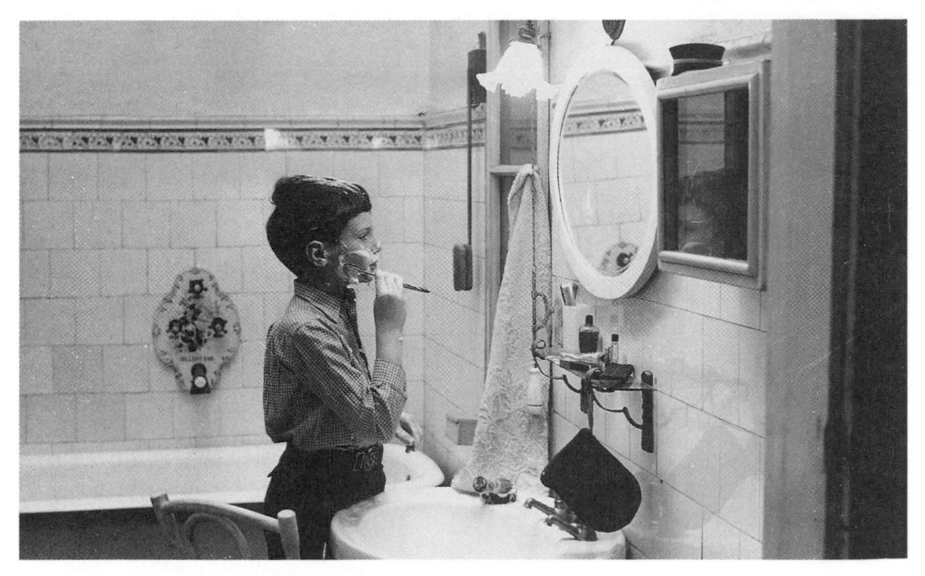

4.3. Takó tries out his dead father's razor. *Father.* HUNGAROFILM.

as we realize he's going to make it, the camera tilts upward from the lone figure of Takó and the focus widens to show a river filled with swimmers. Takó's story is not that of one individual; it is the individualized tale of an entire generation.

By this time, Takó has begun to question the myths he had built up about his father. Swimming across the Danube is something his father had never done, and in doing it, Takó leads his generation to the beginnings of a true adult self-identity. Takó himself achieves this when he accepts the fact that his father was not a fearless partisan hero or a medical pioneer but simply a good and honest man.

En route to this epiphany, Takó learns other perplexing facts. Through his Jewish girlfriend, Anni, he discovers that one's role in life is often accidental and arbitrary. Playing a bit part in a film about World War II, he is at first cast as a victim forced to wear a yellow armband. Suddenly his role is changed, and he becomes a Fascist, wearing an Arrow Cross armband and herding the "Jews" to their destruction.

By the film's end, Takó has learned much. In the final scene, he contemplates his father's grave, years after his father's death. He smiles faintly—a characteristic expression for Bálint, the actor.[14] The Mona Lisa smile announces Takó's reconciliation with his real father—as opposed to the fantasized version—and his own self. The camera pulls back, showing a cemetery full of people memorializing their departed fathers.

In *Father,* as in *You* and *Piety,* Szabó demonstrated a tremendous directorial discipline. Much of the film's emotional impact is due to its narrative restraint. It is the kind of picture whose subtleties linger with the viewer—

4.4. The grown-up Takó with Anni. *Father.* HUNGAROFILM.

from the haunting strains of the third movement of Mahler's *First Symphony* in the background to the quietly touching narrative of Anni as she tells the tragic story of her family.

Father won numerous awards, both at home and abroad. At the age of twenty-eight, István Szabó established himself as one of Europe's most promising young directors. To this day, he himself considers *Father* his finest film. The usually modest Szabó abandons his modesty when discussing *Father;* it is, he has said, "a fantastic miracle"—because, in his words, "it's honest and simple."[15]

Father was the most acclaimed film from Szabó's early period. His next, *Love Film,* was—and remains—one of the two most neglected works of his career (together with *Budapest Tales*) outside Hungary.[16]

Love Film contains several of the ingredients in *Father* and *Daydreaming*—the dialogue of memory and dream, the pain of growing up, and a protagonist confronting obdurate realities not of his own making. Jancsi (András Bálint) and Kata (Judit Halász) were childhood sweethearts, but Kata has emigrated to France in the wake of the 1956 revolt. As the story opens, Jancsi is en route to see her, availing himself of a rare opportunity to travel to the West; it is implicit that Kata cannot return home. But this is not a film about the evils of politics, Communist or capitalist; rather, it is about the pain of emigration and separation, the deceptions of memory, and the hopelessness of a love built on illusion.

The first half of *Love Film* unravels as a dense mosaic of flashbacks and flash-forwards, interweaving past, present, and future, reality and fantasy. As in *Father,* we see events from the protagonist's point of view. At the very beginning, Jancsi recalls scenes from childhood (past), blends them together

4.5. Jancsi and Kata as children. *Love Film.* HUNGAROFILM.

with the border crossings and ticket inspections of his journey (present), expresses the giddiness of anticipation through images of himself turning cartwheels alongside the moving train (fantasy), and conjures up a pretty vision of Kata come to meet him at the station in Fréjus (future). Inspired editing connects these jumbled images in ways that are sometimes verbal and realistic ("Tomorrow I'm going to meet her"), sometimes visual and poetically associative (as in a cut from Jancsi and Kata watching a fish in a bathtub to the voice and face of their childhood swimming instructor), and sometimes simply the continuation of a movement or an action from one scene into the next. As the story progresses, the narrative settles into a more or less chronological pattern, violated when Szabó repeats several key scenes—further invoking the caprice of memory.

As in *Father,* the film begins with a view of reality constructed by the protagonist's mind and moves on to a painful confrontation with the facts. By the film's midpoint, the story moves forward with greater consistency, signaling Jancsi's increasing awareness of the distinction between fact and fancy. Kata is not all he has imagined her to be, and, what's more, her need to abandon him during the daytime for her job tells him she is committed to the life she now lives—a life that cannot be reconnected to his. They part in sorrow, Jancsi returning to Jutka, the woman he left behind in Budapest.

At the end, with Jancsi back in Budapest, Szabó employs a universalizing technique similar to those he used in *Father:* Jancsi sends a telegram to Kata, while dozens of other Hungarians are simultaneously sending telegrams. The soundtrack fills with remembered words and sounds, reminding us that coming to grips with the past does not require us to forget it. The final

4.6. Jancsi visits Kata, the expatriate. How long does our childhood last? *Love Film.* HUNGAROFILM.

image is that of Kata's face, narrating a letter some years later (with references to her French husband, Georges); her face bleaches, like a fading memory, into the screen.

Critics were not impressed by *Love Film,* and it won no awards. Szabó believes that the technical virtuosity so evident in the film may have been excessive given the weight of its message, which, he feels, was little more than a restatement of ideas from *Father.*[17]

To be sure, *Love Film* is an imperfect work. There is a sequence in Paris, following Jancsi's departure from Fréjus, that takes off on a tangent (a statement, presumably, about the lure of the West). There is a scene, poignant but again tangential and too long, among Hungarian expatriates at a nostalgic gathering in Fréjus. Too little attention is paid to Jancsi's present-day life in Budapest, especially his relationship with Jutka, the inexplicably forgiving lover who sees him off on his way to visit Kata and eventually becomes his wife.

And yet, despite its flaws, *Love Film* stands as one of Szabó's most interesting efforts. Szabó's doubts notwithstanding, it does advance the director's exploration of his generation's obsessions. Within the story of two young adults trying to recapture the innocent love they once knew is, as Szabó has expressed it retrospectively, a disturbing question: How long is our childhood? It is a question with a particular poignancy for adults who, in Szabó's words, "are treated as children by the society"—that is, by the Communist state. "The society was happy to have us as children even long into adulthood."[18]

Additionally, *Love Film* presents a passionate statement on the human effects of political conflict and, in particular, the pain of separation by exile. And it accomplishes this through a unique cinematic style that manages to be both dazzling and comprehensible.

> **For me, if a boy and a girl sit down together across a table and look at each other, I expect some great historical event to happen. There must be some reason why they're sitting there.**
>
> **—István Szabó, 1985**

With the completion of *Love Film,* several qualities were now distinctive in Szabó's work. His films showed technical resourcefulness, an intimacy with reality (without being limited by the language of realism), meticulous attention to detail, and a strong social consciousness. If the feature films focused in on personal stories, Szabó's shorts demonstrated his ability to work as well from a community perspective—something that would characterize his projects in the mid-1970s.

Szabó's Second Period

Like *Father, Love Film* told an intimate story that audiences easily understood. In its style, however, *Love Film* resembled the work of Alain Resnais more than that of Truffaut. Szabó played teasingly with time and memory, yet managed not to confuse the forward motion of the narrative. *Love Film* served as a jumping-off point for the more radical directions of Szabó's next works—films that mass audiences, and even critics, would find more difficult: films built around characters in a Brechtian mode, characters purposefully designed to embody classes or types rather than individuals.

Love Film was Szabó's first color film, and it demonstrated his talent for working in this more complex visual medium. All of his subsequent films would be shot in color, sometimes with striking effect.[19]

Szabó's films of the 1970s also took him into new dimensions of his thematic territory. If *Father* is a sketch of an entire generation's childhood, it is still a story about one boy, told in first-person singular. *Love Film,* too, is told in first-person singular, strictly from Jancsi's point of view. During the 1970s, Szabó experimented more with his narrative style, arriving at a highly original community point of view, which he applied to *25 Firemen's Street* and *Budapest Tales.*

The focus of these new stories shifted to the parents of Szabó's generation—they whose decisions determined the contours of the world in which Szabó's generation grew up. Szabó's sources for these stories, in contrast to those of his early period, were not his own experiences, but reminiscences and anecdotes that he heard, as he has put it, "around the dinner table."[20] Because they were not "his" stories but rather those of his elders, Szabó felt more comfortable telling them from "their" point of view—as anecdotes, as dreams, as memories. Aided by the supremely adept camerawork of Sándor Sára, Szabó so convincingly captured their point of view, so completely entered into their stories, that the effect is as if he were narrating from "our" point of view; that is, first-person plural.

What shall I carve on the tree—"I am here" or "I was here"?
—Character in *Budapest Tales*

THE BUDAPEST SERIES

In 1971, Szabó completed *Budapest, Why I Love It,* a series of five short films about his hometown. The individual pieces range from three to twelve minutes in length, all are in color, and none has so much as one word of dialogue. Together, they convey an intricate portrait of this beautiful city on the Danube. Szabó's cinematographer, József Lőrincz, maintains a distant, indifferent camera, photographing these five pieces as if they were documentaries of everyday life.

And yet the only film in this series that is in fact a documentary is *The Square* (*A tér*). This little piece takes place in a small park, full of people on a sunny afternoon. A boy scratches graffiti on the back of a bench; other boys, in separate groups, are climbing a tree, dueling with wooden swords, brawling. There are kids on a seesaw, tykes in a sandbox. A grandmother sits on a bench with several small children; two men on another bench are playing chess, while others are playing cards. Lovers embrace, a boy plays a violin. There are ice-cream cones, a parakeet in a cage, dolls and puppets, hula hoops and—for one little boy who has exhausted his mother's patience—a spanking. *The Square* is four minutes of a warm day in the city, captured by a neutral camera and offered without commentary.

In contrast to the airy and naturalistic tone of *The Square, A Mirror* (*Egy tükör*) projects an aura of dark enchantment. An antique mirror stands in the window of a shop. We see the images of people who have, over the course of time, inspected themselves in the mirror—the young and the old, workers and fine ladies. A nun. Lovers. A Jew in hat and beard, a war veteran, a widow in a black veil, a soldier. They seek a confirmation of their handsomeness, a denial of their plainness. The mirror, mute and dispassionate, reflects all that happens before it—a kiss on the hand, a slap in the face.

Abruptly, the tone of the images darkens. Someone casts a suspicious glance sidewise. Soldiers appear. A dignified old man frowns into the mirror, then turns away and faces a hostile crowd. He frowns again, returns to the flatness of the mirror. His image fades.

A Mirror is a rich and puzzling little film. In only three minutes it offers a statement about the passage of time and the variability of human faces—faces that betray the personalities behind them. The objectivity of the images turns out to be misleading, and yet the flatness and immobility of the reflections leave us with a disquieting sense of incompleteness. Who are these people? What do they mean to tell us, really?

Danube, Fishes, Birds (*Duna, halak, madarak*) focuses on those vital nonhuman elements that inhabit the heart of Budapest. Szabó has filmed the life-giving Danube in a whimsical fantasy of water and air, birds and fish.

A tram runs up to the river bank, then angles off down a street in Pest, and returns to run along the waterfront. A rapid montage follows—fish in an aquarium; gulls flying overhead; bridges, buildings, and other landmarks along the river. Then the images, still in rapid succession, change; the fish appear in a shallow basin or in their aquarium on a balcony behind iron grillwork. Finally, the settings are fancifully jumbled: We see the fish swimming in a telephone booth, one of them poised as if speaking on the phone, and then the birds in the phone booth, the birds perched on seat backs in the tram, the fish inside the tram, and so on. The only signs of humanity are old photos floating on the river, carried gently by the current.

If this film shows Szabó at his most playful, it also shows his thoughtful side. The timelessness of the Danube and its natural life contrasts with the movement of humanity, which seems incidental to the flow of the river; people come and go, but the river remains, majestic and indifferent. The water, the birds, the fish and—yes—the artifacts of human civilization are all interconnected, but can we say that the river and its creatures are "ours"—or are we "theirs"?

Portrait of a Girl (*Lányportré*) returns us to the world of humanity. As in the earlier *You,* Szabó trains his camera on one young woman, but this time his subject is an abstracted representative of all women, and her story touches more than just the immediate present.

As the girl sets off to spend her day, she notices other females who reflect her own past and future—a little girl with a doll, an old woman in a shawl. Soon it is apparent that the camera has entered the young woman's dreams. She leads a parade of everyday people down a street. At home, there are close-ups of her face and hands, mid-shots of her family, her dolls. She sleeps; the camera pulls back to show her bed, inside a tram. Outside, the city passes by.

She stands among spring flowers, the wind blowing her hair. Inside, a tall candle glows; an old woman—the girl's grandmother? or her own future?—sleeps in a chair, covered by her own elaborate crochet work. A cellist plays in the street. A coffin is carried out. An antique clock drifts through the air over the city. A bride appears, and then the whole neighborhood, walking together, the grandma carrying the clock. Finally, the camera holds on a multigenerational group portrait of this community, the bride and groom standing in the rear.

The themes of time and community dominate the longest, and best-known, segment of this series, *A Dream about a House* (*Álom egy házról*). This prize-winning short film is a visual poem reflecting on the events that have taken place over the lifespan of an old apartment building. Generations come and go, repeating an eternal pattern of birth, life, and death. Individuals and families play abstracted roles. We see them as the house itself might—a succession of nameless occupants playing out standardized repetitions of the human story.

In the opening sequence, the tram—one of Szabó's favorite props—rattles along streets in the heart of Pest. Lighting contrasts are sharp as the streetcar passes through deep shadows and tawny, late-afternoon sunlight. The brakes squeal and the tram stops outside the old house; here is where the action will take place. As the tram is left behind, the sound track carries a solo violin playing Bach. There is no other sound. Furniture now appears on the street and sidewalk, and here the inhabitants of the house, young and old, go about their daily lives. They cook, they sew, they deliver bread, they flirt. A fish on a plate appears and reappears, alternately cooked and alive. An old woman resets the hands of a clock (another favored Szabó prop). A young bride and groom move in, and soon they decorate a spindly tree for Christmas. Overlighting now blurs the scene, heightening the abstract quality of the action.

The old woman dies at her sewing machine. The bridegroom, in a brown soldier's uniform, must leave his tearful wife. An elderly gentleman is arrested by officers wearing gray. The grayshirts occupy the building, one or two of them standing guard. But life continues. The bride is seen kissing another man, a young girl unbuttons her blouse and smiles seductively, the fish on a plate reappears. In time, the "grays" are led away by brown-uniformed soldiers. The old man returns from captivity. Everyone embraces him, and the old woman (no longer dead) goes back to her sewing. The old man dies, and the same doctor who had announced the old woman's death confirms his.

The soldier returns to his wife's embrace. He brings another puny tree and decorates it. New people move in. The doctor dies. Now a middle-aged woman assumes the duty of resetting the clock. And the unfaithful bride departs, carrying her suitcase; she pauses, glances back at her husband standing in the doorway, and continues on. On the soundtrack, the music stops. There is again the squeal of the tram; the camera pulls back, and the picture fades out.

A Dream about a House completes this cycle of films, weaving together numerous elements of the symbol system running through the series: the clock, the tram, the fish, the community of interchangeable characters. *Budapest, Why I Love It* is more than a poetic tribute to Szabó's hometown: it is a mosaic of urban life and an impressionistic portrait of humanity.

25 FIREMEN'S STREET AND *BUDAPEST TALES*

From the Budapest series, Szabó moved on to his next feature, *25 Firemen's Street.* The connections are obvious at a glance, and one could get the impression that the Budapest series, while fascinating and complete in itself, served as a sketch pad on which Szabó worked out ideas he put to more dramatic use in *25 Firemen's Street*—a collage-like style, a deep tint of surrealism, the theme of community, and the burden of history.

Szabó's director of photography for *25 Firemen's Street,* Sándor Sára, had worked with Szabó on *Father.* It is Sára's special talent that gives *25 Firemen's*

4.7. Maria amid her ancestors. *25 Firemen's Street.* HUNGAROFILM.

Street its visual textures, rich and yet subdued, inspired by Szabó's careful study of Rembrandt and Brueghel.[21]

In contrast to Lőrincz's emotionally distant camera operating as if objectively, the camera in *25 Firemen's Street* assumes the viewpoint of the characters—but not immediately. First we see the apartment house at 25 Firemen's Street, an old building standing alone in a block undergoing demolition. The small community at number 25 will not live at this address much longer. The camera becomes a voyeur, peeking through their windows on a sultry night; then it steals into their homes and, as they drift one by one into an uneasy sleep, invades their dreams. Their dreams intermingle with memories, and it becomes impossible to tell one from the other.[22]

A woman in her middle years, Mária (played by the Polish actress Lucyna Winnicka), mumbles a quick prayer before floating through the air to become a young girl again. One of her neighbors, Mrs. Gaskóy (Rita Békés), awakens and debates whether or not to swallow yet another sleeping pill. Before settling into the viewpoints of these two people, who will become more or less the central characters, the camera surveys the dreams of several other residents: Mária's son Andris (András Bálint), who dreams of walking in on a beautiful woman as she steps from the bath; Julika (Mari Szemes), who sees herself making love with the younger Andris; a middle-aged man, stumbling about his kitchen in anguish about being left behind by some unnamed others; an elderly man who, awakened by the cries of a dozen babies around him, tries unsuccessfully to quiet them with a song about the great Hungarian patriot, Lajos Kossuth.

Even as the story focuses in on Mária and Mrs. Gaskóy, still more characters populate this surreal world. They come from as far in the past as the First World War, and they bring the narrative forward in time to events that, although abstracted, are recognizable as the aftermath of the 1956 revolt. Mária relives her youthful indecision: should she marry Jancsi or Pista? Mrs. Gaskóy finds a young man in her apartment searching for his violin, and then there is a police raid. An old woman offers sound but chilling advice to her daughter: "Don't wear anything they might kill you for—your brooch, your necklace. . . ." A schoolboy, saying his prayers, invokes Jesus and Stalin. Soldiers, black marketeers, and many more individuals leave their marks on the landscape of Firemen's Street.

The chronological center of Szabó's narrative is the Second World War. It is, of course, a time of horror. Mária and her husband, Dr. Baló, are separated, she to the filth and degradation of prison, he to an unknown fate. They are reunited at war's end, albeit briefly, for the doctor dies—in a reprise of this Szabó obsession, seen before in *Father* and *A Dream about a House.* Meanwhile, Mrs. Gaskóy quietly shelters fugitives in the attic of the family bakery, while a neighbor woman becomes a brutal sergeant of the Fascist Arrow Cross. "We've been bastards, all of us," an old man mumbles, reflecting on the war years. But he is wrong; only some were bastards. Some, like Mrs. Gaskóy, were saints. And some, like the woman who submits Mária to a humiliating body search en route to prison, are just everyday people trying to stay afloat in the current of history; "Forgive me," the woman whispers to Mária.

It is characteristic of Szabó's style at this time that his depiction of the war's horrors is understated. All occurs as if in a dream, tinted by Rembrandt's soft colors; violence is rarely seen, anger is held in check. The suicide of a young woman is shown only in a fragmentary shot of her falling through the air, and the scene completely blurs the line between dream and reality. The most directly violent event is the demolition of the old building—a metaphor that serves for more than merely summarizing the story.

Szabó's judgment on his parents' generation is a picture of complexity. Relating their life experiences is no small feat, but Szabó has accomplished it brilliantly. And more: He has woven the adventures of that generation into a vision of history far more sweeping than the literal time period comprehended by the story.

History, in Szabó's schematic, repeats itself in ironic loops. When Mária returns from prison, she sees the count next door forced from his apartment by the new regime. Mrs. Gaskóy, who never considered herself anything but a good neighbor, receives a hero's recognition for protecting partisans but, when the political winds change again, her bakery is expropriated and nationalized; still later, her fate reverses once more and the woman who administered the expropriation of her bakery now begs for shelter in the attic, like the partisans. And so history moves, folding itself back upon those who imagine they control it—as well as those who have no pretentions to doing so.

4.8. The morning after. The residents watch their home fall to the wrecking crew. *25 Firemen's Street.* HUNGAROFILM.

> Everybody needs a community, a group of human brings to provide acceptance and acknowledgment.
>
> —István Szabó, 1991

Szabó's next feature, *Budapest Tales* (1976), was a direct and conscious outgrowth of *25 Firemen's Street.* Szabó was angered by the public's response to *25 Firemen's Street,* which won only two awards at minor festivals (Locarno and Atlanta) and failed to attract large audiences. He guessed that the public had found the film too complicated, and so he set out to tell "the same story, about the same people, in a very simple way."[23]

Budapest Tales, then, is another community story, told through a simpler narrative.[24] Its simplicity, however, only lies on the surface, above layers of inner story wrapped in an intricate pattern of symbols and metaphors. The protagonists of this film are engaged in an allegorical adventure, struggling to find their way back to civilization from a quasi state of nature. So far abstracted is this drama that the characters and the land they inhabit are unnamed, and the timespan across which the story takes place is only vaguely ascertainable.

The acting ensemble includes two Polish players, Maja Komorowska and Franciszek Pieczka, as well as András Bálint, by now a familiar face in Szabó's films. Several other solid Hungarian actors appear, including József Madaras (well known from numerous roles in Jancsó films) and Ildikó Bánsági (playing her first of several distinguished roles under Szabó's direction).

4.9. Pulling together. *Budapest Tales.* HUNGAROFILM.

In the prologue, black-and-white documentary clips screened to the background music of the Radeczky March tell of a devastating war; we see explosions, destroyed bridges, city buildings in rubble. Abruptly, now in color, we see an overturned tram car, in tilted and rolled camera shots. It is the aftermath of the war, although which war it was is not exactly specified; only the vintage of the tram and the clothing of the protagonists suggest it was World War II. Four survivors emerge from nowhere and find the overturned car beside a riverbank. More refugees appear and, with great effort, they turn the car upright and put it on the tracks. Still others join the group, men and women, and they begin pushing the car across an isolated landscape in the hope that the tracks will lead them to the city they believe is nearby. A new little community takes shape within the tram car, bonded by a myth that develops about the depot at the end of the tracks.

An abandoned warehouse provides stores of food, and distributing the food poses the first explicit question of authority. More such questions arise, and no issue is unimportant: how to defend the community against enemies, what color the car should be painted. The strong-willed rise to the top, expressing their political philosophies to each other in straightforward dialogue—"We ought to decide for them" and "Let's beat the hell out of them." Among the citizens, suspicion and hatred develop. A doctor among them, a wise and sensitive man, is discovered murdered, just inside the forest flanking the tracks.

Trust is a fragile commodity, but the group members know they must pull together if they are to reach their objective. At a point where the track is broken, they devise a way to reinforce the rail—but at the cost of one man's life. He is quickly forgotten, and the car moves on. Later, they must

4.10. A man dies that the tram may continue. *Budapest Tales.* HUNGAROFILM.

cross a river, but the bridge is out; they disassemble the car, float the parts across on a raft, and reassemble them on the other side.

And so the community struggles on, encountering difficulties and overcoming them with determination, bumbling skill, and luck. Rules are proclaimed and broken; the highest moral values are affirmed, and the lowest human traits are displayed. Doubt sometimes clouds over the people's optimism, and all express their fear. In the end, however, they reach the depot that signals their return to civilization. And, in an almost predictable István Szabó touch, other tracks converge with theirs, and other trams carrying other survivors are seen rolling toward the depot.

Szabó consciously styled *Budapest Tales* as a fable; the Hungarian title, *Budapesti mesék,* can be translated as "Budapest Fables" or "Budapest Fairy Tales." Yet this fable offers no explicit moral lesson. Szabó does not judge his characters; he simply leads them through experiences that bring out the best and worst of their human qualities.

Like *Love Film,* which closed Szabó's first filmmaking phase, *Budapest Tales* failed to impress critics. Some tried to read specific meanings into the story and were frustrated, while others found it excessively allegorical and obscure. Even those who viewed the film with some sympathy disagreed on what it was about; Graham Petrie wrote that *Budapest Tales* is "clearly an allegory of Hungarian history since the War," but Karen Jaehne argued that "Hungarian history contributes no necessary or sufficient condition whatsoever for understanding *Budapest Tales.*"[25]

Hungarian critics had no doubt that *Budapest Tales* was specifically about Hungary in the postwar years. There is much in the film to affirm this interpretation, beginning, of course, with the title. In an early scene, a scornful reference to a battered pair of soldiers ("Here comes our bloody army") reflects the humiliation of two wars lost within a third of a century. Arbitrary decision making, reversals of fortune among those who vie for power, and such thinly veiled ideological lines as "You should be happy to be here" smack of the Communist environment. When the exhausted community oversleeps one morning, the clocks are set back so that the day might begin on schedule—a fine metaphor about the rewriting of history, the fudging of Five-Year Plan results, and other reconstructions of truth. Characters whose roles appear to be abstracted—a poet, a thug, a compromiser—resemble real-life public figures whom Hungarian audiences can identify (or imagine they can identify).[26]

Szabó himself has not clearly supported this narrower reading of *Budapest Tales*. His assertion that the film tells the same story as *25 Firemen's Street* is true only in an ambiguous and general way. If *Budapest Tales* is indeed a story about the experiences of a particular Hungarian generation, Jaehne's argument nevertheless holds; there is nothing in the film that uniquely identifies the historical, political, and geographical context. The selfsame story could have been told in Czechoslovakia, Poland, Germany (East or West), or—for that matter—China or Japan. The film depicts any society in the aftermath of a devastating war. And its portrayal of human nature dares to invoke the Hobbes-Locke argument about what it is that motivates human beings to form communities. Whereas *25 Firemen's Street* is a collective memory, *Budapest Tales* is an allegory in the truest sense.

And, as an allegory, *Budapest Tales* begs to be read in a way that reaches beyond specific interpretations. The film is rich with metaphors that give it a universal appeal—the capture and escape of a raven; the birth of twin babies, a new generation, aboard the tram en route to its obscure destination; a blind woman (Komorowska) who "sees" that the tram's color is not yellow, as everyone else pretends, but green. The quest for the depot, which takes on a mythic complexion, can of course be likened to the pursuit of communism; however, it can also be taken as the eternal human quest for community or security.

Szabó professed to have had abstraction in mind when creating *Budapest Tales*.[27] Seen in this light, the film is a philosophical poem about community building, trust, and security—something that eluded most critics, Hungarian and foreign. To be sure, Szabó told this "fairy tale"—the term he prefers to use in describing the film—through allusions to the world he knew. That is why his characters are convincing, and it is why Hungarians recognize specific, real-life individuals. The story's power, however, comes from the fact that the Brechtian characters are recognizable in any community; they represent generalized human qualities—hope, creativity, compassion, violence, and fear.

To understand this film as a broad parable rather than merely an allegory about Hungary helps to place it in the development of Szabó's work. *Budapest Tales* completed a set of films, beginning with *Budapest, Why I Love It*, that departed radically from the personal stories of Szabó's early period. At the same time, it carried one of his strongest early themes—community—to its most explicit statement.

In the same year as *Budapest Tales,* Szabó completed a short film, *City Map* (*Várostérkép,* 1976), in which he returned once again to explicit reflections on his home city, expressed, as in *Budapest, Why I Love It,* in a poetic language.

Urban vignettes captured by the camera of Gábor Szabó—silent church bells, people's faces, a streetcar, still photographs of individuals and families—are punctuated by the recurring image of an old map of Budapest. Again Szabó has created a collage of sights, but, in contrast to *Budapest, Why I Love It,* he has added the sounds of the city. The camera roams along snowy streetscapes and draws close up to doors, iron grillwork, a clock; it finds a family singing a Christmas carol, sees crowds celebrating a public holiday. Gunfire is heard, tanks roll down the street, and a young woman stands before her demolished home. The wartime images are interspersed among peacetime scenes. In a final sequence, people united by personal or professional ties—a family, nuns, old war veterans in uniform, the staffs of a restaurant and of a bakery—are gathered into group portraits, and the specific constituency of each group changes as one member steps out of the scene and another takes his or her place.

Aside from the specific choice of vignettes and the sounds, what distinguishes *City Map* from the earlier Budapest series is the map. Szabó has personified the map, given it the starring role. Instead of an old building, as in *A Dream about a House,* it is the map that sees the city in all its beauty and ugliness.

It is interesting, but *City Map* lacks the freshness of *Budapest, Why I Love It.* Szabó repeats many of his earlier images and takes on no significant new ideas. *City Map* is an artful film, and it might have been a successful addition to the earlier Budapest series in its time; however, following upon *25 Firemen's Street* and *Budapest Tales, City Map* reads like a gratuitous summary at the end of an elegantly written chapter.

NEW VISTAS

If there is anything cinematically conventional about *Budapest Tales,* it is its straight-line narrative progression. It is impossible to say exactly how much time passes in the course of the story, although the growth of the twins born aboard the tram car tells us it is years rather than weeks. Nevertheless, the story itself proceeds from its beginning to its end without any of the startling flashbacks and flash-forwards that run through *Love Film* and *25 Firemen's Street.*

By the end of *City Map,* Szabó's iconography has reached the baroque. Some of the recurring images can be traced back to the filmmaker's early period. The tram and its long-distance equivalent, the train, go back to *Love Film* and even *Father;*[28] the fish to *Love Film;* the weapons of war and the rubble they produce to *Variations on a Theme* and *Piety;* clocks and other timepieces to *Father;* and the river to Szabó's diploma film, *Concert.* Other icons are more specific to this second period of his work—the baker, photo portraits and mirror-glass reflections, the Christmas tree. It is both complicated and superfluous to explain exactly what these images mean; we know—or can reasonably guess—what they signify; and yet fitting them together like jigsaw pieces into a coherent whole is something only Szabó's artistic mind can accomplish.

It had to end; the artist needed to move on. *Love Film* had exhausted Szabó's early themes while contributing something to his aesthetic ideas; *City Map,* on the contrary, depleted his store of aesthetic material while yielding nothing new thematically.

And yet, there was something in the films of Szabó's second period that would lead him into his next artistic phase and lift his career to unexpected heights. It was the theme of role-playing, which is implicit in *Budapest Tales.* In *Budapest Tales,* the characters aboard the tram are obliged to redefine their functions; whether they were barbers or dentists or soldiers in the past becomes secondary to the need to be mechanics, food gatherers, decision makers, and guards.

Role-playing is a central thread in Szabó's next film, *Confidence,* and it dominates the plots of *Mephisto, Colonel Redl,* and *Hanussen.*[29] Szabó employs the motif of role-playing to develop the theme that becomes his obsession during the 1980s—people acting like people they're not in order to achieve fame, power, or security.

If Szabó was disappointed with the reception of *25 Firemen's Street,* he had all the more reason to feel frustration after *Budapest Tales,* which attracted much negative criticism and no awards whatsoever. He realized he needed a different approach if he was to reconnect with the audience and win back the critics. Perhaps this explains, in part, why he startled his followers by his sudden conversion to realism.

It would not be fair to say that Szabó's change of style came about simply because he craved acceptance. Looking back, Szabó's own explanation—"because I became an adult"[30]—tells us that he abandoned experimentalism by conscious choice; he knew the new tasks to which his muse was calling him required a different approach.

Szabó has never been one to subordinate his stories to preordained forms. Although he admired the French *new wave,* he did not make *The Age of Daydreaming* because he wished to mimic Truffaut; he adopted the Truffaut style because it fitted the story he wished to tell. The same is true of *Love Film* and *25 Firemen's Street:* He devised the complicated narratives in order to display the threads of dream and memory woven into his characters' lives. And if, for *Budapest Tales,* his motive was to tell a simple fable, the resulting story was anything but simple.

For his next feature, Szabó chose a story that dictated a straight-line, quasi-third-person narrative. Except for one flashback sequence, the beginning, the middle, and the end follow clearly in that order, and the time that

4.11. Kata, in a rare moment outside, queues for potatoes. *Confidence.* HUNGAROFILM.

passes can be measured in weeks or months. The intensity of the drama and the intimacy of the setting are enough to propel the film; narrative complexity is not needed and, indeed, would be inappropriate. It is to Szabó's credit that he recognized this.

Confidence is the story of a man and a woman trapped in the fierce combat raging in Budapest during the autumn and winter of 1944–1945. The end of the German occupation is near, but the Nazis and their Hungarian Fascist allies are determined to fight to the end. Kata (Ildikó Bánsági) has lost track of her husband, a member of the partisan resistance. In danger from the authorities, Kata has had to flee her home, and she has become separated from her little daughter. A partisan sympathizer gives her false identification papers and arranges refuge for her in the home of an elderly couple on the outskirts of the city. Sharing her one-room hideout is another fugitive—a man—whom she has never before met. According to her documents and her instructions, she must now pretend to be his wife, Mrs. János Bíró.

For their safety, János and Kata must play their roles convincingly, concealing the truth even from the old couple who serve as their hosts. Both find their situation in these close quarters unnerving. Kata feels isolated and fearful for her husband and daughter. János, active in the underground, goes away frequently, leaving Kata even more lonely and anxious; when

4.12. Kata and János. *Confidence.* HUNGAROFILM.

she ventures out on her own, however, he berates her. Their very personal conflict reflects the war going on outside—a war that remains in the background throughout the story.

In the midst of this nerve-wracking situation, Kata and János suddenly find themselves in love, or at least irresistible lust. And yet their passion does not break down the barriers between them. Kata opens herself to János, offers him her trust, her confidence, but he is too much a product of the underground environment to trust her completely. Their love-hate relationship within the confinement of their room affords them little more security than the violent world outside.

And just when this condition begins to seem permanent, the outside world mutates. Budapest is liberated, and they are free to leave. But what do they return to? For Kata, the answer is clear: she returns to her family, whatever the pain of leaving her temporary lover. For János, however, the new era holds a position of responsibility and a continued struggle. But we see János, in the final scene, seeking something else. There is a long queue of people at an agency, searching for loved ones from whom they have been separated. Running up and down the line of people is János, anxiously calling out the name "Mrs. János Bíró"—searching for Kata.

The intimacy of *Confidence* is reminiscent of Szabó's earliest films. Like *Love Film, Confidence* focuses on two people, a man and a woman, and stays with their story to its conclusion. *Confidence* is in fact more intimate and intense than *Love Film,* for it takes place primarily within the confines of Kata and János's one-room hideout.

The acting by Ildikó Bánsági and Péter Andorai is outstanding, and the emotional intensity of their characters is heightened by the fine camerawork of Lajos Koltai. Exteriors—and they are very few—are drab, and every street appears threatening. Inside the refugee couple's room, the play of light and shadows heightens the protagonists' sense of claustrophobia.

Actress Bánsági has testified to the difficulty of creating some of the more powerful scenes—especially the lovemaking scene and those in which the characters fight. During the filming of some scenes, only the two actors plus Szabó and Koltai were allowed on the set, and once Szabó even turned away while Koltai shot the scene.[31]

Confidence marks a turning point for Szabó. Readily comprehensible by the mass international film audience, *Confidence* also pleased many critics for its clean, straightforward drama. The film captured the Silver Bear at the Berlin Festival in 1980 and was nominated for an Academy Award in 1981. Bánsági has commented that the title is applicable to the director himself—that is, Szabó discovered a self-confidence that carried him into the next period of his work and changed his directing style. He began to trust his actors, worked the script with them, heard their opinions. According to Bánsági, Szabó also began to trust himself more, for example by relying on fewer takes per scene.[32]

Thanks to his fine work in *Confidence,* Lajos Koltai now became Szabó's mainstay behind the camera. Koltai directed the photography for the Central European trilogy and stayed on Szabó's team, at the director's insistence, for the British-produced *Meeting Venus.*

After the success of *Confidence,* the stage was set for the beginning of Szabó's career as an international director. His greatest critical and commercial triumph was soon to come.

Szabó's Third Period

> **The Central European experience is the struggle of the individual amid the storms of history.**
>
> **—István Szabó, 1985**

The storms of history swirl around the edges of Szabó's films from the 1970s. They are in the dreams of *25 Firemen's Street,* in the back story of *Budapest Tales,* and off screen in *Confidence.* In Szabó's next films, his protagonists plunge directly into the storms of the twentieth century. They are not primary players in history but individuals whose choices propel them into conflicts that overwhelm them. They are accomplices in those great and tragic crimes that shattered Central Europe.

THE CENTRAL EUROPEAN TRILOGY

Confidence's success opened new possibilities for Szabó. With *Mephisto* (1981), he entered the world of international co-productions, where he discovered the advantages and disadvantages of working with Western producers. The advantages, of course, are money and access to the world cinematic market; the disadvantages are the controlling power of the producer and the constraints of the profit motive. It was a big step for a director whose heart is so strongly entwined with his home country. Szabó took it only after satisfying himself that he could film a story that was to his liking.

And what a choice it was! *Mephisto* proved to be as much a "miracle" as *Father* had been—a perfect match of story, thematic material, directorial style, and something new in a Szabó film: a towering performance by a fresh actor, Klaus Maria Brandauer.

The right story was found in an obscure German novel written by Klaus Mann, the son of Thomas Mann. A German producer, Manfred Durniok of West Berlin, proposed the idea to Szabó and agreed to cooperate with Szabó's MAFILM studio, Objektiv. Szabó asked Hungarian novelist and screenwriter Péter Dobai to draft a screenplay. Szabó streamlined the script and revised it to fit the capabilities of Brandauer, the Austrian stage actor whom Szabó chose for the starring role. It was the first time Szabó shared screenplay credits.

The story is about the rise and corruption of an actor, Hendrik Höfgen (Brandauer). The character of Höfgen is believed to have been modeled after Gustav Gründgens, the brother-in-law of Klaus Mann.[33] In the opening scene, Höfgen, a small-time actor in the cabarets and proletarian theaters of Hamburg, rages backstage while the renowned actress Dora Martin (Ildikó Kishonti) receives a tumultuous ovation onstage. Höfgen lusts for the acclaim of the crowds and dedicates himself to achieving it. Dora Martin recognizes his talent and helps him get a start in Berlin. There he becomes famous just as the Nazis seize power.

When colleagues warn him about the dangers growing in Berlin, Höfgen ignores them. He now has a patron: a Joseph Goebbels look-alike referred to as the minister-president (Rolf Hoppe), who adores Höfgen's acting and knows Höfgen's vulnerabilities. Höfgen's star rises rapidly, and soon he becomes artistic director of the State Theater.

Höfgen's rise is by no means due to any political conversion; indeed, he believes himself apolitical. Before long, however, he becomes helplessly enmeshed in the evil of the Third Reich. He betrays a Jewish friend (Péter Andorai); loses his wife (Krystyna Janda), who becomes a political exile; gives up his part-African mistress (Karin Boyd); confiscates protest leaflets found in his theater; and directs a Hamlet who, in Höfgen's interpretation, stands as a model for the master race.

As the madness of Nazism engulfs him, Höfgen takes on the greatest role of his career: as Mephistopheles. He awes the crowds and impresses the minister-president, who refers to Höfgen as "my Mephisto." Höfgen marries a woman of the aristocracy, Nicoletta von Niebuhr (Ildikó Bánsági). At a high-power soirée, the minister-president proclaims them the quintessential German couple.

At the summit of his career, Höfgen is taken to see the newly constructed

4.13. Art confronts power. *Mephisto.* HUNGAROFILM.

4.14. The true face of Hendrik Höfgen. *Mephisto.* HUNGAROFILM.

Olympic stadium, built to herald the triumph of German culture. Here, the minister-president tells him, he will perform to massive audiences. Suddenly the spotlights come on and Höfgen is blinded. He hears his name echoing from the loudspeakers around the empty stadium and staggers in confusion. His image bleaches and fades into the whitening screen.

Höfgen's inability to see is obviously a reference to the blindness of Faust at the end of Goethe's great drama. The film ends here; we may conjecture that Höfgen's blindness, like that of Faust, signifies that he now finally sees the error of his ways—or perhaps not.

Mephisto is different from all previous Szabó films. There is in *Mephisto* no confusion about time, no memory sequences, no enigmatic symbolism. Its grandiosity is on a scale that cannot be compared to the intimacy of *Father* or *Confidence*. In contrast to the conscious understatement characterizing Szabó's previous work, *Mephisto* speaks in a language that is emphatic, driving home its thesis about the inseparability of art and politics and the necessity of moral choice. For viewers who thought they knew Szabó, the change in style was remarkable—even more so than the change that produced *Confidence*.

International audiences responded enthusiastically, and critical honors accumulated, including an Academy Award for best foreign-language film. At Cannes, Szabó and Dobai shared both the jury prize and the FIPRESCI award for best screenplay. More awards poured in from the world's film capitals—Rome, London, New York; back home, *Mephisto* won the main prize at the Hungarian National Feature Festival, and Szabó was named best director by Hungarian film critics.[34]

Much credit must go to Klaus Maria Brandauer, whose performance propels the film, and the fine international supporting cast, including Bánsági, Hoppe, Boyd, Janda, Andorai, Christine Harbort, and György Cserhalmi. Amid this bounty of talent, it is Brandauer's singular power that lingers in the viewer's memory.

Szabó's choice of Brandauer for the starring role was a courageous one. Although well established on the major stages of Vienna and Salzburg, Brandauer had never before entered the world of film. On screen, Brandauer has a commanding presence; his face is unrelentingly intense, and his eyes seem to hypnotize the camera. He displays a dramatic energy that makes him capable of stealing any scene—as he demonstrated subsequently by costarring with Robert Duvall in Jerzy Skolimowski's *The Lightship* (1985) and Robert Redford and Meryl Streep in Sidney Pollack's *Out of Africa* (1985).

Once discovered, Brandauer proved a difficult actor to direct, and directors other than Szabó have voiced complaints about Brandauer's ego and temperament. It was said that Brandauer refused to attend the premiere of *The Lightship* at the Venice festival because the festival officials would not send a private jet to Salzburg for him. After directing him in *The Lightship*, Skolimowski told an interviewer he wouldn't mind seeing Brandauer "cut into small pieces on the screen."[35]

Nor did Brandauer always behave himself when working with the man who gave him his ticket to stardom. Brandauer eagerly followed Szabó's direction during the shooting of *Mephisto,* but thereafter the actor's strong will and mercurial temperament asserted themselves more and more. By the time *Hanussen* was filmed, Brandauer's ego led to disagreements with Szabó. At times Szabó, whose style of working normally relies on the strict maintenance of directorial authority, found himself obliged to let Brandauer run with the script, or else risk losing control of the filming entirely. Upon the completion of *Hanussen,* it seemed clear to everyone that the Szabó-Brandauer partnership had come to an end.[36]

There is no denying the power of their collaboration in *Mephisto,* however. If it is true that Szabó made a star of Brandauer, it is also true that Brandauer's driving performance in *Mephisto* made Szabó's international career. The whole world recognized the magic in their teamwork, and the message was not lost on *Mephisto*'s producer. It was inevitable that Szabó's next Manfred Durniok production would include his newfound star.

Thus it was that the same core team assembled for the second film in Szabó's international career, *Colonel Redl* (1984). Szabó chose the story from an actual historical incident, with Brandauer specifically in mind for the title role. Dobai again drafted the screenplay, and Lajos Koltai directed the photography.

Colonel Redl is a bizarre and sinister tale about the rise and fall of a powerful army officer in the dying years of the Austro-Hungarian Empire. In an abstract sense, *Colonel Redl* is to *Mephisto* as *25 Firemen's Street* is to *Father,* for in *Colonel Redl* Szabó reached back to the preceding generation whose story helps to explain the catastrophe of the 1930s and 1940s. In Szabó's interpretation, the collapse of the Habsburg Empire (and, by extension, the entire Central European order) presaged the horrors that were to come. The character of Colonel Redl is a personification of the old order's frailty.

The story of Alfried Redl begins as a rags-to-riches tale. A child of mixed ethnicity and the lower middle class, he is nevertheless admitted to an imperial military academy because, his mother tells him, of the munificence of the emperor. For someone of Redl's origins, the army offers the only possibility of advancing into the ranks of the elite. And doing just this becomes Redl's undying ambition.

Moving upward through the ranks of the army, Redl remembers his mother's words and adopts the only political position he believes appropriate for a soldier: he is *kaisertreu*—almost naively loyal to the emperor. He becomes a fanatic about defending the monarchy against its internal enemies. Political conspiracies abound in the empire, with its plethora of restless nationalities, and the army is not immune to trouble. Early in his career, duty requires Redl to report that two other officers, including his longtime friend Kristóf Kubínyi (Jan Niklas), have committed the political sin of criticizing the Austro-Hungarian Compromise of 1867.

While commanding troops on the Russian frontier, Redl cracks down on insubordination. Throughout the ranks there is a feeling that the empire is on the verge of collapse, and discipline is increasingly hard to maintain. Redl fights untiringly for order and against dissent, and the troops come to regard him as an enemy. Rumors spread about Redl—he is a Jew, or a homosexual. Both may be true; either would end his career.

For the moment, however, fortune smiles on Redl. He is called to Vienna and becomes chief military intelligence officer. He is now admired and feared, and he moves among the highest social circles. His job, as he understands it, is to eradicate those who would weaken or destroy the state. The task is more complicated than it appears. In a meeting with the archduke (Armin Müller-Stahl), Redl identifies five officers guilty of high treason—and learns that the arcane complexities of politics within the empire determine which individuals may, and may not, be prosecuted.

Too late, Redl finds himself lost in a political labyrinth. The traitors he has identified are in league with the archduke, who wishes to use them in making his own move against the emperor. Worse, Redl learns by reading his own personnel file that he has influential enemies. They have condemned him, on the record, for the very acts he thought were his duty: spying on, and reporting as traitors, his fellow officers.

Meanwhile, there is talk of war. At a masked ball, the atmosphere is filled with intrigue. For the first time, the hope is expressed that Germany will be the savior of Austria. At midnight, the masks come off and the archduke makes a triumphant entry.

Redl's mask comes off, too. He meets a young boy in circumstances that suggest he is being set up, and they go off for a sexual encounter. As if consciously following the script of a Greek tragedy, Redl allows the boy to pump him for military secrets. Redl knows he is doomed, and, curiously enough, he now appears relieved. Soon, of course, he is arrested. Offered the chance to shoot himself and avoid a public scandal, Redl does so.

In an epilogue, Redl's possessions are auctioned off. Newsreel clips show the archduke's assassination and the opening campaigns of the First World War.

Colonel Redl is a bold drama driven, like *Mephisto,* by the screen presence of Brandauer and held together by a plot filled with intrigue. Yet *Redl* does not have quite the power of *Mephisto.* Some scenes are elliptical, and at times the action, as one American critic has written, "seems weighty and frozen."[37] Brandauer, at once passionate and restrained, is especially convincing in the suicide scene, where he agonizes and paces before finally resolving, in a frenzy, to commit the deed.[38]

The elliptical quality of *Redl* resulted, in large part, from the producer's pressures. Szabó's producer was determined to keep the film within conventional lengths. The circumstances of Redl's life, however, were full of psychological twists and political complications. The overarching context, the demise of the Austro-Hungarian monarchy, defied the constraints of conventional cinema. Dobai's original script was very long and detailed; Szabó cut large portions to satisfy the producers, and even so, the resulting film runs to two and a half hours.

4.15. Colonel Redl confronts his doom. *Colonel Redl.* HUNGAROFILM.

Colonel Redl received many honors, including the special jury prize at Cannes, the British Academy Award for best foreign-language film, and the award for best West German film in 1985. It was clear to all that *Mephisto* was no accident; *Colonel Redl,* despite its flaws, was indisputably the work of a master. István Szabó was now one of the most respected European directors.

For *Mephisto* and *Colonel Redl,* Szabó developed new icons, the most important of which is the mask. The literal masks worn by Redl and the others at the ball remind us of Hendrik Höfgen, who played the role of Mephistopheles in whiteface. Redl began wearing a mask of another sort the minute he first tried to be something he was not; his military uniform, with all its snap and authority, covered up what he really was—an insecure young man from a marginal background with a sexual orientation that was unacceptable in his society. Höfgen's mask, on the contrary, served to expose the actor's true quality—the evil of his complicity in the crimes of his patrons.

Many common strands link *Mephisto* and *Colonel Redl.* The total sense of Szabó's work during the 1980s, however, became clear only with the third film of the Central European trilogy, *Hanussen,* for it is in *Hanussen* that the story stretches from the First World War into the Nazi era and roams from Budapest to Berlin.

> I tell stories about Central European mental diseases.
>
> —István Szabó, 1985

In *Hanussen,* Szabó delved more explicitly into the psychopathology of

Central Europe. Again he chose a story based on a real personality, and again he enlisted Péter Dobai in the task of writing the screenplay.

The opening scene is a World War I battle raging in a churchyard.[39] Klaus Schneider (Brandauer), a sergeant in the Austro-Hungarian army, receives head wounds and is taken to a hospital. During his recovery, a crazed patient threatens to blow up the ward with a grenade. Schneider stops him and, in the process, discovers that he has the power to hypnotize. The physician attending his recovery, Dr. Bettelheim (Erland Josephson), is an early medical practitioner of hypnotism. Bettelheim invites Schneider to work with him after the war in the suicide ward of a teaching hospital in Budapest.

Schneider has been in Budapest only a short time when an old war comrade, Nowotny (Károly Eperjes), persuades him to forsake medicine and use his talent to achieve fame. With Nowotny as his manager, Schneider adopts the stage name of Erik Jan Hanussen and heads for Vienna. On stage, he predicts that an ocean liner will sink; when it does, his reputation spreads—not only can he hypnotize, he can predict the future.

Nowotny now takes Hanussen on tour, along with his new assistant (Adriana Biedrzyńska), formerly a woman journalist whom he has seduced and given a new name, Wally. She becomes his close companion, believing in him and putting up with his rampant infidelities.

Not all goes well on tour. In Karlsbad, now within the newly independent Czechoslovakia, Hanussen stands trial for fraud. He proves his innocence but antagonizes the tribunal by professing himself a citizen of "Central Europe" and declaring his fidelity to the empire—not a popular sentiment in republican Czechoslovakia.

Then it is on to Berlin and greater fame—but also greater danger. Hanussen predicts the crash of the commodity markets, pleases a gathering of industrialists by telling them that the people hate the Weimar Republic, and stuns another audience into silence by predicting that Adolf Hitler will become chancellor. Like Höfgen in *Mephisto*, Hanussen claims to be apolitical, but he cannot avoid being drawn into the web of politics. At a séance, it is revealed that Hanussen has the same birthday as Hitler. At a session with a photographer, a woman who has also photographed Hitler, he strikes poses that resemble those of the Führer.

Inevitably, Hanussen falls into peril. He meets an exotic dancer, Valery de la Meer (Grażyna Szapołowska), who turns out to be Váli Tóth, a childhood friend. Symbolically, Váli's family had owned a pharmacy that burned to the ground, giving Schneider/Hanussen nightmares about fire persisting into adulthood. He has an affair with Váli, despite the dangerous fact that she is the mistress of Berlin's chief of police. The chief sends his subordinate, Captain Becker (Michał Bajor), to disrupt one of Hanussen's performances. Hanussen turns the tables—he calls Becker onto the stage and humiliates him by forcing him, under hypnosis, to crow like a cock.

During another performance, Hanussen hypnotizes a woman from the

4.16. Hanussen persuades the hypnotized woman to torch the curtain. *Hanussen.* HUNGAROFILM.

audience and persuades her to set fire to the stage curtain. Later, Hanussen predicts the burning of the *Reichstag.* This is too much for the sinister political forces who are now positioning themselves in Berlin. They ban the sale of newspapers reporting Hanussen's prediction.

Hanussen and Wally are taken by car into a forest. It is the moment of revenge for Captain Becker, who has abducted them. Becker orders Hanussen to climb onto a tree branch and crow like a cock, and then executes him and Wally. The film ends with a newsreel clip: the *Reichstag* fire.

Hanussen is replete with symbols, iconic elements, and lines of dialogue that yield clues, subtle and bold, about the complicated message running through the story. Gone are the explicit masks seen in *Mephisto* and *Colonel Redl*—although, in a sense, the haunting face of Klaus Maria Brandauer is its own kind of mask, and the benign faces of those he hypnotizes (like the torch woman) are masks concealing their destructive potential.

Back again is the figure of the doctor, whose wisdom and humaneness stand in contrast to the madness of the world around him. In persuading Schneider to come to Budapest, Dr. Bettelheim tells him, "Your gift must be used to help others." Appearing again in Berlin, Bettelheim offers a piece of good advice that Hanussen ignores: get out of Berlin.

Another resurrected icon is the train. It is while riding a train that Klaus Schneider decides to change his name to Hanussen, completing his transition to an identity that is tied up with a tragic destiny.

Hanussen contains new elements, however, including the dominant

4.17. Hanussen's humiliation. *Hanussen.* HUNGAROFILM.

motif of fire: the fire of Schneider's childhood memory, the fire set by the woman onstage, and ultimately, of course, the *Reichstag* fire. These all index the cataclysm into which Germany, and all of Europe, will soon plunge.

For the first time in a Szabó film, religion becomes a motif.[40] The first spoken words are the Lord's Prayer, murmured in fear by Sgt. Schneider in the heat of the churchyard battle. Schneider's transformation to the all-knowing Hanussen makes an atheist of him. During his trial in Karlsbad, Nowotny suggests that if Hanussen is acquitted, they should go to a church and give thanks; Hanussen retorts, "To whom?" In the end, Hanussen turns back to God when confronting his executioner. He prays in vain for his dignity—"Dear God, please don't let him make me crow"—and then, in desperation for his soul, mutters the Lord's Prayer once more.

The doomed man's pathetic prayers confirm that *Hanussen* is a story about humanity's need to believe in something. Erik Jan Hanussen is the charlatan desperate people follow when they feel abandoned by those powers, earthly and sacred, who have betrayed their faith.

The names of characters, and even the casting choices, give further clues about Szabó's message. "Dr. Bettelheim" was not a random name for the psychiatrist; Szabó no doubt had Bruno Bettelheim in mind. The name of Hanussen's photographer, who seeks to portray human perfection, is Henni Stahl—an obvious reference to Leni Riefenstahl. Again Szabó chose an international cast, and, true to the Central European melting pot Hanussen himself stands for, the players jumble their own national origins: Szapołowska (as Váli Tóth, a Hungarian) and Biedrzyńska (as Wally, an Austrian) are Poles; Eperjes (as Nowotny, probably a Czech/Austrian) and

György Cserhalmi (as the Berliner Trantow-Waldbach) are Hungarians; and Josephson (as Bettelheim, a Hungarian Jew) is a Swede.

Hanussen plays out a dialectic of nationalism and "Central Europeanism." Just as strongly as Hanussen identifies with Central Europe, Bettelheim considers himself a Hungarian, not a Jew, as he makes clear during a touching scene in a Berlin café. He hears an elderly matron across the room singing a Hungarian song and quietly sings along with her. One must wonder if this is not a profession from the soul of director Szabó, also a Jew with deep attachments to his specific homeland within Central Europe.

The critics' consensus is that *Hanussen* is a weak link in the Central European trilogy. An English critic put it well, writing that *Hanussen* "doesn't reach the concentrated intensity of the two earlier films; it's sometimes sketchy and . . . over-explicit."[41] A French critic noted that Szabó, having taken awards at Cannes during his two previous appearances there, this time (1988) went home empty-handed, and justly so: "With the passage of time, the team of István Szabó and Klaus Maria Brandauer has lost its sharpness, and the type of films the two men make . . . is reaching its limitations."[42]

Reaching its limitations, perhaps—but not yet a bad film. *Hanussen* is a gripping story with many fine Szabó touches, including a few moments of playfulness. For example, when soldiers bury World War I combat victims in a new cemetery that is soon to be consecrated by the emperor, they inscribe on two grave markers the names "Franz Josef" and "Kaiser Wilhelm." Their commanding officer had ordered them to give unknown victims whatever names they wished—but, as he now berates his soldiers, he meant "real names—Wajda, Menzel, Jancsó." Szabó thus compounds the joke with a play on the names of three other prominent Central European film directors.

The critics are right, however; neither these witty touches nor the apt metaphor of the charlatan makes *Hanussen* a great film. Szabó himself, perhaps overly self-critical, considers it a failure. There is something missing in the drama, and Szabó believes he knows what it is. In real life, the clairvoyant was a Jew, or part Jewish. Dobai wrote the character's Jewishness into the screenplay, but Szabó took it out. He was afraid that, in his words, "to tell the story of a Jewish man who collaborated with the Nazis and wanted only to save himself would make the film anti-Semitic." This may be a rationalization on the part of a director for whom the subject of the Jews is very personal and painful. In retrospect, Szabó believes that this change robbed the story of its real tragedy.[43]

If *Hanussen* is the weakest of the three Szabó-Dobai-Brandauer films, it nevertheless completes the cycle; without it, an essential part of the Central European saga would be lacking. *Hanussen*'s geographic sweep, from Budapest to Berlin, connects the idea of *Mitteleuropa*. In addition, *Hanussen* focuses the story on the populist dimension of Nazism: the appeal of the charlatan, the desire to overcome insecurity by knowing the future, and the danger of speaking the truth.

The dialectic of nationalism and Central Europeanism, nowhere more explicit than in *Hanussen,* brings together the complex thesis permeating the entire trilogy. The peoples and cultures occupying the heart of Europe are bound together, whatever their singular caprices. Their common history is a conflict between security and identity, between the deceptive comfort of authority and the uncertain appeal of freedom. *Mephisto, Colonel Redl,* and *Hanussen,* produced during the last decade of the Cold War, express a complex sentiment many Central Europeans were already beginning to voice. Just as much as they longed to reaffirm their national identities and revalidate their specific cultures, they also longed to escape the destructive obsessiveness of nationalism that for nearly two centuries had brought their communities into conflict.

The events that began to unfold in Central Europe from 1989—one year after the release of *Hanussen*—have made of Szabó a prophet. That same dialectic continues to play itself out as the nations of the region redefine their collective identities and grope for new models of security.

Meeting Venus: *Another Turning Point?*

In 1991, Szabó completed a film that appeared to mark yet another major change in his career. *Meeting Venus* took Szabó out of the co-production milieu and into a contract with one producer only—a foreign one. The film was shot in Hungary, and Hungarian production resources were used; however, for *Meeting Venus* István Szabó had only one boss: David Puttnam, the head of Enigma Productions Ltd. in London. The screenplay is the product of a collaboration between Szabó and Michael Hirst, and the cinematography is by Lajos Koltai.

Meeting Venus centers on a multinational production of Richard Wagner's opera *Tannhäuser.* At first glance, the film has little in common with the Szabó works of the 1970s and 1980s. It is a contemporary story, set mostly in Paris—outside Szabó's familiar Central Europe. In contrast to Szabó's traditional preference for dramatic stories with just a touch of wit, *Meeting Venus* is a comedy, albeit with a serious underlying message.

It doesn't require deep analysis, however, to spot some customary Szabó touches. Like *Confidence, Meeting Venus* has two dominating actors at its center. American star Glenn Close plays a soprano in the opera production, and a previously little-known Danish actor, Niels Arestrup, plays the conductor. Like the Central European trilogy, *Meeting Venus* also features an ensemble of able supporting actors from a multiplicity of countries.

Already in the two lead roles, it is apparent that Szabó is up to one of his casting tricks from the 1980s; the diva played by Close is Swedish, and the conductor played by Arestrup is a Hungarian. With few exceptions, the supporting cast is similarly mixed. Erland Josephson, the Swedish veteran best known for his roles in Bergman films, plays the managing director of the Opéra Europa, Jorge Picabia, a Spaniard; Czech character actor Marian Labuda plays the tenor Von Schneider, a German from the former German

4.18. Part of the Tannhäuser cast, with diva Karin Anderson and conductor Zoltán Szántó in the center. *Meeting Venus.* Warner Brothers.

Democratic Republic; Parisian actress Maite Nahyr plays Maria Krawiecki, a Polish soprano; and this only begins to list the players in this cosmopolitan stew. All performances are strong, and especially impressive is the acting of newcomer Arestrup.

A number of gifted singers contribute their voices to the music. Close sings with the voice of Kiri Te Kanawa; Labuda's singing is dubbed by René Kollo, and Nahyr's by Waltraud Meier.

The common language among the musicians is English—"broken English," as Szabó has described it, for only one of the performers of the Opéra Europa is an anglophone (American tenor Stephen Taylor, played by American actor Jay O. Sanders). Each has his or her own prejudices and complexes, personal and nationalistic, and all believe themselves worthy of being stars.

Into this volatile mix steps Zoltán Szántó (Arestrup), freshly arrived from Budapest. He brings a baton case full of Hungarian complexes—now that we are free, do we really belong in Europe? I've proven myself in Budapest; do I have the talent to make it in Paris? But he also brings a genuine dedication to music, and he expects the same of his performers.

Zoltán's first challenge is taming the diva, Karin Anderson (Close). Karin, cast in the role of Elizabeth, makes it clear that she does not consider the upstart Hungarian her master.

Zoltán runs into other problems. The musicians are unhappy about their wages and do not fail to complain about them. Their union requires them to take coffee breaks and limits their working hours so severely that Zoltán despairs over the amount of time available for rehearsal. He begins to feel that he is the only one in the entire production who really cares about the music.

The complications pile up. Outside, environmental activists angrily protest the production's sponsor, a corporation ironically named Eurogreen. Inside, Thomas, the stage manager (François Delaive), refuses to allow anyone else to raise or lower the curtain. He's usually there when needed—but not always. The Opéra Europa's administration is bogged down in bureacracy. Picabia, an idealistic old socialist, sympathizes with the musicians' union and refuses to pressure them. In a letter to his wife Edith (Dorottya Udvaros), Zoltán muses, "Everything moves so slowly here, apparently because of democracy."

As if the offstage difficulties are not enough, personal rivalries surface among the cast. When these erupt in conflicts one day, Zoltán sits down at the piano and bangs out an improvised song about all the national groups and "how they hate each other."

This inspired act of frustration wins Karin over, and soon the maestro and the diva fall madly in love. That gets Zoltán in trouble with other members of the cast—not to mention his wife—and when his mixed-up passion explodes outside Karin's room, he gets in trouble with the police, once in Paris and once in Budapest.

Somehow, the company makes it to the night of the big performance, which is about to be telecast around the world. And then, at the last minute, Thomas announces he is on strike. The curtain cannot be raised.

Thinking fast, Zoltán comes up with a solution. They will perform *Tannhäuser* concert style, with the principals standing onstage in front of the closed curtain. The chorus will file in from the rear of the auditorium and sing from the aisles. It is not easy to sell this idea to the stage director/set designer, Von Binder (Dieter Laser), but he has little choice. Zoltán insists it will work; the music alone will carry it.

And he is right. The audience is stunned, first by the style of the production and then by the quality. The musicians know they are giving the performance of their lives. In the end, Zoltán has triumphed.

There are a number of weaknesses in *Meeting Venus*. Most obviously, the final crisis and its resolution seem contrived. It is hard to believe that one crew member could stymie such an important production, and almost as hard to believe that the impromptu "nonstaging" of the opera could be such an overpowering achievement.[44]

Szabó's ensemble approach, following numerous little stories in a fashion reminiscent of Robert Altman, is good for showing the petty conflicts permeating the company, but it extracts a cost in terms of the central characters' story. Zoltán and Karin's initial feud is unconvincing; the conflict between them seems more cogent in the maestro's narrative than in the action—a rather clumsy way of projecting it. As a result, their falling in love is predictable and trite. Still, their passion for each other is reasonably convincing, as is the passion of Zoltán's inevitable clash with Edith.

More seriously, the connection that is meant to hold together this "inner" story of Zoltán's two loves and the "outer" story of the *Tannhäuser* production is obscure. One presumes that Zoltán's scrambled love life is supposed to equate with Tannhäuser's being torn between Venus and Elizabeth, a titanic conflict between sacred and profane love. But our only real clue comes in Zoltán's opening pep talk to his musicians. *Tannhäuser,* he says, is not a period piece, it is about us: "How should we live? What is important, Venus or Elizabeth?" This grandiose theme becomes muddled and trivialized amid the antics of the musicians, crew, and opera staff. As for Zoltán, he never resolves his own personal dilemma.

And yet on another level, the story succeeds very well. The conflicts among performers, conductor, staff, and crew are an elegant metaphor for the lumpy process of European unification. In addition, Zoltán's personal complexes aptly portray the doubts and insecurities of Hungarians as they struggle, in the unfamiliar atmosphere of post-communism, to relate to the rest of Europe.

And moving further into the abstract, we find a forceful comment about the power of art. *Meeting Venus* asks, What value do beauty and creativity retain in a world preoccupied with everyday wants and needs? Its answer is that art will triumph. This is hardly an original libretto, but it deserves the reaffirmation it receives in Szabó's film.

Once again drawing comparisons to earlier Szabó works, we can see several familiar themes. The theme of creativity echoes a motif in *Mephisto* and emphasizes the universal appeal Szabó is aiming for in *Meeting Venus:* "Everybody has a creative part in his soul. The creative process is everybody's problem, whether you are an opera singer, a filmmaker, or a baker."[45]

The theme of community is obvious, as well, in this tale of a polyglot band of artists struggling to pull together. Like the refugees in *Budapest Tales,* the musicians must overcome their personal differences if they are to achieve something worthwhile.

The theme of Hungarity reveals itself in Zoltán's inner struggle, recalling the sequence in *Love Film* about Hungarians in exile. Judit Pintér reads this as the latest in Szabó's many autobiographical references, reflecting this time on the identity of the artist and the quandary of remaining true to one's creative instincts while working abroad.[46]

And finally, Szabo's own favorite theme—security—recurs, as the Siamese twin of Zoltán's Hungarity. As the first-person narrator of *Meeting Venus,* Zoltán admits us into his troubled psyche as he seeks proof that he is competent to conduct a world-class operatic production. Combined as it is with a question of personal identity, it is a problem like that facing the young Takó in *Father.*

Szabó's Career: One More Look

Have István Szabó's films changed because he has become an international director? The obvious answer is yes. His films have become more ambitious, his cinematic language more assertive. He now works with major stars and in languages other than his native Hungarian. He commands the attention of a world audience, and he is aware that, wherever his personal muse leads him, his films must play to that wider audience.

Have Szabó's films, as a result, lost something vital? The answer to this question is more complicated. Although none can deny the power of *Mephisto* and *Colonel Redl*, many Hungarian critics believe Szabó took a wrong turn during the 1980s. They are uneasy with the cosmopolitan flavor and commercial-studio polish of his recent films. They criticize him for not taking on Hungarian themes and note that, in his eagerness to work with international stars, Szabó has relegated his own favorite Hungarian actors and actresses—whose talents are considerable—to secondary roles. And they criticize Szabó's retreat from formal innovation, mourning, in a way, the passing of the young István Szabó.

It is true that Szabó has broadened his thematic focus and polished the look of his films. The Szabó who claims to have become an adult through the adoption of a greater realism has dramatically changed his approach to storytelling. Without knowing the truth, it would be hard for even an experienced student of film to tell that *Meeting Venus* is the work of the director who made *Father, 25 Firemen's Street,* and *Budapest Tales.*

Whatever judgment one makes of these changes, it is not accurate to ascribe them wholly to the internationalization of Szabó's career. The crucial change in Szabó's narrative style emerged in *Confidence,* a purely Hungarian film. Working with major stars did not immediately accompany co-production, for Klaus Maria Brandauer was unknown when Szabó chose him for *Mephisto*. And as for the polish of Szabó's films, much of that quality is the product of his able Hungarian crews, including first and foremost his director of cinematography, Lajos Koltai.

And it is not accurate to infer that Szabó has intentionally tailored his stories to the world market. It is true that *Mephisto,* the first part of the Central European trilogy, originated with the West German producer, Manfred Durniok.[47] However, the story immediately appealed to Szabó, and he seemed to realize that making this film would represent a logical step in the development of his work. And well it did. The work of his first period focused on his own age cohort. The work of his second period focused on his parents' generation. Szabó's next work led him to an inquiry into those historical forces that defined the sociopolitical environment of his era.

Meeting Venus is Szabó's original story, based on his own experience with the Paris Opéra a decade or so earlier. Szabó first told David Puttnam of the idea in the wake of his triumph with *Mephisto,* and eventually Puttnam teamed him up with Michael Hirst for the screenplay. If the work is flawed, it is not because Szabó has pandered to popular tastes (which he has not), but because the story is too ambitious to be contained within the format of a feature film.

Szabó has changed, yes. But filmmakers must change if their work is to remain fresh. Szabó has grown over the years; his films have become more sophisticated, and his message more complex.

THE FILMMAKER'S MESSAGE

> Every filmmaker has only one message, because he has only one life; and in this one life, there is only one important experience. The form is not important; sometimes you change the form, because it is boring to do the same thing. . . . But your experience is the same, and you only try to express that experience in another way.
>
> —István Szabó, 1991

István Szabó is never reluctant to talk about the meaning of his films. All of them, he maintains, are primarily about the individual's search for security. A young boy, weighed down by insecurity, attempts to find self-confidence by following in his dead father's elusive footsteps. An anonymous band of refugees searches for a lost Eden in an unlikely vehicle. An ambitious but vulnerable soldier vainly pursues security in the upper ranks of the imperial army. Whether his characters desire self-fulfillment, pure love, peace of mind, fame, or respect, Szabó insists that their basic yearning is for security—the security of self-identity, of a stable life, of acceptance by their fellow humans.

Other readings of Szabó's message are plausible. Judit Pintér, for example, emphasizes the theme that dominated the earliest of the director's features: searching for identity. The search for individual identity, so powerful in *Father;* the search for the identity of Szabó's generation, as depicted in *The Age of Daydreaming* and *Love Film;* and the search for the community's identity, as dramatized in *25 Firemen's Street* and *Budapest Tales*—this theme recurs in Szabó's international films, too, in different colorations. Who are Hendrik Höfgen, Alfried Redl, Klaus Schneider? They are gifted individuals whose confusion about their identities mirrors the condition of their societies, morally disoriented and adrift in a perilous world.

Closely tied up with identity is role-playing. This theme, nearly hidden in *Budapest Tales,* is developed in *Confidence* with startling subtlety and in the Central European trilogy with unmistakable boldness. There are traces of the theme in Szabó's work going back to his early short, *You,* and implicit expressions of it in *Father.* Role-playing is an obvious element in *Meeting Venus,* although in this most recent film it serves more as a framework around the story than as a central issue.

Identity is inseparable from another important Szabó theme, community. The quiet heroes of Szabó's earliest features define their identities in relation to their community—or, more to the point, they discover they cannot define themselves as individuals without reference to their community. In the films of Szabó's second period, the community does not simply stand as a reference point for the identity of Szabó's characters: It defines them. The films of the Central European trilogy portray the community out of kilter, unable to offer a secure sense of identity to its citizens, who all too willingly become pawns in a power game and followers of false prophets. Finally, *Meeting Venus* is a study of community-building in the new European order.

Szabó agrees that identity and community are important in his films. However, he argues, they are important in the way they relate to the dominant issue of security. Community relates to security because, in Szabó's words, "a very important part of the feeling of security is to be accepted by other people." Identity is important because security is first and foremost a personal, psychological question. Szabó sees contemporary Europeans in a vacuum because they have found nothing to replace the God they once believed in—a God who could not, or would not, protect them from the perils that arose in this most violent of centuries.

Security very much pertains to human emotions. When talking about *Meeting Venus,* Szabó, a man whom actors and actresses have often found disconcertingly unemotional, punches this issue home with the conviction of a religious convert. *Meeting Venus,* he says, is a story about people discovering something essential about the difference between real emotions and creative emotions. "Is it possible," Szabó asks—as if he is asking himself—"to create emotions that will reach the audience without drawing upon your own true emotions?" This, he insists, is a question of security. The artist, like all individuals, must search within his or her own soul to find the path to genuine security.[48]

DOCTOR TO THE HUMAN CONDITION

Following the U.S. release of *Mephisto,* an American reporter dubbed Szabó "Doctor to the Human Condition."[49] It was an apt attribution to this filmmaker who at times seems obsessed by the character of the physician. There is a doctor character in most of Szabó's features, as well as in his prize-winning short *A Dream about a House.* And as if that is not enough, Szabó, in a rare acting performance, even played the part of a doctor in Gyula Gazdag's *Standoff* (*Túsztörténet,* 1989).

To this day Szabó, who has never escaped doubts about his career choice, thinks frequently about the profession he did not choose. He likes to believe he has approached his filmmaking career as a doctor might—to seek some solutions to the maladies of the human condition, some means of healing or providing therapy.

Nowhere is this more evident than in *Hanussen,* where the one unambiguously positive character is Dr. Bettelheim. If only the world followed Bettelheim's example—if only the gifted personalities among us dedicated their talents to healing rather than self-aggrandizement—then maybe, Szabó seems to be saying, the great tragedies of history could be prevented.

But why physicians? Why not world leaders? Szabó does not appear to be interested in politicians, and he denies that his films have any specific political aim. In fact, it has often been said of Szabó that he has deliberately avoided making direct political statements. By nature insecure, the young Szabó felt burned by official disapproval of his first feature, *The Age of Daydreaming,* and he approached his work thereafter with great circumspection. He remained reluctant to take a political stand and, in private, admitted to fears that he might somehow be compelled to do so.

And yet, no Central European artist with any social sensitivity could have remained uninvolved with the political issues of the past thirty years. István Szabó may not have made a *Man of Iron* or an *Angi Vera,* but neither did he ignore the central problems of his era—unfreedom, injustice, conformity, hypocrisy, and deceit. Szabó may have purposefully sidestepped questions of political right versus wrong, but he took great pains to display the negative human effects of bad politics.

It should not be forgotten that *Father,* for example, was one of the first Hungarian films to make explicit reference to the tragic 1956 uprising—and to portray sympathetically those who fought or demonstrated for national liberation. Further, the references in *25 Firemen's Street* and *Budapest Tales* to the ugliness of the postwar revolution may be inferential or abstract, but they are unmistakable. Such cinematic references pushed against the boundaries of the Communist regime's tolerance as of the mid-1970s.

Even as the logic of István Szabó's artistic vision pulled him backward in time, into the first four decades of this century, he did not fail to raise questions that were meaningful in his own day. Released in 1981, *Mephisto* was very contemporary. Its theme concerns the relationship between the artist and the state, and—as those who are close to Szabó have acknowledged—it applied to the Hungary of 1981 as much as to the Germany of the 1930s in which the story was set.[50]

THE TRILOGY SYNDROME AND ITS PITFALLS

Prior to *Meeting Venus,* one could readily analyze Szabó's career in terms of three trilogies. The first and third of these we have already identified. The middle period, including Szabó's works between *Love Film* and *Mephisto,* presents us with a slight complication, but it, too, can be seen to comprise a trilogy (counting the series *Budapest, Why I Love It*) plus the transitional film *Confidence.*

Each of the trilogies displays a great deal of consistency in both story and style. Szabó himself, as we have seen, consciously set out to repeat the story of *25 Firemen's Street* when he developed *Budapest Tales,* and, in addition, he has confessed that "*Love Film* is a little bit of a remake of *Father,* and *Hanussen* is a tiny bit of a remake of *Mephisto* and *Colonel Redl.*"[51]

Numerous directors whose aesthetic and thematic ideas cannot be confined within one feature film have succeeded brilliantly by making trilogies; one thinks of Satyajit Ray's *Apu* trilogy, Andrzej Wajda's early trilogy about Poland during and after World War II, and Ingmar Bergman's trilogy about faith and unbelief (*Through a Glass Darkly,* 1961; *Winter Light,* 1962; and *The Silence,* 1963). Can we compare István Szabó's trilogies to these masterpieces?

There can be no disputing the moments of greatness in Szabó's career. Certainly *Father* and *Mephisto* are great films, and it is the present critic's judgment that the trilogy of Szabó's middle period has been universally underestimated. At the same time, however, it does appear that the freshness and depth of Szabó's storytelling tend to peter out in the third installment of each trilogy. By this measure Szabó's trilogies compare unfavorably, for example, to the Wajda trilogy, which reaches its powerful culmination in its third part, *Ashes and Diamonds* (*Popiół i diament,* 1958). Szabó's works, particularly the Central European trilogy, are more comparable to Francis Ford Coppola's *Godfather* trilogy; the first *Godfather* (1972) was audacious and startling, and the second (1974), intelligent and probing. The third *Godfather* (1991), however, failed to match the quality of the first two.

Hanussen is a better film than *Godfather III,* but nevertheless it, too, is a comedown from its two predecessors. No one has expressed more disappointment about *Hanussen* than István Szabó. Rightly, Szabó does not believe the problem with *Hanussen* is that the film, after *Mephisto* and *Colonel Redl,* was superfluous—which is a large part of the problem with *Godfather III*—but rather that the film didn't tell the whole story: "It was a big, big mistake, the greatest mistake of my life. . . . I knew the truth about this character, and I didn't tell the truth."[52]

To István Szabó, not telling the truth is a serious artistic infraction. However others may judge the quality of *Hanussen*—and there is reason to judge it less harshly than Szabó does—it remains a failure in the eyes of this director's sharpest critic: himself.

HUNGARIAN, CENTRAL EUROPEAN, OR INTERNATIONAL?

> **Filmmaking is a very insecure profession, because experience doesn't help. Experience can be a bad thing; when you've had success with something, you think you can do it again in the same way. You can't. You have to start every film from point zero.**
>
> **—István Szabó, 1991**

During the 1980s, Szabó became one of the first directors from East-Central Europe to work regularly in international co-productions. The benefits of co-production are obvious: greater production funds, international stars, ready access to world distribution markets, and hard-currency professional fees greatly exceeding directors' salaries in forints, złoty, or Czechoslovak crowns. With the 1990s has come the end of state monopolies in the film industries at home; the national cinemas are in a financial crisis, and as a result, co-production has become even more enticing.

One fact of life that East European directors working in the West have learned is that they no longer have the artistic autonomy they took for granted in their home studios. There was a great irony in the socialist film industries: ultimately, the state was the arbiter of what was artistically permissible, but within the political boundaries, the director had a great deal of freedom. There were no producers bankrolling films with their own money, and therefore there was no one to enforce restrictions dictated by marketing considerations. Socialist film directors were free from the censorship of the commercial market—or, more accurately stated, the censorship of those whose interests in films were bound up with the uncertain rules of the market.

Success in the commercial environment requires a filmmaker to fit his or her artistic vision into the producer's interests, which usually have less to do with artistic vision than with profitability. The ability to excite mass audiences is, of course, crucial. This has sometimes been a hard lesson. For every Miloš Forman who has succeeded in the West, there are a Jerzy Skolimowski and a Dezső Magyar who have not.

István Szabó has become, arguably, the most successful East-Central European director to "go west" without emigrating. As of the time of this writing, no other East-West co-production has achieved the acclaim or the audience of *Mephisto,* and no two have equaled the consecutive results of *Mephisto* and *Colonel Redl.* The fate of *Hanussen* demonstrates, however, that Szabó cannot take his success for granted. Clearly *Meeting Venus* was not the beginning of a new upward climb; but neither does it appear to be the continuation of a downtrend begun by *Hanussen.*

Nor is it clear how Szabó will balance the weight of his artistic vision with the requirements of the commercial film market in the remainder of his career. He appears to have accepted and accommodated the power of the producer, although not, in every instance, happily.

The fate of the script for *Colonel Redl* is a case in point. One cannot say whether *Colonel Redl* would have been stronger or weaker had Szabó stuck more closely to Péter Dobai's original screenplay. Perhaps the longer, more complex script would have made *Colonel Redl* the masterpiece it was not; perhaps, on the other hand, it would have made the story convoluted and wearisome. The fact is that the result was significantly different from the original vision.[53]

So, too with *Hanussen*—and more. As Dobai has attested, Szabó's producer, Arthur Brauner, flew in frequently from Berlin to take an active part in the shooting while cast and crew were at work in Budapest. Such an active role is, of course, standard among American and West European producers, but Hungarians see it as interference in the artistic process.[54]

While yielding to producers' interests in some matters, Szabó insists he will not undertake film projects designed solely by commercial standards. In a 1985 interview, Szabó stated categorically that he would work only with stories that he found artistically and intellectually compelling. Stories filmed in co-production, he said, must treat problems common to the countries of co-production; in other words, he cannot be expected to make films that are of interest primarily to Germans or Britons or Americans—no matter what currency the production costs are paid in.[55] Signing an exclusive contract with Enigma did not change Szabó's position, and *Meeting Venus,* his first film of the 1990s, shows that he is still working with themes of his own choosing.

Just as the Central European trilogy broadened Szabó's thematic focus outward from Hungary, *Meeting Venus* takes aim at a still wider target: the new Europe of the 1990s, a continent whose national borders have been thoroughly perforated but whose populations still pull in their own separate directions. *Meeting Venus* reflects Szabó's consciousness of the new Europe struggling for that greater sense of community emerging, in all of its complexity, in the final decade of this turbulent century. And, consistent with

Szabó's characteristic point of view, *Meeting Venus* portrays that new, emerging community with a Central European irony.

Szabó continues to reveal his own dialectic of identity. "In his thinking," András Bálint has said, "he is a Middle European Jew."[56] And yet, like the character of Dr. Bettelheim in *Hanussen,* Szabó repeatedly demonstrates his special sentiments for his homeland. As Bettelheim sings along with the old Hungarian woman in the Berlin café, Szabó holds tight to his Hungarian domicile. When discussing a contract with foreign producers, Szabó asks them to "come to Budapest and work with my crew and my people."[57]

Szabó professes to having never had a desire to work in Hollywood. He says he can imagine himself making an American film only if it were a story about Central European emigrants in the United States.[58]

Neither Szabó's affection for his homeland nor his obsession with its complexes makes him immune to the effects of his experiences abroad; however, his attention remains focused on his own home territory, the source of all his artistic inspirations—"Central Europe is my landscape," he has said—and, rather than diluting or diffusing his consciousness, Szabó's international experiences have given him a new point of view from which to reinterpret his own life and that of his kinfolk. Living temporarily in London while completing the post-production for *Meeting Venus,* Szabó admitted to a touch of homesickness: "I can be walking in Brompton Road, but my daily problems are my problems in Budapest.[59]

Szabó very much wants to maintain his connections to Hungarian cinema. He muses about once again directing a purely Hungarian-produced film, for which he says he has a screenplay in the planning—"a very simple, black-and-white, cheap Hungarian film . . . a really simple, contemporary project." At the same time, he mourns the dilemma of the contemporary Hungarian cinema, now staggering under the loss of state sponsorship and desperately short of financial resources. "I feel as if I'm standing in a cemetery," Szabó has said, "watching a burial ceremony, throwing flowers into the grave."[60]

The Hungarian film industry's financial difficulties began in the mid-1980s, while cinema was still totally financed through the Ministry of Culture. Szabó was then the chief of Objektiv Studio and the head of the film program at Budapest's Academy of Dramatic and Cinematographic Art. In 1990 he resigned the latter position, prompting speculation in Budapest that he was forsaking Hungary for the greener pastures of the West.

The accusation is not new. Ever since *Mephisto,* Budapest critics have accused Szabó of betraying Hungarian cinema. Instead of fighting for the advancement of the national cinema, the argument goes, Szabó was off making the Central European trilogy with foreign money.

There were indeed fights being fought, both political and artistic. Szabó assiduously avoided the risky territory staked out, for example, by Gábor in *Angi Vera,* András Kovács in *The Stud Farm* (*Ménesgázda,* 1978), Károly Makk in *Another Way* (*Egymásra nézve,* 1982), and Márta Mészáros in *Diary for My Children* (*Napló gyermekeimnek,* 1982, 1984). Nor did Szabó join those who were on the cutting edge of formal innovation. He left the search for a new aesthetic to his younger colleagues—Gábor Body and András Jeles, for example.[61]

Hungarian critics have long played a positive role, educating public tastes and pushing artists to higher standards. Many of the critics, however, have failed to overcome the instinctive parochialism of their culture, and the criticism aimed at Szabó would appear to reflect that narrow perspective. Rightly, Szabó feels he has continued to make a contribution to Hungarian cinema. He has shown the way to connect his own film culture with that of the outside world, and he has helped keep Hungarian art alive amid the increasingly perilous environment of world cinema. And he has done this while remaining true to his own artistic instincts.

It is no coincidence that István Szabó's perspective has become more cosmopolitan at a time when his countrymen have begun to refocus their community perspectives and adopt a broader sense of identity; indeed, Szabó was a few years ahead of his time when he followed the vision that led to the Central European trilogy. The trilogy, as one of his more sympathetic Hungarian critics has recognized, was a logical continuation of Szabó's work.[62] *Meeting Venus* represents a further step.

It has sometimes been said that great artists retell their autobiographies throughout their careers, each time in a different aspect or form. István Szabó's films certainly have that quality about them, beginning with the stories of young Hungarians very much like himself and continuing through to artists in conflict with their own hearts or souls.

But Szabó's stories, with their deeply humanistic tone, are not his alone. If we recall, one final time, the image of Hendrik Höfgen in the Olympic stadium overwhelmed by his self-confrontation, we might be reminded not only of Faust but also of *Jedermann* (Everyman), who, in the final scene of the medieval morality play, hears accusatory voices. Those voices are like the reflections in *A Mirror;* they are like the theater curtain set ablaze by the hypnotized woman in *Hanussen;* and they are like the silence of the adult Takó at his father's graveside. They are, in other words, messengers bringing us the truth about ourselves.

NOTES

The author gratefully acknowledges the support of the Seattle Arts Commission and the National Endowment for the Humanities, as well as the generous assistance of Hungarofilm. Thanks are also due to István Szabó, Péter Dobai, András Bálint, Ildikó Bánsági, Péter Andorai, and Judit Pintér. Finally, the author expresses his gratitude to Katalin Vajda and Annamária Róna, whose assistance during the author's visits to Budapest has always been gracious and indispensable, and also to Márta Horányi.

1. Interview with the author, March 6, 1991.
2. See David Paul, "Hungary: The Magyar on the Bridge," in *Post New Wave*

Cinema in the Soviet Union and Eastern Europe, ed. Daniel J. Goulding (Bloomington and Indianapolis: Indiana University Press, 1989), pp. 172–214.

3. Other directors whose work Szabó now professes to respect particularly include Jiří Menzel, Wim Wenders, Bernardo Bertolucci, and Woody Allen.

4. Ildikó Bánsági, interview with the author, September 28, 1990.

5. Szabó does not like to discuss the question of his own Jewishness. In interviews, he shies away from the subject. Explicitly Jewish characters appear in his films, but their roles are never the principal ones. Szabó admits to having intentionally—perhaps wrongfully—avoided the issue of Jewishness when he rewrote Péter Dobai's script for *Hanussen,* which originally called for a protagonist who was a Jew (see the discussion of *Hanussen,* later in this chapter).

6. András Bálint, interview with the author, September 28, 1990.

7. Marshall McLuhan, *Understanding Media: The Extensions of Man* (New York: McGraw-Hill, 1964).

8. Judit Pintér, interview with the author, March 20, 1991.

9. Nevertheless, according to Pintér, the public criticism upset Szabó and caused him to be politically cautious in his subsequent work.

10. Karen Jaehne, "István Szabó: Dreams of Memories," *Film Quarterly* 32, 1 (Fall 1978): 30.

11. Ibid., p. 31.

12. Interview with the author, March 5, 1991.

13. Szabó interview, March 5, 1991.

14. Years later, Szabó would refer to that smile as "the usual, familiar, Andy Bálint-ish intellectual smile." In "Szabó István levelé Bálint András-hóz" ("A Letter from István Szabó to András Bálint"), *Színházi élet* (Budapest) (October 1990): 35.

15. For Szabó, *Father* is of course a very personal story—indeed, autobiographical. "I am not responsible for the quality of the film," he has said. Enough time has passed that he can analyze its success objectively: "Theoretically, I know why it's a good film. In *Father,* my message and my knowledge about filmmaking were on the same level. That's very important." In contrast, he says, *The Age of Daydreaming* is a film in which he wanted to say everything, but his filmmaking ability was inadequate. In *Love Film,* his technical abilities were at a higher level, but his message was comparatively trivial. (Szabó interview, March 5, 1991.)

16. *Love Film* was received more enthusiastically at home than abroad. András Bálint, who played the lead role, considers it Szabó's most popular film among Hungarians. Interview with the author, September 28, 1990.

17. Szabó interviews, March 5–6, 1991.

18. Szabó interview, March 5, 1991.

19. See Jaehne, "István Szabó: Dreams of Memories," for an excellent discussion of color in *Love Film* and *25 Firemen's Street.*

20. Szabó interview, March 5, 1991.

21. As told to Jaehne, pp. 34–35.

22. While conceiving this extraordinary narrative, Szabó drew upon Dylan Thomas's *Under Milk Wood,* seeking a visual form for the dream-narrative style of Thomas's radio play. (Szabó interview, March 5, 1991.)

23. Szabó interview, March 5, 1991.

24. *Budapest Tales* tells only one story, common to all of its characters. In this it differs from *25 Firemen's Street,* which tells several characters' stories and weaves them together—an approach that Robert Altman would develop successfully two years later in *Nashville* (1975).

25. Graham Petrie, *History Must Answer to Man* (Budapest: Corvina Kiádó, 1978), p., 226; Jaehne, "István Szabó: Dreams of Memories," pp. 37–40. Jaehne's discussion of *Budapest Tales* is perhaps the most favorable critical response the film attracted at the time of its release.

26. Judit Pintér interview, March 20, 1991.

27. Jaehne, "István Szabó: Dreams of Memories," p. 37.

28. Jaehne points out (p. 38) that the young adult Takó makes his crucial decision to seek information about his father while on a train, passing through a vaguely remembered village.

29. The author is indebted to Judit Pintér for having pointed out this connection between *Confidence* and Szabó's films of the 1980s.

30. Szabó interview, March 5, 1991.

31. Ildikó Bánsági, interview with the author, September 28, 1990.

32. Bánsági interview. Bánsági's co-star, Péter Andorai, has explained, however, that Szabó's trust for the actors went only so far. After discussing and analyzing and revising the script with Szabó, he and Bánsági were not allowed to improvise on the set; the script was, in a sense, frozen. Péter Andorai, interview with the author, March 20, 1991.

33. Although not a first-rate novel, *Mephisto* had gained some notoriety because it was alleged to have been written as the grudge story of a homosexual, and because it was banned both in the Third Reich and, for a while, in the Federal Republic of Germany.

34. Interestingly, Péter Dobai has pointed out that it was not until after the Academy Award that *Mephisto* first gained widespread recognition in Hungary. Péter Dobai, interview with the author, March 19, 1991.

35. John Powers, "Under Western Eyes," *American Film* 12 (December 1986): 42. In another interview, Skolimowski said that, during the filming of *The Lightship,* "Brandauer's arrogance reached a level I've never before encountered. . . . he has a mentality that is truly very special. . . ." Michel Ciment, "Entretien avec Jerzy Skolimowski," *Positif* 300 (February 1986): 6.

36. To this day, Szabó refuses to speak ill of Brandauer. Szabó has summed up their relationship with a balanced appraisal: "We are friends. We fought each other and hated each other for a few hours, but we knew our friendship and our common creative work were more important than our stupid macho vanity." Szabó admires Brandauer's unrelentingly serious approach to acting—an attitude that is consistent with Szabó's toward his own job. (Szabó interview, March 5, 1991.)

37. David Edelstein, in the *Village Voice,* October 8, 1985, p. 60.

38. Not all will agree that Brandauer's performance in *Colonel Redl* is comparable to that in *Mephisto*. Péter Dobai, for example, feels that Brandauer played the suicide scene brilliantly but that his performance otherwise failed to live up to that scene. Szabó had shot the suicide scene first; Dobai maintains that thereafter, because Brandauer had already "killed himself," he played the rest of the film as "a dead man." (Dobai interview, March 20, 1991.)

39. As such, the scene recalls the opening sequence of Andrzej Wajda's classic *Ashes and Diamonds.*

40. There had been religious references in earlier Szabó films—for example, the All Souls' Day segment of *Piety,* a Catholic burial in *Father,* and the prayer of the schoolboy in *25 Firemen's Street*—but as incidental references only.

41. Margaret Walters, in *Listener* 121, 3111 (April 27, 1989): 32.

42. Jean Gili, in *Positif* 329–330 (July-August 1988): 74.

43. Instead, Szabó created the character of Bettelheim to carry the burden of Jewishness: "But imagine," he has said, "if the Bettelheim character and the Hanussen character had been the same. . . ." (Szabó interview, March 6, 1991.)

44. In an interview with Janet Maslin, Szabó noted that the story of *Meeting Venus* is loosely based on his own experience as stage director for an opera in Paris approximately ten years earlier. When asked if he had encountered problems comparable to those depicted in his film, Szabó replied that the real-life problems were worse. Janet Maslin, "'Meeting Venus' Sings of Politics," *The New York Times,* November 10, 1991, Sec. 2, pp. 17–18.

45. Szabó interview, March 5, 1991.

46. Pintér interview, March 20, 1991.
47. John W. Hughes, "'Mephisto': István Szabó and 'the Gestapo of Suspicion,'" *Film Quarterly* 35, 4 (Summer 1982): 14.
48. Szabó interviews, March 5–6, 1991.
49. Claudia Dreifus, "Doctor to the Human Condition," interview with István Szabó, *The Progressive* 46, 8 (August 1982): 47–49.
50. Dobai interview, March 19, 1991: also Péter Andorai, interview with the author, March 20, 1991.
51. Szabó interview, March 6, 1991.
52. Szabó interview, March 5, 1991.
53. Pintér interview, March 20, 1991.
54. Dobai interview, March 19, 1991. In this light it is interesting that *Mephisto,* by far the most successful film of the trilogy, does not appear to have been crucially influenced by commercial, as opposed to artistic, considerations in either the development of the screenplay or the production of the film.
55. Szabó interview, September 25, 1985.
56. Bálint interview, September 28, 1990.
57. Szabó interview, March 6, 1991.
58. Ibid.
59. Ibid.
60. Ibid. In fact, Szabó's first film after *Meeting Venus* was *Sweet Emma, Dear Böbe* (*Édes Emma, draga Böbe*), a low-budget Hungarian film released early in 1993, too late to be included in the present essay.
61. See Paul, "Hungary: The Magyar on the Bridge."
62. Judit Pintér interview, March 20, 1991.

Five Makavejev

Daniel J. Goulding

From his earliest days as an amateur filmmaker (1953–1958) and as an award-winning documentarist (1958–1964), Dušan Makavejev established himself as one of the most prolific and inventive of a younger generation of filmmakers, theorists, and critics who spearheaded Yugoslavia's *new film* (*novi film*) movement of the sixties and early seventies. Beginning in 1965, he made a series of distinctive and witty feature films that won for him a substantial international critical attention: *Man Is Not a Bird* (*Čovek nije tica,* 1965), *Love Affair, or the Tragedy of a Switchboard Operator* (*Ljubavni slučaj ili tragedija službenice PTT,* 1977), *Innocence Unprotected* (*Nevinost bez zaštite,* 1968), and *WR: Mysteries of the Organism* (*WR: Mysterie organizma,* 1971).

During his Yugoslav period, Makavejev created increasingly complex and multilayered film collages that challenged the viewer to move freely within the films' open spaces and multiple imagistic associations. The nexus of his thematic concerns also grew more complex and multidimensional in its implications. He remained throughout the period an ironic, irreverent, and sophisticated gadfly who stung with wit and cunning; debunked the rituals of reification and cant; challenged officially sanctioned myths; exposed the obscenity of repressive power even when it was dressed in the illusory garb of sanctioned bureaucratic niceties; explored the actual and metaphorical realms of desire, sexuality, and eroticism; and celebrated the uniqueness and liberating spirit of the individual.

Makavejev's career in the West, following in the wake of the stormy controversy and shelving of his film *WR: Mysteries of the Organism* in Yugoslavia, has been erratic and restlessly nomadic. His film *Sweet Movie,* a French, Canadian, West German co-production (1974), raised as much controversy and outright condemnation in the West as his previous film *WR* had raised in Yugoslavia. As a result, Makavejev found himself unable to find backing for another film until seven years later, when he made a critical and commercially successful comeback with his Swedish-produced film *Montenegro* (1981), followed four years later by *The Coca-Cola Kid* (1985), produced in Australia, and by *Manifesto* (1988), a U.S.-Yugoslav co-production. In all three of these films, Makavejev abandoned his earlier experiments with radical narrative discontinuities and multiple montage/collage imagistic structures. He did not abandon, however, his central thematic concerns and his predilection for bizarre episodes, surrealistic images, and sharp social and political satire.

The present chapter synthesizes and reexamines the ways in which Makavejev's earlier films reflected and critiqued Yugoslav social and political reality, as well as the way they probed and interrogated the ideological substrata and political myths of both East and West. Special attention is devoted to his pivotal films *WR* and *Sweet Movie*—the former transgressing the boundaries of the allowable in Yugoslavia and the latter doing the same in the West. Finally, an attempt is made to identify and assess the thematic and imagistic continuities and discontinuities of his last three films with those of his earlier, more avant-garde works.

Born in Belgrade on October 13, 1932, Makavejev lived out his childhood and teen years against a troubled canvas of dramatic and convulsive events. Those few years witnessed the disintegrating final throes of Yugoslavia's prewar monarchy: Nazi Germany's savage bombing of Belgrade; swift defeat, dismemberment, and obliteration of Yugoslavia's old boundaries; harsh occupation by multiple enemy forces; armed guerrilla resistance; civil war waged among Partisans, Ustashi and Chetniks; postwar establishment of a newly founded Federal Socialist Republic; the ruins of war and Stalinist reconstruction; the expulsion in 1948 of Yugoslavia from the Cominform following Tito's split with Stalin; and the prolonged crisis from 1948 until Stalin's death in 1953. Even with such a brief litany of events, it is easy to see why little semblance of social, cultural, and political "normalcy" began to assert itself in Yugoslavia until the early fifties. In the specific realm of film culture, the decade of the fifties was an important transitional period, leading away from the sterile aesthetic dogmas of socialist realism and naive filmmaking of the initial postwar years to the more fully liberated and fecund *new film* tendencies of the sixties and early seventies.

It was in this decade of ferment and change that Makavejev began his film career. While Makavejev earned his diploma in psychology from the philosophy faculty in Belgrade in 1955, he had already made his primary commitment to film. He directed his first amateur film, *Jatagan mala,* in 1953 at age twenty-one, pursued professional studies in film at the Academy of Dramatic Arts in Belgrade, established himself as a gifted and prolific film essayist and critic, and began writing and directing documentary films professionally in 1958.

Early Works

In the fifties and early sixties the liveliest venue for film experimentation and expression in Yugoslavia was not in feature film production but in the areas of amateur, documentary, short, and animated films. Makavejev was one of many young cineastes who began their film careers in the amateur film movement and who later became leading feature film directors (as well as film writers, cinematographers, and film editors) associated with *new film* tendencies of the next decade.

Makavejev early allied himself with vanguard film activities through his five-year creative involvement with Belgrade's amateur film club "Beograd," under whose sponsorship he made four films: *Jatagan mala* (1953), *The Stamp* (*Pečat*, 1956), *Anthony's Broken Mirror* (*Antonijevo razbijeno ogledalo*, 1957), and *Don't Believe in Monuments* (*Spomenicima ne treba verovati*, 1958). While amateur film clubs operated under looser ideological guidelines than professional cinema, several of the early experiments by the Belgrade group aroused the concern of more conservative official ideologues, still wed at the time to socialist realism, and led to the banning (even for showing in amateur film festivals) of some of the *kino klub*'s more irreverent offerings. Among these was Makavejev's last amateur film, *Don't Believe in Monuments*, which ironically and elliptically portrays the vain attempts of a young girl to make love to a nude reclining male statue.

Eclectic in approach, the major participants in Belgrade's *kino klub* eschewed aesthetic conformity and experimented with a wide variety of themes and styles, including the poetic, symbolic films of Marko Babac, some of them inspired by the work of Maja Deren; experiments in surrealism by Kokan Rakonjac and Babac; political satires by Makavejev; and love stories with social overtones by Dragoljub Ivkov. Nonetheless, the more talented among the Belgrade group, although highly individualistic and sometimes bitingly acerbic among themselves, were united in their criticism of conformist, establishment films and increasingly impatient to move from the wings of amateur film to the center stage of Yugoslav film production. Makavejev made his move into professional filmmaking in 1958 with his first documentary, *Damned Holiday* (*Prokletni praznik*), produced by Zagreb Film.

From 1958 to 1964 Makavejev completed thirteen documentary films in which he continued to experiment with expressive-realist montage structures and surrealist-inspired film collages.[1] His satiric wit was aimed at "sacred" topics of the time, including workers' self-management (*What Is a Workers' Council?* [*Šta je to radnički savet*], 1959), Communist May Day parades (*Parade* [*Parada*], 1962), and youth workers' brigades (*Smile 61* [*Osmejh 61*], 1961). He also wittily reflected upon and critiqued various dimensions of everyday Yugoslav reality, beauty contests in *Miss Yugoslavia 62* (*Ljepotica 62*, 1962), children at play in *Down with Fences* (*Dole plotovi*, 1962), and the assault of urban pressures on village life in *New Domestic Animal* (*Nova domaća životinja*, 1964). In the film *One Potato, Two Potato* (*Eci pec pec*, 1961) Makavejev experimented with cut-out collage techniques, and he gained his first experiences with 35mm color film in *Beekeeper's Scrapbook* (*Slikovnica pčelara*, 1958) and *Colors Dreaming* (*Boje sanjaju*, 1958).

One of the most intricately structured and thematically characteristic of Makavejev's early documentaries was his film *Down with Fences*. It opens with a series of *tableaux vivants* of four boys variously posed against a decaying and scaling wall with jaunty music playing on the sound track. These images are followed by those of children riding tricycles or pushing scooters in and out of open passageways. From these simple opening images, a complex montage is built up that contrasts images of children playing and constantly moving with those in which children are stationary and looking through or being looked at behind railings, fences, and openings in walls. Extreme camera angles are used to suggest containment and imprisonment, including, for example, a high-angle shot of children trapped and dwarfed by gray-walled buildings surrounding an enclosed courtyard. The sound of childrens' voices swells and then is muted. There is the image of a small boy playfully making his way through white sheets hung out to dry, only to come out against an inpenetrable wall. Increasingly more ominous images are then interjected: close-ups of spikes on fences, barbed wire, sinister gaping windows, growling dogs, the hands of children clinging to the top of a fence. Then everything begins to change and an ebullient visual and aural epiphany is built up. Children find holes in the fences and walls, pour out of the enclosed playgrounds and courtyards, climb over large chain-link fences, tumble across wooden slatted ones, and rush through previously closed passageways. The last handwritten message at the end of the film is "Down with fences!" A film ostensibly about children at play is thus transformed into an enlarged metaphor of human freedom, creativity, and spontaneity playing itself out against social constraint and repression—a theme that Makavejev develops with much greater dimensionality and nuance in his later films.

In addition to his film work during this period, Makavejev also played an increasingly important role in promoting *new film* tendencies through his frequent film essays and critiques, which appeared in a number of progressive Yugoslav weeklies and journals, including, among others, *Student, Književne novine, Sineast,* and *Film danas.*[2] By the early sixties, Yugoslavia's vanguard of film critics, theorists, and film artists had rallied loosely and with varying degrees of commitment under the banner of *novi film* (*new film*) or *open cinema.* While lacking a specific program or coherent aesthetic perspective, the advocates of *new film* sought (1) to increase the latitude for individual and collective artistic expression and to free film from dogmatism and bureaucratic control; (2) to promote stylistic experimentation in film form and film language—influenced initially by French *nouvelle vague* and vanguard Italian cinema, and later in the sixties by *new wave* tendencies in East European countries, most notably Czechoslovakia and Poland; (3) to involve film in the expression of *savremene teme* (contemporary themes), including the right to critique the darker, ironic, alienated, and gloomier side of human, societal, and political existence; and (4) to do all of these things within the context and premises of a Marxist-socialist state—at a time in Yugoslavia's evolution when these very premises were a focal point for heated philosophical and ideological debate.

New film was associated with the larger trends of the period toward greater decentralization and democratization of Yugoslav society, sometimes referred to as Yugoslavia's "second revolution," and claimed for itself the right to serve as a critic of all existing conditions. *New film* creators numbered themselves among those who favored humanistic, democratic socialism and self-government over Stalinist positivism and bureaucratic statism; who aligned themselves with Marx's earlier notions of *praxis* over ideological dogmatism, conformity, elitism, and cults of personality; who vigorously and critically confronted the founding myths of the postwar Yugoslav state (the National War of Liberation and its aftermath and Workers' Self-Management), often endowing these themes with new contemporary relevance and urgency; who explored the sources of humanity's alienation in a society that claimed, theoretically at least, to have eliminated its causes; and who created a series of open metaphors about contemporary human and societal conditions that resisted closure and that refused to offer easy and optimistic answers to the questions they posed.[3] It was in this atmosphere, which Makavejev had helped to create, that he contributed his first two feature films, *Man Is Not a Bird* (*Čovek nije tica,* 1965) and his international success *Love Affair, or the Tragedy of a Switchboard Operator* (*Ljubvani slučaj ili tragedija službenica PTT,* 1967). Both films metaphorically connect simple intimate love stories with larger satiric social commentary. Both films also fuse documentary realism, associational editing, and expressive uses of camera angle, compostion, and lighting with boldly original leaps into the surreal.

Man Is Not a Bird

> A woman from Pirot
> went crazy over a guy. . . .[4]
> —Hypnotist

The film *Man Is Not a Bird* is set in a small industrial town in the copper mining basin of Bor in eastern Serbia, where a large copper smelting factory is undergoing modernization. A highly skilled engineer from Slovenia, Jan Rudinski (Janez Vrhovec), is brought in to direct the installation of new machinery and speed up production. He is middle aged, serious, stolid, and devoted to his work. He finds a modest sleeping room with a family, whose daughter, Rajka (Milena Dravić), is a vivacious and pretty young hairdresser. Rudinski and Rajka are attracted to each other, and a love affair develops. It is Rajka who takes the initiative in overcoming Rudinski's conventional reserve and doubts when they first make love. Rudinski, however, becomes more deeply involved in his work and sees Rajka less and less. One evening while they are walking across the bleak expanse of the factory yard, with its piles of gray slag, Rajka chides him for working too hard and being married to his work. As Rajka and Rudinski become increasingly separated, she is pursued by a virile and ruggedly handsome young truck driver, Boško. A magnetic physical attraction develops between them.

When Rudinski has completed his work—even ahead of the tight schedule alotted—a chorus and symphony orchestra are brought from Belgrade to celebrate the event. Before the concert, Rudinski receives a medal and a commendation for his exceptional achievement. The orchestra plays

5.1. Rajka (Milena Dravić) and Rudinksi (Janez Vrhovec). *Man Is Not a Bird.* BFI Stills, Posters and Designs.

Beethoven for the edification of the workers. In the meantime, Boško and Rajka are joyously consummating their mutual desires in the cab of his truck to the swelling chords of the "Ode to Joy," the sublime finale to Beethoven's *Ninth.*

The next morning Rudinski questions Rajka closely about where she was during the concert. At first she is evasive, but then tells him she was with a young man. She assures Rudinski that it meant nothing to her. He is, however, stonily unforgiving and grasps her hard by the wrists. She falls down as she pulls away from his grip, is frightened, and runs away. The last shot of the film is a long aerial one of the tiny figure of Rudinski, walking slowly across the vast gray expanse of the factory yard. He has been rewarded for his work but has lost an opportunity to open his life to spontaneity, tenderness, and joy.

Makavejev enriches this simple story of romance and sexual attraction with satirical social commentary. Throughout the film the uninhibited, exuberant, and machismo lifestyle of the workers is satirically contrasted to planned and rationalized socialist self-management objectives. Near the beginning of the film, the factory manager is on the phone to Belgrade, arranging for the appearance of the symphony orchestra and commenting on how much the workers are ecstatically transfigured by classical culture. The film then cuts to a workers' café, where the men are so inspired by the provocative torch singing of a buxom female entertainer that they dash their glasses against the floor and walls, and become so raucous that the local police intervene. The workers are also caught up in the mesmerizing entertainment of a hypnotist and by snake swallowers, trapeze artists, belly dancers, and other circus performers, who symbolize life as an abundance of sensations and attractions and as a means of release, through laughter, from the grinding realities of daily existence.

In a factory tour, the manager tells the vistors that modern machines have freed man from alienating and brutish labor. His speech is carried over the sound track while the film depicts grimy and sweating workers breaking coal and feeding the copper-smelting furnaces—enveloped by unventilated hellish vapors, and framed against black, soot-covered ironwork grids. Barbulović (Stojan Aranđelović), a large-framed, muscular worker, is singled out as the perfect model of the "new worker." He is shown energetically doing the work of three men—calling up associations of post war Yugoslav "shock workers" and the legendary Russian shock worker Stakhanov. Barbulović, however, is depicted off the job as a provincial brute who spends his time drinking, whoring, and brutalizing his wife. A self-management committee discusses the problem of missing copper wire. The film cuts to two gypsy workers wrapping the bare waist and torso of one of them from a large spool of copper wire. The worker then puts on his shirt and walks out of the plant. While Rudinski is hard at work directing the installation of machines, a worker is inspired to swing over the machines on a rope ladder, declaring that he is a bird. Rudinski stolidly proclaims that "man is not a bird"—a statement that proves sadly prophetic in his case.

While *Man Is Not a Bird* is structured somewhat more conventionally than Makavejev's later films, it is nonetheless rich with inter-referential imagistic associations and teasing ironies and ambiguities. Some of the most interesting of these are prompted by the hypnotist, who introduces the film while the titles are being run, appears later in the film performing his stage act for the enraptured and enthusiastic workers and townspeople, and provides the film's concluding voice-over narration. In the beginning of the film, the hypnotist is introduced from a low angle shot standing before microphones, his head framed by a suspended black circular stage decoration. He is dressed entirely in black, including a high-necked, long-sleeved overblouse. He tells the story of the girl from Pirot who "went crazy over this guy"—a story that underscores the powerful magnetizing force of sexual attraction and the difficulties of breaking such "spells," even with hypnosis. The figure of the hypnotist (a real hypnotist whom Makavejev recruited for the film and who advertised himself as "the youngest hypnotist in the Balkans") is presented ambiguously—both humorously as a clever entertainer and teller of tall tales and, more ominously, as a black-shirted charismatic conjurer and manipulator. The ambiguity of his *persona* is further enlarged when his stage act is depicted in the film. He hypnotizes several adult men and women workers recruited from the audience and induces them to engage in absurd or gross behaviors for the enthusiastic amusement of the audience. At one point he tells them they are birds and they begin to flap their arms and circle the stage in illusory imitation of freedom and flight. At the conclusion of the film, the voice of the hypnotist is heard on the sound track saying, "Listen to my explanation please. I will make everything clear. I don't want you to say that I used magic." He then gives the Greek derivation of the word hypnosis and explains that hypnosis is "an artificial sleep, under which a man carries out any order. Even to kill."

Paradoxically, the only character to "see through" the hypnotist's act and to derive understanding from it is the most mesmerized (oppressed) character in the film—Barbulović's wife (Eva Ras). She is introduced in the film in the miserly surroundings of her worker's flat with shot compositions strongly reminiscent of the opening scene in *Mother,* Pudovkin's famous film version of the Gorky novel. She is shot from above, and placed in weak and cowering positions before the towering frame of Barbulović. In this scene Barbulović bullies and threatens her for having the audacity to complain that he has given his mistress the new red dress he bought for his wife. Later, in the town market, the wife meets the mistress, who is wearing the red dress; she attacks her and tries to remove it. The wife and mistress are hauled into the local police station, with an unrepentant Barbulović protesting that he bought the dress for his wife and that he has the right to take it away. He then crudely enunciates his patriarchal rights: "I feed her. I clothe her. I can beat her. She is my wife." After seeing the hypnotist's act, however, Barbulović's wife tells a female friend that now she sees that the hypnotist is like her husband, and "all officials": "That's how we go on believing everything. . . . He says 'shut up' . . . and you do. . . . You do what he pleases." At the end of her struggle toward revelation, she smilingly declares: "No more hypnosis!" Later in the film, she sits with her female friend at the concert while Barbulović anxiously and unsuccessfully tries to locate her. Near the end of the film, she is at the circus seated beside the young worker who declared himself to be a bird, and they are having a relaxed and pleasurable conversation. It is now Barbulović who wears an anxious and concerned expression as he vainly searches for his wife (who, significantly, is never given a name in the film) and is left to wonder where she has gone and with whom.

The magnetic and subversive force of sexual attraction spoken of by the hypnotist is most satirically and complexly evoked in the montage sequence in which Beethoven's "Ode to Joy," performed in the factory for the workers, is intercut with Rajka and Boško having sexual intercourse in the cab of his truck. The final shots of this bravura sequence (the filmmaker here is himself taking on something of the role of "hypnotist" and conjurer of illusions) begins with a close-up of Rudinski's face expressing joy as he becomes increasingly caught up in the sublimities of the music—having earlier looked around anxiously to see if Rajka was present at the concert. The close-up of Rudinski is cut directly to a matching close-up of Rajka's face illumined in the half-light of the truck cab. Her face also expresses joy and pleasurable anticipation, associated however, in this case, with the sexual "ode to joy" that she now plans to compose with her young lover. As the two lovers become entwined in quietly intense lovemaking, there are two cuts to the conductor urging the choir and orchestra to the climactic finale of "Ode to Joy." The last of these shots is a side-angle view of the conductor making vigorous and accelerated thrusting motions. At the height of his *furioso* performance, the film cuts to a quiet close-up of Rajka's face, her head tilted backward as she experiences orgasm. The film then cuts back to the end of the concert and sustained applause—including a cut to a medium shot of Rudinski helping to lead a standing ovation. These last juxtapositions, of course, create the satiric *double entendre* that the audience (including Rudinski) is not only applauding the concert performance but also the performance of Rajka and Boško. The sequence as a whole is also reciprocally satiric and ironic. The "Ode to Joy" playing on the sound track—with its elevated theme of joy in the collective brotherhood of man based in God's love—is ironically (though in no sense condescendingly) associated with the intensity of private, joyous sexual fulfillment. Reciprocally, Schiller's and Beethoven's elevated poetic and musical themes, as well as the manner of their performance, are eroticized and sexualized. In fact, the music and its performance are filmically depicted as far more orgasmic than the sexual coupling of Rajka and Boško!

The above montage sequence also suggests many other imagistic associations. Rudinski's delighted appreciation of the concert is contrasted to the polite but bewildered and uncomprehending expressions of the workers in the audience whose pleasures (not demeaned in the film) run to the Rabelaisian and carnivalesque. Rudinski's rapturous expression filmically juxtaposed to Rajka's evokes the togetherness in joy that they had previously experienced as well as their current separation and growing estrangement. The surrender of Rudinski to the "collective" joy expressed in Beethoven's music is associated with his devotion to the "collective" interests of the factory and the sacrifice this has entailed. Makavejev, a member of the Yugoslav Communist party and an informed Marxist at the time, is not presenting easy didactic answers to the complex and often paradoxical relationships among collective societal interests and individual desires and freedoms.

Throughout the film there are contrasting and often ambiguous images related to humankind's aspirations to freedom and "flight." There is the worker swinging high above the machinery on a rope ladder, the simulated flight of the hypnotized workers, the aerial flight of trapeze artists, the symbolic "flight" of Barbulović's wife, the orgasmic flight of lovers, and the ecstatic flights of poetry and music. The associational pathways connecting these images are left open and multidimensional. In the final image of the film, for example, a sense of melancholy and poignancy is created by framing Rudinski in long shot, alone and dwarfed, in a vast expanse of grayness. There is a feeling created of his lost opportunity to open his life to tenderness, joy, and spontaneity. At the same time, the top of the frame contains a swath of light, and Beethoven's "Ode to Joy" is playing on the soundtrack.

5.2. Image of flight. *Man Is Not a Bird.* BFI Stills, Posters and Designs.

At one level, the "Ode to Joy" ironically adds to the feeling of melancholy. At another level, however, it recalls not only Rudinski's capacity to take flight with Beethoven's music and Schiller's poetic expression of noble sentiments but also his capacity to take sensual flight with Rajka. The final image, therefore, ambiguously suggests both a human defeat and the human capacity, even within the stolid Rudinski, to transcend his earlier declaration that "man is not a bird."

Makavejev's first feature film reveals an original and imaginative capacity to create open metaphors free of dogmatism and closure. Openness, however, does not extend to vacuity. The most important targets of Makavejev's well-stocked quiver of satiric arrows are clearly identified: official cant and ideological dogma, repressive mechanisms of individual and social control, public pomp and propagandistic ritual, official hypocrisy, and mesmerizing and charismatic leaders who "hypnotize" followers into "choosing" their own unfreedom.

Love Affair, or the Tragedy of a Switchboard Operator

> **Men live their beautiful, wild lives quite close to magnificent ideas and progressive truths. My film is dedicated to those interesting, vague, in-between places.[5]**
>
> **—Makavejev**

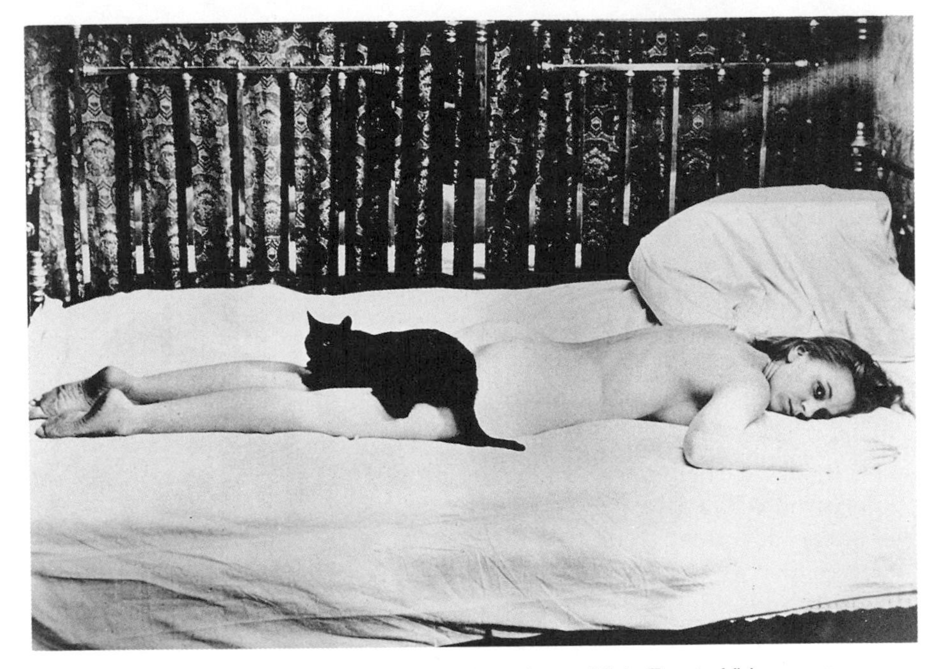

5.3. Isabella (Eva Ras) and her pet kitten. *Love Affair.* Facets Video.

Makavejev's ironic vision is given greater scope and complexity in his second feature film, *Love Affair, or the Tragedy of a Switchboard Operator* (1967)—his first significant international success. In this film, Makavejev experiments more fully with discontinuous narrative structure and with filmic collage. He also tempers and blends the expressive-realist montage style of *Man is Not a Bird* (influenced primarily by Vertov and Eisenstein) with a looser improvisatory "realism" associated with French *nouvelle vague.* The story upon which the wider associations of the film is built takes place in Belgrade, and portrays a warm and humorous love affair that ends in bizarre tragedy. Isabella (Eva Ras), a vivacious, sensual, and free-spirited switchboard operator, who has enjoyed several affairs, meets a kind, serious, and somewhat older sanitary inspector, Ahmed (Slobodan Aligrudić). They end up in Isabella's apartment, where she takes the initiative in prompting their first tender and joyous sexual union. They live together and enjoy an uncomplicated period of idyllic sensuality and domesticity, in which trivialities and offbeat moments are infused with humor and warmth—she preparing delicious food and caring for her pet black kitten, he bringing home a record player and a new shower.

Ahmed, whose area of expertise is rat extermination, is called out of town for several weeks on special assignment. During his absence Isabella has a brief affair with a young postal worker, the office lothario Mića (Miodrag Andrić)—an infidelity predicted by her close female friend and co-worker Ruža (Ružica Sokić), who dabbles in fortune telling. Later, Isabella discovers she is pregnant, but the film leaves the question open as to whether the father is Mića or Ahmed.

After Ahmed's return, the relationship begins to sour, and joy darkens into anxiety and tension. Ahmed discovers the hospital report announcing Isabella's pregnancy. Believing that he now knows the cause of her anxiety and markedly changed mood, and that it is he who is the father, Ahmed happily reassures Isabella of his desire and intent to marry her. Instead of responding as Ahmed anticipates, however, Isabella strongly rejects his proposal and the enslaving entrapment which she now believes such a marriage would involve. Ahmed, deeply wounded by Isabella's rejection, goes on a drunken binge and determines to commit suicide by throwing himself into an antique Roman well, which has become part of the city's sewer system. Isabella follows him, and in her struggle to prevent Ahmed from taking his own life, she accidentally falls into the murky and fetid waters of the well and drowns. Ahmed is later arrested and charged with murder.

Makavejev greatly enlarges the resonances of this love story—which he envisioned as "sympathetic and comic, erotic and a bit neurotic, like all human relationships"[6]—by his adoption of a nonlinear narrative strategy and by his insertions of various types of film material not directly connected to the narrative development.

A sense of ambivalence and tragedy is introduced from the outset of Isabella's and Ahmed's affair. Immediately after their first accidental meeting on the streets of Belgrade, the film cuts to a flash-forward of the retrieval of Isabella's body from the brackish waters of the Roman well—with expressive close-ups and expressionistic renderings of the dark, dank passageways leading to the bottom of the well, and high angle shots peering down into the well from its large surface opening. The shots of the corpse render its identity ambiguous at this point in the film, so that a viewer seeing the film for the first time may not make a direct connection between the corpse and Isabella.

A second flash-forward, however, reduces or eliminates the ambiguity. At the conclusion of one of the most tender and warmly intimate scenes between Isabella and Ahmed, the film cuts to the cold and sterile confines of an autopsy room where Isabella's nude corpse is rolled in on a cart for examination. The two temporally disjunctive narrative strands of the film, however, are finally joined and resolved near the end of the film—with the arrest of Ahmed by the police. But the film then delivers a final narrative surprise. It ends on a long shot of Isabella and Ahmed happily descending the staircase of Isabella's apartment building—depicted as they had been at the highest moment of their brief love affair. Playing on the sound track is the stirring Mayakovsky/Eisler revolutionary Communist song that Ahmed had earlier played for Isabella on the record player he had brought to her as a gift.

In addition to nonlinear narrative development, Makavejev further enlarges the film's web of imagistic associations with the interjection of (1)

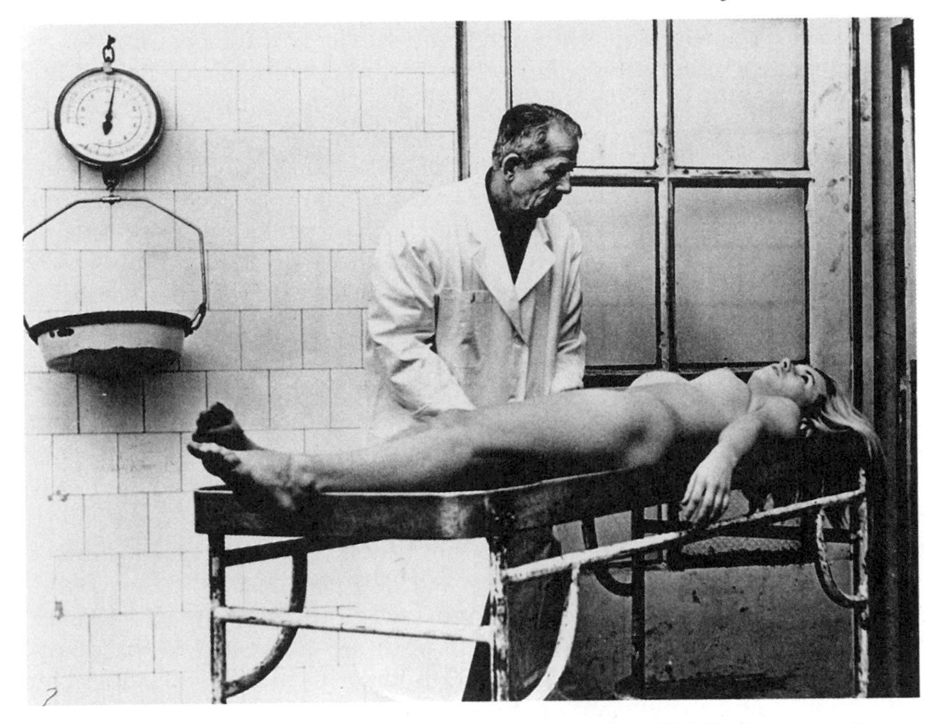

5.4. Isabella's corpse in the autopsy room. *Love Affair.* BFI Stills, Posters and Designs.

lectures by a kindly and elderly Belgrade sexologist, Professor Aleksandar Kostić, concerning phallic adoration in early cultures, a learned disquisition on the hen's egg as the perfect unit of reproduction, and an analysis of the nature of coitus and its representation in paintings; (2) a detached, rational, and sometimes gruesomely illustrated voice-over and lecture by a noted criminologist, Dr. Živojin Aleksić, on the psychology of murder and of modern means of detection and the identification of corpses; (3) footage from a Dziga Vertov film depicting the fall of the Romanovs—featuring a segment in which Orthodox churches are being sacked and the steeples pulled down so that only rounded cupolas remain; (4) a parodic pseudo-documentary on the problems of rat infestation and extermination; and (5) a brief *belle epoque* erotic film depicting a nude couple posing in a series of *tableaux vivants* on a revolving platform to the accompaniment of the tinkling sounds of a music box.

Makavejev enriches the context of the film's love story by anchoring it in the polarities and tensions of Yugoslav reality in a period (the late sixties) of rapid political, social, and economic change. Makavejev's film vividly evokes the forces of modernity and Western cultural values, and of older forms of Communist political orthodoxy clashing with steadily strengthening forces of cultural liberalization, socialist pragmatism, and economic experimentation. The energy and vitality of these opposing forces are imaginatively and satirically evoked in the opening sequences of the film—following upon the sexologist's prologue and the intercutting of the film's opening titles with erotic slides. In these opening sequences, Isabella and her friend Ruža are depicted on the job at the switchboard and afterwards on the busy streets of Belgrade sharing intimate and joking comments about their love affairs, enjoying pedicures, sharing refreshments bought at a kiosk, and being swept along in the pedestrian traffic as they pass by shopping windows, Communist flags being readied for a parade, a large propaganda poster depicting Mao Tse Tung surrounded by young women and children who are gazing adoringly up at him, a huge banner of Lenin draped on the side of a building, and a large float passing through the crowded street with two giant forward-tilting tubes of toothpaste and a box of soap powder surrounded by pretty young women smiling and waving to the passersby. Streets are being torn up and new buildings erected, while the air is filled with contrasting strains of Communist party songs, popular music, and folk tunes. In this vibrant opening montage, a number of witty imagistic associations are suggested. The float that advertises toothpaste and soap powder is satirically connected to the giant image of Lenin and the propaganda poster of Mao, and both are connected to the sexologist's opening lecture on phallic adoration in early cultures—illustrated by slides that show fanciful giant phalluses posed in relation to smiling young women, much like the young women posing with the giant phallic tubes of toothpaste on the float. Such phallocentric associations deliver a double satiric critique of commodity fetishism on the one hand and eroticized reification of charismatic leaders on the other.

The larger tensions and polarities in society are reflected in the relationship between Isabella and Ahmed. Isabella is a member of the Hungarian minority in Yugoslavia, attempting to adopt a modern, liberated lifestyle free of Balkan male domination. She has financial independence (though a clearly limited and limiting job), and her own apartment in the city, and she freely chooses her lovers. Ahmed is a member of the Moslem Slav minority, its history rooted in five centuries of Turkish rule, which represents the most traditional and conservative expression of a male-ordered and -dominated social structure. His quiet formality and kindness mask deeper layers of fiery pride and passionate ferocity. Early in their relationship, Isabella playfully refers to Ahmed as "Suleiman the Turk," and he calls her "Eve"—referring both to the temptation she represents and to Ahmed's earlier assertion that she is the first "modern" woman with whom he has become sexually involved. Later, when Ahmed and Isabella are sharing a finger dessert together, he happily asks, "Am I a sultan or not?" Playful allusions, however, take on a hard and bitter edge when Isabella rejects Ahmed's proposal of marriage and concludes by emphatically declaring, "I don't want to be your slave."

Ahmed also embodies more recent forms of tradition and conformity. He was orphaned by the war, became a member of the Communist party, and expresses an uncomplicated and orthodox belief in its history and precepts—precepts that he puts to work in his socialist-determined role as rat exterminator. He lives frugally and alone in a small cupola-shaped apartment on the roof of a building; the dark, cramped interior is sparsely furnished. One of the few wall decorations is a photograph of a military scene from the Second World War. By contrast, Isabella's apartment, though quite modest, is airy and open, with tasteful and whimsical decorative touches. She invests even simple domestic chores with a certain flair and imagination—especially in the sequence where the film deftly portrays her elaborate preparation of Hungarian blueberry strudel to the accompaniment of the "Grand March" from *Aida*!

The contrasting attitudes of Isabella and Ahmed to communism's revolutionary past is brought out most vividly in the sequence where he brings a phonograph player to Isabella's apartment—which they are now sharing—and plays a record of a song written by Mayakovsky, a famous poet of the Russian revolution, to music composed by Hanns Eisler. The song "March of Time" has been translated into German and presented to Ahmed by his "friends from East Germany." Ahmed plays the record from the second-floor balcony of Isabella's apartment, which overlooks the proletarian, activity-filled interior courtyard of the building complex. The sequence ends with an up-angle shot of Ahmed, virtually at attention, transfixed by the rousing revolutionary sentiments expressed in the song. Isabella, by contrast, is standing relaxed by his side with a look of tolerant amusement. Ahmed is at his most rapt when the song triumphantly promises ". . . a future of joy/Since the commune is at the door/Be faithful to your oath!/Time, march forward."

The Eisler/Mayakovsky song expresses an ambivalent duality that pervades the entire film. Its lofty, life-affirming idealism, expressed in the promise of a "future of joy," is antithetically undercut by the aggressive march rhythm and the regimented, militaristic, death-oriented command to "Go, make your assault/Crush to death the rotten vermin/Fight boldly!" The song's admonition to annihilate "rotten vermin" is satirically amplified in the parodic documentary on rat extermination which occurs later in the film—a sequence in which Ahmed is depicted as part of a "vanguard of humanity" boldly invading antiquated outhouses, garbage dumps, and abandoned lots to seek and destroy the pestilential horde. The mock militaristic and rhetorical exaggeration of this sequence ends with an ironic contrapuntal poem—composed for the film by the Serbian writer Dušan Radović—which looks at the question of rat extermination from the unaccustomed vantage point of the rat!

Isabella's and Ahmed's sensual and tragic love affair is contrasted to a modern, rationalized, cool, and indifferent world. Scenes of the postmortem examination of Isabella's body are accompanied by lectures on detection and the identification of corpses. The tragic and bizarre circumstances of Isabella's death are missed altogether by rationalized methods of police detection and a pompous, self-righteous, and beside-the-point criminologist's lecture on the psychology of murder. Makavejev satirizes both the criminologists' and the sexologist's reductionist attempts to explain away the irrationalities, complexities, and mysteries of life—which ironically may reveal themselves most fully in such seemingly random intimate trivialities and "senseless" moments as those depicted in the film.

Can humanity be "reconstructed"? The question is raised rhetorically and satirically in the film's opening title: WILL MAN BE REMODELED? WILL THE NEW MAN PRESERVE CERTAIN OLD ORGANS? If the answer to that question involves ideological restructuring from without (the Communist promise to remodel a new man), then the film's answer appears to be quite wittily in the negative. More richly than in his first feature film, Makavejev explores the elusive and paradoxical intersections and contradictions of *eros* and *thanatos* as they express their mysterious and powerful imperatives within the individual psyche and on the larger social order. The film, despite its sometimes disturbing images of repressive violence and death, is ultimately life-affirming and celebrates sensual liberation, joy, humor, spontaneity, and creativity as anti-death mechanisms of counter-repression.

The film that elaborates most fully upon Makavejev's thematic preoccupations in *Man Is Not a Bird* and *Love Affair* is his most widely discussed and influential film, *WR: Mysteries of the Organism.* On the way toward making that film, however, Makavejev's path was pleasantly diverted by his discovery in the Belgrade Film Archives of a neglected and long-forgotten Serbian "talkie," *Innocence Unprotected,* made in 1942 during the Nazi occupation of Belgrade—a film which he resurrected as the core of his own film by the same name.

Innocence Unprotected

The innocent and the beautiful have no enemy but time.[7]

—Yeats

The original *Innocence Unprotected* is a naive, romantic melodrama featuring the death-defying exploits of a real-life Balkan superman and folk hero,[8] Dragoljub Aleksić, who is a versatile and daring stuntman, strongman, aerial acrobat, and escape artist. Not only did Aleksić play himself in the feature role of the film (acting and singing with charming ineptitude) but, with some professional help, he also directed and produced it. In the film, Aleksić, integrates footage of his most daring acrobatic stunts, filmed professionally over a period from 1929 to 1940, with an artlessly written and performed romantic melodrama. In the melodrama, the orphaned heroine, Nada, repeatedly fends off the unwelcome importunings of a rich but vile suitor, Petrović, who is encouraged in his suit by Nada's even more vile stepmother. Nada's heart, however, belongs entirely to the strongman Aleksić, whom she describes (to Petrović) as a man with "nerves of steel, the strength of a giant, and a heart of gold." In the climactic scene, Aleksić rescues Nada from an attempted rape by a drunken Petrović, who is actively encouraged to perform this despicable

5.5. The young Aleksić balancing on the "Pillar of Death." *Innocence Unprotected.* BFI Stills, Posters and Designs.

act by Nada's unrelentingly vindictive stepmother. In his most daring stunt in the film, Aleksić lassos a chimney stack and swings by a rope from one building to the next, crashing through the upper story window of Nada's apartment, subduing Petrović in hand-to-hand combat, and claiming his true love! Into this melodramatic text are interpolated previously shot film segments of Aleksić's death-defying acrobatic stunts (including climbing the "pillar of death" precariously balanced on a small wheel, escaping from a suspended iron cage just before an explosive charge detonates and severs it from its aerial perch, and hanging by his teeth while suspended from the undercarriage of a plane flying over Belgrade—this latter stunt helped in some measure by trick photography).

Despite the film's naiveté, it attracted enormous audiences during its premiere engagement in occupied Belgrade and easily outsold the professionally better-made German film playing at a nearby theater. The initial success of the film prompted an inquiry by Nazi officials to determine how such a film could be made entirely outside official channels. To prevent possible confiscation, Ivan Živković, who portrays Aleksić's brother and served as the film's co-producer, buried a print of the film in a farmyard until after the liberation. Ironically, the postwar Communist officials in Yugoslavia were also perplexed by how such a film could have been made outside Nazi channels and Aleksić was charged with enemy collaboration. Only after a vigorous defense was Aleksić able to clear himself of the charges. The film print, meanwhile, was rescued from its barnyard archive, only to gather dust and anonymity in the more sanctified environs of the Belgrade Film Archives—not even finding its way into Yugoslav film histories or official filmographies.

In his "new edition" of *Innocence Unprotected* Makavejev completely recontextualizes the original film and endows it with fresh new meanings and satiric implications. First, he embellishes the original black-and-white film by tinting some of the frames and adding vivid splashes of color in others—including giving the heroine a pair of bright red lips in one scene, adding color to a chair and mugs of beer in a cafe scene, giving a black eye to a villain in the final fight scene, and painting a Yugoslav flag on the dress of a young girl dancing the kolo. Makavejev also embellishes the film's sound track by adding parodic political and folk songs. Second, Makavejev intercuts the original film with other archival film material from the same period, including documentary footage of war-damaged Belgrade, Nazi and quisling propaganda films, and newreel segments. Third, Makavejev intercuts contemporary scenes in color, which he directed, of interviews and staged routines involving the now white-haired but still vigorous Aleksić and five other members of the original cast and crew of *Innocence Unprotected.* Aleksić can still hang by his teeth, bend iron bars, break boards over his head, and absorb the shock of detonated explosive charges going off in a pipe which he has placed in his mouth. He reenacts (on crutches) the consequences of a near-fatal accident he suffered as a young acrobat, and the defense he made of his innocence when accused of being an enemy collaborator and is posed by Makavejev and his crew in a series of heroic strongman *tableaux vivants.*

Much of the satiric wit and charm of this film arises from the fresh connections that Makavejev invites the viewer to make among disparate and incongruous film texts. One of the most fertile of these associational complexes relates to the naively heroic *persona* of Aleksić—a *persona* that emerges as a mixture of Aleksić's self-promotion and guileless faith in his prowess (not always justified) and Makavejev's sly embellishments—especially in the staged reenactments and *tableaux vivants* that he orchestrates in the latter sequences of the film.

There has been critical speculation since the film's release that Aleksić the strongman-acrobat represents, in part, a parody of Yugoslavia's famous leader Marshal Tito, who exercised undisputed leadership over Yugoslavia from the war years until his death on May 4, 1980. There are many suggestive associations in the film to support such a conclusion. Most of these implications are indirect, however, since even in Yugolslavia's liberal atmosphere of the late sixties Tito's name and legend were sacrosanct and a taboo subject for political caricature and parody.

The only direct visual connection of Aleksić with Tito occurs near the end of the film, when Aleksić is reenacting his defense against the charge of collaboration and Makavejev places him in a hearing room (probably simulated) alongside a Communist flag and in front of a large photograph of Tito.[9] Tito is in his familiar all-white marshal's uniform

5.6. The middle-aged Aleksić posed in a heroic *tableau vivant. Innocence Unprotected.* BFI Stills, Posters and Designs.

and military cap and posed in a manner that mimics Aleksić's earlier *tableaux vivants* heroic posturing, as stage-managed by Makavejev. In the segment of the film where the present-day Aleksić is demonstrating his iron-bending prowess, he reveals that he learned how to work iron in his early days as a locksmith. Makavejev gives prominence to this fact in the opening titles of the film, where Aleksić is identified as a "Locksmith and Acrobat." Tito began his career as an apprentice locksmith and was a member of the Ironworkers' Union during his early days as a Communist party activist. Aleksić also bears some physical resemblance to Tito, with his relatively short, sturdy build, peasant vitality, and seeming indestructability. At a metaphorical level, Aleksić's repeated near escapes from death and resourceful balancing acts suggest the legendary stories of Tito's narrow escapes as an illegal party organizer, his leadership of the Partisans during the war, in which he repeatedly led his forces through the encircling rings of vastly superior enemy forces, and the diplomatic tight-wire act he performed after the war in charting Yugoslavia's independent course between East and West. All of these associations are given additional parodic lift in the Aleksić "theme song," which was written especially for Makavejev's new version of *Innocence Unprotected* and which is jauntily played and sung under the opening titles, and twice more in the middle and latter half of the film. Each verse of the song ends with the refrain "Oh, Aleksić/We'll support you, in everything you do." The comic-strip idolatry expressed in the song is not far removed from that which is invited by Tito propaganda slogans and songs ubiquitous in Yugoslavia at the time, including, for example, "Comrade Tito/We swear to you/That from your path/We will not stray," and "We are Tito's; Tito is ours."[10]

Makavejev further enlarges his satiric treatment of Communist icons and sacred texts by adding the "Internationale" to the sound track of the original *Innocence Unprotected* at the point when Aleksić is performing his most complex and involved aerial stunt. Two iron cages are suspended high in the air with Aleksić bound and chained in one, and his assistant handcuffed in the other. Aleksić breaks loose from his cage a moment before an explosive charge severs it from its moorings and plunges it to the ground. He then swings over to his assistant, frees him, and carries him away at the precise moment that another explosive charge dislodges the second cage and also sends it earthward. As Aleksić flies through the air carrying his assistant, the Communist "Internationale" reaches its triumphant conclusion that the victory will be decisive and that the battle, though hard fought ". . . will unite us, one and all." The film then cuts to the villain Petrović, who supplies the unintended punchline: "I don't believe it!"

But this film is much more than witty political parody. Makavejev's intercutting of period archival film material with the original *Innocence Unprotected* provides an innovative and evocative perspective on the early years of the war and the occupation of Belgrade. The overall effect of these interlaced materials is to further enlarge upon the "innocence" of *Innocence Unprotected*–with its naiveté, air of honest enthusiasm, resourcefulness, seeming obliviousness to the harshness and deprivations of the time, and the uncomplicated, cartoon-like moral universe of good and evil which it portrays. Contrasted to that is a collage of documentary, newsreel, and propaganda film images that portrays a morally ambiguous and perverse world of human suffering, calamitous events, and cynical manipulation.

The shock and destruction of war is captured in the documentary footage of war damage suffered in Belgrade following Nazi Germany's savage bombing attack begun on Sunday, April 6, 1941, under the code name "Operation Punishment." The footage contains haunting images of collapsed buildings, rubble-strewn streets, corpses being hauled away on crude carts, and a lone man and woman wandering aimlessly through the ruins. An even more shocking image occurs in a later documentary film segment of a naked, filth-covered, half-dead child lying in a shallow pit listlessly picking up pieces of straw. These images provide an ironic counterpoint to the crude Nazi propaganda poster representations of gigantic smiling German soldiers posing as liberators and protectors of the Serbs against the apelike Russian Bolsheviks. And the crude Nazi propaganda segments are contrasted at other points in the film with documentary footage of German soldiers at rest, and one brief segment in which a row of German soldiers take castor oil, fall out of rank, make faces, and behave in clownish human ways—suggesting, of course, that not all German soldiers were descended from Attila the Hun. But the most fascinating film segments from the times are those that depict quisling leaders and their German puppetmasters manipulating the worst strains of Serbian nationalism and chauvinism and tying them in with folk culture and the Serbian Orthodox church. It was, of course, a part of the propagandist aims of the enemy occupiers to exploit Yugoslavia's volatile interethnic and national rivalries as a means of diminishing united resistance and of fostering a new Fascist culture. The film segment that depicts the Serbian quisling leader General Milan Nedić giving a speech in support of *Nova Srbija* (The New Serbia) and the one that depicts the carefully orchestrated funeral procession of an assassinated quisling leader are vivid examples of that policy in operation.

Viewed against the background of the times in which it was made, *Innocence Unprotected* is quite innocent indeed—and all the more charming for being so. Makavejev was right to label it "a good old Serbian film," not because it had any artistic legitimacy, but because it emerges remarkably unspoiled in a very spoiled time. Nor did the makers of the flm escape the harsher realites and moral choices of the time. Ana Milosavljević (Nada), Pera Milosavljević (Servant, loyal to Nada), and Ivan Živković (Aleksić's brother) served in the Army of Liberation; Stevan Mišković (cinemotographer) was a Partisan cameraman; and Vera Jovanović (the wicked stepmother) was in the Banjica concentration camp for a year.

Another level of complexity is added to Makavejev's film by his intercutting between past and present. Time itself proves to be the one thing against which innocence cannot be protected. Three of the film's survivors meet at the gravesite of the actor who played the villain Petrović (Bratoljub Gligorijević) and one of them wryly remarks: "We'll all end up here one day." On a rooftop setting, Vera Jovanović, dressed in top hat and tails, gamely dances and sings a faded period piece: a bawdy song about a girl named Freda who had ". . . lots of things to please lots of people." Her song is followed (in a park setting) with a satirical tune, performed ably if a bit off-key by the aging Pera Milosavljević, which states that in politics "You get the fat prize, if you cling to those who rise." Even the seemingly indestructible Aleksić shows signs of wear.[11] In one shot of him posed in black trunks, the camera slowly travels up his body in close-up, revealing the inevitable traces of the rough fingerprints of time—the crevices and sags that mark a still-muscular frame. In these latter sequences, Makavejev achieves poignancy without any hint of sentimentality and with his usual Brechtian distancing—attained through the use of irony and through the constant shifting among disparate film texts. In the end, Makavejev has succeeded, with a sophisticated blend of wit, compassion, and irony, in liberating Aleksić's film from the imprisoning cage of obscurity. He has also succeeded in making it perform marvelous and daring new tricks without destroying its essential core of naive enthusiasm and innocent charm.

Innocence Unprotected did not attract as large a domestic audience as had Makavejev's two quite successful previous films, and in some theaters it played to nearly empty houses.[12] The film's lack of a contemporary "love story," of well-known, talented, and popular actors and actresses, and of sexual explicitness and nudity contributed in some measure to the film's more modest (though not negligible) domestic audience appeal. The film was critically well received internationally and won several festival awards, including a Silver Bear and International Film Critics' Award at Berlin in 1968.

In his next and most controversial and widely discussed film, *WR: Mysteries of the Organism,* Makavejev significantly enlarges the scope of his satirical political critique, the complexity of his film collage structure, and the boldness of his fantasy psychosexual/political paradigms and "investigations." The title of the film *WR* stands for both Wilhelm Reich and World Revolution.

WR: Mysteries of the Organism

> **. . . a black comedy, political circus, a fantasy on the fascism and communism of human bodies, the political life of human genitals, a proclamation of the pornographic essence of any system of power and authority over others.[13]**
>
> **—Makavejev**

In his film *WR,* Makavejev explores more fully than in his previous works the realms of erotic and sexual liberation as a foil to repressive power. He uses the psychoanalytic theories of Wilhelm Reich as a touchstone for wide-ranging political commentary and satire. In his later writings,[14] Reich developed the theory that, unless a mysterious universal phenomenon called "orgone energy" is discharged naturally through sexual union, neurosis will erupt. He developed an Orgone Accumulator to aid patients in tapping into this energy resource. In the late 1950s, Reich was jailed in the United States for his unorthodox therapeutic techniques, his Orgone Accumulators were confiscated as health hazards, and all of his books were burned (including earlier works that had nothing to do with the Orgone Accumulator).

Makavejev's film is divided into two sections that are continuously intercut. The first intersperses a documentary account of Wilhelm Reich's life, work, persecution, and death in a Pennsylvania prison with examples of bioenergetic and primal-scream therapies of contemporary Reichian practitioners and various scenes and interviews reflecting contemporary America (circa 1969-1970). The second section is a fictional story set in Yugoslavia, which centers on Milena (Milena Dravić), a liberated young woman whose attempt to spread the gospel of Reichian sexual freedom to a perfectly formed and handsome but politically conditioned Russian skating star is finally

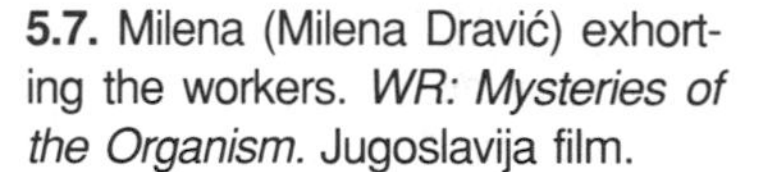

5.7. Milena (Milena Dravić) exhorting the workers. *WR: Mysteries of the Organism.* Jugoslavija film.

rewarded with decapitation by his ice skates. Milena's roommate, Jagoda (Jagoda Kaloper), practices Reichian sexual freedom with unusual devotion and pursues the doctrine with unflagging enthusiasm in her sexual couplings with Ljuba "the Cock" (Miodrag Andrić).

In the context of the film, the United States and the Soviet Union are monuments to sexuality misdirected into power politics and militarism. The principal symbols of American repression are the right-wing excesses of the McCarthy era, in which pathologies of "Get the Commies" were combined with suppression of intellectual unorthodoxy and the contemporary (at the time the film was made) U.S. militarism in Vietnam. Stalin is the preeminent symbol of Soviet repression. In the context of the film he gradually absorbs Lenin and takes on his guise. The contemporary symbol of the repressive Stalinist-Leninist orthodoxy is represented in the politically conditioned Russian ice-skating champion Vladimir Ilyich (after Lenin's first name), whose perfectly formed lips speak nothing but Socialist clichés.

Yugoslavia represents a separate path to socialism, espousing humanistic self-management socialist doctrine but not always living up to its claims. It is Milena's self-appointed task to enliven self-management and self-regulating socialism by preaching the doctrine of liberation through orgasm—"Only by liberating both love and labor can we create a self-regulating worker's society"—and she admonishes the workers to "fuck merrily and without fear."[15]

Makavejev assumes an ironic and satirical attitude toward all forms of

5.8. "Death to male fascism—freedom to female people." Milena in surrealist revolutionary pose. *WR: Mysteries of the Organism.* Facets Video.

dogmatism and cant—including an affectionately satirical handling of Milena's naive, simplistic, and rhetorical presentation of Reichian sexual politics. He satirizes both conventional sexual taboos and mechanical and doctrinaire revolts against them (from Jackie Curtis's bisexuality to Betty Dobson's paintings of men and women masturbating). He adopts an ironic view of New Left anti-Vietnam protests by interspersing scenes of Tuli Kupferberg of the "Revolting Theater" prowling the New York streets, autoerotically caressing his rifle while the song he wrote for the Fugs plays on the sound track: "Kill, kill, kill for peace."

There are extended scenes of vigorous and joyful sexual intercourse in the film but, ironically, no orgasms. Scenes of sexual intercourse are separated by dissolves and inserts, which provide a structural filmic equivalent to Reich's belief that we live in an age of incomplete sexuality, in which sex has become subservient to politics, institutionalism, and dogma. This notion is further conveyed in the repetition of motifs in which arousal is followed by freezing. The most widely discussed example of this motif is the sequence in which the editor of *Screw* magazine, Jim Buckley, has his penis manipulated to erection by the sculptress Nancy Godfrey, who then makes a plaster cast of its erect state. Later, a shot of the replica of Buckley's penis in rigid clear pink plastic is followed by a film segment from *The Vow,* Chiaurelli's idealized portrayal of Stalin, in which Stalin proclaims, "Comrades, we have successfully completed the first stage of communism"[16]—a juxtaposition that equates the powerful but repressive Stalin with a frozen phallus and emphasizes the frozen nature of the revolution under Stalinist centralized, hierarchical dogmatism. The image of Stalin is then followed by a cut to a segment of film depicting a patient in a Nazi-run insane asylum catatonically and methodically pounding his head against the wall. A Communist hymn is on the sound track intoning: "We thank the Party/Our glorius Party/For bringing happiness/To every home!" The film then cuts to a medium shot of Tuli Kupferberg facing the camera and energetically masturbating his toy M-16 rifle. The montage sequence as a whole suggests the film's paradigmatic core of repressive associations among and between communism, fascism, U.S. militarism, and authoritarian institutional insanities.

The complex and ambivalent relationship between Yugoslavia and the Soviet Union is metaphorically mirrored in the brief love affair between Milena and the Russian ice skater Vladimir Ilyich (Ivica Vidović). Milena sees Vladimir perform during a guest tour in Yugoslavia and falls instantly and romantically in love with him. Despite her views concerning complete sexual freedom, Milena approaches Vladimir with diffidence and a touch of awe. In their first encounters, Vladimir speaks in socialist clichés and takes a condescending view toward Yugoslavia's separate path to socialism: "We Russians . . . we do respect your efforts to find your own way. You are a proud and independent people. But we are confident you will learn from your own experience that our way is best!" Milena responds that "time will tell who's closest to the best," and Jagoda chimes in, "The closest kin will do you in"[17]—a clear allusion to the Soviet-led Warsaw Pact invasion of Czechoslovakia in 1968, which made an enormous impact on Makavejev and Yugoslav public opinion.

As Vladimir begins to relax in the free ambience of Milena and Jagoda's apartment, he is inspired, at one point, to observe, "Well, I've been to the East and I've been to the West, but it was never like this!"[18] On a romantic stroll with Milena along a snow-covered riverbank, Vladimir declares, "I like being here! I confess there's much I don't understand. But your people are wonderful."[19] They kiss romantically to the melancholy strings of the Hungarian gypsy song "Like a Beautiful Dream." Vladimir at first yields to the sensual moment and then reasserts (in words that Makavejev borrowed from Lenin) his rigid, doctrinaire character: ". . . nowadays if you stroke anybody's head, he'll bite off your hand! Now you have to hit them over the head, hit them on the head mercilessly . . . though in principle we oppose all violence."[20] Milena attempts to turn Vladimir back to a more sensual mood, but he slaps her face, and she falls down. Vladimir is filled with remorse and asks her to forgive him. Milena begins to hit him hard around the head and shoulders and makes an impassioned plea:

> You love all mankind, yet you're incapable of loving one individual: one single living creature. What is this love that makes you nearly knock my head off?

5.9. Jagoda (Jagoda Kaloper) helps Milena entertain Vladimir Ilyich (Ivica Vidović) under the watchful gaze of Reich and Freud. *WR: Mysteries of the Organism.* BFI Stills, Posters and Designs.

> You said I'm lovely as the Revolution. You gazed at me like a picture. . . . But "Revolution" mustn't touch! What's a baby to a male? A matter of a second! Everything else is the woman's job!
>
> Meanwhile you put your body to the service of Art! Your magic flood-lit figure serves the needs of the masses!
>
> A bunch of lies is what you're serving . . . the People and the Party! A toy balloon is what it is . . . not a revolution! A petty human lie dressed up as a great historical truth! Are you capable, you rotten louse, of serving the needs of the species by taking the one basic position for an ecstatic flight to the target . . . like an arrow . . . or a vigorously hurled . . . spear?[21]

After delivering this key speech in the film, Milena continues to strike Vladimir bitterly and unthinkingly until he stands up in front of her, tears in his eyes, and they kiss passionately. After prolonged and copious love-making (not shown in the film), Vladimir severs Milena's head from her body with his ice skates (also not shown) in an effort to reassert his authoritarian rigidity and perhaps, by metaphorical extension, as Vogel suggests, to reclaim his Communist virginity from Yugoslav revisionism.[22]

The last two scenes of the film metaphorically pose the possibility, despite the past, for reconciliation. Milena's severed head, on a white tray in the autopsy room, speaks and bitterly equates (as did Reich) Stalinist-Leninist orthodoxy with fascism:

> Cosmic rays streamed through our coupled bodies. We pulsated to the vibrations of the universe. But he couldn't bear it. He had to go one step further. Vladimir is a man of noble impetuousness, a man of high ambition, of immense energy. . . . He's romantic, ascetic, a genuine Red Fascist!

Despite these deformations and perversions of the revolutionary spirit, however, Milena declares: "Even now I'm not ashamed of my Communist past!"[23]

Blood on his hands, filled with remorse—his rigid doctrinaire mask dissolved—Vladimir wanders near a gypsy camp in the snowy landscape. With his arms outstretched, he appeals to an unknown God in words written and sung by the Russian underground poet Bulat Okudjava:

> O Lord, my God, my green-eyed one,
> Before the earth stops turning
> and all our pain is done
> Before this day is through
> And the fires are still burning
> Grant to each some little thing
> And remember, I'm here too.[24]

Awakened sensuality and love have placed Vladimir in touch with his humanity and the hope of redemption. During the last lines of Vladimir's song, the film cuts to a shot of Milena's smiling head and then to the shot of a photograph of a smiling Reich, the author of this political miracle, and the film ends.

In the Yugoslav segments of the film, Makavejev goes much further than in previous films in satirizing and parodying the more conservative icons and symbols of Yugoslavia's revolutionary past—especially those pertaining to the National War of Liberation. In a kozara snake dance spontaneously organized on the balconies of Milena's tenement building, a Partisan song is sung with new lyrics celebrating love and sexual freedom and ending with "Life without fucking isn't worth a thing."[25] The indefatigable Ljuba is serving his required term in the Yugoslav People's Army and announces to the ever-receptive Jagoda, "I'm Ljuba the Cock. I mount guard by day and girls by night."[26] In one scene, Milena comes to her apartment when Jagoda and Ljuba are coupling on the couch. Jagoda cheerfully introduces her guest as Comrade Ljuba. "He came for a little rest. He didn't even finish his tea. Ever ready, our military! Ah, the People's Army!"[27] In a particularly vigorous coupling, Jagoda exults, "Onward People's Soldiers,"[28] and in another sequence, Ljuba mounts Jagoda from the rear and triumphantly exclaims, "War of Liberation."[29]

Echoes of the student protests at Belgrade University and elsewhere in 1968 are captured in the character of Radmilović, the "natural man" (Zoran

Radmilović), a tempestuous and angry young radical, who attacks a Mercedes belonging to a high party official, jumps on the hood, and shouts a slogan that had been used in the student demonstrations and festooned on university walls: "Down with the Red Bourgeoisie!"[30] He uses the same slogan in another scene, in which he has blocked traffic and is hosing the cars, shouting: "Screw you all! Down with the Red Bourgeoisie."[31] He scornfully denounces symbols of consumerism, including Steak Esterhazi, Mitsuko perfume, and "Marx Factor."

WR shares and expands upon the thematic and stylistic concerns of Makavejev's other films made during the Yugoslav period. As Eagle has perceptively demonstrated, Makavejev's films mirror, in part, the humanistic Marxist critique that was prevalent in Yugoslavia (and elsewhere in Eastern Europe) in the late sixties.[32] Yugoslav Marxists associated with the internationally well-known journal *Praxis* asserted that there could be "no free society without free personality" and attacked orthodox communism in terms closely paralleling those of Makavejev. They especially singled out the repressive consequences of dogmatism, bureaucratism, party elitism, and charismatic leadership (the cult of personality). They were also concerned with unmasking propagandistically constructed myths, fetishes, taboos, and sacred texts. But Makavejev's satiric critique is ultimately more radical and idiosyncratic than theirs in its orientation. He implicates Lenin in his critique of Stalinism, which the *Praxis* group studiously avoided. More significantly, he called not merely for "socialism with a human *face*," but one with a human *body* as well.

Ironically, Makavejev's most liberating film appeared at a time when antireform and middle-of-the-road party elements were regaining the upper hand in Yugoslavia. A vigorous counteroffensive against *new film* tendencies was launched in 1969 under the banner of *black film*, and reached its highest peak of intensity and effectiveness in 1971 and 1972. The campaign was stimulated, in part, by events occurring on the larger political stage: the 1968 student demonstrations in Belgrade, the Warsaw Pact invasion of Czechoslovakia, and especially the Croatian nationalist-separatist crisis of 1971. In the Croatian crisis, Tito personally intervened to purge the ranks of top Croatian party officials supporting nationalist-separatist goals. As a *quid pro quo*, he supported the campaign in Serbia aimed against non-establishment Marxists (especially philosophers associated with the journal *Praxis*), members of the non-Marxist "humanistic intelligentsia," radical students, and artists. Makavejev's film was caught in the vortex of these events and was effectively kept from domestic distribution by action of the Executive Committee of the Regional Cultural Commission of Vojvodina. The film was subjected to a special screening in Novi Sad, capital of the autonomous region of Vojvodina, where the film had been produced by Neoplanta film. Approximately 800 largely hostile viewers were in attendance, representing SUBNOR (Veterans of the War of Liberation) and a local Novi Sad community organization. The screening was followed by heated public discussion, with Dušan Makavejev and representatives from Neoplanta film present to defend the film against polemic attack. Although the film was initially cleared for domestic distribution by the Commission on Cinematography of the Regional Cultural Commission, this decision was later overruled by the Cultural Commission's Executive Committee, which placed a freeze on the licensing of the film for domestic distribution. In an equally controversial move, the public prosecutor of Serbia restrained the film from being shown at the Pula festival (Yugoslavia's annual showing of domestically produced feature films). Widespread protests against these actions were unsuccessful.[33] Makavejev's film was never formally banned (formal censorship, under Yugoslav law at the time, required a full court proceeding). The film was simply not allowed to be seen and remained on the shelf for sixteen years (until 1987). Makavejev was later dismissed from the party, and he moved to Paris to continue his film career in the West.

WR also provoked widespread discussion and controversy internationally. It was shown at a number of major festivals and won several awards, including the prestigious Luis Buñuel Prize in 1971 at Cannes. Vanguard critics in the West hailed Makavejev as a bold and innovative cinemarxist and placed him on the leading edge of what was termed a "second wave" of critically and commercially nonconformist cinema—the "first" being the French *nouvelle vague* of the early sixties.

Makavejev's growing international reputation helped him to secure funding for his first film made outside of Yugoslavia, but it did not compensate for the disruption of many personal and artistic associations which he had nurtured in Yugoslavia and that had contributed substantially to the remarkable thematic and stylistic continuity, growth, and evolution of his earlier films, as well as their strong grounding in Yugoslav social and political realities. Among his strongest artistic collaborators were the cinematographer Aleksandar Petković, whose work with Makavejev dated from their days together in the Belgrade amateur film club; the scenarist/director Dragoljub Ivkov, another "graduate" of the *kino klub*, who collaborated closely with Makavejev in providing art direction for *Man Is Not a Bird* and *WR;* and Branko Vučićević, one of the most influential scenarists of the *new film* movement, who served as an assistant director on *Love Affair* and *Innocence Unprotected* and whose sardonic wit complemented well Makavejev's own. But Makavejev's most important and constant source of artistic collaboration was preserved in his move to the West. His wife Bojana Marijan, a talented musicologist who put together the complex sound collage for *WR*, has been an artistic collaborator and assistant director on all of Makavejev's subsequent films.

In *Sweet Movie*, his first film made in the West, Makavejev continued to develop and to elaborate upon the stylistic and thematic concerns expressed in *WR*. Indeed, *Sweet Movie* is, in many ways, a remake of *WR*, painted in even wilder and more surrealistic hues. Like *WR* it delivers an ironic and satiric double critique of the degeneration of Communist ideals and practice in the East, and the trivialization of human values, excessive self-interest, and consumer-oriented narcissism and commodity fetishism in the West.

Makavejev moves even further than in *WR* toward allegorical typage rather than "realistic" characterizations (reflecting Pudovkin's and Eisenstein's "theory of types" as well as tendencies in surrealist art and Brechtian drama). Some of the characters are presented as broad lampoons and parodic caricatures. Makavejev also moves much further in breaking social taboos and film conventions—even transgressing, as Bart Testa has cogently argued, the conventions and "decorum" of the "art film" and the art film audience toward which it was primarily aimed.[34]

Sweet Movie was the *succès de scandale* at the 1974 Cannes Film Festival, generating enormous controversy and a number of angry critical denunciations. It premiered in New York's D. W. Griffith Theater on October 8, 1975—with four minutes of scatological material deleted—and precipitated equally vociferous controversy.[35] Some critics defended the film's courage, originality, and progressive insights, while others found it egregiously offensive. Some mainstream critics were especially perplexed. Jay Cocks, writing for *Time* (November 3, 1975), declared that *Sweet Movie,* ". . . full of unenlightened lunacy, is not really a film at all. It is a social disease." And Frank Rich of the *New York Post* wrote on October 3, 1975, that "*Sweet Movie* drowns itself in tedium." Taking a somewhat more charitable view, Vincent Canby (*New York Times,* October 10, 1975) observed that ". . . for a film so full of concern for the political and social sanity of man, *Sweet Movie* is, paradoxically, elitist. If one doesn't share Mr. Makavejev's knowledge of the history of communism and Reichian psychology, much of it is incomprehensible." He concludes that the "overall work remains a courageous example of a personal kind of filmmaking that, for me, leads nowhere."

Some vanguard critics who had beaten the critical drum for Makavejev's earlier films were also quite negative in their evaluations of *Sweet Movie.* These attitudes are perhaps best illustrated by Richard Roud's remark that *Sweet Movie* was "a critical disaster," and expressed his own view that there has always been ". . . a streak of opportunistic vulgarity in Makavejev and in *Sweet Movie* that streak, as it were, took over. Let us hope it is only a temporary lapse."[36] Two sequences in the film were especially troublesome to viewers and critics. One of these involved scenes of Otto Muehl's real-life radical therapy commune in Vienna, in which members of the commune are vividly depicted playing with and spitting food at each other, vomiting, defecating, and urinating. The other scene is a totally fictional one depicting Anna Planeta's seduction of four prepubescent boys.

Scandal had already attached itself to *Sweet Movie* several months before its completion and release. The Canadian actress Carole Laure, who plays a major role in the film (Miss World), dropped out of the project before completing her scenes. She complained of the role's demeaning physical requirements and expressed fear that continued involvement in the film would be damaging to her career. She was apparently rather traumatized by her encounters with Otto Muehl's radical therapy commune and dropped out of the film before all of these scenes were shot. As originally conceived, Carole Laure's character was to provide the dramatic and narrative line for the film. The episodes at the commune were to have affected a "rebirth" and transformation of "Miss World" into a radical revolutionary. Instead, it was necessary for Makavejev to spend an additional two months rewriting the film's script to include two separate but intercut story sequences; one centering on Miss World, and the other centering on a new major character, the militant Marxist prostitute Anna Planeta. The Polish-French actress Anna Prucnal was contracted to play the new part.[37] The controversy and scandal surrounding this film (understandable given the provocative nature of its content) should not obscure the prescience of its satirical political critique—a critique made all the more relevant by the recent dramatic collapse of Communist systems in East and Central Europe and the former Soviet Union.

Sweet Movie

> Is there life after birth?[38]
> —Makavejev

In this film Makavejev continuously intercuts two bizarre fictional stories as well as other insertions and filmed material—the most important of which is the Nazi documentary film of the exhumation and examination of the corpses of hundreds of Polish officers murdered by the Red Army in 1939 in Katyn forest.

The first fictional narrative concerns the sexual adventures and misadventures of a Canadian beauty who wins the title of Miss World 1984 for being judged the virgin with the most exquisitely formed hymen. Her prize is marriage to the wealthiest bachelor in the world, the billionaire Texan, Mr. Kapital, Aristoteles Aplanalpe (John Vernon). He whisks her away in his plane and discourses expansively on his worldwide acquisitions, including a recent purchase of Niagara Falls, which he plans to convert into "a fantastic quadraphonic extravaganza unaffected by weather conditions and in living color." Before consummating the marriage, Aplanalpe engages in an elaborate cleansing ritual with rubbing alcohol to ensure absolutely antiseptic conditions. Having completed these loving labors, he then removes his gold-painted erect penis (a visual pun on the James Bond film *Goldfinger*) from his white, cherry decorated shorts and urinates on his eager and prostrate bride—an unexpected perversity that prompts from her an understandably prolonged scream of loathing and protest. Despite her protests, she is then passed into the hands of the black superstud, Jeremiah Muscle (Roy Callender), where she suffers even more varied forms of sexual degradation. Jeremiah finally packs her in a suitcase and sends her off to Paris where she escapes and falls (this time willingly) into the arms of the superstar singing sensation, El Macho (Sami Frey), who wins her over with his sequined eyelids and electronically hyped ersatz Spanish love ballad recorded under the Eiffel tower. Following the recording, they make love and become locked together in sexual embrace. They are separated by an emergency team while tourists, including a group of nuns, look on.

5.10. Anna Planeta (Anna Prucnal) steering the ship "Survival" through Amsterdam harbor. *Sweet Movie.* BFI Stills, Posters and Designs.

Somewhat later, Miss World is carted by wheelbarrow into the real-life Milky Way Commune, headed by Dr. Otto Muehl, whose radical therapy consists of inviting the members of the commune to regress toward the womb, break through earlier learned physical taboos—what Reich termed "body armor"—and to recapture the freedom and joy of playing with their own and others' genitalia and with their food and body excretions. Miss World regresses to a fetal position, sleeps in a crib, is suckled by the black, ample breasted Momma Communa (Marpessa Dawn), and, at one point, rather catatonically rubs a man's flaccid penis across her cheek.

Finally, Miss World's odyssey of sexual exploitation, unredeemed by the ministrations of the Milky Way Commune, ends all too sweetly in a large pool of chocolate that is especially constructed for an elaborately produced TV commercial to sell candy. Her nude body is covered with liquid chocolate and she writhes seductively to orgasm before expiring by suffocation—as an excited cameraman zooms in for the final big close-up.

The second discontinuous narrative line involves vain attempts by the radical prostitute Anna Planeta (a decadent version of the Milena character in *WR*) to breathe some life into the moribund myths of the worldwide Communist revolution. She captains a ramshackle ship called "Survival" with an enormous figurehead of Marx on its prow. Limp strands of his beard drag in the water as the ship plies its way through the harbor and canals of Amsterdam. Anna stands proudly on the head of Marx as the old Italian

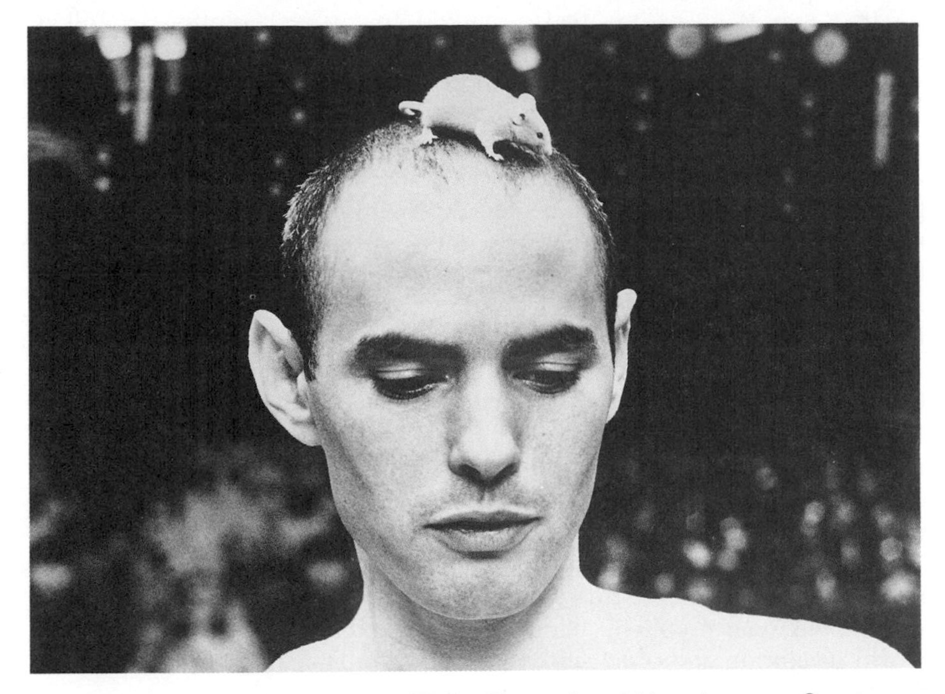

5.11. The sailor Luv Balkunin (Pierre Clementi) and his pet mouse. *Sweet Movie.* Facets Video.

revolutionary song, "The whole world is our country; our law is freedom," is heard on the sound track. Later she sings the film's theme song (with lyrics written by Makavejev and Anne Lonnberg): "Is there life on earth? Is there life after birth?"

The interior of the ship is a shrine to the fallen heroes of the revolution; its martyrs and assassins—huge fading collage photographs of Trotsky, Stalin, Lenin, the Kremlin leadership presiding over a parade in Red Square adorn the walls, and a clutter of other memorabilia recall the corpses of the past. Stuffed in the hold of the ship as well are vats of sugar, lollipops, and candy eggs, which Anna uses, along with the sweets of her body, to lure passengers aboard.

An especially eager passenger is a young Russian sailor, Luv Balkunin (Pierre Clementi), carrying a pet mouse under his hat, who comes aboard and makes love to Anna on the prow of the ship in broad daylight to the cheers of the shore's onlookers. Later they make love in a huge bed of sugar. Following the sailor's orgasm, Anna plunges a knife through the sugar into his gut and mixes the blood and sugar into a thick paste. The sailor at first laughs and welcomes his martyrdom—explicitly linking himself to the martyred sailor (Vakulinchuk) in Eisenstein's *Battleship Potemkin*— but then his head suddenly jerks backward, his mouth opens in a final death spasm, and he resembles more nearly the frozen death mask of one of the corpses dug up in Katyn Wood. Anna had remarked that the revolution is "full of corpses." The sailor replied, "The whole world is full of corpses." In the film Anna added to the world's body count by luring four young boys to their martyrdom after first seducing them with candy and the allures of her body.

Anna's story ends when the Amsterdam police arrest her and carry her off half-naked, screaming and kicking, while the bodies of the sailor, the four boys, and other victims are laid out in plastic bags along the shore. In the concluding (and most complex) sequence of the film, images of the row of body bags are intercut with images of Miss World expiring in the vat of chocolate, and with the grisly (black and white) images of exhumed corpses from Katyn Wood. The final cut of the film is from these corpses to the corpses of the young boys, also shot in black and white. As the camera holds on this final scene, the boys begin miraculously to stir and to emerge from their plastic entombment. The frame then freezes, color bleeds back into the screen image, the final film credits are superimposed, and the film ends by evoking the possibility of regeneration and rebirth even in the midst of such widespread entropy and deformation of human values.

A film that begins with cartoonlike comic charade and pornographic parody (or parodic pornography), *Sweet Movie* ends by offering a complexly ironic (and even prophetic) vision of the death throes of the Communist world revolution and of advanced consumer capitalism—what Norman O. Brown called the "excremental vision of the West."

In *Sweet Movie,* Makavejev goes even further than in *WR* in associating orthodox Communist culture with the antihuman distortion of human sexuality into eroticized martyrdom and revolutionary sacrifice. He also broadens his satiric critique of Stalinist communism's distortions, falsifications, and perversions of history, of its crimes against humanity, and of its betrayal of revolutionary ideals. In her most impassioned speech in *WR,* Milena accuses Vladimir of serving "a bunch of lies," and calls the revolution "a toy balloon . . . a petty lie dressed up as a great historical truth." In *Sweet Movie,* these verbal accusations are given greater satiric and parodic *visual* amplification by allegorizing the world revolution as a ramshackle boat called "Survival" captained by a militant prostitute—appropriately named "Planeta." A cross between a demented good ship lollipop and a little shop of Communist horrors, it carries in its hold the repressed secrets and crimes of the revolution's faded martyrs and assassins. The ship is also stuffed with tattered myths that are as shoddy as the material goods and sweets it carries. When Luv asks Planeta if she is afraid or ashamed of her Communist past, she responds, "I brought a lot of sugar, but I can't get rid of the bitter taste." Milena in *WR,* on the other hand, had confidenly declared that "Even now I'm not ashamed of my Communist past." The greater sense of disillusionment expressed in Planeta's assessment of communism's revolutionary past is consistent with the greater underlying sense of disillusionment and entropy that pervades most of the film.

Even Marx is not spared Makavejev's satiric wit—though he is handled with bittersweet and even affectionate irony. Early in the film, Marx makes his appearance as a novelty commodity item. His likeness is carved on the bowl of a pipe which Aplanalpe is smoking and which he proudly shows to Miss World—explaining to her in expansive and ignorant terms exactly who Marx was and what he symbolized. But the most important iconic representation of Marx is as the giant masthead of the Planeta's ship. He is represented as sad-eyed, bedraggled, and rather worn and tacky. Near the end of the film a giant water-filled plastic tear is affixed to one of Marx's eyes. A satiric association is evoked that is not far different from the one in Woody Allen's film *Hannah and Her Sisters*, when Frederick (Max von Sydow) caustically condemns TV evangelists and remarks: "If Jesus came back, and saw what's going on in his name, he'd never stop throwing up."[39]

The ironically qualified but nonetheless "positive" coda which ended Makavejev's other films is also clearly present in *Sweet Movie*—depicted in the efforts of the participants of the Milky Way Commune to shed encrusted repressions and when they gather around and sing the "Internationale" near the end of the film, and especially in the miraculous rebirth of the four boys in the final scene. But the hope is more circumscribed. The evocative power of the images of decomposed, mud-caked corpses from Katyn Wood lingers on. They are potent reminders of a corpse-strewn century and of political cover-ups and repression of historical realities. They also lend metaphorical weight to the fictional martyrdom of the sailor in the vat of sugar—his sugar-encrusted face a perfect mimic of their dirt-encrusted death masks. Miss World's death by suffocation—her face a mask of chocolate (mud, excrement)—mimics and completes this triptych of death.

Sweet Movie was censured and banned in several countries, portions were deleted in others, and black-out bars (vertical and horizontal) were added in some prints to cover genital areas. It received practically no distribution in the East or West, and the scandal that the film provoked dogged Makavejev for several years, making it difficult to get other projects off the ground.

Makavejev was certainly not idle during the seven years that lapsed between the making of *Sweet Movie* and the making of his comeback film *Montenegro*. He was a frequent guest of film festivals and of film schools, and was a visiting professor at both Harvard University and Columbia University in 1977–1978. Makavejev's opportunity to write and direct the film *Montenegro* resulted primarily from his friendship and mutually admiring relationship with the gifted Swedish producer Bo Jonsson, who worked closely with Makavejev in putting the project together. During the mid-seventies, Makavejev also made initial contacts in Australia, which matured a decade later in the making of *The Coca-Cola Kid*.

In both *Montenegro* (1981) and *The Coca-Cola Kid* (1985) Makavejev abandoned his experiments with discontinuous narrative structure and multiple levels of montage associations. He did not abandon, however, his predilection for bizarre shifts of plot, surrealistic images, and sharp social and political satire. In both films the balance of his satirical critique shifts westward. In his surrealistic comedy *Montenegro*, he provides a witty

5.12. Luv finds martyrdom in a vat of sugar. *Sweet Movie.* BFI Stills, Posters and Designs.

examination of the crazy, neurotic, perverse, and murderous urges that may lie just under the smooth, repressed, and conformist surfaces of bourgeois life and values. In *The Coca-Cola Kid* he exposes the lunacy of market-driven psychology and product fetishism. In both films, sexuality—expressed, repressed, misdirected, or exploited—remains a central and powerful force in Makavejev's subversive universe—messy, unpredictable, and anarchic.

Montenegro

> Expatriates are his subjects.
> Iconoclasm is his homeland.[40]
> —Annette Insdorf

Montenegro, a Swedish co-production made in English to reach an export market, takes place in Stockholm. It focuses on an American, Marilyn Jordan (Susan Anspach), married to a successful Swedish businessman who travels worldwide selling ballbearings. They live in a wealthy suburb of Stockholm with two children, a girl and a boy, who are being molded into perfect replicas of their parents; an eccentric grandfather (John Zacharias), who imagines himself to be Buffalo Bill; and a newly acquired pet dog. Marilyn busies herself with women's clubs, cleaning, cooking, reading trashy novels, and

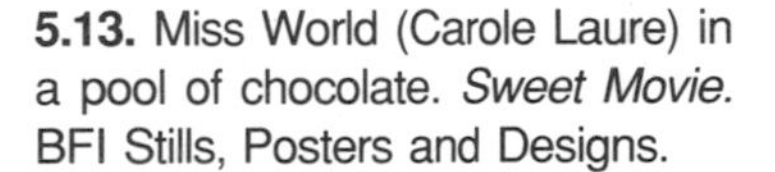

5.13. Miss World (Carole Laure) in a pool of chocolate. *Sweet Movie.* BFI Stills, Posters and Designs.

attempting (without success) to interest her husband Martin (Erland Josephson) in amorous play. Martin is the personification of the anti-Reichian man: rigidly unresponsive, emotionally disengaged and distant, aloof and supercilious in his contacts with others, and egoistically impervious to his own callousness. The actor Erland Josephson's close association with Bergman roles of a related kind (e.g., *Scenes from a Marriage*) enlarges the parodic implications of this characterization.

Laboring under the leaden boredom of her narrow routines and sterile existence, Marilyn is quietly coming apart at the seams and beginning to break out in unsettling behaviors. One night, after another unsuccessful attempt to interest her husband in sex, she deliberately snuffs her cigarette out on the bed coverlet, and laughs as her husband frantically runs to the bathroom to douse its smoldering remains in the bathtub. She later puts poison in the dog's dish and observes with curiousity what existential decision it will make: after a few tentative passes, the dog finally decides not to take the bait. Beginning to notice that his wife is behaving a bit erratically, Martin contacts and then invites a psychiatrist Aram Pazardijan (Per Oscarsson) for dinner to observe his wife's behavior. The most penetrating psychological insight that the psychiatrist can muster, however, is to tell Marilyn—out of earshot of her husband—that "I like your legs."

On a sudden impulse, Marilyn decides to go with her husband to Brazil—an invitation he had only halfheartedly offered. She is delayed at the airport by customs officials (because of a large pair of garden shears detected in her bag) and she misses the plane. Martin, in the meantime, has also missed the plane while waiting for Marilyn, gives up trying to locate her, and returns home. It proves to be a three-day wait. Marilyn has fallen in with a free-spirited band of Yugoslav guest workers who adopt her as their own and jolt her into a free, anarchic realm of surrealistic experiences unlike any she has yet encountered.

Marilyn's first encounter is with Tirke (Patricia Gelin), an ill-dressed, shy young Yugoslav woman who has also been detained at the airport while a customs official, with nose upturned, inspects the contents of her beat-up suitcase which is tied together with a rope. He retrieves several bottles of homemade šljivovica whose contents are so potent that even after they have been poured down the drain, a match must be lit and tossed into the sink to burn off the excess fumes. The official also confiscates Tirke's smoked pig—despite her pathetic pleas in broken English that "Eet ess very important. Eet ees very important." Marilyn and Tirke, as companion sufferers at the hands of callous officialdom, are drawn to each other, and Tirke introduces Marilyn to her "sponsor," Alex Rossignol (Bora Todorović). Alex is dressed in a long, fake leather coat, black-and-white oxfords, and mismatched suit and tie, has slicked-back hair, and carries a boom box playing loud Serbian popular songs. He is part-owner, with his ex-wife Rita (Lisbeth Zachrisson), of an illegal bootleg club called the "Zanzi Bar" located on the seamy side of Stockholm in an abandoned distillery (which also serves as makeshift living quarters for several other Yugoslavs). Alex invites Marilyn to hop into his battered station wagon, which has "Zanzi" emblazoned on one side, and offers to take her home. Marilyn demurely gets in along with Tirke and a bleating lamb held in the lap of a handsome, quiet, and vulnerable young Yugoslav with the nickname "Montenegro" (Svetozar Cvetković)—a zookeeper Marilyn had met earlier when her family came to him at the Stockholm zoo to purchase their pet dog. Instead of taking Marilyn home, Alex drives her to the Zanzi Bar complex, where she spends the next two nights.

Marilyn's first close encounter of a surrealist kind occurs immediately upon her arrival at the Zanzi Bar. A man with a knife protruding from his forehead must be rushed to the hospital emergency room. He sits quietly beside Marilyn in the front seat of the station wagon and eventually breaks the silence by complaining "I think I have a fever." Alex is completely unsympathetic, however, and tells him that his brother was completely justified in plunging the knife into his forehead because he had been cheating at cards! Before going into the emergency room, Alex arranges for one of the hospital orderlies to take a photograph of the entire group (including Marilyn). The man with the knife protruding from his forehead rises magnificently to the occasion and smiles broadly with the rest.

Later, in the interior of the Zanzi Bar, Marilyn grows ever more relaxed and a bit tipsy from drinking potent home brew. Suddenly, Alex leads several men clustered around Marilyn in a Serbian folk chant with his own Serbo-Croatian lyrics added: "I swear above to the sky of blue: How nice it would be fucking you." Marilyn asks Tirke what they are singing. Tirke answers sincerely that "It's very nice. It's about you." The next verse is given an even more plaintive intonation: "Dear girl, take off your equipage. So I can park my jeep in your garage." Marilyn is smiling rather dreamily through all of this. But then the mood turns more dangerous. A silent rivalry has developed between Alex and Montenegro over Marilyn. They go outside and fight a duel with shovels. At first there is an air of boisterous fun. When Montenegro gains the advantage over Alex the game seems played out. Alex, however, tricks Montenegro into letting down his guard and strikes him with a violent blow that sends him to the ground unconscious with a serious head wound. Alex dismisses the wound as insignificant, but Marilyn, thoroughly frightened, runs to Montenegro, discovers that he has stopped breathing and revives him with mouth-to-mouth resuscitation.

After a strenuous, emotional day and evening, Alex's ex-wife Rita leads Marilyn to bed in the makeshift upper floor of the brewery where, still half-intoxicated, she is gently tucked in and goes to sleep to the cooing of pigeons. She awakes in the wee hours of morning to the breathy serenade of Alex and Rita making love vigorously in the same bed. Just as Rita bids a cheery "hello" to Marilyn, the bed collapses and coitus is interrupted. Rita jokes that Alex never finishes anything, declares to Marilyn that "We don't need him anyway," and cuddles up to her in a warm, sensual (possibly lesbian) embrace.

Marilyn's culminating experiences at the Zanzi Bar occur the next night. Fireworks announce the club's special holiday (New Year's Eve) offerings. Tirke, coached by Alex and Rita, opens with her new act, in which she is improbably costumed as a Tahitian dancer covered with long strands of fake leaves and flowers. She removes the strands of leaves while dancing an erotic duel with a remote-controlled toy tank sporting a large dildo protruding from its cannon. In an adroitly edited sequence, Tirke finally loses the duel, engenders wild applause, and is hoisted triumphantly upward on a forklift platform. Following this class act, Alex introduces Marilyn as "Suzy Nashville" from the "land of immigrants." Marilyn woos the appreciative audience with a soft rendering of "Give Me a Little Kiss," aiming the lyrics especially at Montenegro, who is roasting the once-bleating lamb on a spit.

Following Marilyn's number, the ambience of the club subtly alters—becomes more bluesy, mellow, and soft-focused. A dreamy waltz is being played on the piano. The dance floor is filled. Montenegro and Marilyn dance with their separate partners until they are quite close and then adroitly exchange their partners for one another. In a space to themselves, Marilyn hoists herself on Montenegro's tall frame, and with her legs wrapped around him, he slowly swirls her off the dance floor—to the back room of the distillery where he lives. Marilyn asks to make love. At first Montenegro refuses. Marilyn becomes angry and attacks him physically and curses him. As they struggle, passion overtakes them both, and they end up making love quietly and intensely. Makavejev, however, satirically undercuts the sensual moments he has created and "deconstructs" the stereotypical voyeuristic gaze of

5.14. Tirke (Patricia Gelin) prepares for her erotic dance/duel with a toy tank. Alex (Bora Todorović) operates the remote control. *Montenegro.* BFI Stills, Posters and Designs.

the camera by cutting to the hens and the chicken-feed which share Montenegro's modest abode. He also satirically cuts to a fireworks display at the moment of sexual climax—a pun on an old film cliché. More significantly, he cuts to a close-up of a bottle of champagne being uncorked. The camera pulls back to reveal Dr. Pazardijan perversely seducing Marilyn's husband Martin into participating in a decadent *ménage à trois* with the psychiatrist and his half-clothed female secretary.

In the blue-tinted morning after, Marilyn makes her way through the scattered debris of the courtyard outside the Zanzi Bar. The film cuts to a close-up of blood intermingling with water going down a drain. The camera pans right to reveal the naked corpse of Montenegro lying under the makeshift shower in his room—the blood flowing from a head wound. While there is a suggestive presumption that Marilyn may have murdered him, Montenegro's death and its cause are left deliberately ambiguous and unexplained.

In the film's final scene, Marilyn is depicted back in the bosom of her family who, along with the psychiatrist, are gathered around the dinner table. Marilyn is standing and passing out pieces of fruit. The mood is one of surface good cheer. But a title is superimposed on the screen that mordantly announces in capital letters: "THE FRUIT WAS POISONED." The image freezes, Marilyn's theme song plays on the sound track, and the film ends.

Within its surrealistic comedic framework, *Montenegro* introduces sharply observed satirical commentary on themes of societal and cultural displacement, alienation, and expatriation—themes that Dušan Makavejev, of course, has experienced firsthand. The theme of expatriation is lightly introduced in the opening titles of the film, which pose the question, "Why do you live here? Isn't it nicer where you come from?"—followed by a close-up of a chimpanzee framed behind the bars of his cage in the zoo nodding his head uncertainly in the affirmative. The chimpanzee behind bars is visually equated with Montenegro, who is later introduced in a similar close-up framed behind the bars of the Stockholm zoo's central monkey cage. Not only Montenegro but also all of the main characters of the film are presented as displaced expatriates. The psychiatrist is from a family of refugees from Armenia. Marilyn is a double exile—a displaced American in Stockholm who is also trapped in a sterile frostbitten marriage. The Yugoslav "guest workers" are expatriates from economically marginal fringes of Europe who are welcome to perform the menial jobs that more-prosperous Europeans disdain: as long as the economy supports their presence, they do not overstay their welcome, and they refrain from propping their muddy boots on Western Europe's banquet table and breathing garlic in the face of polite society. Makavejev had originally planned to begin his film with a dedication to the immigrants and guest workers of Europe:

> This film is dedicated to the new invisible nation of Europe, the fourth largest, of 11 million immigrant and guest workers who moved north to exploit rich and prosperous people, bringing with them filthy habits, bad manners, and the smell of garlic.[41]

While Makavejev did not include the above text in the final version of the film, the statement expresses well his satiric approach to the problems of economic exploitation, social displacement, and ostracism of European immigrant workers. In typical fashion he avoids heavy-handed and bitter polemic and political schematizing in favor of exuberant satire and Rabelaisian exaggeration. His guest workers are larger than life "types" (or stereotypes) of his fellow countrymen—types that Makavejev skillfully employs to turn the tables on those who do the stereotyping! Even Marilyn's husband, a native Swede, is presented as something of an expatriate—not only because of his constant travels abroad, but also because of his detached, alienated behavior. Early in the film, the psychiatrist tells Martin, "Everyone has to come from somewhere." "Not me," says Martin, "I'm from here"—a reply that satirically underscores that Martin's "here" is, in reality, a "nowhere."

Without losing its comedic framework (albeit, at times, dark and sardonic), *Montenegro's* satire shifts from the global Cold War ideologies examined in *WR* and *Sweet Movie* to focus more fully on underlying repressive institutional structures and values, gender discrimination, and economic exploitation. In this film, Makavejev returns to a sharply satirical Reichian critique of the institution of marriage—viewing it as the perfect training ground for libidinal repression, gender-role differentiation, and docile acceptance of the larger repressive patriarchal social order.[42] It is not merely the Jordans' stereotypical suburban bourgeois marriage that is the target of Makavejev's satire, but marriage among the proletarian guest workers as well. The rough equality that Rita asserts with Alex—as co-owner of the Zanzi Bar and as one who is free to express her sexual preferences and to puncture Alex's chauvinistic pretensions—is related, in no small measure, to her decision to assume the status of *ex*-wife. Rita's choice is not dissimilar to the one symbolically taken by Barbulović's wife in *Man Is Not a Bird,* and the one preemptively taken by Isabella in *Love Affair.*

Montenegro was a solid international critical and commercial success that earned back its modest production budget of 2-1/2 million dollars several times over.[43] Makavejev's next film, *The Coca-Cola Kid* (made on a budget of 3 million dollars), was an even larger commercial success—both in its theatrical release and in its subsequent release in the videocassette market. It was also the first and only film in which Makavejev surrendered primary scripting responsibilities to another artist, the Australian writer Frank Moorhouse. Makavejev met Moorhouse for the first time in 1975 in Sydney where Makavejev had come to attend a screening of his film *Sweet Movie* during the 1975 Sydney Film Festival. A sympathetic relationship developed between them which eventually led to their close collaborative work on the screenplay of *The Coca-Cola Kid* (thirteen versions, over an eight-year period) based on two collections of Moorhouse's short stories: *The Americans, Baby* and *The Electrical Experience.* The talented producer David Roe put together the financial and artistic resources to make the film—including a seed grant from the Australian Film Commission—and negotiated with the Coca-Cola Company and its representatives in Australia the disclaimer that appears in the opening of the film.

The Coca-Cola Kid

> **When you don't see a Coca-Cola sign, you have passed the borders of civilization.**
>
> **—A Coca-Cola Company brochure**

In production for two years, *The Coca-Cola Kid* was shot entirely on location in Sydney, in the picturesque Blue Mountains west of Sydney, and in the small towns of Redfern, Lithgow, and Katoomba, which dot the landscape of the Blue Mountains region. The film centers on the efforts of a top American Coca-Cola troubleshooter, Becker (Eric Roberts) a.k.a. "The Coca-Cola Kid," to breathe new life into the Australian Coca-Cola operation and to double or triple the annual sales. He soon discovers that there is an area (Anderson Valley) in Australia in which not a single bottle of Coke is sold, and where the soft-drink market is monopolized by an entirely local product of nine multi-flavored drinks manufactured in a 1920s old-fashioned steam-operated bottling factory run by an irascible local land baron, T. George McDowell (Bill Kerr).

Becker launches a campaign to oust McDowell from his monopoly control of the valley and win him over to the proposition of signing up with Coca-Cola. In a war of wits and physical intimidation, McDowell staves off for a time the imperialistic incursion of Coca-Cola into his local marketing sanctuary. In the end, however, he chooses quixotically and defiantly to blow up his own factory rather than capitulate to Becker's terms for continuing in business. Becker is so impressed with McDowell's rugged, old-fashioned, conservative, and stubborn brand of defiant capitalism and idiosyncratic entrepreneurial integrity that he loses his taste for being an international marketing troubleshooter and succumbs instead to the multiple charms and regenerative possibilites of beginning a new life in Australia.

It is not only T. George's rugged individualism and independent-minded Australian ethos that prompts Becker to turn in his corporate Coca-Cola badge for a new and uncertain future, but also the powerful sexual forces unleashed by Terri (Greta Scacchi), who is assigned to serve as Becker's secretary and who, by comedically contrived coincidence, is also the runaway daughter of T. George McDowell. Terri is immediately and strongly attracted sexually to Becker and persists in her attempts, even against considerable odds, to break through the repressed rigidities of his Reichian "body armor" and his clichéd inner identification with his public persona as heroic representative of Coca-Cola. He sees Coke not just as a brown-colored bubbly drink but as a worldwide cultural icon and symbol of American freedom, effervescent vitality, ubiquitous pauses that refresh, messianic harbinger of the American Way of Life to "more countries than are members of the United Nations," and sacramental elixir for creating, in Becker's words, "worldwide fellowship." Despite Becker's formidable defenses, Terri finally has her way with him near the end of the film when they make love in his hotel room, covered in a blizzard of down and feathers.

Terri's young daughter, nicknamed DMZ (Rebecca Smart), is the first person in Australia to befriend Becker and to uncover the vulnerable, "kid" side to his nature. Her nickname was given by her mother and father (Chris Haywood), now divorced, who declared the daughter a "demilitarized zone" in their ongoing verbal and physical marital warfare—a warfare that continues even after the divorce. At the end of the film, Becker decides to shed his corporate identity, to don jeans, sneakers, and an open-necked casual shirt, and to make a commitment to a new life shared with Terri, DMZ, their cockatoo, and a small mouse that Becker earlier befriended and presented to DMZ as a pet.

While *The Coca-Cola Kid* adopts a less sardonic, darkly laced comedic framework than *Montenegro,* it nonetheless resonates with several of Makavejev's recurring imagistic and thematic preoccupations. Becker emerges in the film as a surrealistically constructed allegorical "type"—not fully understandable in conventional dramatic realist terms; i.e., accessible through motivational analysis. He resembles the character construct of

5.15. T. George McDowell (Bill Kerr) leads a song for his new drink, "McCoke." *The Coca Cola Kid.* BFI Stills, Posters and Designs.

Vladimir, the Russian ice-skating champion, in *WR*. Both are true believers in the systems they rigidly and faithfully serve. Both are puritanical and repressed. Both are charismatic heroes—Vladimir the perfect embodiment of Stalinist-Leninist socialist orthodoxy expressed as People's Artist and Champion; Becker as the perfect embodiment of the American Way of Life expressed as heroic Marketing Whiz Kid and International Troubleshooter. The Coca-Cola Kid, however, is also depicted as a rather strange and alien being—even to his bosses in Coca-Cola's international office in Atlanta, Georgia. He is compulsively neat, robotically disciplined, speaks with an idiosyncratic, off-the-wall southern accent, and is a walking compendium of marketing clichés and management-by-objectives jargon, which he stirs together with charismatic, single-minded evangelical zeal and the fanaticism of a true believer. Becker's status as an outsider is established in the opening of the film. Before his plane lands at the Sydney airport, the pilot announces to the passengers that because of Australia's distinctive ecology, it is necessary to spray the plane for any foreign insects. The spray settles heavily around Becker's head—satirically connoting that he is exactly the pest they are after!

As in others of Makavejev's previous films, a repressed, puritanical male is "liberated" or partially liberated by a bright, independent, and sexually relaxed and free female. In previous films, most notably in *WR*, such ecstatic sexual release carries in its wake the release of other powerful and mur-

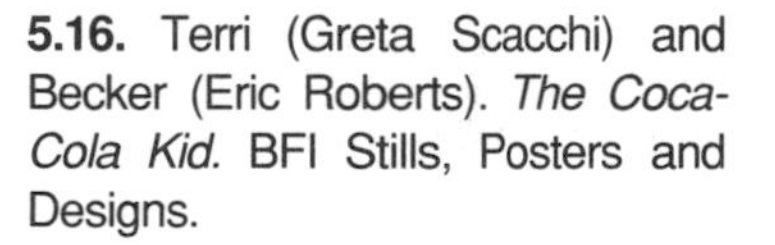

5.16. Terri (Greta Scacchi) and Becker (Eric Roberts). *The Coca-Cola Kid.* BFI Stills, Posters and Designs.

derous forces of counter-repression. *The Coca-Cola Kid,* however, follows a simpler psychological pattern. As in Makavejev's other films, sexuality and sexual energy remain a central and powerful subversive force which Terri embodies in the film. Some critics have complained that Terri's immediate and strong sexual attraction to Becker and her dogged persistance in continuing to pursue him after every rebuff is "unmotivated" and inexplicable. Such criticism apparently rests on the assumption that sexual attraction is rationally determined and always fixes on the most sensible object of desire!

Makavejev's fondness for animals and animal imagery is given especially prolific expression in this film. A small field mouse (Mickey), a kangaroo with a wounded paw (Malcolm), a camel, an office aquarium full of colorful tropical fish, and a pet cockatoo all make their brief entrances and exits. The sound track is filled with subtle blends of indigenous insect and animal sounds—creating an important ambience throughout the film. An overall metaphorical impression is created of a culture in which people live on easy, natural, and intimate terms with other members of the animal kingdom. This contrasts with the film *Montenegro,* in which an opposite impression is created of a culture in which people segregate fellow animals into zoos, cages, or as carefully disciplined pets. In a more generic sense, Makavejev uses animals as metaphorical reminders of the part of human nature that is most often denied, repressed, or sanitized, or flushed or hosed away. He also, of course, metaphorically associates animals with particular characters in his films (including, among others, the hen and hen's eggs with the sexologist in *Love Affair;* a pet black kitten with Rudinski in *Man Is Not a Bird,* with Isabella in *Love Affair,* and, in a more sinister way, with the psychiatrist in *Montenegro;* the pet mouse with the sailor in *Sweet Movie* and with Becker in *The Coca-Cola Kid;* the black lamb—sacrificial?—and the caged chimpanzee with Montenegro in *Montenegro*).

In *The Coca-Cola Kid,* the more vulnerable and open side of Becker's character is first revealed by his attitude and behavior toward animals. Early in the film, he adopts a little field mouse as a companion and pet when he finds it in his bedroom slippers on the night of his arrival in Sydney. Later in the film, Becker gallantly offers to take a wounded kangaroo (Malcolm) to a veterinarian when the kangaroo and its owners Juliana (Kris McQuade) and Mrs. Haversham (Colleen Clifford) crash land on the side of a lonely road after their bush plane has narrowly missed hitting the car that Becker is driving. It is thus early established in the film that Becker relates more easily to animals than he does to people—offering the first hints that his mechanically constructed facade may eventually crumble under the impact of the "Down Under" cultural ethos.

As in previous Makavejev films, some of the most imaginative and subtle satiric effects in *The Coca-Cola Kid* are achieved by the interplay of visual imagery and the film's musical sound track and songs (adapted and original). Makavejev and his wife Bojana Marijan formed a close creative relationship with William Motzing, who composed the original music score for the film, and with Tim Finn, who composed and wrote three of its original songs—a creative relationship that produced some of the film's most amusing and sophisticated scenes. Especially effective is the scene of the studio session in which an original Coca-Cola jingle, written and composed by Tim Finn, is being recorded by a group of Australian rock musicians under the watchful eye of Becker. The musicians are charged with creating an "authentic" Australian sound to serve as a vehicle for "naturalizing" Coca-Cola into the Australian culture. Integrated into the band are indigenous percussion instruments and a marvelously constructed native horn played by "Bushman" (Tony Barry). With wry humor and satiric invention, the musicians undermine Becker's attempt to exploit indigenous cultural expression and inventiveness as a means of promoting American cultural hegemony. In the end, it is difficult to say who has been Americanized and who has been Australianized! Throughout the film, Makavejev and Moorhouse reject simplistic one-way models of American economic and cultural imperialism—suggesting that the resiliency, eccentricity, and complexity of indigeneous cultures are not so easily subverted or subsumed by international marketeers and popular-culture merchants.

Despite the rather weak, sentimental, and arbitrary ending, the somewhat softer satiric bite, and the relative lack of ironic complexity when compared to Makavejev's previous films, *The Coca-Cola Kid* is nonetheless an imaginative, humorous, and significant addition to his total work. It satirizes the marketing mechanisms and processes of cross-cultural influences and international image-making and, like his earlier films, affirms the liberating power of individual creativity—including its quirky, eccentric, and bizarrely atypical manifestations. Some of the darker strains of Makavejev's sardonic wit reassert themselves in his next and most recent film, *Manifesto* (1988).

Manifesto

> **After the fall of great empires, new governments appeared. They took themselves very seriously. Life became hard for revolutionaries. However, ice cream was sold and enjoyed as if nothing had changed. . . .[44]**
>
> —Makavejev

Manifesto (1988), inspired by Emile Zola's story *Pour Une Nuit d'Amour (For a Night of Love),* is a United States/Yugoslav co-production shot entirely on location in Slovenia—still a republic of Yugoslavia at the time the film was made. Following upon sixteen years of self-selected exile, the film *Manifesto* provided Makavejev the opportunity to return to his native country and to renew and strengthen old personal friendships and creative ties, as well as to generate a host of new ones.

Following in the wake of the First World War's devastation of Europe, a wave of social revolutions rolled across the continent. The early 1920s witnessed the Berlin Spartacist uprising and the Vienna General Strike, the establishment of workers' soviets in Munich and Budapest, and mass factory occupations throughout Italy. While all of these insurgencies were forcefully suppressed, the bourgeois social order of Europe was profoundly shaken by these events and by the shocks and assaults made on those ideologies and values which supported the older order. Makavcjev's film satirically portrays these larger tidal forces playing themselves out in a small provincial town on the rippled edge of Central Europe.

Made in English to increase its potential international audience, *Manifesto* is a dark comic fable set in an unnamed Central European country in the year 1920. It focuses on a convoluted plot to assassinate an equally unnamed, newly crowed king during his planned visit to the fictional provincial town of Waldheim (a satiric reference to Austria's recent controversial president). Waldheim is, in reality, Skofja Loka, a picturesque thirteenth-century Slovenian fortified town that stood on a once-important trade route from Trieste to Munich.

The planned visit of the new king to Waldheim is preceded by the appearance of the king's head of secret police, Avanti (Alfred Molina). Upon arriving by train in Waldheim, Avanti combines forces with the not very bright local chief police inspector, Hunt (Simon Callow), and his men (whose slapstick ineptitude is reminiscent of the Keystone Kops) to provide security for the king and to keep a sharp eye on suspected revolutionaries and potential assassins.

Arriving on the same train as Avanti is the beautiful young aristocrat Svetlana (Camilla Søeberg), who is returning to Waldheim and to the fading splendor of her family estate after having spent several years in the sophisticated cultural centers of Europe. During her sojourn, the innocent-appearing Svetlana has been politically radicalized and sexually liberated. She carries a gun under her petticoats and is a key figure in the ring of revolutionaries who plan to assassinate the king. She is bold enough to flirt with Avanti, whose interest in undercover sexual dalliances clearly outweighs his interest in undercover spy work. In their first encounter, and throughout the film, Svetlana cleverly outmaneuvers him on both fronts.

In the course of the film the web of revolutionary intrique draws into its net innocent and unwary accomplices, the assassination itself never takes place, and, typical of previous Makavejev films, several corpses pile up on the turbulent shores of sexual desire and revolutionary zeal. The two most ardent revolutionaries in the film are given the comic opera names Rudi Kugelhopf and Lily Sacher—names of popular Austro-Hungarian pastries of the time.

Rudi, a local schooteacher—portrayed by the charismatic Yugoslav actor Svetozar Cvetković, who also played the title role in *Montenegro*—is selected to fire the fatal shots at the king. Early in the film, however, he is arrested and sent for political reeducation to the notorious Bergman Sanatorium, presided over by Dr. Lambroscu. With the help of an inventive array of Rube Goldberg torture contraptions, the diabolical Dr. Lambroscu (Patrick Godfrey) sadistically turns against its practitioners the Marxist slogan "From each according to his abilities to each according to his needs." Rudi is imprisoned in a large enclosed wheel/treadmill device, "The Permanent Revolution Rotor"—a satirically mocking reference to the Marxist "Wheel of Destiny." No matter how fast Rudi treads, the wheel goes nowhere, and its direction can be reversed at will by Lambroscu.

Later in the film, Rudi is smuggled a gun baked in a loaf of bread. During his visit to Waldheim, the king makes an inspection tour of the Bergman Sanatorium, providing Rudi with the perfect opportunity to carry out the assassination. Instead he shouts, "Long live the king!"—not because he has been reeducated as a royalist, but because he has decided to adopt the role of revolutionary martyr rather than the role of assassin. His choice is spectaculary fulfilled near the end of the film. A fire accidentally starts in Lambroscu's laboratory. It spreads to the outer wooden rims of the wheel/treadmill. Rudi begins to run—his eyes aglow with revolutionary zeal. He shouts revolutionary slogans interspersed with "Momma, Momma. My heart is on fire." He runs faster and faster in the burning treadmill. Images of rising laboratory fumes, all-engulfing flames, erratically dancing spires of light and shadow, odd-angled shots of the treadmill's criss-crossing imprisoning grid—all conspire to give a wild and expressionistic ending to Rudi's self-selected martyrdom. Rudi's death links him to the martyred sailor in *Sweet Movie* and to Makavejev's theme of the Communist revolution's antihuman distortion of sexuality into eroticized martyrdom and revolutionary sacrifice. It also satirically suggests that the death rattles of the Communist world revolution were present in its cradle.

The second ardent revolutionary, Lily Sacher (Lindsay Duncan), does

5.17. Rudi (Svetozar Cvetković), imprisoned in "The Permanent Revolution Rotor," has just received from Svetlana (Camilla Søeberg) the loaf of bread with the gun baked inside. *Manifesto.* BFI Stills, Posters and Designs.

not begin the film that way. She is a childhood friend of Svetlana and a dedicated elementary schoolteacher who attempts to protect her young charges from the adult world's corrupt values and loose sexual mores. Despite her best efforts, however, several of the more bizarre sexual trysts in the film are witnessed by wide-eyed children and innocent animals. One of the most curious of these is performed in the branches of a large tree by the artist/photographer Wango (Chris Haywood) and his model Olympia (Tanja Bošković). Their sexual coupling is aided by a specially constructed hoisting device, which holds them both in proper position to create this avant-garde piece of living sculpture. Much to Lily's dismay, the children are quite pleased with the day's field trip and their unanticipated lesson in art.

Later in the film, however, Lily is falsely arrested and sent to the Bergman Sanatorium for a major "mouth washing, brain washing, and character washing treatment." This time, however, Lambrusco's efforts create an effect quite opposite the one intended—converting the mild, sexually repressed Lily into a wild-eyed and eager revolutionary. She escapes from the clinic with Svetlana's help, pausing only to take the gun/phallus concealed in Rudi's pants, and pledges herself completely to the revolutionary cause.

The only relationships depicted in *Manifesto* that reveal traces of Zola's *For a Night of Love* are those among Svetlana (Zola's Mademoiselle Thérèse de Marsanne), Emile (Zola's Colombel), and Christopher (Zola's Julien). Emile (Rade Šerbedžija) is a servant of the Vargas estate who has enjoyed privileged access to Svetlana since her teen years. Their illicit sexual liaison is tempestuous and rife with ambivalence—a mixture of loathing and lust, of class envy and class hatred, of violent resistance and passionate surrender. In their most turbulent sexual scene in the film, Emile breaks into Svetlana's private chambers on the very night that the king and his party, on their last night in Waldheim, are being entertained at the Vargas mansion and its spacious gardens. During the course of their usual turbulent foreplay, Emile accidentally slips on pieces of artificial fruit that Svetlana has thrown on the floor. Emile and Svetlana laugh as he loses his balance and begins to slip and fall backward. Alas, however, Emile strikes his head hard against the stone fireplace. Svetlana is alarmed and runs to him. Emile attempts to rally with a gallant smile, but his wound is fatal. Svetlana withdraws her hand from the back of his head. It is covered with blood.

After washing away the blood on her hands, Svetlana rolls Emile's body into a carpet—with five small puppies cavorting and whimpering around the corpse. Shortly thereafter, members of the king's ever-alert secret service come into Svetlana's chambers to clear the way for the king. Several times they politely and nonchalantly step over the rolled-up carpet as they complete their security check. The king passes through Svetlana's chambers, also politely stepping over the corpse, as he makes his way to her balcony to address the evening's guests in the garden below. The king (Enver Petrovci) is depicted as a rather mild-mannered dolt—the product, it would appear, of too much royal inbreeding. He concludes his little speech with a tribute to Svetlana: "Your beauty, youth, and innocence represent the future of our country."

Another character who bears traces of Zola's original story is Christopher (Eric Stoltz), a diffident, shy postal clerk who has been obsessively in love with Svetlana for more than ten years (similar to Julien's obsessive love for Thérèse in *For a Night of Love*). The window of his modest second-floor apartment overlooks the town square and provides a direct view of the Vargas mansion and of the balcony leading to Svetlana's private chambers. Early in the film, Christopher is shown at the window of his apartment playing the flute (another Zola touch). The sweet sounds of the flute linger in the night air and, like an unseen lover's voice, lure Svetlana to her balcony. Upon her appearance, however, Christopher ceases playing the flute and retreats from his window into the shadows. As Svetlana walks back into her chambers through the lace curtains, she slips off her silk nightgown—her nude body now wrapped in shadows and dim half-light.

Later in the film, Christopher conceals from Hunt a compromising letter from Svetlana to Rudi concerning the assassination plot against the king. When Christopher is no longer under the watchful eye of the secret police, he burns the letter and delivers a note to Svetlana pledging his secrecy and

5.18. Svetlana expresses her ambivalent desire/loathing for Emile (Rade Šerbedžija). *Manifesto.* Cannon Pictures, Inc., and MGM/UA Telecommunications, Inc.

fealty to her—if not to her cause. On the night of Emile's accidental death, Svetlana summons Christopher to her private chambers. He enters her room in total awe and romantic confusion. He confesses the long vigil of his love and the many love letters he has written without having the courage to send them. Touched by his story, Svetlana leads him gently to her bed and they make passionate love.

Afterward, Svetlana unrolls the carpet and reveals to Christopher the nature of her "problem." Christopher, still dazed by the wonder of the night, agrees readily to dispose of the corpse. In the dead of the night, with church bells tolling, Christopher struggles with his heavy burden through the town's deserted streets. He carries Emile's body onto the old arched stone bridge at the edge of town. He strains to lift the heavy corpse over the rail and into the churning water below. Just as he seems at the point of accomplishing his mission, however, one of Emile's arms locks around Christopher's neck and carries them both down into the dark waters below. The next day the bodies of Christopher and Emile are found wedged among the rocks in the shallows downstream, still locked in deadly embrace, and the two men are falsely implicated by Hunt and Avanti in a criminal conspiracy against the king. Once again, Makavejev has created a world in which authority is so ordered (or disordered) that the innocent are as likely to be punished for their virtues as the guilty for their vices. Christopher, in particular, has paid a heavy price for his "night of love," and joins the gallery of other "innocent" casualties in

Makavejev's ironic universe: Isabella in *Love Affair,* Milena in *WR,* and Montenegro in *Montenegro.*

Insinuating himself throughout the film's winding plot is Avanti, the head of the king's secret police, whose attention is more often focused on sexual affairs than affairs of state. Unable to seduce Svetlana, he seduces her mother Stella (Linda Marlowe) instead. He also uses his snaky charm to seduce Tina (Gabrielle Anwar), a sweet- and pure-looking fifteen-year-old ice-cream vendor. Unfortunately for Avanti, however, Tina turns out to be a tough, street-wise "Lolita" who turns the tables on Avanti and ends up dictating the terms of their sexual engagement.

In the concluding scene of the film, Avanti and Svetlana are once more on a train—this time leaving the town of Waldheim. They embrace and kiss in Svetlana's compartment. In the meantime, Lily Sacher—elementary schoolteacher turned zealous and romantic revolutionary—is boldly moving across the top of the rapidly moving train, a red scarf wrapped around her neck dramatically trailing in the wind. Lily leans down the side of the train and peers upside down through the window of Svetlana's compartment. The gun is in her hand. Lily and Svetlana exchange smiles. Avanti looks startled. Lily says: "Let's go!" The screen fades to black. A gunshot is heard and the film ends. It is left unresolved whether Avanti is added to the film's body count. More significantly, the film does not attempt to resolve the ambivalences suggested in the character of Svetlana, just as Zola, in fictional circumstances very different from those in Makavejev's film, leaves unresolved the enigmatic character of Thérèse. Svetlana suggests both an aristocrat playing at being a revolutionary and a revolutionary dissembling her role as an aristocrat: she is both sexually liberated and a slave to unruly desires—including more than a hint of sadomasochistic impulses released in her relationship with Emile; both a victim and a victimizer and, in a lighter and more farcical vein, both a dabbler in sexual intrigue as a means of advancing the cause of the revolution and a dabbler in the cause of the revolution as a means of advancing sexual intrigue. The presence of such ambiguities and contradictions not only provides evocative pathways connecting *Manifesto* to Makavejev's earlier films but also gives a tougher and chewier center to this film than its light, lushly colored, picturesque, farcical, comic-opera surface might at first suggest.

Conclusion

At the time of this writing Makavejev is involved with two new projects. The first of these, for which funding has already been secured, is to write and direct a feature film on the aftermath of the fall of the Berlin Wall and of German reunification—focusing on the complex and ambivalent attitudes that have surfaced following the initial period of euphoria (to be released in 1993 with the title *Gorilla Bathes at Noon*). The second project, in its preliminary first-draft stage, is a fictional feature film with the working title *Ecstasy.* It is conceived as a sequel to *WR* in which Milena, her severed head surgically restored, provides the focus for wide-ranging satirical comment on the dramatically changed and rapidly evolving "new world order" taking shape since the collapse of communism in East and Central Europe and the former Soviet Union.[45] Originally planned as a co-production involving Yugoslav, Russian, and German funding, the project may be sidetracked or reformulated because of the tragic and bloody internecine warfare in Yugoslavia and the volatile and uncertain financial condition of the cinema industries in Russia and the other newly declared and recognized independent countries in the former Soviet Union.

It remains to be seen whether Makavejev's original and distinctive ironic cinematic vision will continue to find expression in the emerging political and cultural landscape of the nineties. Throughout his career he has been a bold challenger of boundaries (political and aesthetic) as well as a frequent border crosser (in the literal sense)—expatriate, guest artist, and cross-cultural filmmaker. Whether made in the "East" or in the "West," Makavejev's films provide a consistently off-beat, often Rabelaisian, and surrealistic view of individual sexual dynamics and their connections to the larger cultural, societal, and political order. The creative space he occupies intersects East and West, but belongs to neither—existing somewhere in the interstices and folds of a world whose major ideologies and political polarites he has always viewed with an ironic and skeptical eye. He has maintained a unique stance—whose implications take on fresh relevance in view of recent sweeping changes—especially as it is expressed in his most far-reaching and complex political film satires, *WR* and *Sweet Movie*. However much he may wrap it in irony and qualify it with satirical skepticism, Makavejev has always remained an exuberant celebrant of the liberating power of individual creativity (including its quirky, eccentric, and bizarrely atypical manifestations) against social conformity, institutional rigidity, and the obscenities of repressive power.

NOTES

1. Makavejev's amateur and documentary films are no longer in distribution—even in Yugoslavia. I am grateful to Predrag Golubović, director of the Institut za film in Belgrade, and to Miroljub Vučković, program editor, for arranging special archival viewings of all but two of these films during my visit to Belgrade in June 1991.

2. The most important of Makavejev's early critical writings on film were collected and published in 1960 in his book *Poljubac za drugaricu parolu*.

3. For a more complete definition and analysis of *new film* tendencies in Yugoslavia during the sixties and early seventies and the controversies surrounding their development, see Goulding, *Liberated Cinema: The Yugoslav Experience*, pp. 62–84.

4. Unless noted otherwise, all direct quotations from the films are taken from the films themselves.

5. Amos Vogel, "Makavejev: Toward the Edge of the Real . . . and Over," p. 191.

6. Ibid.

7. Quoted in Robin Wood, "Dušan Makavejev," p. 32.

8. For a recent and imaginative analysis of Serbian folkloric traditions as they relate to Makavejev's filmic representation of Aleksić, see Andrew Horton, "The Mouse Who Wanted to F--k a Cow," pp. 225–32.

9. Horton incorrectly states that nowhere in the film is a direct connection made between Aleksić and Tito. See Andrew Horton, p. 230.

10. *Druže Tito/Mi ti se kunemo/Da sa tvoga/Puta ne skrenemo* and *Mismo Titovi. Tito je nas.*

11. In 1985, Aleksić died at age seventy-five in relative obscurity—a resident of an old-people's home. An enterprising reporter form *Politika* picked up on the story which led to an interesting feature in *NIN* by Bogdan Tirnanić titled "Prvi crpski superman" ("The First Serbian Superman"), pp. 37–38.

12. See, for example, discussions of film attendance and audience responses in *Slobodna dalmacia,* February 21, 1969, and *Filmski svet,* March 13, 1969.

13. Amos Vogel, "Makavejev," p. 192.

14. For a clear and helpful discussion of distinctions between earlier and later writings by Reich and their influence on Makavejev's films see James MacBean, *Film and Revolution,* pp. 230–53.

15. Dušan Makavejev, *WR: Mysteries of the Organism,* p. 31.

16. Ibid., p. 130.

17. Ibid., p. 105.

18. Ibid., p. 127.

19. Ibid., p. 135.

20. Ibid., p. 136. For a complete text of Lenin's remarks from which this speech was derived, see "Let's Put the Life Back in Political Life—An Interview with Dusan [*sic*] Makavejev," p. 18.

21. Ibid., pp. 139–40.

22. Amos Vogel, *Film as a Subversive Art,* p. 153.

23. Dušan Makavejev, *WR: Mysteries of the Organism,* p. 142.

24. Ibid., p. 144.

25. Ibid., p. 88.

26. Ibid., p. 95.

27. Ibid., p. 69.

28. Ibid., p. 76.

29. Ibid., p. 78.

30. Ibid., p. 65. Other slogans that arose out of the student demonstrations in 1968 were: "Into tomorrow without those who ruined yesterday," "Let's dismiss incompetent politicans," "Enough of unemployment," "We struggle for a better man, not a better dinar," "More schools, fewer automobiles," "Free information media," "Down with corruption," "Down with the princes of socialism," and "There is no socialism without freedom, no freedom without socialism."

31. Ibid., p. 72.

32. Herbert Eagle, "Yugoslav Marxist Humanism and the Films of Dušan Makavejev," pp. 131–47.

33. The most complete set of documents detailing the official actions taken with regard to the film and the polemic that surrounded these actions was put together for internal use by Neoplanta film. See *Dokumentacija za internu upotrebu,* pp. 518–1009.

34. Bart Testa, "Reflections on Makavejev: The Art Film and Transgression," pp. 232–44.

35. A completely restored version of the film is available in videocassette from Facets.

36. Richard Roud (ed.), *Cinema: A Critical Dictionary,* vol. 2., p. 657. (Roud's remarks are in a footnote to an entry on Makavejev by Robin Wood.)

37. For a discussion of the Carole Laure episode, see Edgardo Cozarinsky and Carlos Clarens, "Dušan Makavejev Interview," pp. 49–51.

38. The opening line of *Sweet Movie*'s "theme" song.

39. Woody Allen, *Hannah and Her Sisters,* p. 102.

40. Annette Insdorf, from her review of *Montenegro* for the *New York Times,* November 8, 1981.

41. J. Hoberman, "Slavs of Love," *Village Voice,* November 4–10, 1981, p. 54.

42. For a brief but clear discussion of Reich's analysis of sexually repressive patriarchal family structures and his differences with Freud, see James MacBean, *Film and Revolution,* pp. 231–33.

43. For a summary of *Montenegro's* early international box office returns, see "*Montenegro,* Hot Swedish Export Item," *Variety,* March 24, 1982.

44. The "Foreword" to *Manifesto.*

45. Personal interview/conversation with Dušan Makavejev, June 21, 1991.

SELECTED BIBLIOGRAPHY

Andrei Tarkovsky

BOOKS BY TARKOVSKY

Tarkovsky, A. *Lekcii po kinorezhissure* (*Lectures on Film Directing*). Ed. Konstantin Lopushansky. Leningrad: Lenfilm, 1989.

———. *Sculpting in Time: Reflections on the Cinema.* Translated by Kitty Hunter-Blair. Revised edition. London: Faber and Faber, 1989. First published in 1986.

———. *Time within Time: The Diaries 1970-1986.* Translated by Kitty Hunter-Blair. Calcutta: Seagull Books, 1991. First published in German as *Martyrolog: Tagebücher 1970–1986.* Translated by Vera Stutz-Bischitzky and Marlene Milack-Verheyden. Frankfurt a. Main/Berlin: Limes, 1989. (*N.B.* The two texts are quite similar but not identical and do not contain exactly the same extracts.)

INTERVIEWS WITH TARKOVSKY

"Between Two Worlds." *American Film* (November 1983): 14, 75–79.

"Entretien" with Boleslav Edelhajt. *Cahiers du Cinéma* 392 (février 1987): 36–39, 41.

Ekran 65: Sbornik. Moscow: Iskusstvo, 1966, pp. 154–57.

"My delayem filmy" ("We Make Films"). *Kino* no. 10 (1981): 16–18.

"O kinoobraze" ("About the Film Image"). *Iskusstvo kino* no. 3 (1979): 80–93.

"Strasti po Andreyu" ("The Passion According to Andrei"). *Literaturnoe obozrenie* no. 9 (1988): 74–80.

"Vstat na put" ("Finding the Way"). *Iskusstvo kino* no. 2 (1989): 109–30.

SCRIPTS

Andrei Rublev. *Iskusstvo kino* no 4 (1964): 139–200; no. 5 (1964) 125–58. Original script of *Andrei Roublev* published in two parts (April and May). Afterword ("Vozrozhennyi Rublev") by V. G. Pashuto no. 5 ([1964]: 159–60).

Andrei Rublev. Translated by Kitty Hunter-Blair. London: Faber and Faber, 1991.

Hoffmanniana. Munich-Paris: Schiemer/Mosel, 1988 (in French). First published in *Iskusstvo kino* no. 8 (1976): 167–89.

Mashina zhelaniy (*The Wish Machine*). Script of *Stalker* by Arkady and Boris Strugatsky, published in *Sbornik nauchoy fantastiki* 25 (1981): 7–39.

Mirror. Published in *Kinoscenarii.* Moscow: Goskino, 1988, pp. 122–54.

Le Sacrifice. Munich-Paris: Schirmer/Mosel, 1987. (Also published in German as *Opfer.*)

BOOKS ON TARKOVSKY

Andrej Tarkowskij. Reihe Film 39. Munchen: Carl Hanser Verlag, 1987 (essays by various authors).

Ciment, Gilles, ed. *Andrei Tarkovski.* Dossier Positif. Paris: Editions Rivages, 1988 (essays and interviews from the magazine *Positif,* 1969–1988). (*N.B.* The essays are reprinted without editorial correction and many contain serious factual inaccuracies.)

de Baecque, Antoine. *Andrei Tarkovski.* Collection "Auteurs." Paris: *Cahiers du Cinéma,* 1989.

Estève, Michel, ed. *Andrei Tarkovsky. Etudes cinématographiques,* nos. 135–38. Paris: Lettres Modernes, 1983.

Gauthier, Guy. *Andrei Tarkovski.* Filmo 19. Paris: Edilig, 1988.

Kovács, Bálint András, and Akos Szilágyi. *Les Mondes d'Andrei Tarkovski.* Translated (from Hungarian) by Veronique Charaire. Lausanne: L'Age d'Homme, 1987.

Le Fanu, Mark. *The Cinema of Andrei Tarkovsky.* London: The British Film Institute, 1987.

Sandler, A. M., ed. *Mir i filmy Andreya Tarkovskogo* (*The World and the Films of Andrei Tarkovsky*). Moscow: Iskusstvo, 1991. (Some new, some reprinted articles, reminiscences, Tarkovsky's letters and interviews.)

Tarkovskaya, Marina, ed. *O Tarkovskom.* Moscow: Progress Publishers, 1989. (Reminiscences by various friends and co-workers.)

Turovskaya, Maya. *Tarkovsky: Cinema as Poetry.* London: Faber and Faber, 1989.

———. *7 1/2 ili filmy Andreya Tarkovskogo* (*7-1/2, or The Films of Andrei Tarkovsky*). Moscow: Iskusstvo, 1991. (Russian version of *Tarkovsky: Cinema as Poetry* with additional interviews.)

ARTICLES, REVIEWS, AND OCCASIONAL PIECES

Anninsky, Lev. "Popytka ochishcheniya" ("A Purification Attempt"). *Iskusstvo kino* no. 1 (1989): 24–37.

Batkin, Leonid, "Ne boyas svoyego golosa" ("Unafraid of One's Own Voice"). *Iskusstvo kino* no. 11 (1988): 77–101.

Demin, Viktor. *Pervoye lico* (*The First Person*). Moscow: Isskustvo, 1977, pp. 263–73.

"Glavnaya tema-sovremenost" ("The Main Theme Is Contemporaneity"). *Iskusstovo kino* no. 3 (1975): 1–18.

Green, Peter. "The Nostalgia of the Stalker." *Sight & Sound* (Winter 1984/85): 50–54.

Hyman, Timothy. Review of *Solaris. Film Quarterly* (Spring 1976): 54–58.

Johnson, Vida T., and Graham Petrie. "Andrei Tarkovskii's Films." *Journal of European Studies* 20, Part 3 (September 1990): 265–77.

Loysha, Viktor. "Takoye kino" ("That Kind of Cinema"). *Druzhbanarodov* no.1 (1989): 214–32.

Marshall, Herbert. "Andrei Tarkovsky's *Mirror.*" *Sight & Sound* (Spring 1976): 92–95

Mikhalkovich, V.I. *Andrei Tarkovsky.* Scientific Popular Series. Moscow: Znanie, 1989.

Mitchell, Tony. "Andrei Tarkovsky and *Nostalghia.*" *Film Criticism* VIII, 3 (1984): 2–11.

———. "Tarkovsky in Italy." *Sight & Sound* (Winter 1982/3): 54–56.

Montagu, Ivor. "Man and Experience: Tarkovsky's World." *Sight & Sound* (Spring 1973): 89–94.

Petric, Vlada. "Tarkovsky's Dream Imagery." *Film Quarterly* (Winter 1989–90): 28–34.

Petrie, Graham, and Ruth Dwyer, eds. *Before the Wall Came Down: Soviet and East European Filmmakers Working in the West.* Lanham, MD: University Press of America, 1990. (Contains chapters on *The Sacrifice* by A. Heidi Karriker and Jim Leach and on *Nostalghia* by Anna Makolkina.)

Salynsky, Dmitry. "Rezhisser i mif" ("Director and Myth"). *Iskusstvo kino* no. 12 (1989): 79–91.

Soloviev, Vladimir. "Zamysel, poetika, film" ("Concept, Poetics, Film"). *Neva* no. 10 (1972): 194–201.

Yermash, Filip. "On byl khudozhnik" ("He was an Artist"). *Sovietskaya kultura,* September 9, 1989, p. 10, and September 12, 1989, p. 4.

Zak, Mark. *Andrei Tarkovsky: Tvorchesky portret.* Moscow: Soyuzinformkino, 1988.

———. *Kinorezhissura* (*Film Directing*). Moscow: Iskusstvo, 1989, pp. 98–127.

Zorkaya, Neya. "Zametki k portretu Andreya Tarkovskogo" ("Remarks towards a Portrait of Andrei Tarkovsky"). *Kino panorama* 2 (1977), pp. 144–65.

———. "Filmy i rezissery" ("Films and Directors"). In *Problemysovremennogo kino,* edited by S. I. Yutkevich. Moscow: Iskusstvo, 1976.

DOCUMENTARY FILMS ON TARKOVSKY

Baglivo, Donatella. *Andrei Tarkovsky: A Poet in Cinema*, Ciak Studio: Italy, 1983.

Leszczylowski, Michal. *Directed by Andrej Tarkovskij*. Swedish Film Institute, 1988.

GENERAL WORKS

Cohen, Louis Harris. *The Cultural-Political Traditions and Developments of the Soviet Cinema, 1917–1972*. New York: Arno Press, 1974.

Golovskoy, Val, with John Rimberg. *Behind the Soviet Screen: The Motion-Picture Industry in the USSR, 1972-1982*. Ann Arbor: Ardis, 1986.

Lem, Stanislaw. *Solaris*. 1971. Harmondsworth: Penguin Books, 1981. Translated by Joanna Kilmartin and Steve Cox. First published in Polish in 1961.

Leyda, Jay. *Kino: A History of the Russian and Soviet Film*. Princeton: Princeton University Press, 1973.

Strugatsky, Arkady, and Boris Strugatsky. *Roadside Picnic/Tale of the Troika*. 1977. New York: Pocket Books, 1978. First published in Russian in 1972.

Tarkovsky, Arseny. *Stikhotvoreniya* (*Poems*). Moscow: Khudozhestvennaya literatura, 1974.

Zorkaya, Neya. *The Illustrated History of the Soviet Cinema*. New York: Hippocrene Books, 1990.

Miloš Forman

BOOKS

Boček, Jaroslav. *Looking Back on the New Wave*. Prague: Československý Filmexport, 1967.

Foll, Jan. *Miloš Forman*. Prague: Československý filmový ústav, 1989.

Forman, Miloš, John Guare, Jean-Claude Carrière, and John Klein. *Taking Off* (screenplay). New York: New American Library, 1971.

———, Jaroslav Papoušek, and Ivan Passer. "*Les Amours d'une Blonde.*" *L'Avant Scène du Cinema* no. 60 (June 1966): 7–34.

Hames, Peter. *The Czechoslovak New Wave*. Berkeley and Los Angeles: University of California Press, 1985.

Liehm, Antonín J. *The Politics of Culture*. Translated by Peter Kussi. New York: Grove Press, 1973.

———. *Closely Watched Films: The Czechoslovak Experience*. New York: International Arts and Sciences Press, 1974.

———. *The Miloš Forman Stories*. Translated by Jeanne Němcová. New York: International Arts and Sciences Press, 1975.

Škvorecký, Josef. *All the Bright Young Men and Women*. Translated by Michael Schonberg. Toronto: Peter Martin Associates, 1971.

ARTICLES AND ESSAYS

Adair, Gilbert. "What's Opera, Doc?" (*Amadeus*). *Sight and Sound* 54, 2 (Spring 1985): 142–43.

Arkadin (pseud). "Film Clips" (interview with Miloš Forman). *Sight and Sound* 35, 1 (Winter 1965–66): 46.

Arnault, Hubert, and André Cornand. "Entretien avec Miloš Forman." *Image et Son* no. 221 (November 1968): 39–47.

Benayoun, Robert. "Les Temps par Lambeaux ou Time in Rags" (*Ragtime*). *Positif* 250 (January 1982): 79–82.

Blue, James, and Gianfranco de Bosio. "Entretien avec Miloš Forman." *Cahiers du Cinéma* no. 174 (January 1966): 62–63.

Bourget, Jean-Loup. "Eloge du Gaspillage" (*Valmont*). *Positif* no. 346 (December 1989): 2–4.

Cameron, Julia. "Miloš Forman and *Hair:* Styling the Age of Aquarius." *Rolling Stone,* April 19, 1979, pp. 85–86.

———. "Twyla Tharp Lands on Her Feet." *Rolling Stone,* April 19, 1979, p. 87.

Ciment, Michel. "Une Experience americaine" (two interviews with Miloš Forman). *Positif* 179 (March 1976): 14–23.

———. "Entretien avec Miloš Forman." *Positif* 220–21 (July-August 1976): 19–28.

———. "Entretien avec Miloš Forman." *Positif* 285 (November 1984): 21–28.

———. "Entretien avec Miloš Forman." *Positif* 346 (December 1989): 5–9.

Collet, Jean. "Les Amours d'une Blonde." *Cahiers du Cinéma* no. 176 (March 1966): 75–76.

Combs, Richard. "One Flew Over the Cuckoo's Nest." *Sight and Sound* 45, 2 (Spring 1976): 120.

———. "Sentimental Journey." *Sight and Sound* 46, 3 (Summer 1977): 153.

———. "Ragtime." *Monthly Film Bulletin* 49, 578 (March 1982): 46–47.

———. "Amadeus." *Monthly Film Bulletin* 52, 612 (January 1985): 14–15.

Dyer, Peter John. "Peter and Pavla." *Monthly Film Bulletin* 32, 382 (November 1965): 161.

———. "Star Crossed in Prague." *Sight and Sound* 35, 7 (Winter 1965-66): 34–35.

Forman, Miloš. "Chill Wind on the New Wave." *Saturday Review,* December 23, 1967, pp. 10–41.

Gelmis, Joseph. Interview with Miloš Forman. In *The Film Director as Superstar.* New York: Doubleday, 1970.

Gow, Gordon. "Peter and Pavla." *Films and Filming* 12 (December 1965): 27–28.

———. "Red Youth." *Films and Filming* 12 (February 1966): 32–33.

———. "A Blonde in Love." *Films and Filming* 12 (July 1966): 16–17.

———. "The Firemen's Ball." *Films and Filming* 15 (February 1969): 41–44.

———. "A Czech in New York." *Films and Filming* 17 (September 1971): 20–24.

———. "Taking Off." *Films and Filming* 18 (November 1971): 20–24.

———. "One Flew Over the Cuckoo's Nest." *Films and Filming* 22 (April 1976): 30–31.

———. "Hair." *Films and Filming* 25 (August 1979): 33–36.

Humphries, Reynold, and Genevieve Buzzoni. "One Flew Over the Cuckoo's Nest." *Framework* 11, 5 (Winter 1976–1977): 23–24.

Jacobson, Harlan. "As Many Notes as Required." *Film Comment* 20, 5 (September-October, 1984): 50–55.

Langley, Lee. "Taking Off in the West." *The Guardian* (London and Manchester), August 18, 1971, p. 8.

Liehm, Antonín J. "Forman Talks Cuckoo." *Take One* 5 (August 1976): 19–20.

———. "Miloš Forman: the Style and the Man." In David W. Paul (ed.) *Politics, Art and Commitment in the East European Cinema* (London: Macmillan, 1983), pp. 211–24.

Pulleine, Tim. "Hair." *Sight and Sound* 48, 4 (Autumn 1979): 261–62.

Shaffer, Peter. "Making the Screen Speak." *Film Comment* 20, 5 (September-October 1984): 50–57.

Sineux, Michel. "Les Coucous de Midwich." *Positif* 131 (October 1971): 53–56.

———. "Big Mother Is Watching You (*One Flew Over the Cuckoo's Nest*)." *Positif* 179 (March 1976): 11–13.

———. "Une Trilogie Américaine." *Positif* 220–21 (July-August 1976): 16–18.

———. "Quasi una Fantasia (*Amadeus*)." *Positif* 285 (November 1984): 29–31.

Škvorecký, Josef. "Miloš Forman." In Christopher Lyon (ed.), *The International Dictionary of Films and Filmmakers: Volume 2, Directors/Filmmakers.* London: Firethorn Press, 1986).

Stein, Harry. "A Day in the Life: Miloš Forman." *Esquire,* May 8, 1979, pp. 82–83.

Strick, Philip. "A Blonde in Love." *Monthly Film Bulletin* 33, 389 (June 1966): 89.

———. "The Firemen's Ball." *Monthly Film Bulletin* 36, 420 (January 1969): 6.

Sturhahn, Larry. "*One Flew Over the Cuckoo's Nest:* An Interview with Miloš Forman." *Filmmakers Newsletter,* December 1975.
Svitak, Ivan. "Les héros de l'aliénation." *Image et Son* no. 221 (November 1968): 51–69.
Téchiné, André. "Le sourire de Prague." *Cahiers du Cinéma* no. 174 (January 1966): 60–63.
Thomson, David. "Redtime." *Film Comment* 18, 1 (January–February 1982): 11–16.
Uhde, Jan. "Ragtime ve Formanově virtuózním rytmu." *Zapad* no. 1 (1982): 26–29.
Walsh, Michael. "*Amadeus,* Shamadeus." *Film Comment* 20, 5 (September–October 1984): 50–52.
Wilson, David. "The Firemen's Ball." *Sight and Sound* 38, 1 (Winter 1968–69): 46.
———. "Taking Off." *Sight and Sound* 40, 4 (Autumn 1971): 221–22.

Roman Polanski

Belmans, Jacques. *Roman Polanski.* Paris: Editions Seghers, 1971.
Bisplinghoff, Gretchen, and Virginia Wright Wexman. *Roman Polanski: A Guide to References and Resources.* Boston: G. K. Hall, 1979.
Butler, Ivan. *The Cinema of Roman Polanski.* New York: Barnes, 1970.
Cawelti, John G. "*Chinatown* and Generic Transformation in Recent American Films." In *Film Theory and Criticism,* Gerald Mast and Marshall Cohen, eds. New York: Oxford, 1979, 559–79.
Chappetta, Robert. "Rosemary's Baby." *Film Quarterly* 22, 3 (Spring 1969): 35–38.
Durgnat, Raymond. "Repulsion." *Films and Filming* 11(August 1965): 28–29.
Harker, Jonathan. "Two Men and a Wardrobe." *Film Quarterly* 12, 3 (Spring): 53–55.
Houston, Beverle, and Marsha Kinder. "Rosemary's Baby." *Sight and Sound* 38, 1 (Winter): 17–26.
Kiernan, Thomas. *The Roman Polanski Story.* New York: Delilah/Grove, 1980.
Lawton, Anna. "The Double: A Dostoevskian Theme in Polanski." *Literature/Film Quarterly* 9, 2 (1981): 121–29.
Leach, James. "Notes on Polanski's Cinema of Cruelty." *Wide Angle* 2, 1 (1978): 32–39.
Leaming, Barbara. *Polanski, A Biography: The Filmmaker as Voyeur.* New York: Simon and Schuster, 1981.

István Szabó

BOOKS

Holloway, Ronald, and Dorothea Holloway, *O Is for Oberhausen: Weg zum Nachbarn.* Oberhausen, Germany: City of Oberhausen, 1979.
Koopmanschap, Eric. *De Hongaarse film* no. 29, VNFI Verkenningen. Hilversum, Netherlands: verenigd Nederlands Filminstituut, 1980.
Magill, Frank N., ed. *Magill's Survey of Cinema: Foreign Films.* Los Angeles: Salem Press, 1986.
Nemes, Károly. *Films of Commitment: Socialist Cinema in Eastern Europe.* Budapest: Corvina Kiádó, 1985.
Passek, Jean-Loup, Jacqueline Bribois, and Philippe Haudiquet, eds. *Le cinéma hongrois.* Paris: Centre d'art et de culture Georges Pompidou, 1979.
Paul, David, ed. *Politics, Art and Commitment in the East European Cinema.* London: Macmillan, and New York: St. Martin's Press, 1983.
Petrie, Graham. *History Must Answer to Man.* Budapest: Corvina Kiádó, 1978.

ARTICLES

Dreifus, Claudia. "Doctor to the Human Condition." *The Progressive* 46, 8 (August 1982): 47–49.

Hughes, John W., "'Mephisto': István Szabó and 'the Gestapo of Suspicion,'" *Film Quarterly* 35, 4 (Summer 1982): 13–18.
Jaehne, Karen. "István Szabó: Dreams of Memories," *Film Quarterly* 32, 1 (Fall 1978): 30–41.
Paul, David. "Hungary: The Magyar on the Bridge." In *Post New Wave Cinema in the Soviet Union and Eastern Europe,* ed. Daniel J. Goulding. Bloomington and Indianapolis: Indiana University Press, 1989, pp. 172–214.
Riegel, O.W. "What Is 'Hungarian' in the Hungarian Cinema," Three-part article in *New Hungarian Quarterly* 17, 63 (Autumn 1976): 185–93; 17, 64 (Winter 1976): 206–15; and 18, 65 (Spring 1977): 201–10.
Rubenstein, Lenny. "Dreams and Nightmares: An Interview with István Szabó." *Cinéaste* 12, 2 (1984), p. 36.

PERSONAL INTERVIEWS
István Szabó. (Budapest) September 28, 1985; (London) March 5 and 6, 1991.
Péter Andorai. (Budapest) March 20, 1991.
András Bálint. (Budapest) September 28, 1990.
Ildikó Bánsági. (Budapest) September 28, 1990.
Péter Dobai. (Budapest) March 19, 1991.
Judit Pintér. (Budapest) March 20, 1991.

Dušan Makavejev

BOOKS
Allen, Woody. *Hannah and Her Sisters.* New York: Random House, 1986.
Blaževski, Vladimir, ed. *Dušan Makavejev: 300 Čuda.* Belgrade: Studenski kulturni centar, 1988.
Breton, André. *What Is Surrealism? Selected Writings.* Edited by Franklin Rosemont. New York: Pathfinder Press, 1978.
Carroll, Noel. *Mystifying Movies: Fads and Fallacies in Contemporary Film Theory.* New York: Columbia University Press, 1988.
Goulding, Daniel J. *Liberated Cinema: The Yugoslav Experience.* Bloomington: Indiana University Press, 1985.
Hoffman, Katherine, ed. *Collage: Critical Views.* Ann Arbor: U.M.I. Press.
Makavejev, Dušan. *Poljubac za drugarica parolu.* Belgrade: Nolit, 1960.
———. *WR: Mysteries of the Organism.* New York: Avon Books, 1972.
Matthews, J. H. *Languages of Surrealism.* Columbia: University of Missouri Press, 1986.
———. *The Imagery of Surrealism.* Syracuse: Syracuse University Press, 1977.
Oesterreicher-Mollwo, Marianne. *Surrealism and Dadaism.* Oxford: Phaidon Press, 1979.
Petrie, Graham, and Ruth Dwyer, eds. *Before the Wall Came Down: Soviet and East European Filmmakers Working in the West.* New York: University Press of America, 1990.
Paul, David W. ed. *Politics, Art and Commitment in the East European Cinema.* New York: St. Martin's Press, 1983.
Sher, Gerson. *Praxis: Marxist Criticism and Dissent in Socialist Yugoslavia.* Bloomington: Indiana University Press, 1977.
Sitney, P. Adams. *Modernist Montage: The Obscurity of Vision in Modernist Cinema and Literature.* New York: New York University Press, 1990.
Vogel, Amos. *Film as a Subversive Art.* New York: Random House, 1974.
Walsh, Martin. *The Brechtian Aspect of Radical Cinema.* London: The British Film Institute, 1981.

INTERVIEWS
Aćin, Zdenka. "Zašto smo srećni." In *Makavejev: 300 Čuda,* edited by Vladimir Blaževski. Belgrade: Studenski kulturni centar, 1988.

Cozarinsky, Edgardo, and Carlos Clarens. "Dušan Makavejev Interview." *Film Comment* no. 3 (May-June, 1975): 47–51.

"Let's Put the Life Back in Political Life—An Interview With Dusan [*sic*] Makavejev." *Cineaste* no. 2 (1974): 14–18.

Lopate, Phillip, and Bill Zavatsky. "An Interview with Dušan Makavejev." In Dušan Makavejev, *WR: Mysteries of the Organism*. New York: Avon Books, 1972.

Mekas, Jonas. "Movie Journal." A three-part interview with Makavejev in *The Village Voice*, January 13 and 20 and February 3, 1972.

Sitton, Robert, James Roy MacBean, and Ernest Callenbach, "Fight Power with Spontaneity and Humor: An Interview with Dušan Makavejev." *Film Quarterly* (Winter 1971–1972): 3–9.

Unpublished Personal Interviews on March 15–16, 1989, February 4, 1990, and June 21, 1991.

ARTICLES, CHAPTERS, OCCASIONAL PIECES

Armes, Roy. "Dušan Makavejev: Collage and Complication." In Roy Armes, *The Ambiguous Image: Narrative Style in European Cinema*. Bloomington: Indiana University Press, 1976.

Callenbach, Ernest. "Montenegro." *Film Quarterly* no. 3 (Summer 1982): 48–51.

Cavell, Stanley. "An Afterimage—On Makavejev On Bergman." In *Films and Dreams: An Approach to Bergman*, edited by Vlada Petrić. New York: Redgrave Publishers, 1981.

Dokumentacija za internu upotrebu. Prepared by Svetozar Udovički. Neoplanta film, 1971. (A 1,009-page mimeo report containing all important documents pertaining to the controversy in Yugoslavia over Makavejev's film *WR: Mysteries of the Organism*).

Eagle, Herbert. "Yugoslav Marxist Humanism and the Films of Dušan Makavejev." In *Politics, Art and Commitment in the East European Cinema*, edited by David W. Paul. New York: St. Martin's Press, 1983.

Hoberman, J. "Slavs of Love." *The Village Voice*, November 4–10, 1981, p. 54.

Horton, Andrew. "The Mouse That Wanted to F--k a Cow: Makavejev's Cinematic Carnival Laughter." In *Comedy/Cinema/Theory*, edited by Andrew Horton. Berkeley: University of California Press, 1991.

Insdorf, Annette. "Expatriates Are His Subject, Iconoclasm Is His Homeland." *New York Times*, November 8, 1981, D p. 13.

Kuspit, Donald B. "Collage: The Organizing Principle of Art in the Age of the Relativity of Art." In *Relativism in the Arts*, edited by Betty Craig. Athens: The University of Georgia Press, 1983.

MacBean, James Roy. "Sex and Politics: Wilhelm Reich, World Revolution, and Makavejev's *WR: Mysteries of the Organism*." In James Roy MacBean, *Film and Revolution*. Bloomington: Indiana University Press, 1975.

Popov, Raša. "Imago Makavejev." In *Dušan Makavejev: 300 Čuda*, edited by Vladimir Blaževski. Belgrade: Studenski kulturni centar, 1988.

Rosenberg, Harold. "Collage: Philosophy of Put-Togethers." In Harold Rosenberg, *Art on the Edge*. New York: Macmillan Publishing Company, 1975.

Stojanović, Miroljub. "O tradiciji i konvencijama u delu Dušana Makavejeva." In *Dušan Makavejev: 300 Čuda*, edited by Vladimir Blaževski. Belgrade: Studenski kulturni centar, 1988.

Taylor, John Russell. "Dušan Makavejev." In John Russell Taylor, *Directors and Directions: Cinema for the Seventies*. New York: Hill and Wang, 1975.

Testa, Bart. "Reflections on Makavejev: The Art Film and Transgression." In *Before the Wall Came Down: Soviet and East European Filmmakers Working in the West*, edited by Graham Petrie and Ruth Dwyer. New York: University Press of America, 1990.

Tirnanić, Bogdan. "Prvi srpski superman." *NIN*, November 24, 1985, pp. 37–38.

Ulmer, Gregory L. "The Object of Post-Criticism." In *The Anti-Aesthetic: Essays on Postmodern Culture,* edited by Hal Foster. Port Townsend, Washington: Bay Press, 1983.

Vogel, Amos. "Makavejev: Toward the Edge of the Real . . . and Over." *Film Comment* no. 6 (November-December 1973): 190–93.

Wood, Robin. "Dušan Makavejev." In *Second Wave,* edited by Ian Cameron. New York: Praeger, 1970.

———. "Dušan Makavejev." In *Cinema: A Critical Dictionary, Vol. II.,* edited by Richard Roud. London: Secker and Warburg, 1980.

FILMOGRAPHY

Andrei Tarkovsky

DIPLOMA FILM

Katok i skripka (*The Steamroller and the Violin*). Production: Mosfilm, Moscow, USSR (Children's Film Unit); color; running time: 46 mins. Released: 1960.

DOCUMENTARY FILM

Tempo di Viaggio (*Time of Travel*). Production: RAI Television, Rome, Italy; color and black and white; running time: 60 mins. Released 1981.

FEATURE FILMS

Ivanovo detstvo (*Ivan's Childhood;* American title: *My Name Is Ivan*). Production: Mosfilm, Moscow, USSR; black and white; running time: 95 mins. Released: 1962. Production supervised by G. Kuznetsov; screenplay by Mikhail Papava, Vladimir Bogomolov; based on the novella *Ivan* by Bogomolov; directed by Andrei Tarkovsky; photography by Vadim Yusov; edited by G. Natanson; art direction by Yevgeny Chernyaev; music by Vyacheslav Ovchinnikov. Cast: Nikolai Burlyaev (Ivan), Valentin Zubkov (Captain Kholin), E. Zharikov (Lieutenant Galtsev), S. Krylov (Corporal Katasonych), Nikolai Grinko (Lt.-Col. Gryaznov), V. Malyavina (Masha), Irina Tarkovskaya (Ivan's mother).

Andrei Roublev. Production: Mosfilm, Moscow, USSR; black and white and color; running time: 185 mins. Released: 1971 (completed 1966). Production supervised by Tamara Ogorodnikova; screenplay by Andrei Mikhalkov-Konchalovsky, Andrei Tarkovsky; directed by Andrei Tarkovsky; photography by Vadim Yusov; edited by Lyudmila Feiginova; art direction by Yevgeny Chernyaev; music by Vyacheslav Ovchinnikov. Cast: Anatoly Solonitsyn (Andrei Roublev), Ivan Lapikov (Kirill), Nikolai Grinko (Daniil the Black), Nikolai Sergeyev (Theophanes the Greek), Irina Tarkovskaya (Fool), Nikolai Burlyaev (Boriska), Rolan Bykov (Buffoon), Yuri Nikulin (Sacristan), Mikhail Kononov (Foma), Yuri Nazarov (Grand Duke/his brother), Bolot Ishalenev (Tartar Khan).

Solaris. Production: Mosfilm, Moscow, USSR; color and black and white; running time: 165 mins. Released: 1972. Screenplay by Andrei Tarkovsky, Friedrich Gorenstein; based on the novel by Stanislaw Lem; directed by Andrei Tarkovsky; photography by Vadim Yusov; edited by Lyudmila Feiginova; art direction by Mikhail Romadin; music by Eduard Artemyev, J. S. Bach (Choral Prelude in F Minor). Cast: Natalia Bondarchuk (Hari), Donatas Banionis (Kris Kelvin), Yuri Yarvet (Snaut), Anatoly Solonitsyn (Sartorius), Vladislav Dvorzhetsky (Berton), Sos Sarkissyan (Gibarian), Nikolai Grinko (Kris's father), Olga Barnet (Kris's mother).

Zerkalo (*Mirror*). Production: Mosfilm, Moscow, USSR; color and black and white; running time: 106 mins. Released: 1975. Produced by E. Vaisberg; screenplay by Andrei Tarkovsky, Alexander Misharin; directed by Andrei Tarkovsky; photography by Georgy Rerberg; edited by Lyudmila Feiginova; art direction by Nikolai Dvigubsky; music by Eduard Artemyev, J. S. Bach, Giovanni Batista Pergolesi, Henry Purcell; poems by Arseny Tarkovsky, read by the poet. Cast: Margarita Terekhova (Masha, Alexei's mother/Natalia, Alexei's wife), Filip Yankovsky (Alexei, aged five), Ignat Daniltsev (Alexei/Ignat, aged twelve), Oleg Yankovsky (Alexei's father), Nikolai Grinko (Boss in printing shop), Alla Demidova (Lisa), Yuri Nazarov (Military

Instructor), Anatoly Solonitsyn (Doctor, passing by), Innokenty Smoktunovsky (voice of Alexei, the Narrator), Larissa Tarkovskaya (Rich Doctor's wife), Maria Tarkovskaya (Alexei's mother as an old woman).

Stalker. Production: Mosfilm, Moscow, USSR; color and black and white; running time: 161 mins. Released: 1979. Production supervised by Aleksandra Demidova; screenplay by Arkady and Boris Strugatsky; based on their novella *Roadside Picnic;* directed by Andrei Tarkovsky; photography by Alexander Knyazhinsky; edited by Lyudmila Feiginova; art direction by Andrei Tarkovsky; music by Eduard Artemyev. Cast: Alexander Kaidanovsky (the Stalker), Anatoly Solonitsyn (the Writer), Nikolai Grinko (the Professor), Alyssa Freindlikh (Stalker's wife), Natasha Abramova (Stalker's daughter).

Nostalghia. Production: Opera Film, Rome, Italy, for RAI TV Rete 2; in association with Sovinfilm (USSR); color and black and white; running time: 126 mins. Released: 1983. Produced by Renzo Rossellini, Manolo Bolognini; screenplay by Andrei Tarkovsky, Tonino Guerra; directed by Andrei Tarkovsky; photography by Giuseppe Lanci; edited by Erminia Marani, Amadeo Salfa; music by Verdi, Wagner, Beethoven, Debussy. Cast: Oleg Yankovsky (Andrei Gorchakov), Erland Josephson (Domenico), Domiziana Giordano (Eugenia), Patricia Terreno (Gorchakov's wife), Delia Boccardo (Domenico's wife).

Offret (*The Sacrifice*). Production: Swedish Film Institute, Stockholm, Sweden/ Argos Films, Paris, France; in association with Film Four International, London, England; color and black and white; running time: 149 mins. Released: 1986. Produced by Anna-Lena Wibom (Swedish Film Institute); screenplay by Andrei Tarkovsky; directed by Andrei Tarkovsky; photography by Sven Nykvist; edited by Andrei Tarkovsky, Michal Leszczylowski; music by J. S. Bach, "Erbarme Dich" from the *St. Matthew Passion;* Swedish and Japanese folk music. Cast: Erland Josephson (Alexander), Susan Fleetwood (Adelaide), Valérie Mairesse (Julia), Allan Edwall (Otto), Gudrún Gísladóttir (Maria), Sven Wollter (Victor), Filippa Franzén (Marta), Tommy Kjellqvist (Little Man).

Miloš Forman

DOCUMENTARIES

Visions of Eight (*The Decathlon segment*), Wolper Pictures, USA, 1973.

FEATURE FILMS

Konkurs (*Talent Competition*). Production: Barrandov Film Studios, Prague, Czechoslovakia; black and white; running time: 90 mins. Released: 1963. Screenplay by Miloš Forman and Ivan Passer; directed by Miloš Forman; photography by Miroslav Ondříček; edited by Miroslav Hájek; music (part two) by Jiří Suchý and Jiří Šlitr. Cast: (part one) Vladimír Pucholt (Vláda), Václav Blumenfeld (Vašek), Jan Vostrčil and František Zeman (conductors): (part two) Věra Křesadlová, Markéta Krotká, and Ladislav Jakim (participants in audition), Jiří Suchý and Jiří Šlitr (themselves).

Černý Petr (*Black Peter/Peter and Pavla*). Production: Barrandov Film Studios, Prague, Czechoslovakia; black and white; running time: 89 mins. Released: 1963. Screenplay by Miloš Forman and Jaroslav Papoušek; directed by Miloš Forman; photography by Jan Němeček; edited by Miroslav Hájek; art direction by Karel Černý; music by Jiří Šlitr. Cast: Ladislav Jakim (Petr), Vladimír Pucholt (Čenda), Pavla Martínková (Pavla); Jan Vostrčil (Petr's father); Božena Matušková (Petr's mother).

Lásky jedné plavovlásky (*Loves of a Blonde/A Blonde in Love*). Production: Barrandov Film Studios, Prague, Czechoslovakia; black and white; running time: 82 mins. Released: 1965. Screenplay by Miloš Forman, Jaroslav Papoušek, and Ivan Passer; directed by Miloš Forman; photography by Miroslav Ondříček; edited by Miroslav Hájek; art direction by Karel Černý; music by Evzen Illín. Cast: Hana

Brejchová (Andula), Vladimír Pucholt (Mila), Josef Šebánek (Mila's father), Milada Jezková (Mila's mother), Vladimír Menšík (Vacovsky), Ivan Kheil (Manas), Jiří Hrubý (Burda), Josef Kolb (social director), Jan Vostrčil (army officer).

Hoří, má panenko! (*The Firemen's Ball/Like a House on Fire*). Production: Barrandov Film Studios, Prague, Czechoslovakia; Carlo Ponti, Rome, Italy; color; running time: 71 mins. Released: 1967. Screenplay by Miloš Forman, Jaroslav Papoušek, and Ivan Passer; directed by Miloš Forman; photography by Miroslav Ondříček; edited by Miroslav Hájek; art direction by Karel Černý; music by Karel Mareš. Cast: Jan Vostrčil (Chairman of the Ball Committee), Josef Kolb (Josef), Milada Jezková (Josef's wife), Josef Šebánek (committee member), Jan Stöckl (President), František Svět (old man), Josef Kutálek (Ludva), Stanislav Holubec (Karel), Antonín Blažejovský (Standa), František Debelka, Karel Valnoha, Josef Řehořek, Vratislav Čermák, Václav Novotný, František Reinstein, František Paska, Ladislav Adam (committee members).

Taking Off. Production: Universal Pictures, USA. A Forman-Crown-Hausman production in association with Claude Berri; color; running time: 92 mins. Released: 1971. Produced by Alfred W. Crown; screenplay by Miloš Forman, John Guare, Jean-Claude Carrière, and John Klein; directed by Miloš Forman; photography by Miroslav Ondříček; edited by John Carter; art direction by Robert Wightman. Cast: Lynn Carlin (Lynn), Buck Henry (Larry), Linnea Heacock (Jeannie), Georgia Engel (Margot), Tony Harvey (Tony), Audra Lindley (Ann Lockston), Paul Benedict (Ben Lockston), Vincent Schiavelli (Mr. Schiavelli), David Gittler (Jamie), Rae Allen (Mrs. Divito), Corinna Cristobal (Corrina Divito), Allen Garfield (Norman), Barry Del Rae (Schuyler).

One Flew Over the Cuckoo's Nest. Production: Fantasy Films, USA; color; running time: 134 mins. Released 1975. Produced by Saul Zaentz and Michael Douglas; screenplay by Lawrence Hauben and Bo Goldman: based on the novel by Ken Kesey; directed by Miloš Forman; photography by Haskell Wexler, Bill Butler, and William A. Fraker; edited by Lynzee Klingman and Sheldon Kahn; production design by Paul Sylbert; art direction by Edwin O'Donovan; music by Jack Nitzsche. Cast: Jack Nicholson (R. P. McMurphy), Louise Fletcher (Nurse Ratched), William Redfield (Harding), Will Sampson (Chief Bromden), Brad Dourif (Billy Bibbit), Sydney Lassick (Cheswick), Christopher Lloyd (Taber), Danny De Vito (Martini), Delos V. Smith, Jr. (Scanlon), Marya Small (Candy), Louisa Moritz (Rose), Dean R. Brooks (Dr. Spivey), Scatman Crothers (Turkle).

Hair. Production: United Artists, USA. CIP Filmproduktions; color; running time: 121 mins. Released: 1979. Produced by Lester Persky and Michael Butler; screenplay by Michael Weller; based on the musical play by Galt MacDermot (music), Gerome Ragni, and James Rado (book and lyrics); directed by Miloš Forman; photography by Miroslav Ondříček; edited by Stanley Warnow and Alan Heim; production design by Stuart Wurtzel; choreographed by Twyla Tharp; music by Galt MacDermot. Cast: John Savage (Claude), Treat Williams (Berger), Beverley D'Angelo (Sheila), Annie Golden (Jeanie), Dorsey Wright (Hud), Don Dacus (Woof), Cheryl Barnes (Hud's fiancée), Richard Bright (Fenton), Nicholas Ray (General).

Ragtime. Production: Ragtime Productions, USA. A Sunley production; color; running time: 155 mins. Released: 1981. Produced by Dino De Laurentiis; screenplay by Michael Weller; based on the novel by E. L. Doctorow; directed by Miloš Forman; photography by Miroslav Ondříček; edited by Anne V. Coates, Antony Gibbs, and Stanley Warnow; production design by John Graysmark; art direction by Patrizia Von Brandenstein and Anthony Reading; music by Randy Newman. Cast: Howard E. Rollins (Coalhouse Walker, Jr.), Elizabeth McGovern (Evelyn Nesbit), James Olson (Father), Mary Steenburgen (Mother), Brad Dourif (Younger Brother), Mandy Patinkin (Tateh), Debbie Allen (Sarah), James Cagney (Rhinelander Waldo), Moses Gunn (Booker T. Washington), Kenneth McMillan (Willie Conklin), Pat O'Brien (Delmas), Donald O'Connor (dance instructor), Jeff Demunn (Houdini), Robert Joy (Harry K. Thaw), Norman Mailer (Stanford White).

Amadeus. Production: Saul Zaentz Company, USA; color; running time: 159 mins. Released: 1984. Produced by Saul Zaentz; screenplay by Peter Shaffer; adapted from his play; directed by Miloš Forman; photography by Miroslav Ondříček; edited by Nena Danevic and Michael Chandler; production design by Patrizia Von Brandenstein; art direction by Karel Černý; costume design by Theodor Pištěk; musical direction by Neville Marriner. Cast: F. Murray Abraham (Salieri), Tom Hulce (Mozart), Elizabeth Berridge (Constanze), Simon Callow (Schickaneder), Roy Dotrice (Leopold Mozart), Jeffrey Jones (Emperor Josef II), Christine Ebersole (Catarina Cavalieri), Charles Kay (Orsini-Rosenberg), Kenny Baker (Parody Commendatore), Lisabeth Bartlett (Papagena), Barbara Bryne (Frau Weber), Roderick Cook (von Strack), Patrick Hines (Kappelmeister Bonno), Herman Meckler (Priest).

Valmont. Production: Claude Berri and Renn Productions, France, Timothy Burrill Productions, Great Britain; color; running time: 140 mins. Released: 1989 (USA), 1991 (Great Britain). Produced by Paul Rassam and Michael Hausman; screenplay by Jean-Claude Carrière; based on themes from *Les Liaisons Dangereuses* by Choderlos de Laclos; directed by Miloš Forman; photography by Miroslav Ondříček; edited by Alan Heim and Nena Danevic; production design by Pierre Guffroy; costume design by Theodor Pištěk; music by Christopher Palmer. Cast: Colin Firth (Valmont), Annette Bening (Marquise de Merteuil), Meg Tilly (Mme de Tourvel), Fairuza Balk (Cécile de Volanges), Sian Phillips (Mme de Volanges), Jeffrey Jones (Gercourt), Henry Thomas (Danceny), Fabia Drake (Mme de Rosemonde), T. P. McKenna (the baron), Isla Blair (the baroness).

Roman Polanski

SHORT FILMS

Rower (*The Bicycle*), State School for Theater and Film, Łódź (SSTF-Łódź), Poland, 1955–57 (unfinished); *Śmiech* (*The Smile*), SSTF-Łódź, Poland, 1957; *Rozbijemy zabawe* (*Breaking Up the Party*), SSTF-Łódź, Poland, 1957; *Morderstwo* (*The Crime*), SSTF-Łódź, Poland, 1957–1958; *Dwaj ludzie z szafa* (*Two Men and a Wardrobe*), SSTF-Łódź, Poland, 1959; *Lampa* (*The Lamp*), SSTF-Łódź, Poland, 1959; *Gdy spadaja anioły* (*When Angels Fall*), SSTF-Łódź, Poland, 1959; *Le Gros et Le Maigre* (*The Fat and the Lean*), Claude Joudioux-A.P.E.C., France, 1961; *Ssaki* (*Mammals*), Studio Se-Ma-For, Poland, 1962.

FEATURE FILMS

Nóż w wodzie (*Knife in the Water*). Production: Kamera Film Unit of Film Polski, Warsaw, Poland; black and white; running time; 94 mins. Released: 1962. Produced by Stanisław Zylewicz; screenplay by Roman Polanski, Jerzy Skolimowski, Jakub Goldberg; directed by Roman Polanski; photography by Jerzy Lipman; edited by Halina Prugar; music by Krzysztof Komeda. Cast: Leon Niemczyk (Andrzej), Jolanta Umecka (Krystyna), Zygmunt Malanowicz (the hiker).

La Rivière des Diamants (*A River of Diamonds*). Episode in the film *Les Plus Belles Escroqueries Du Monde* (*The Beautiful Swindlers*). Production: Ulyssee Productions, Primex Films, Lux Films, Vides Cinematografica, Toho Company, Caesar Films, Paris, France; black and white; running time: 33 mins. Released: 1964. Produced by Pierre Roustang; screenplay by Roman Polanski, Gérard Brach; directed by Roman Polanski; photography by Jerzy Lipman; edited by Rita von Royen; music by Krzysztof Komeda. Cast: Nicole Karen (Young Woman), Jan Teulings (Seducer).

Repulsion. Production: Compton/Tekli Film Productions, London, England; black and white; running time: 104 mins. Released: 1965. Produced by Gene Gutowski; screenplay by Roman Polanski, Gérard Brach; directed by Roman Polanski; photography by Gilbert Taylor; edited by Alastair McIntyre; art direction by Seamus Flannery; music by Chico Hamilton. Cast: Catherine Deneuve (Carol), Ian Hendry (Michael), John Fraser (Colin), Yvonne Furneaux (Helen), Patrick Wymark (Landlord), Renée Houston (Miss Balch), Helen Fraser (Bridget).

Cul-de-sac. Production: Compton/Tekli Film Productions, London, England; black and white; running time: 111 mins. Released: 1966. Produced by Gene Gutowski; screenplay by Roman Polanski, Gérard Brach; directed by Roman Polanski; photography by Gilbert Taylor; edited by Alastair McIntyre; art direction by George Lack; music by Krzysztof Komeda. Cast: Donald Pleasance (George), Françoise Dorléac (Teresa), Lionel Stander (Richard), Jack MacGowran (Albert), Iain Quarrier (Christopher).

The Fearless Vampire Killers (first released as *Dance of the Vampires*). Production: Cadre Films-Filmways, Inc., London, England; color and panavision; running time: 107 mins. Released: 1967. Produced by Gene Gutowski; screenplay by Roman Polanski, Gérard Brach; directed by Roman Polanski; photography by Douglas Slocombe; edited by Alastair McIntyre; art direction by Fred Carter; music by Krzysztof Komeda. Cast: Jack MacGowran (Professor Abronsius), Roman Polanski (Alfred), Alfie Bass (Shagal), Jessie Robbins (Rebecca), Sharon Tate (Sarah), Ferdy Mayne (Count von Krolock), Iain Quarrier (Herbert), Terry Downes (Koukol).

Rosemary's Baby. Production: Paramount/William Castle Enterprises, New York, USA; color; running time: 137 mins. Released: 1968. Produced by William Castle; screenplay by Roman Polanski; based on the novel by Ira Levin; directed by Roman Polanski; photography by William Fraker; edited by Sam O'Steen, Robert Wyman; art direction by Joel Schiller; music by Krzysztof Komeda. Cast: Mia Farrow (Rosemary Woodhouse), John Cassavetes (Guy Woodhouse), Ruth Gordon (Minnie Castevet), Sidney Blackmer (Roman Castevet), Maurice Evans (Hutch), Ralph Bellamy (Dr. Sapirstein), Angela Dorian (Terry), Charles Grodin (Dr. Hill).

Macbeth. Production: Playboy Productions/Caliban Films, London, England; color; running time: 140 mins. Released; 1971. Produced by Andrew Braunsberg; screenplay by Roman Polanski, Kenneth Tynan; based on play by William Shakespeare; directed by Roman Polanski; photography by Gil Taylor; edited by Alastair McIntyre; art direction by Fred Carter; music by Third Ear Band. Cast: Jon Finch (Macbeth), Francesca Annis (Lady Macbeth), Martin Shaw (Banquo), Nicholas Selby (Duncan), John Stride (Ross), Stephan Chase (Malcolm), Paul Shelley (Donalbain), Terence Bayler (Macduff), Diane Fletcher (Lady Macduff), Andrew Laurence (Lennox), Keith Chegwin (Fleance), Maisie MacFarquhar (Blind Witch), Vic Abbot (Cawdor).

Che? (*What?*). Production: C. C. Champion, Rome, Italy/Les Films Concordia, Paris, France/Dieter Geissler Produktion, Munich, Germany; color; running time: 112 mins. Released: 1973. Produced by Carlo Ponti; screenplay by Roman Polanski, Gérard Brach; directed by Roman Polanski; photography by Marcello Gatti, Giuseppe Ruzzolini; edited by Alastair McIntyre; art direction by Franco Fumagalli; music by Claudio Gizzi. Cast: Sydne Rome (Nancy), Marcello Mastroianni (Alex), Hugh Griffith (Joseph Noblart), Romolo Valli (Giovanni), Guido Alberti (Priest), Gianfranco Piacentini (Tony), Roger Middleton (Jimmy), Roman Polanski (Mosquito).

Chinatown. Production: Long Road Productions, Paramount-Penthouse Presentation, New York, USA; color and panavision; running time: 130 mins. Released: 1974. Produced by Robert Evans; screenplay by Robert Towne; directed by Roman Polanski; photography by John A. Alonzo; edited by Sam O'Steen; art direction by W. Steward Campbell; music by Jerry Goldsmith. Cast: Jack Nicholson (Jake Gittes), Faye Dunaway (Evelyn Mulwray), John Huston (Noah Cross), Darrell Zwerling (Hollis Mulwray), Perry Lopez (Lieutenant Escobar), John Hillerman (Yelburton), Diane Ladd (Ida Sessions), Roy Jenson (Mulvihill), Roman Polanski (Thug with Knife), Dick Bakalyan (Loach), James Hong (Evelyn's Butler), Belinda Palmer (Katherine Mulwray), Curly (Burt Young).

Le Locataire (*The Tenant*). Production: Marianne Productions, Paris, France; color and panavision; running time: 125 mins. Released: 1976. Produced by Andrew Braunsberg; screenplay by Roman Polanski, Gérard Brach; based on the novel by Roland Topor; directed by Roman Polanski; photography by Sven Nykvist; edited by

Françoise Bonnot; art direction by Claude Moesching, Albert Rajau; music by Philippe Sarde. Cast: Roman Polanski (Trelkovsky), Isabelle Adjani (Stella), Shelley Winters (Concièrge), Melvyn Douglas (Monsieur Zy), Jo Van Fleet (Mme Dioz), Bernard Fresson (Scope), Lila Kedrova (Mme Gadérian).

Tess. Production: Renn Productions, Paris, France/Burrill Productions, London, England; color and panavision; running time: 190 mins. Released: 1980. Produced by Claude Berri; screenplay by Roman Polanski, Gérard Brach, and John Brownjohn; based on the novel by Thomas Hardy; directed by Roman Polanski; photography by Geoffrey Unsworth, Ghislain Cloquet; edited by Alastair McIntyre, Tom Priestly; art direction by Jack Stephens; music by Philippe Sarde. Cast: Nastassia Kinski (Tess), Peter Firth (Angel Clare), Leigh Lawson (Alec d'Urberville), John Collin (John Durbeyfield), Rosemary Martin (Mrs. Durbeyfield), David Markham (Reverend Clare), Arielle Dombasle (Mercy Chant).

Pirates. Production: Carthago Films in association with Accent-Cominco, Paris, France; color and panavision; running time: 117 mins. Released: 1986. Produced by Tarak Ben Amar; screenplay by Roman Polanski, Gérard Brach, John Brownjohn; directed by Roman Polanski; photography by Witold Sobochinski; edited by Herve de Luze, William Reynolds; music by Philippe Sarde. Cast: Walter Mattau (Captain Red), Cris Campion (Frog), Damien Thomas (Don Alfonso), Charlotte Lewis (Dolores), Olu Jacobs (Richmond), David Kelley (Surgeon), Roy Kinnear (Dutch), Emilio Fernandez (Angelino), Wladislaw Komar (Jesus), Luc Jamati (Gonzalez), Robert Durning (Commander of Marines).

Frantic. Production: Warner Brothers/Mount Company Production, New York, USA; color; running time: 120 mins. Released: 1987. Produced by Thom Mount, Tim Hampton; screenplay by Roman Polanski, Gérard Brach; directed by Roman Polanski; photography by Witold Sobochinski; edited by Sam O'Steen; music by Ennio Morricone. Cast: Harrison Ford (Dr. Richard Walker), Betty Buckley (Sondra Walker), Emmanuelle Seigner (Michelle), Dominique Virton (Desk Clerk), Yves Reignier (Inspector), John Mahoney (Williams), Jimmie Ray Weeks (Shaap), Yorgo Voyagis (Kidnapper), David Huddleston (Peter).

István Szabó

SHORT FEATURES

Koncert (*Concert*), Academy of Dramatic and Cinematographic Art, Hungary, 1961; *Variáciok egy témára* (*Variations on a Theme*), Béla Balázs Studio, Hungary, 1961; *Te* (*You*), Béla Balázs Studio, Hungary, 1963; *Budapest, amiért szeretem* (*Budapest, Why I Love It*), series of short films including *A tér* (*The Square*); *Egy tükör* (*A Mirror*); *Lányportré* (*Portrait of a Girl*); *Duna, Halak, Madarak* (*Danube, Fishes, Birds*); and *Álom egy házról* (*A Dream about a House*), MAFILM, Hungary, 1971.

DOCUMENTARIES

Kegyelet (*Piety*), MAFILM, Hungary, 1967. *Várostérkép* (*City Map*), MAFILM, Hungary, 1976.

FEATURE FILMS

Álmodozások kora (*The Age of Daydreaming*). Production: MAFILM Studio 3, Budapest, Hungary; black and white; running time: 97 minutes. Released: 1964. Screenplay by István Szabó; directed by István Szabó; photography by Tamás Vámos; edited by Sándor Zákonyi; music by Péter Eötvös; sound by György Pintér. Cast: András Bálint (Janos), Ilona Béres (Éva), Judit Halász (Habgab), Kati Sólyom (Anni), Béla Asztalos (Laci), Tamás Erőss (Matyi), László Murányi (Gergely), Cecília Esztergályos (Ági, the dancer), Miklós Gábor (Flesch, the chief engineer).

Apa (*Father*). Production: MAFILM Studio 3, Budapest, Hungary; black and white; running time: 95 minutes. Released: 1966. Screenplay by István Szabó;

directed by István Szabó; photography by Sándor Sára; music by János Gonda; art direction by Béla Zeichán. Cast: András Bálint (Takó as an adult), Dani Erdély (Takó as a child), Klári Tolnay (Mother), Miklós Gábor (Father), Kati Sólyom (Anni).

Szerelmes film (*Love Film*). Production: MAFILM Studio 3, Budapest, Hungary; color; running time: 130 minutes. Released: 1970. Screenplay by István Szabó; directed by István Szabó; photography by József Lőrincz; music by János Gonda. Cast: András Bálint (Jansci), Judit Halász (Kata).

Tuzoltó utca 25 (*25 Firemen's Street*). Production: MAFILM Budapest Studio, Budapest, Hungary; color; running time: 97 minutes. Released: 1973. Screenplay by István Szabó; directed by István Szabó; photography by Sándor Sára; music by Zdenkó Tamássy; art direction by József Romvári. Cast: Rita Békés (Mrs. Gaskóy), Lucyna Winnicka (Mária), Péter Müller (János, Mária's husband), András Bálint (Andris), Mari Szemes (Julika), Ági Mészáros (Aranka), Margit Makay (Mária's mother), Károly Kovács (Mária's father).

Budapesti mesék (*Budapest Tales*). Production: Hunnia Studio, Budapest, Hungary; color; running time: 91 minutes. Released: 1976. Screenplay by István Szabó; directed by István Szabó; photography by Sándor Sára; music by Zdenkó Tamássy. Cast: Maja Komorowska, Ági Meszáros, Ildikó Bánsági, András Bálint, Franciszek Pieczka, Károly Kovács, József Madaras, Simon Surmiel, Zoltán Huszárik, Vilmos Kun, Sándor Halmágyi, Rita Békés.

Bizalom (*Confidence*). Production: MAFILM Objektiv Studio, Budapest, Hungary; color; running time: 117 minutes. Released: 1979. Screenplay by István Szabó; based on a film story by Erika Szántó and István Szabó; directed by István Szabó; photography by Lajos Koltai; art direction by József Romvári. Cast: Ildikó Bánsági (Kata), Péter Andorai (János Bíró).

Mephisto. Production: MAFILM Objectiv Studio, Budapest, Hungary, in cooperation with Manfred Durniok Productions, Berlin, Federal Republic of Germany: color; running time: 144 minutes. Released: 1981. Produced by Manfred Durniok; screenplay by István Szabó and Péter Dobai; directed by István Szabó; photography by Lajos Koltai. Cast: Klaus Maria Brandauer (Hendrik Höfgen), Krystyna Janda (Barbara Bruckner), Ildikó Bánsági (Nicoletta von Niebuhr), Karin Boyd (Juliette Martens), Rolf Hoppe (the Minister-President), Christine Harbort (Lotte Lindenthal), György Cserhalmi (Hans Miklas), Martin Hellberg (Professor), Christian Graskoff (Cäsar von Muck), Péter Andorai (Otto Ulrichs), Ildikó Kishonti (Dora Martin), Tamás Major (Oskar H. Kroge).

Oberst Redl (*Colonel Redl/Redl Ezredes*). Production: MAFILM Objektiv Studio, Budapest, Hungary, in collaboration with Manfred Durniok Productions, Berlin, Federal Republic of Germany; ORF, Vienna, Austria; and ZDF, Mainz, Federal Republic of Germany, color; running time: 149 minutes. Released: 1984. Produced by Manfred Durniok; screenplay by István Szabó and Péter Dobai; directed by István Szabó; photography by Lajos Koltai. Cast: Klaus Maria Brandauer (Alfried Redl), Armin Müller-Stahl (the Archduke), Gudrun Landgrebe (Katalin Kubínyi), Jan Niklas (Kristóf Kubínyi), Dorottya Udvaros (Clarissa), Károly Eperjes (Lieutenant Jaromil Schorm), András Bálint (Dr. Sonnenschein), Athina Papadimitriu (singer), László Gálffi (Velocchio), László Mensáros (Colonel Ruzitska), Róbert Ráthonyi (Baron Ullman), Tamás Major (Grandfather Kubínyi), György Bánffy (Aide-de-camp to the Archduke), Ágnes T. Katona (Willhelmina).

Hanussen. Production: MAFILM Objektiv Studio, Budapest, Hungary; CCC Filmkunst, Berlin, and ZDF, Mainz, Federal Republic of Germany; Hungarofilm and MOKÉP, Budapest, Hungary; color; running time: 118 minutes. Released: 1988. Produced by Arthur Brauner; screenplay by István Szabó and Péter Dobai; directed by István Szabó; photography by Lajos Koltai; edited by Zsuzsa Csakány; music by György Vukán; sound by György Fék; art direction by József Romvári. Cast: Klaus Maria Brandauer (Klaus Schneider/Erik Jan Hanussen), Erland Josephson (Dr. Bettelheim), Ildikó Bánsági (Nurse Betty), Walter Schmidinger (Propaganda Chief),

Károly Eperjes (Nowotny), Grażyna Szapołowska (Váli Tóth/Valery de la Meer), Colette Pilz-Warren (Dagma), György Cserhalmi (Count Trantow-Waldbach), Michał Bajor (Captain Becker).

Meeting Venus. Production: Enigma Films, London, United Kingdom; distributed by Warner Brothers, Fujisankei, and British Sky; color; running time: 119 minutes. Released: 1991. Produced by David Puttnam; screenplay by István Szabó and Michael Hirst; directed by István Szabó; photography by Lajos Koltai; edited by Jim Clark; casting by Patsy Pollock; costume design by Catherine Leterrier; production design by Attila Kovács; music by Richard Wagner. Cast: Glenn Close (Karin Anderson), Niels Arestrup (Zoltán Szánto), Erland Josephson (Jorge Picabia), Macha Meril (Miss Malikoff), Johanna ter Steege (Monique Angelo), Maite Nahyr (Maria Krawiecki), Victor Poletti (Stefano del Sarto), Maria de Medeiros (Yvonne), Jay O. Sanders (Stephen Taylor), Marian Labuda (von Schneider), Ildikó Bánsági (Jana), Dieter Laser (von Binder), Roberto Pollak (Isaac Partnoi), Moscu Alcalay (Jean Gabor), Johara Rácz (Dancer), Étienne Chicot (Toushkau), Rita Scholl (Delfin van Delf), André Chaumeau (Étienne Tailleur), François Delaive (Thomas), and Dorottya Udvaros (Edith).

Dušan Makavejev

AMATEUR FILMS

Jatagan Mala, Kino Klub "Beograd," Belgrade, 1953; *Pečat* (*The Stamp*), Kino Klub "Beograd," Belgrade, 1956; *Antonijevo razbijeno ogledalo* (*Anthony's Broken Mirror*), Kino Klub "Beograd," Belgrade, 1957; *Spomenicima ne treba verovati* (*Don't Believe in Monuments*), Kino Klub "Beograd," Belgrade, 1958.

DOCUMENTARIES

Prokletni praznik (*Damned Holiday*), Zagreb film, Zagreb 1958; *Slikovnica pčelara* (*Beekeeper's Scrapbook*), Zagreb film, Zagreb 1958; *Boje sanjaju* (*Colors Dreaming*), Zagreb film, Zagreb 1958; *Šta je to radnički savet* (*What Is a Worker's Council?*), Zagreb film, Zagreb 1959; *Eci pec pec* (*One Potato, Two Potato . . .*), Avala film, Belgrade, 1961; *Pedagoška bajka* (*Educational Fairy Tale*), Avala film, Belgrade, 1961; *Osmjeh 61* (*Smile 61*), Sutjeska film, Sarajevo, 1961; *Film o knjizi A.B.C.* (*Film about an ABC Book*), Sutjeska film, Sarajevo, 1962; *Parada* (*Parade*), Dunav film, Belgrade, 1962; *Dole plotovi* (*Down with Fences*), Zora film, Belgrade, 1962; *Ljepotica 62* (*Miss Yugoslavia 62*), Sutjeska film, Sarajevo, 1962; *Nova Igračka* (*New Toy*), Zagreb film, Zagreb 1964; *Nova domaća životinja* (*New Domestic Animal*), Dunav film, Belgrade, 1964.

FEATURE FILMS

Čovek nije tica (*Man Is Not a Bird*). Production: Avala film, Belgrade, Yugoslavia; black and white; running time: 80 mins. Released: 1965. Produced by Dušan Perković; screenplay by Dušan Makavejev; directed by Dušan Makavejev; photography by Aleksandar Petković; edited by Ljubica Nešić; art direction by Dragoljub Ivkov; music by Petar Bergamo. Cast: Milena Dravić (Hairdresser), Janez Vrhovec (Engineer Rudinski), Eva Ras (Barbulović's wife), Stojan Aranđelović (Barbulović), Boris Dvornik (Truck Driver), Roko Ćirković (Hypnotist), Živojin Pavlović (Neighbor).

Ljubavni slučaj ili tragedija službenice PTT (*Love Affair, or The Tragedy of a Switchboard Operator*). Also released in English as *Love Affair* and *Love Affair: Or, The Case of the Missing Switchboard Operator.* Production: Avala film, Belgrade, Yugoslavia; black and white; running time: 70 mins. Released: 1967. Produced by Aleksandar Krstić; screenplay by Dušan Makavejev; directed by Dušan Makavejev; photography by Aleksandar Petković; edited by Katarina Stojanović; art direction by Vladislav Lašić; music by Dušan Aleksić. Cast: Eva Ras (Isabella), Ružica Sokić (Isabella's friend), Slobodan Aligrudić (Ahmed), Miodrag Andrić (Mića), Dr. Aleksandar Kostić (Sexologist), Dr. Živojin Aleksić (Criminologist).

Nevinost bez zaštite (*Innocence Unprotected*). Production: Avala Film, Belgrade, Yugoslavia; color and black and white; running time: 78 mins. Released: 1968. Produced by Boško Savić; screenplay by Dušan Makavejev; directed by Dušan Makavejev; photography by Branko Perak; photgraphy for Aleksić's film by Stevan Mišković; edited by Ivanka Vukasović; music by Vojislav Kostić, Aleksandar Popović. Cast: Dragoljub Aleksić (himself), Ana Milosavljević (Nada), Vera Jovanović (Wicked Stepmother), Bratoljub Gligorijević (Petrović), Ivan Živković (Aleksić's brother), Pera Miroslavljević (Servant), Stevan Mišković (himself).

WR: Misteria organizma (*WR: Mysteries of the Organism*). Production: Neoplanta film, Novi Sad, Yugoslavia; color; running time: 86 mins. Released: 1971. Produced by Srđan Ilić, Bert Koetter, Stevan Petrović; screenplay by Dušan Makavejev; directed by Dušan Makavejev; photography by Aleksandar Petković; edited by Ivanka Vukasović; art direction by Dragoljub Ivkov; music by Bojana Marijan. Cast: Milena Dravić (Milena), Jagoda Koloper (Jagoda), Ivica Vidović (Vladimir Ilyich), Zoran Radmilović (Radmilović), Miodrag Andrić (soldier), Tuli Kupferberg, Jackie Curtis, Živka Matić, Nikola Milić, Dragoljub Ivkov, Milan Jelić.

Sweet Movie. Production: V. M. Production (Paris), Mojack Films (Montreal), and Maran Films (Munich); color; running time: 99 mins. Released: 1974. Produced by Helene Vager, Richard Hellman, Vincent Malle; screenplay by Dušan Makavejev and Joel Santoni; directed by Dušan Makavejev; photograpy by Pierre Lhomme; edited by Yann Dedet; art direction by Jocelyn Joly, Christian Lamarque; music by Manos Hadjidakis. Cast: Carole Laure (Miss World 1984), Pierre Clementi (*Potemkin* sailor), Anna Prucnal (Anna Planeta), Sami Frey (El Macho), Jane Mallet (PDG), Otto Muehl and his commune (themselves), Marpessa Dawn (Mama Communa), John Vernon (Mr. Kapital), Roy Callendar (Jeremiah Muscle).

Montenegro. Production: Viking Film and Europa Film, Stockholm, Sweden; color; running time: 97 mins. Released: 1981. Produced by Bo Jonsson; screenplay by Dušan Makavejev with additional scenes and dialogue by Branko Vučićević, Bojana Marijan, Arnie Gelbart, Bo Jonsson, Donald Arthur; directed by Dušan Makavejev; photography by Tomislav Pinter; edited by Sylvia Ingemarsson; art direction by Radu Boruzescu; music by Kornell Kovach. Cast: Susan Anspach (Marilyn Jordan), Erland Josephson (Martin Jordan), Bora Todorović (Alex Rossignol), Per Oscarsson (Dr. Aram Pazardjian), Patricia Gelin (Tirke), Lisbeth Zachrisson (Rita Rossignol), Svetozar Cvetković (Montenegro).

The Coca-Cola Kid. Production: Cinema Enterprises with support from the Australian Film Commission, Australia; color; running time: 94 mins. Released: 1985. Produced by David Roe; screenplay by Frank Moorhouse based on his short stories published in *The Americans, Baby* and *The Electrical Experience;* directed by Dušan Makavejev; photography by Dean Semler; edited by John Scott; art direction by Anni Browning; music by William Motzing. Cast: Eric Roberts (Becker), Greta Scacchi (Terri), Bill Kerr (T. George McDowell), Chris Haywood (Kim), Kris Mcquade (Juliana), Max Gillies (Frank), Tony Barry (Bushman), Paul Chubb (Fred), David Slingsby (Waiter), Tim Finn (Philip), Colleen Clifford (Mrs. Haversham), Rebecca Smart (DMZ).

Manifesto. Production: Cannon Film (USA) and Jadran film (Zagreb, Yugoslavia); color; running time: 94 mins. Released: 1988. Produced by Menahem Golan and Yoram Globus; screenplay by Dušan Makavejev inspired by *For a Night of Love* by Emile Zola; directed by Dušan Makavejev; photography by Tomislav Pinter; edited by Tony Lawson; art direction by Veljko Despotović; music by Nicola Piovani. Cast: Camilla Søeberg (Svetlana), Alfred Molina (Avanti), Simon Callow (Hunt), Eric Stoltz (Christopher), Lindsay Duncan (Lily Sacher), Rade Šerbedžija (Emile), Svetozar Cvetković (Rudi), Chris Haywood (Wango), Patrick Godfrey (Dr. Lambroscu), Linda Marlowe (Stella), Gabrielle Anwar (Tina), Enver Petrovci (the king), Ronald Lacey (Conductor), Tanja Bošković (Olympia), Željko Duvnjak (Martin), Danko Ljustina (Baker).

CONTRIBUTORS

Herbert Eagle, Professor of Slavic Languages and Literatures at the University of Michigan, has written extensively on film theory, literary theory, and contemporary East European literature and film. He has published several books and numerous articles in leading journals in Slavic studies and film.

Daniel J. Goulding, Professor of Film Studies and Theater Arts at Oberlin College, has lectured and published widely on film and related subjects. His book *Liberated Cinema: The Yugoslav Experience* received the first "Close-up" award from the Yugoslav Film Institute. His most recent book, for which he is editor and contributor, is *Post New Wave Cinema in the Soviet Union and Eastern Europe.*

Peter Hames, Principal Lecturer in Film Studies in the Department of History of Art and Design at the North Staffordshire Polytechnic in England, wrote the critically acclaimed book *The Czechoslovak New Wave* and contributed the chapter on Czechoslovakian cinema for *Post New Wave Cinema in the Soviet Union and Eastern Europe.* He organized the first major retrospective of Czech and Slovak films at the National Film Theatre in London and has written articles for *Sight and Sound, Films and Filming, The Movie, New Statesman,* and other journals.

Vida T. Johnson, Associate Professor of Russian Language and Literature at Tufts University, received her Ph.D. in Slavic languages and literatures from Harvard. A specialist in literature, she has recently begun to publish significant work in film. She is co-author (with Graham Petrie) of a soon to be published book on the films of Andrei Tarkovsky.

David Paul, writer and film critic, is the editor of and a contributor to *Politics, Art and Commitment in the East European Cinema* and wrote the chapter on Hungarian film for *Post New Wave Cinema in the Soviet Union and Eastern Europe.* His articles on film have appeared in recent volumes of *Film Quarterly, Film Comment, Cinéast,* and other journals. Paul's earlier writings include two books and numerous articles on politics and society in Eastern Europe. He received his doctorate in political science from Princeton University.

Graham Petrie, Professor of Film and English literature at McMaster University in Canada, is the author of *History Must Answer to Man: The Contemporary Hungarian Cinema, The Cinema of François Truffaut,* and *Hollywood Destinies: European Directors in America, 1921–1931.* He has published a novel and numerous articles, and recently co-authored (with Vida Johnson) a soon to be published book titled *Tarkovsky: A Visual Fugue.*

INDEX